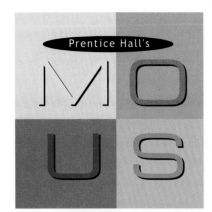

Prentice Hall's

MOUS

TEST PREPARATION GUIDE FOR

PowerPoint® 2000

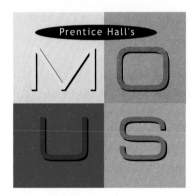

TEST
PREPARATION
GUIDES
SERIES

**Emily Ketcham,
Series Editor**

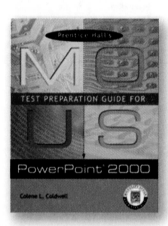

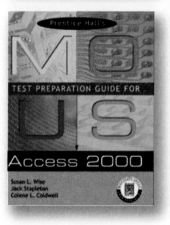

TEST PREPARATION GUIDE FOR

PowerPoint® 2000

Colene L. Coldwell

Upper Saddle River, New Jersey

Editor-in-Chief: Mickey Cox
Acquisitions Editor: Lucinda Gatch
Assistant Editor: Jennifer Cappello
Development Editor: Sue Wise
Managing Editor: Monica Stipanov
Editorial Assistant: Mary Toepfer
Director of Strategic Marketing: Nancy Evans
Marketing Manager: Kris King
AVP/Director of Production & Manufacturing: Michael Weinstein
Manager, Production: Gail Steier de Acevedo
Project Manager: Tim Tate
Manufacturing Buyer: Natacha St. Hill Moore
Associate Director, Manufacturing: Vincent Scelta
Book Design: David Levy
Cover Design: Pisaza Design Studio, Ltd.
Full Service Composition: Impressions Book and Journal Services, Inc.

© 2001 by Prentice Hall

Printed in the United States of America

ISBN: 0-13-027742-8

Library of Congress Cataloging-in-Publication Data

Coldwell, Colene.
    Prentice Hall's MOUS test preparation guide for PowerPoint 2000 / Colene Coldwell.
      p.   cm.—(Prentice Hall's MOUS test preparation guides series)
    ISBN 0-13-027742-8 (pbk.)
      1. Electronic data processing personnel—Certification.   2. Microsoft
software—Examinations—Study guides.   3. Microsoft PowerPoint (Computer file)
I. Title: MOUS test preparation guide for PowerPoint 2000. II. Title. III. Series.

QA76.3 .C653 2000
006.6'869—dc21   00-057446

Contents

Appendix

Preface

A flash of insight—

...and I saw the kind of book that people would really use—even enjoy using—and that would help them learn. That insight led to the creation of this new series, Prentice Hall's MOUS Test Preparation Guides for Office 2000.

This series has two main objectives: to provide students with a clear, direct and comprehensive source for gaining computer expertise, and to support instructors with superior resources to enhance their teaching.

This book is designed for people like these:

- Busy adults who want to get right to the point.
- Beginners who don't want to be overwhelmed with jargon and unnecessary details.
- Experienced users whose goal is to pass the MOUS certification exam.

Five elements combine to make this series so effective:

Condensed steps cover each skill precisely, without burying you in unnecessary examples and too many words.

 Thought Questions challenge students to apply what they've learned.

 Tips from a Pro give inside information about the application. More than just a way to cram for the exam, this book provides expert guidance so you can use Microsoft Office like a professional.

 MOUS objectives are specifically addressed and clearly labeled in each chapter so you will be ready for certification.

 MOUS PinPoint software supplies interactive tutorials and timed tests so you gain hands-on experience using the software and taking the MOUS exams.

○ **Feature: You cover the subject without getting covered up.**

Straightforward guide to learning—Short, pithy explanations for each skill take a What-Why-How-Results approach. You'll find it easy to learn these key aspects:

- The core concepts for each skill
- Why it's important, or why you'll use it
- How to do it, step-by-step
- What to expect as a result

This means you can quickly find answers, see how to do a skill, and gain expertise. The tasks are covered, but not covered up. Just the facts, ma'am.

○ **Feature: You gain insight into how professionals use the skills.**

Use your skills like a master—The **Tips from a Pro** feature adds to your knowledge so you can handle tasks like a professional. You not only learn how to perform each skill, but also how to select and use the features appropriately, along with some alternatives and shortcuts to the traditional method. For example, **Tips from a Pro** cover these topics:

- How to format a document so people will want to read it.
- What to include when adding a chart to a document.
- Ways to set up a form so people will fill it out correctly and completely every time.
- The best way to use lines and borders in a table.
- Pitfalls to avoid in proofing spelling.
- And many more.

○ **Feature: You zero in on MOUS objectives for success.**

A MOUS bible—For each application, we cover every MOUS objective—at both Core and Expert levels—in one slim book. This means the answer you need for every MOUS skill is close at hand. You can use this book to teach yourself or to help you review your skills.

○ **Feature: You learn hands-on with PinPoint.**

MOUS PinPoint Software—This series is designed to work hand in hand with the engaging PinPoint Software, created by Kelly Temporary Services for training professionals. It matches the book with its short, to-the-point approach, and strongly reinforces the skills you need to prepare for the certification exam.

MOUS PinPoint software contains these elements:

- *Trainers:* Over a hundred interactive computer-based skill drills for each application, with demonstrations and immediate feedback
- *Evaluations:* Sample MOUS certification exams with real-life testing conditions.

I'm hooked on MOUS PinPoint, and here's why:

- It zeroes in on a single skill. When you can successfully complete each task, you can utilize these skills in your real life to help get your work done.
- Instant feedback lets you know whether you've performed the task correctly.
- Not sure how to do it? Click Show Me, and a short explanation and demonstration models the skill, then lets you try it yourself.
- It times how long it takes you to complete a single skill. Like Beat The Clock, this brings out a spirit of competition, and makes you want to try harder and work faster than the timer!

Result: accomplishment and expertise

Learners who use this MOUS Test Prep Guide and its accompanying MOUS PinPoint software are well prepared to pass the MOUS certification exam. Not merely a way to cram for the test, this series expertly guides you to competent use of Microsoft Office to accomplish your day-to-day tasks.

Supplements Package

Student Supplements

Companion Web site (www.prenhall.com/phmoustest)   Includes student data files as well as test questions that allow students to test their knowledge of the material and get instant assessment.

Instructor Supplements

Instructor's Resource CD-ROM   Includes Instructor's Manuals, Test Manager, PowerPoint slides, and data and solutions files for all four Office applications.

Companion Web site (www.prenhall.com/phmoustest)   Includes the Instructor's Manuals, PowerPoint slides, and data and solutions files for all four Office applications, all available for download.

Acknowledgments

I would never have been able to write this book without the contributions of many different people—both friends and colleagues. My dear friend Emily Ketcham, who developed the model for this series, not only encouraged me to write this text but also provided ongoing suggestions and support. The Baylor Business School, specifically Dean Terry Maness and G. W. Willis, allowed me to uses their wonderful resources. Sue Wise provided invaluable ideas regarding the technical development of the manuscript.

Everyone that I have interacted with at Prentice Hall and Impressions Book and Journal Services has been delightful to work with—true team members! I would specifically mention Lucinda Gatch, who championed and cleared the path for this series, and Monica Stipanov who helped keep me on task and focused (not always an easy job, I must say). I would also like to mention and thank Tim Tate and Keith Kline for their help.

Finally, I want to thank and acknowledge my husband, Kendall. His unfailing support and encouragement would not fit within the pages of this text.

Colene L. Coldwell
Baylor University

Features and Benefits

Why the books in this series are the ultimate interactive MOUS test preparation guides:

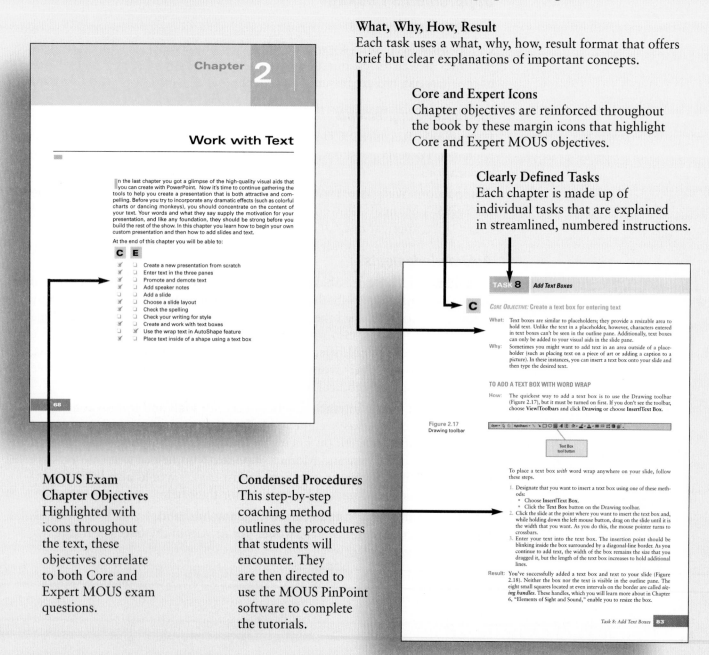

What, Why, How, Result
Each task uses a what, why, how, result format that offers brief but clear explanations of important concepts.

Core and Expert Icons
Chapter objectives are reinforced throughout the book by these margin icons that highlight Core and Expert MOUS objectives.

Clearly Defined Tasks
Each chapter is made up of individual tasks that are explained in streamlined, numbered instructions.

MOUS Exam Chapter Objectives
Highlighted with icons throughout the text, these objectives correlate to both Core and Expert MOUS exam questions.

Condensed Procedures
This step-by-step coaching method outlines the procedures that students will encounter. They are then directed to use the MOUS PinPoint software to complete the tutorials.

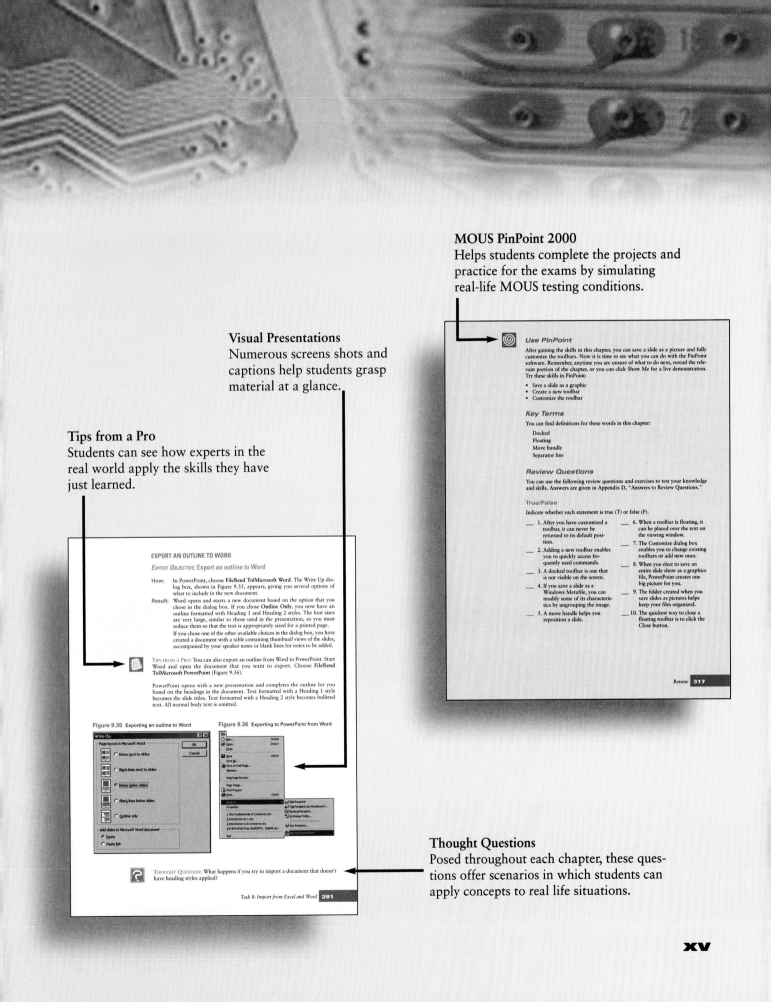

MOUS PinPoint 2000
Helps students complete the projects and practice for the exams by simulating real-life MOUS testing conditions.

Visual Presentations
Numerous screens shots and captions help students grasp material at a glance.

Tips from a Pro
Students can see how experts in the real world apply the skills they have just learned.

Thought Questions
Posed throughout each chapter, these questions offer scenarios in which students can apply concepts to real life situations.

Start
with Windows

Before you begin using the Microsoft Office 2000 programs, you need to know a little bit about Windows. What you see when your computer is first turned on and ready to use is Windows. It is a type of software known as the operating system, and it is what the computer uses to direct its computing processes.

We humans use the operating system for starting programs we want to use for work or pleasure (such as Word, Excel, PowerPoint, Access, or Solitaire) and for managing the contents of our computers.

This chapter will cover the basic skills for all of these versions of Windows:

- ○ Windows 2000
- ○ Windows Millennium Edition (ME)
- ○ Windows 98

At the end of this chapter you will be able to:

- ❑ Explain what an operating system does
- ❑ Name items on the Windows desktop
- ❑ Start programs
- ❑ Handle windows
- ❑ Use menus and dialog boxes
- ❑ Manage the contents of your computer
- ❑ Customize the desktop

TASK 1   *Turn on the Computer*

What: The first step in learning to use the computer is to turn it on.

Why: Well, I guess you know why.

How: Follow these steps to turn on the computer and start Windows.

1. Look on the front of the computer for a button to push. Often the button is marked with a circle with a vertical line, like this: ○ Alternatively, you may have a switch labeled with a line and circle. The line means On, and the circle means Off. If you've found the correct button, you'll hear the computer begin to hum and perhaps see some lights flash.

2. You may have to turn on the monitor as well. Often the switch is under its "chin." When you're successful, you'll see a green light, and after a little warm-up time, you'll see something appear on the monitor.

3. Watch as some numbers and words go by, and then a colorful screen appears while Windows is loading.

4. Depending on how Windows is set up on your computer, you may have to *log on*, that is, type in your user name and password. Check with your instructor to find out what you should type. Here's how to log on:

   1. Type your name in the first box.
   2. Press the Tab key on the keyboard.
   3. Type your password in the second box.
   4. Press **Enter**.

5. Do you see the small hourglass on your screen? That means that Windows is busy.

Result: When the computer has finished ***booting up***, or starting, you will see the Windows screen shown in Figure 1. The hourglass image you may have noticed earlier has changed into a small arrowhead.

TASK 2   *Explore the Windows Desktop*

What: Examine Figure 1 to see the names of each of the items on the screen.

Why: You will need to learn the names of the elements shown on the screen so you can refer to them quickly when they are mentioned in this book or on the MOUS exam. The Windows desktop shown in Figure 1 contains the following elements:

Desktop is the term for the entire Windows screen, including the background. Like your physical desk, it contains the documents you're working on, as well as handy tools to help you get your work done.

Icons are small pictures that represent tools, programs, or documents you can use. This desktop has the following icons:

- ❍ *My Documents* is a handy folder where you can store documents that you work on.
- ❍ *My Computer* is a way to view and manage the contents of your computer.
- ❍ *My Network Places* is a way to view and manage your computer's connections to a network or the Internet. (In Windows 98, you'll see **Network Neighborhood** instead. It's used to manage all the resources connected by a network to your computer.)
- ❍ *Recycle Bin* is a temporary storage place for items you discard or delete from your computer.
- ❍ *Internet Explorer* is a computer program known as a *browser*, which is used to see information found on the World Wide Web.
- ❍ *Microsoft Outlook* is Office 2000's program for sending e-mail and managing personal information such as schedules, contacts, and tasks.

Mouse pointer is controlled by your mouse, touchstick, touchpad, or other pointing device.

Start button, when you click it, reveals a menu or list of choices of things to do.

Quick Launch toolbar contains buttons that, when you click them, start programs.

Taskbar contains a button for each task your computer is currently processing. (There are none shown here.)

The *clock* helps you keep track of how long till lunchtime or your next appointment.

 TIPS FROM A PRO: What you see on your computer may look a little different from what you see here. You may have different icons, different pictures, or different colors. You may see underlined words and additional images.

Figure 1 The Windows screen

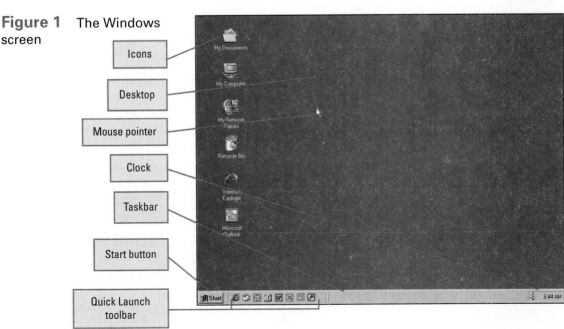

What: A major strength of using Windows is being able to use a pointing device. All pointing devices use similar techniques: point, click, double-click, right-click, and drag. Common pointing devices include these:

1. A mouse, a rolling device you use with your entire hand, consisting of buttons and possibly a wheel;
2. A touchstick, a small, rubbery knob in the middle of a laptop computer's keyboard you wiggle with your fingertip, combined with one or two buttons you click with your thumb;
3. A touchpad, a rectangular area often found below the keyboard of a laptop computer that you use by touching or tapping with your finger.

You use the pointing device to control the ***mouse pointer*** on screen, that little picture that often resembles an arrow or an hourglass.

Why: When you use the mouse (or other pointing device) to give directions to the computer, you don't have to type a million commands. Instead, use the mouse to indicate things on screen that you want to use or actions you want to do.

How: Every pointing device has five major techniques. Read about these techniques for the pointing device that you have (Tables 1 through 3).

Table 1 Mouse Techniques

Technique	How to do it	Effect on screen
Point	Roll the mouse on the surface in a certain direction.	The mouse pointer (often an arrow) moves in the same direction. Try pointing to the clock. You will see today's date appear.
Click	Tap the left mouse button with your index finger (assuming you're right-handed).	Selects (or sometimes opens) whatever the mouse pointer is pointing to on screen. Click the Start button to see the menu appear. Click again to make it disappear.
Double-click	Same as above, only do it two times quickly. If it doesn't work, try holding the mouse very still and clicking twice in a row even more quickly.	Opens whatever the mouse pointer is pointing to on the screen. You'll use this later.
Right-click	Click the right mouse button with your middle finger (assuming you're right-handed).	Shows a ***shortcut menu***, a short menu with a variety of commands. Try this out: Point to the middle of the desktop and right-click. Click a blank area to get rid of the shortcut menu.

Technique	How to do it	Effect on screen
Drag	Point to something on screen, and then click and hold down the left button while you move the mouse.	Moves the item you pointed to from one place to another. Also used to select more than one item. You'll use this later.
Scroll	Rotate the wheel toward or away, or click the wheel button and move the mouse. (Available only on a mouse that has a wheel button between the left and right buttons)	Moves the contents of a list or window up or down. You'll use this later.

Table 2 Touchstick Techniques

Technique	How to do it	Effect on screen
Point	Push the touchstick in a certain direction.	The mouse pointer (often an arrow) moves in the same direction. Try pointing to the clock. You will see today's date appear.
Click	Tap once quickly on a button below the keyboard.	Selects (or sometimes opens) whatever the mouse pointer is pointing to on screen. Click the Start button to see the menu appear. Click again to make it disappear.
Double-click	Same as above, only do it two times quickly. If it doesn't work, try tapping twice in a row even more quickly.	Opens whatever the mouse pointer is pointing to on the screen. You'll use this later.
Right-click	Tap once on the right button.	Shows a shortcut menu, a *short menu* with commands you can choose from. Try this out: Point to the middle of the desktop and right-click. Click a blank area to get rid of the shortcut menu.
Drag	Point to something on the screen, and then hold down the left button while you push the touchstick in a certain direction.	Moves the item you pointed to from one place to another. Also used to select more than one item. You'll use this later.

Table 3 Touchpad Techniques

Technique	How to do it	Effect on screen
Point	"Draw" with your finger on the touchpad in a certain direction.	The mouse pointer (often an arrow) moves in the same direction. Try pointing to the clock. You will see today's date appear.
Click	Tap once lightly on the touchpad, or tap the button.	Selects (or sometimes opens) whatever the mouse pointer is pointing to on screen. Click the Start button to see the menu appear. Click again to make it disappear.
Double-click	Tap two times quickly. If it doesn't work, try tapping twice in a row even more quickly.	Opens whatever the mouse pointer is pointing to on the screen. You'll use this later.
Right-click	Tap once quickly on the right button.	Shows a shortcut menu, a *short menu* with commands you can choose from. Try this out: Point to the middle of the desktop and right-click. Click a blank area to get rid of the shortcut menu.
Drag	Place the mouse pointer on something, and then hold down the left button while you "draw" on the touchpad with your finger in a certain direction.	Moves the item you pointed to from one place to another. Also used to select more than one item. You'll use this later.

 TIPS FROM A PRO: Do you see underlined words beneath each icon when you point to it? If so, you're using Web-style Windows, rather than classic Windows. With Web-style Windows, you use slightly different techniques with your pointing device. Table 4 shows the main differences. You'll learn how to change from one style to the other in Task 9.

Table 4 Pointing and Clicking in Classic and Web-style Windows

When you do this . . .	What happens in classic Windows	What happens in Web-style Windows
Point	No effect	Selects an item
Click	Selects an item	Opens an item
Double-click	Opens an item	Unnecessary—just click once

Result: As you become proficient in using your pointing device, you will be able to tell the computer what you want to do with little effort. You'll learn when to use each of these techniques for using Windows and Office 2000.

Note: From this point on, this book will use the term "mouse" for all pointing devices.

What: An obvious place to start using Windows is the Start button. (A *button* is a rectangular area you can click to access a command or action.) When you move the mouse pointer to the Start button and click, the *Start menu* appears, as you see in Figure 2. It contains a list of choices or commands. Some of the choices are followed by a right-pointing triangle. That means when you choose them, another menu will appear.

Figure 2   Start menu

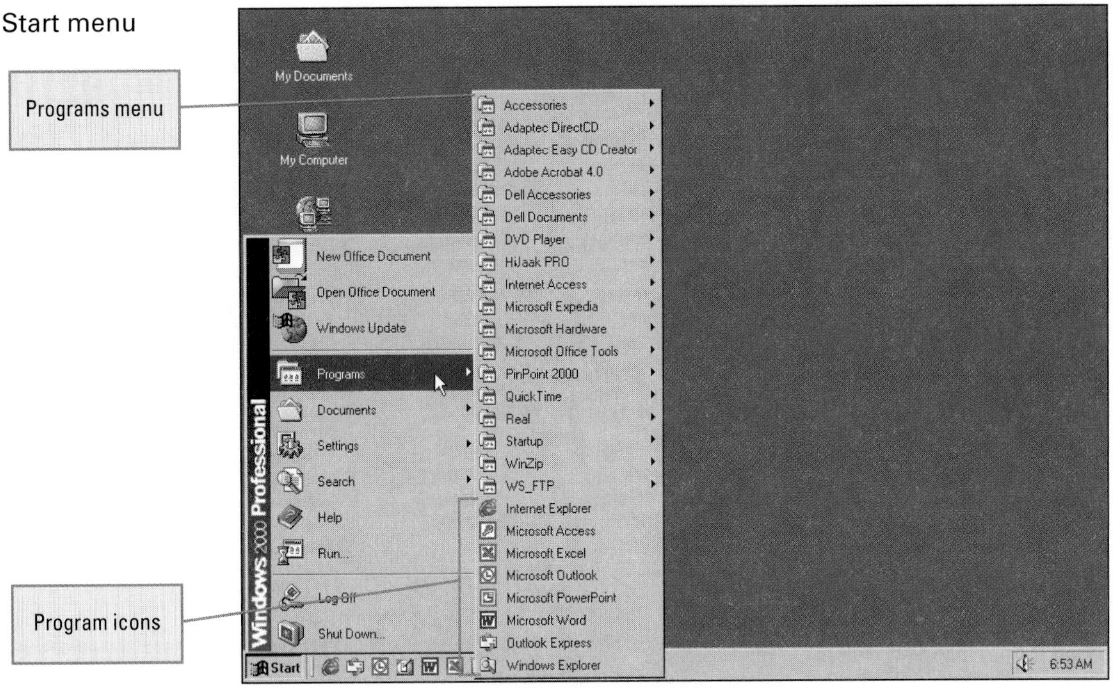

Programs menu

Program icons

Why: A menu provides a set of choices for you. You don't have to remember what command to type to tell the computer what to do.

How: Use a menu this way.

1. Click the **Start** button, and the Start menu appears.
2. Move the mouse up or down to highlight or select different items on the menu.
3. Point to **Programs**, and the Programs menu appears. Point to **Accessories**, and the Accessories menu appears. You can click a program icon (something without a right-pointing triangle) to start a program. For example, you could click **Calculator** on the Accessories menu.
4. Or click away from the menu to make it go away without starting anything.

Result: When you choose something from the menu, the menu disappears, and the computer gets busy doing what you told it to do. You can choose from items listed on the Start menu to begin working on your computer. These are the ones you'll use often:

- ○ **Programs** gives a list of programs you can access and use.
- ○ **Help** offers information and assistance for any technique or feature of Windows.
- ○ **Log Off** enables someone else to use the same computer. If you're working in a computer lab, you'll probably use this command instead of Shut Down.
- ○ **Shut Down** is what you choose when you're ready to turn off your computer.

 TIPS FROM A PRO: Always choose **Shut Down** before turning off the power to your computer. See Task 10 to learn how to do this.

TASK **5**   *Handle Windows*

What: When you start a program or open a folder, it opens in a rectangular area called a ***window***, shown in Figure 3. On the taskbar, you will also see a button associated with the window. You can open several different items, each in its own window. For every open window, a button appears on the taskbar.

All windows have the same elements, some more and some less, that you can use to change the window's size, move it around on the screen, see what's in it, and close it.

Figure 3   Two windows

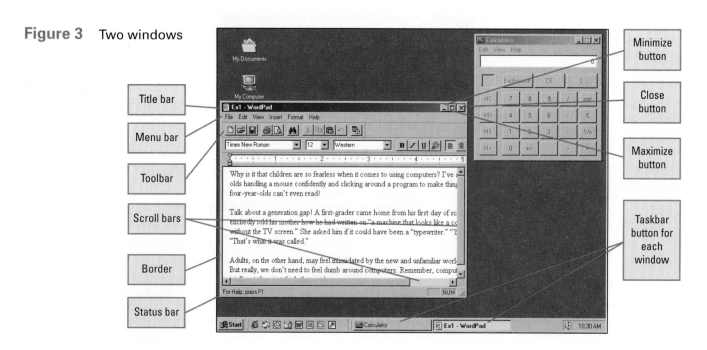

Why: All windows have certain elements in common, and once you learn to use them, you will feel comfortable in any program.

MAXIMIZE A WINDOW

How: A window can be *maximized* or enlarged so that it fills the entire screen (Figure 4). You can do this two ways:

○ Click the **Maximize** button.
○ Double-click the **title bar**.

Figure 4 Two windows, one maximized

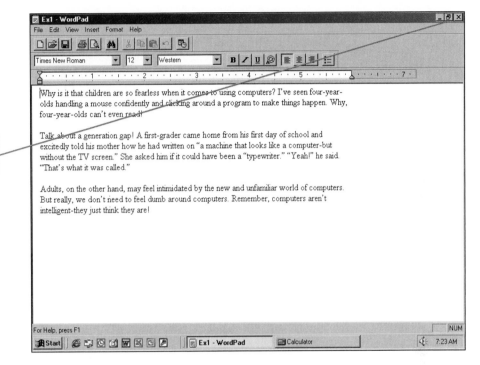

Restore button replaces Maximize button.

Result: The window fills the screen, and the Maximize button disappears, as it no longer applies. In its place is the Restore button that you can click to restore the window to its intermediate size. The maximized window covers the other windows, but you can tell what's open by the buttons on the taskbar.

 TIPS FROM A PRO: When you maximize a window, can you still see the taskbar? If not, you can still access it. Try moving the mouse pointer to the bottom edge of the screen. Sometimes the taskbar will pop into view. If not, you can see it again when you minimize the window, as you'll learn shortly. You'll learn how to customize the taskbar in Task 9 to make it appear or always remain on screen.

RESTORE A WINDOW

How: You may want to *restore* a maximized window to its intermediate size. You can do this in two ways:

- ○ Click the **Restore** button (the one that replaced the Maximize button).
- ○ Double-click the **title bar**.

Result: The window shrinks back to its original size, an intermediate size that does not fill the entire desktop. The Restore button is replaced with the Maximize button.

 THOUGHT QUESTION: Look back at Figure 3. Why do you suppose the Calculator does not have a Maximize or Restore button?

MINIMIZE A WINDOW

How: Whether a window is maximized or middle-sized, you may find that it is in the way when you want to look at something else on the screen. To *minimize* a window so that it appears only as a button on the taskbar, click the **Minimize** button, near the top-right corner of the window.

Figure 5   Two windows, one minimized.

This window is minimized.

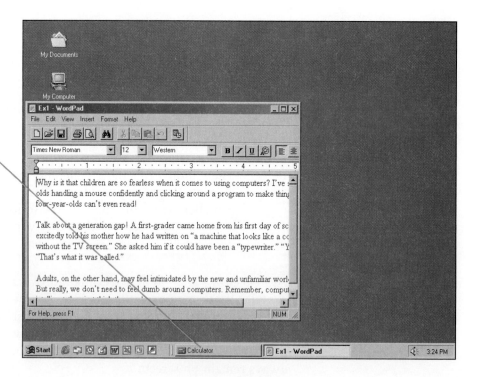

Result: The window seems to disappear, but it is still available. It's just put aside temporarily while you do other things on your Windows desktop.

SWITCH AMONG SEVERAL WINDOWS

How: With two or more windows open at a time, you can work on more than one thing at a time. This is called **multitasking**. The windows may overlap each other or one may be maximized or minimized, but no matter what, a button for each appears on the taskbar. To tell the computer which window you want to use, do one of these:

○ Click the window's button on the taskbar.
○ Click somewhere within the window you want, if you can see it.

Result: The window you choose immediately comes to the front of all the other windows. Its title bar has a brighter color, and its button on the taskbar appears pushed in. This window is called the **active window**.

MOVE A WINDOW

How: When one window overlaps another, or perhaps covers an icon on the desktop that you want to use, you can move the window on the desktop. To do this, place the mouse pointer on the title bar and drag.

Result: The window moves in the direction you drag it. (Of course, this doesn't work on a window that has been maximized or minimized.)

SIZE A WINDOW

How: Besides maximizing or minimizing a window, you can change its height and width to suit your needs.

1. Place the mouse pointer over the border until it turns into a two-headed arrow, as you see in Figure 6.
2. Drag the border inward or outward to change the dimensions of the window.

Figure 6 Change the size of a window

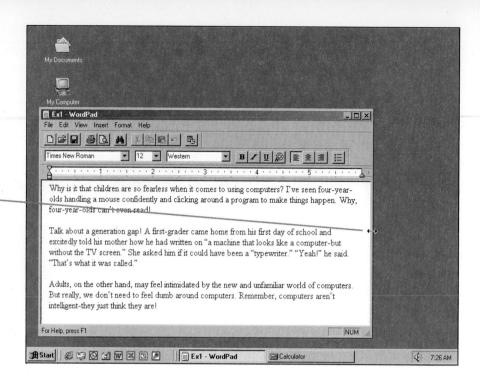

Mouse pointer becomes a two-headed arrow.

Result: The height or width of the window changes, so you can see more or less of the window's contents.

TIPS FROM A PRO: If you place the mouse pointer on the corner, it turns into a diagonal two-headed arrow. Now when you drag, you can change both the height and width at the same time.

SCROLL IN A WINDOW

How: When the contents of a window do not entirely fit within a window, *scrollbars* appear along the right or bottom edge, as in Figure 7. Use your mouse along with the scrollbars to bring the other contents of the window into view:

○ Click an arrow at either end of the scrollbar to move a little bit at a time. Click and hold the arrow to scroll slowly.
○ Drag the box from one end to the other or anywhere in between to see a different part of the contents.
○ Click above or below the box to scroll up or down one screen.
○ Rotate the mouse wheel, if you have one, to look at the contents above or below at the current screen.

Figure 7 Window with scrollbars

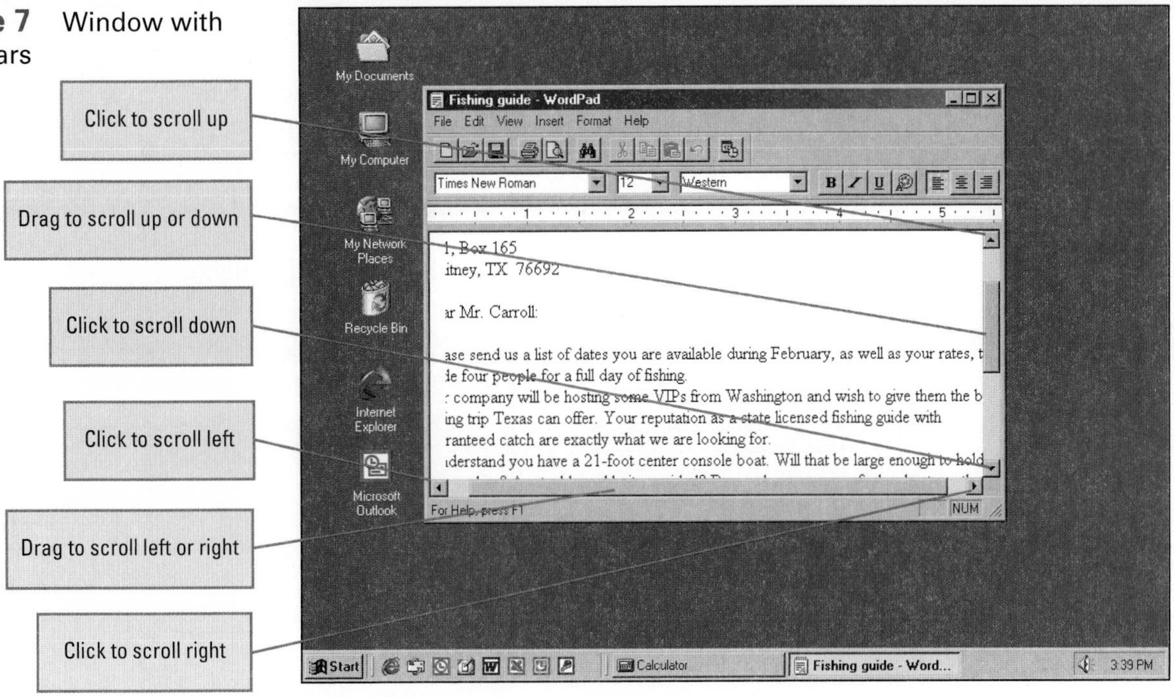

Click to scroll up

Drag to scroll up or down

Click to scroll down

Click to scroll left

Drag to scroll left or right

Click to scroll right

Result: You can view all the contents of a window, even the material that is currently out of view.

CLOSE A WINDOW

 How: When you are completely through using a window, click the **Close** button on the top-right corner.

Result: This removes the window from the screen and removes its button from the taskbar. It is no longer using the computer's processing resources.

TASK **6** *Interact with Programs*

What: When you've got a program open in a window, no matter what program it is, you interact with it the same general way. Just below the title bar is the *menu bar*, containing a series of words that drop down a menu of commands when you click them.

Some commands require you to make more specific choices. For example, the Print command enables you to specify answers to these questions: What pages do you want to print? What printer do you want use? What order do you want the pages printed? To make your choices, the program presents you with a *dialog box*, a rectangular message box that you can click or type in.

Why: Using menus and dialog boxes is how we humans tell the computer what we want it to do. When you can quickly find the commands you need and make choices easily in the dialog box, you'll be showing your expertise.

TASK 6: Interact with Programs   **13**

USE MENUS

How: Here's how to use a menu on the menu bar.

1. Click a word on the menu bar to drop down the menu.
2. Click a command to choose it, or click away from the menu to make it go away without choosing anything.

Look at Figure 8 to see how to read a menu.

Figure 8 Menu commands

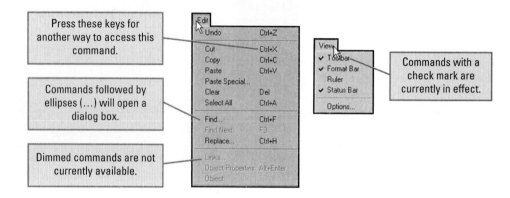

Result: When you choose a command, the program obeys or, if the command is followed by ellipses (...), opens a dialog box for you to make more choices.

TIPS FROM A PRO: Typical commands that appear in many programs are always found on the same menu. For example, you can count on finding the Print command on the File menu, and the Copy command on the Edit menu.

USE DIALOG BOXES

How: Although the choices that appear in various dialog boxes are specific to the command, the way you interact with any dialog box is the same. Each element shown in Figure 9 works a different way to make it easy for you to specify what you want.

○ Type in a *text box* to give the computer your information.
○ Click a *check box* to insert or remove a check next to a choice.
○ Click the down arrow on a *drop-down list* to see more choices to click.
○ Click a choice in a *list box,* or scroll to see more choices.
○ Click one *option button* among the choices given.
○ Click the up or down arrows on a *spin box* to increase or decrease a number.
○ Use a *command button* just as you use the Start button. Click OK to accept the choices and put them into effect, or click Cancel to make the dialog box go away without making any change.
○ Click a *tab* to see another screen of choices on a related topic.

❍ Click the *Help* button (the question mark in the title bar) and then click any element in the dialog-box for pop-up help on what it does.

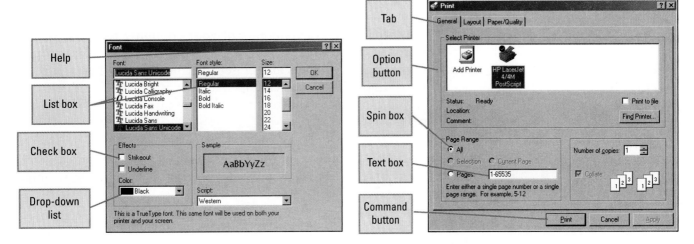

Figure 9 Typical dialog box elements

Result: When you make your choices in the dialog box and click **OK**, the command takes effect. If instead you want the dialog box to go away and not make changes, click **Cancel** or press the **Esc** key.

 TIPS FROM A PRO: To advance from one text box to another, press the **Tab** key. This is faster than clicking with the mouse because you leave your hands on the keyboard and continue typing your information.

TASK 7 — View the Contents of Your Computer

What: Computers store information such as documents, pictures, spread-sheets, databases, and programs in *files*. Files are organized into *folders*, and folders can be placed inside other folders, just as pieces of paper are placed into manila folders and then in hanging folders and organized in the various drawers of a filing cabinet. A folder that contains another folder is called a *parent folder*; and a folder that is inside another folder is often called a *subfolder*.

Like the separate drawers of a filing cabinet, the computer has several *disk drives* that read the information stored there. The drives available on your computer are named with letters of the alphabet:

1. A 3 1/2-inch floppy disk drive is named drive A.
2. An internal hard disk drive is named drive C (a second hard disk, if you have one, would be named drive D).
3. A CD-ROM or DVD-ROM drive is usually named drive D (or E, if you have two hard disks).

4. Other drives, such as a Zip drive and ones available over a network, will be named with subsequent letters.

Windows offers two resources that let you see the contents of the computer: My Computer and Windows Explorer. In both of these, when you look at what's stored in your computer, you can view it several different ways.

Why: You need to see the contents of your computer to know what's stored on it and where everything is, just as you know what's found in the various drawers and closets of your home. When you see a file or folder listed, you can open it, copy it, rename it, or delete it, or you can make a shortcut to it. You'll learn all these skills in the next tasks.

 TIPS FROM A PRO: As you view the file contents of your computer, you'll notice a variety of icons. The icon is a way to see what kind of file it is. Some common icons are shown in Table 5.

Table 5   Common Windows Icons

Icon	File type
	Folder
	Word document
	Excel worksheet
	PowerPoint presentation
	Access database
	Web page
	Text file

USE MY COMPUTER

How: Follow these steps to open My Computer and view its contents various ways.

1. Move the mouse pointer to the **My Computer** icon on the desktop. (If you are using Web-style Windows, the mouse pointer will turn into a pointing hand.)
2. Double-click (or if you are using Web-style Windows, click once) on the icon. My Computer opens in a window on the screen, similar to Figure 10.

Figure 10 My Computer

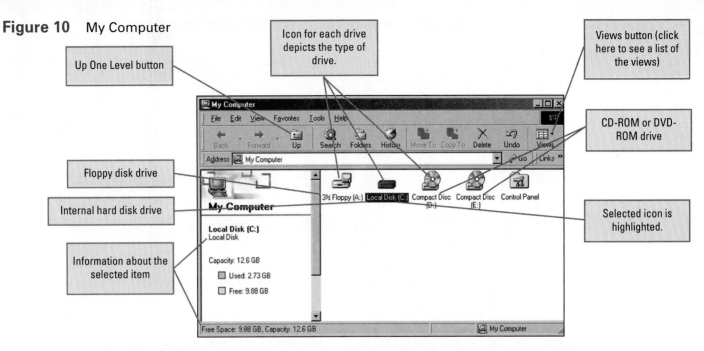

Up One Level button

Icon for each drive depicts the type of drive.

Views button (click here to see a list of the views)

CD-ROM or DVD-ROM drive

Floppy disk drive

Internal hard disk drive

Information about the selected item

Selected icon is highlighted.

3. Click to *select* an icon for a drive (for Web-style Windows, just point to it with the mouse pointer and pause). The icon appears darker, and information appears on the left and on the status bar.

4. Double-click an icon (or click once in Web-style Windows) to open it and see its contents. *Note*: You have to insert a disk into the floppy, CD, or DVD drive before you try to open it.

5. Click the **Views** button several times in succession to get the views shown in Figure 11. You can also click the arrow next to the button and choose a view from the list that appears.

○ **Large Icons view** shows all the folders and files in alphabetical order across the rows.

○ **Small Icons view** lists across the rows all the folders and then the files in alphabetical order.

○ **List view** lists all the folders and then the files in alphabetical order vertically, down the column.

○ **Details view** shows not only the file name and type, but also the size and date it was created or last modified. You can click the column headings to sort the files in order by name, by type, by size, and by date.

○ **Thumbnails view** displays a small version of the file. This is particularly useful for pictures and other graphics.

Figure 11 Five views

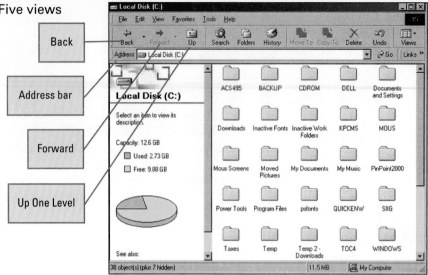

(a) Large icons view

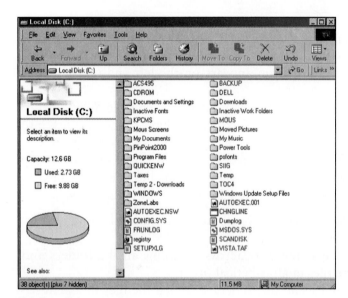

(b) Small icons view

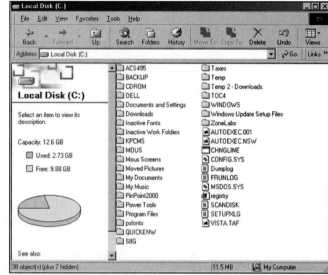

(c) List view

Click a column heading to sort the files on that column; click it again to reverse the sort order.

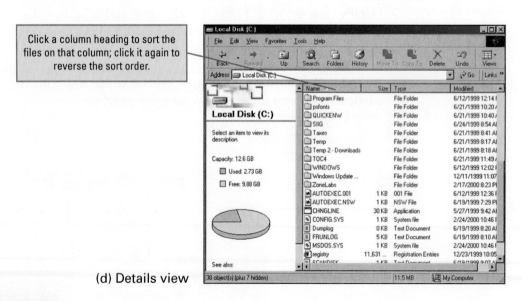

(d) Details view

Start with Windows

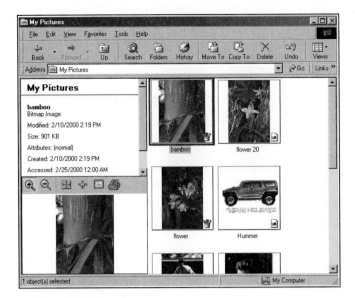

(e) Thumbnails view

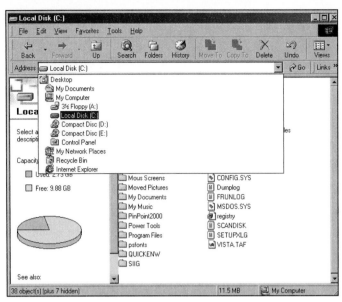

Figure 12 Address bar shows a list of drives

6. Double-click a folder to see its contents (click once in Web-style Windows).

7. Click the **Up One Level** button on the toolbar to see the parent folder or drive that contains the items you are currently viewing.

8. Click the **Back** button to retrace your steps in viewing various drives and folders in reverse order. Click the **Forward** button to step through them again.

9. Click the **Address** bar's down arrow to choose a different drive, as you see in Figure 12.

Result: You can click buttons to change views, and you can control which folder or drive's contents are on display. Viewing the contents is the first step to managing the contents of your computer, which you'll learn in Task 8.

 TIPS FROM A PRO: You can also use the Address bar to access the Web. Just type the address for a Web page and press **Enter**, and My Computer will transform into the Web browser, Internet Explorer.

ACCESS WINDOWS EXPLORER

How: To access Windows Explorer do one of these:

❍ Click the **Start** button, choose **Programs**, and then click **Windows Explorer**. (You may have to click the downward-pointing triangle on the bottom of the Programs menu to see more choices.) In Windows ME, click the Start button, choose Programs, select Accessories, and then click Windows Explorer.

○ Open **My Computer** and transform it into Windows Explorer. To do this, click the **Folders** button. (In Windows 98, click the **View** menu, choose **Explorer Bar**, and click **Folders**.)

Windows Explorer adds one feature to My Computer: the *Folders pane*. As you see in Figure 13, the Folders pane shows a list of drives and folders, with the folders indented beneath the drive, and subfolders indented even more, something like an outline.

To use Windows Explorer, use these techniques:

○ Scroll up and down to see more drives and folders.
○ Click a **+** next to a drive or folder to expand it to show the folders contained inside.
○ Click a **–** next to a drive or folder to collapse the subfolders and take up less space in the Folders pane.
○ Click a drive or folder to see its contents on the right side of the window.

Result: Using the Folders pane makes it easy to navigate around the various drives and folders to view their contents. When you click a drive or folder, it appears dark, or selected. This is the *current drive* or *current folder*, the one whose contents are listed in the right side of the window. Click a different drive or folder in the Folders pane to change which one is current.

 TIPS FROM A PRO: The name of the current drive or folder also appears on the title bar of the window, on the address bar, and on its taskbar button as well.

 THOUGHT QUESTION: Can you have both a current drive *and* a current folder? Can you change the current folder without changing the current drive?

Figure 13 Windows Explorer

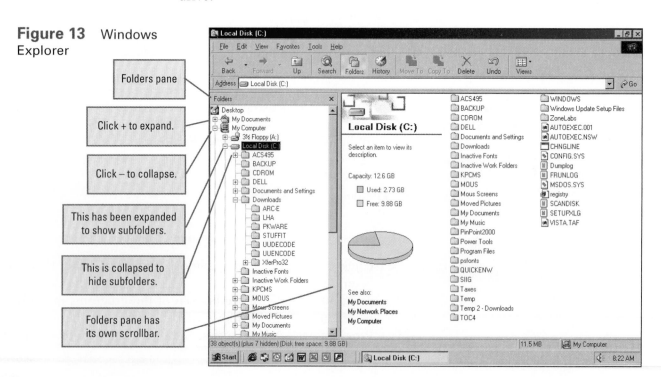

Folders pane

Click + to expand.

Click – to collapse.

This has been expanded to show subfolders.

This is collapsed to hide subfolders.

Folders pane has its own scrollbar.

What: Besides just looking around, you can use My Computer and Windows Explorer to manage the contents of your computer. Here are some of the tasks you can easily do:

❍ Create a folder to organize your stuff.
❍ Rename a file or folder.
❍ Copy a file or folder to another location.
❍ Move a file or folder to a different drive or folder.
❍ Use Send To as a quick way to make a copy.
❍ Delete a file or folder.

Why: You can use these skills to get organized. For example, you might take all the files, including pictures, charts, and documents, that pertain to a certain project and place them in a new folder you've created to specifically hold them. Or you can look on the CD that accompanies this book and copy the files needed for the exercises and projects to your hard disk or floppy disk so you can work on them. You can delete unwanted files, and when you have an important item you've been working on, you can use these skills to create a *backup* copy to store it in a separate location, just in case something happens to the original.

CREATE A FOLDER

How: Follow these steps to create a folder.

1. Open My Computer or Windows Explorer.
2. Choose where you want the folder to be.

   ❍ In My Computer, view the drive or folder that you want to contain the new folder.
   ❍ In Windows Explorer, use the Folders pane to select the drive or folder that you want to contain the new folder.

3. Click **File** and choose **New** and then click **Folder**. A new folder named *New Folder* appears, with its name surrounded by a rectangle, as you see in Figure 14.
4. Type the name of the folder and press **Enter**.

Result: The new folder appears both in the window and in the Folders pane.

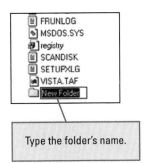

Type the folder's name.

Figure 14   Creating a folder in Windows Explorer

TIPS FROM A PRO: If you happen to click away before you type the name for the new folder, you can still rename it later.

RENAME A FILE OR FOLDER

How: Follow these instructions to rename a file or folder.

1. Select the item you want to rename.
2. Right-click to see the shortcut menu shown in Figure 15.
3. Click (with either button) the **Rename** command. The menu goes away, and a rectangle appears around the name, indicating that you can type.
4. Type the new name and press **Enter**.

Result: The rectangle disappears from around the name, and the file or folder is renamed.

 TIPS FROM A PRO: The shortcut menu is *context-sensitive*, meaning that the choices shown on it depend on what you were pointing to when you right-clicked. This type of menu is sometimes called a context menu. The commands in Figure 15 are the ones you can use for managing files and folders. You'll see other commands on the shortcut menu when you right-click other items on screen.

Figure 15 Shortcut menu

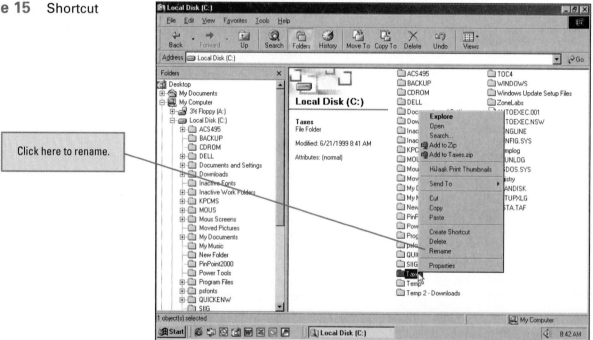

Click here to rename.

COPY OR MOVE A FILE OR FOLDER USING THE FOLDERS PANE

How: The Folders pane makes it easy to copy or move items. You can simply drag the items from the right side to the left.

 TIPS FROM A PRO: You can copy and move several items at the same time, if you want. To do this, you first have to select several items. Here are some techniques for selecting several items at once:

○ Drag a rectangular area surrounding the items you want to select.

○ Press and hold the **Shift** key and click the first and last items; the items you clicked and all the items in between will be selected.

○ Press and hold the **Ctrl** key and click each item you want, without selecting items between.

These techniques are for selecting items in classic Windows; if you're using Web-style Windows, hold down **Shift** or **Ctrl** while you point rather than clicking to select.

1. Scroll up or down the Folders pane, and expand as necessary until you see the destination for the file or folder.

2. Select on the right side of the window the file or folder you want to copy or move.

3. Right-drag (that is, drag while holding down the right mouse button) the selected item to the Folders pane until the destination is highlighted or selected. You can see this operation in Figure 16.

Figure 16 Dragging to the Folders pane

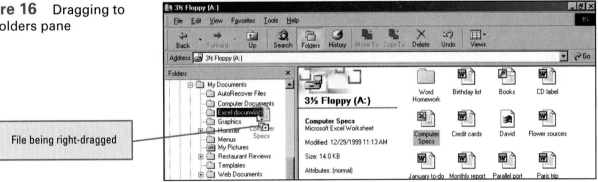

4. Release the mouse button, and a shortcut menu appears with several choices, as you see in Figure 17:

○ **Move here.** This is a good choice for organizing your files and folders.

○ **Copy here.** This is the choice when you want a second copy as a backup.

○ **Create shortcut(s) here.** You'll learn about shortcuts in Task 9.

○ **Cancel.** Choose this if you don't want to do any of the above.

Figure 17 Choose whether to move or copy

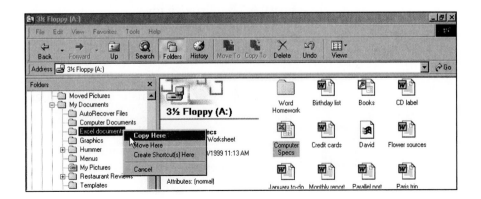

5. Click to choose **Move** or **Copy**, or click **Cancel** to change your mind.

Result: If you chose Move, the file or folder is removed from one location and placed in the new location. This is a good choice for when you are rearranging and organizing your files and folders on your hard disk. If you chose Copy, the file or folder is duplicated and appears in both locations. This is good for making backups on another disk.

  TIPS FROM A PRO: If you make a mistake in the copy or move process, click the **Undo** button and then try again.

COPY OR MOVE A FILE OR FOLDER IN MY COMPUTER

How: Windows provides several methods for copying. The instructions below use the buttons on the toolbar, but the Copy to Folder and Move to Folder commands are also available on the Edit menu. Select the item(s) you want to copy.

1. Click either the **Copy To** or **Move To** button. This opens the dialog box shown in Figure 18.
2. Expand the drives and folders as necessary, and scroll until you see the destination.
3. Click the destination and click **OK**, or click **New Folder** to create a new folder to contain the items.

Figure 18 Browse for Folder dialog box

Figure 19 Copying in progress

Result: You may see an animation of the move or copy process, as shown in Figure 19. This is called a progress bar.

 TIPS FROM A PRO: Here's another way to create a folder. Click the **New Folder** button, as you see in Figure 18, if you want to create a new folder to contain the items you are moving or copying.

COPY OR MOVE IN WINDOWS 98

How: Working in Windows 98 is just a little different from working in newer versions of Windows. Instead of the Copy To button, you use the Copy and Paste buttons, and in place of the Move To button, you use the Cut and Paste buttons, shown in Figure 20. The Cut, Copy, and Paste commands are also available on the Edit menu.

Figure 20 Windows 98 toolbar has Cut, Copy, and Paste buttons

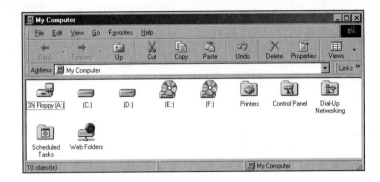

1. Select the item you want to copy.
2. To make a duplicate of an item, click **Copy**; to move an item, click **Cut**.
3. Navigate to and select the destination where you want the item to be placed. (In classic Windows, each folder may open in its own My Computer window, and therefore the Back and Forward buttons may be disabled.)
4. Click **Paste**.

Result: When you paste, you see an animation of the process.

TIPS FROM A PRO: You can use these same Cut, Copy, and Paste commands to move and duplicate lots of things besides just files and folders. For example, you can copy or cut a picture or a bit of text from inside one document and paste it into another. The copied or cut item is placed on the *clipboard*, a temporary storage place provided by Windows. Then you can paste it wherever you want.

USE SEND TO

How: An easy way to make a backup copy of the file is to use the Send To command.

1. Select the file or folder you want to back up.
2. Right-click the file, and then choose **Send To** on the shortcut menu, as shown in Figure 21.
3. Click the destination from the submenu. *Note:* you must first insert a floppy disk into the drive before you choose 3 1/2 Floppy A:.

TASK 8: Manage the Contents of Your Computer **25**

Figure 21 Send To command

Choose **3 1/2 Floppy (A)** to make a backup onto a floppy disk.

Choose **My Briefcase** to coordinate files between two computers.

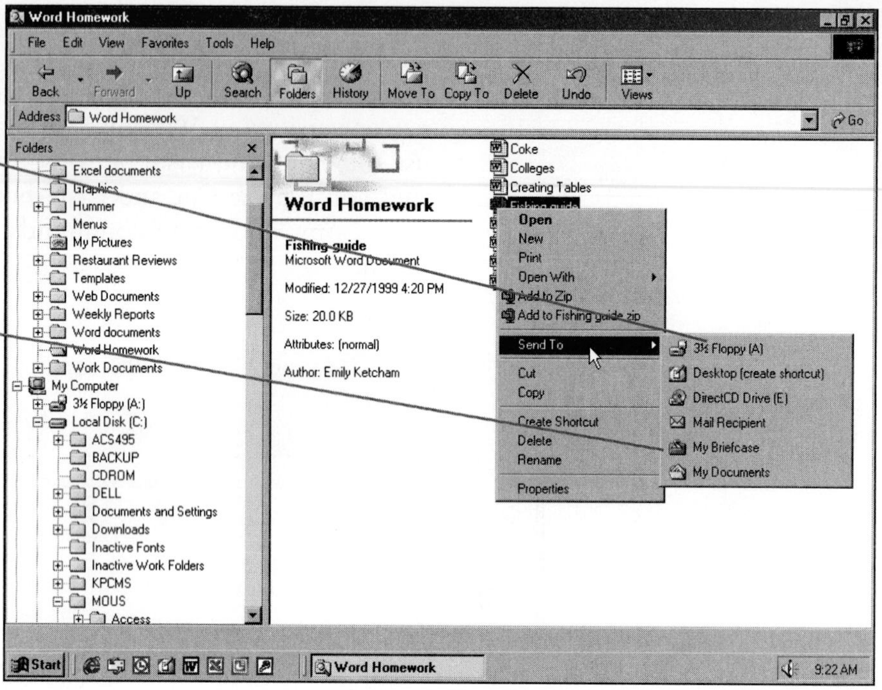

Result: The Copying dialog box appears, showing the process, just as you saw when you used the Copy To button.

DELETE A FILE OR FOLDER

How: When you've got unwanted files or folders on your disk, it's easy to remove them in My Computer or Windows Explorer.

1. Select the file or folder you want to delete.
2. Click the **Delete** button, or press the **Delete** key on the keyboard, or choose **Delete** from the **Edit** menu.
3. Click **OK** to confirm the delete, or **Cancel**.

Result: A dialog box appears, as in Figure 22, confirming whether you want to delete the selected item. When you click OK, the item will be deleted.

If you're deleting an item from your hard disk, Windows will move it to the Recycle Bin instead of permanently deleting it. This Windows feature temporarily stores deleted items, giving you a chance to change your mind and retrieve them, just as you can paw through the wastepaper basket looking for a bill or letter you've tossed by mistake.

Figure 22 Confirming
the delete

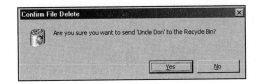

 THOUGHT QUESTION: Why is the Recycle Bin only available on your hard disk, and not for files deleted from a floppy disk?

USE THE RECYCLE BIN TO RESTORE A DELETED FILE

How: To recover a file you've deleted from your hard disk, open the Recycle Bin.

1. Double-click the **Recycle Bin** on the Windows desktop, in My Computer, or in Windows Explorer's Folders pane. (Click once to open, if you are using Web-style Windows.)
2. Select the item you want to retrieve.
3. Right-click and choose **Restore**, as you see in Figure 23.

Figure 23 Restoring a deleted file from the Recycle Bin

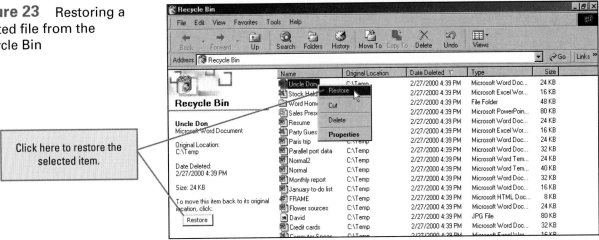

Click here to restore the selected item.

Result: The file is restored to the folder from which it was originally deleted.

 TIPS FROM A PRO: If you delete a folder, you delete all the files contained in it. Only the folder is shown in the Recycle Bin, but the files are there also, even though their names aren't listed. Restoring the folder restores the files as well.

EMPTY THE RECYCLE BIN

How: Deleted items sent to the Recycle Bin are still taking up space on your hard disk. You must empty the Recycle Bin to permanently delete the files and thus make room on your hard disk.

1. Right-click the **Recycle Bin**.
2. Choose **Empty Recycle Bin** from the shortcut menu, shown in Figure 24a.
3. Click **Yes** to confirm that you want to permanently delete the files, or click **No** if you're not sure (Figure 24b).

Figure 24 Emptying the Recycle Bin

(a) Using the shortcut menu   (b) Confirming the delete

Result: The files are now permanently deleted, making more space available on your hard disk. If you wanted to restore them now, you have to go to the trouble and expense of getting and using special recovery software.

 **TASK 9** | *Customize Windows*

What: One of the nice features of using Windows is the capability to customize it. This task covers just a few of the items you can customize.

Why: You can show your personality or just get things arranged the way you like so you can work efficiently.

CHANGE THE MOUSE

How: If you're left-handed, you'll especially like the capability to customize the way the mouse works.

1. Click the **Start** button, choose **Settings**, and click **Control Panel**. This opens the window shown in Figure 25.

Figure 25 Control Panel is used to customize the features of your computer

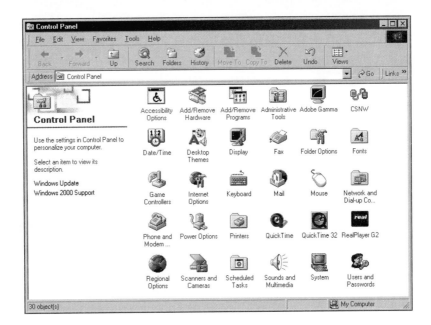

2. Double-click the icon for **Mouse** (or click once if you are using Web-style Windows). This opens the Mouse Properties dialog box.

3. Click the **Buttons** tab, if necessary, to see the dialog box shown in Figure 26. *Note:* Your dialog box may have different options.

4. Specify whether you prefer to use the mouse right-handed or left-handed, that is, which button you want to use regularly to choose things and which button you want to use to get the shortcut menu. Look through the various tabs in the dialog box, and make other adjustments you need, such as changes to the double-click speed or the motion of the mouse, or even the appearance of the mouse pointer.

5. When you're finished making choices, click one of the following buttons:

   ○ **Apply** to make the change and see its effect immediately, leaving the dialog box open for more changes.
   ○ **OK** to make changes and close the dialog box.
   ○ **Cancel** to close the dialog box without making any changes.

Figure 26 Customize the mouse

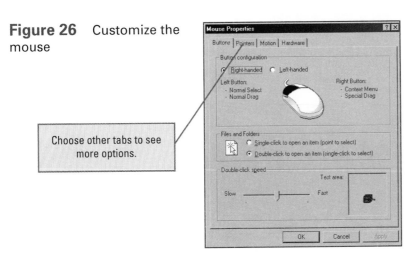

Choose other tabs to see more options.

Result: If you clicked OK, the choices you made in the Mouse dialog box are put into effect. Enjoy the new settings for your mouse!

 Tips from a Pro: The **Control Panel** contains a number of other icons for you to customize to best fit your computer's hardware and your own preference. Open them up, explore a little, and click **Cancel** to leave without making any changes.

CHANGE THE DISPLAY

How: You can access the Display Properties dialog box to customize its appearance without even opening the Control Panel.

1. Right-click an empty area of the Windows desktop.
2. Choose **Properties** from the shortcut menu.
3. Look through the various tabs on the dialog box to see choices for customizing all sorts of features of the desktop. Here are some of the things you can do:

   ○ Change the design that appears on the desktop (Figure 27).
   ○ Set a screen saver to come on when your computer is idle.
   ○ Change the colors of the window elements, such as the title bar.
   ○ Change the resolution and number of colors that your monitor displays.

4. After you've made your choices, click one of the following buttons:

   ○ **Apply** to make the changes and see its effect immediately, leaving the dialog box open for more changes.
   ○ **OK** to make the changes and close the dialog box.
   ○ **Cancel** to close the dialog box without making any changes.

Figure 27 Customize the display

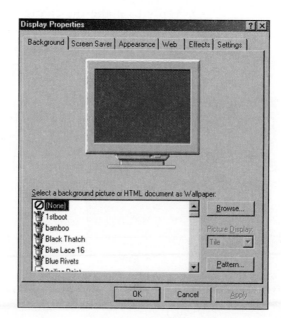

Result: You can show your individuality by your choices and make Windows a more pleasant environment to work in.

TIPS FROM A PRO: Here's how you change to (or from) Web-style Windows:

For Windows 2000

1. In My Computer or Windows Explorer, choose the **Tools** menu and click **Folder Options**.
2. Click the **General** tab, if necessary, to see the dialog box in Figure 28a.
3. Click to choose the top choice of each pair for Web-style windows, or the bottom choice of each pair for classic Windows, or any combination of Web-style and classic style that you prefer.

For Windows 98

1. In My Computer or Windows Explorer, choose the **View** menu, and click **Folder Options**.
2. Click the **General** tab if necessary, to see the dialog box in Figure 28b.
3. Choose **Web-style** (or **Classic style**, if you want to use that instead); or choose **Custom** and click **Settings** to open the Custom Settings dialog box, where you can choose any combination of Web-style and Classic style.
4. Click **OK**.

Figure 28   Folder Options dialog box

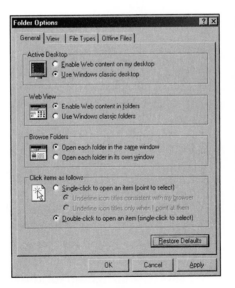

(a) In Windows 2000

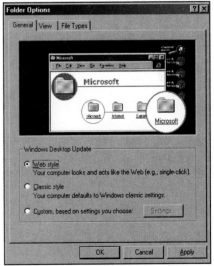

(b) In Windows 98

CUSTOMIZE THE TASKBAR

How: You have to change the settings for the taskbar before you can use the PinPoint tutorials and tests. Here's how to do that:

1. Place the mouse pointer on a blank area of the taskbar and right-click to see the shortcut menu in Figure 29.

Figure 29 Taskbar shortcut menu

2. Click Properties to see the dialog box shown in Figure 30.

Figure 30 Taskbar properties

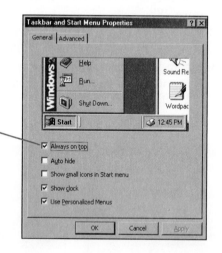

To use PinPoint, click to remove checks from these two boxes.

3. Choose one or more of these choices, and click **OK**:

   ○ **Always on Top** keeps the taskbar on screen even when a window is maximized.
   ○ **Auto Hide** minimizes the taskbar so that it appears as a line on the bottom of the screen. When you move the mouse pointer to it, the taskbar reappears.
   ○ **Show Small Icons in Start Menu** makes the Start menu shorter in height. (Not too useful.)
   ○ **Show Clock** displays the digital clock in the tray on the right side of the taskbar. (Very handy.)
   ○ **Show Personalized Menus** (not available in Windows 98) enables you to see only the menu selections on the Programs menu that you use most often, hiding the rest until you click the down arrow at the bottom of the Programs menu.

Result: The taskbar and Start menu behave the way you prefer.

TIPS FROM A PRO: Before you use the PinPoint software, you must remove checks from the Always on Top and Auto Hide choices in the Taskbar Properties dialog box.

ADD SHORTCUT ICONS TO THE DESKTOP

How: The Windows desktop, like your physical tabletop, should keep all the things you use often close at hand. You can create a *shortcut icon* right on the desktop as a way to quickly access your favorite file, folder, program, or Web page.

1. Use My Computer or Explorer and look around the various drives and folders to find the item you want to access quickly.
2. Right-click and from the shortcut menu choose **Send To** and then click **Desktop (Create Shortcut)**.

Result: A shortcut icon appears on the desktop. You can tell that it's a shortcut not only by its name, but by the small crooked arrow that appears on the corner, as in Figure 31.

You can rename a shortcut by right-clicking and choosing **Rename**, as you did before. You can delete shortcuts from the desktop by selecting it and pressing the **Delete** key. *Warning*: Do NOT delete icons from the desktop if they are not shortcut icons. This might delete a program. A better way to remove unwanted programs is through the Control Panel.

Figure 31
Shortcut icon

 THOUGHT QUESTION: Examine your Windows desktop. Which icons are shortcuts, and which are the actual programs?

ADD BUTTONS TO THE QUICK LAUNCH TOOLBAR

Figure 32
Quick Launch toolbar

How: Rather than cluttering up your desktop with shortcut icons, you can put buttons on the Quick Launch portion of the taskbar (Figure 32). They'll be handy all the time, even when a window is maximized.

1. Use My Computer or Windows Explorer and look around the various drives and folders to find the item you want to access quickly.
2. Select the item and right-drag (that is, drag with the right mouse button) to the Quick Launch toolbar.
3. To rearrange the icons, drag left or right. To delete an icon, drag it to the Recycle Bin.

Result: Your favorite programs, files, or folders are always handy.

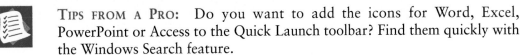 TIPS FROM A PRO: Do you want to add the icons for Word, Excel, PowerPoint or Access to the Quick Launch toolbar? Find them quickly with the Windows Search feature.

1. Click **Start**, choose **Search**, and click **For Files or Folders** (or in My Computer, click the **Search** button). This opens the Search Assistant, shown in Figure 33.

2. In the **Search for Files or Folders Named** box, type one of the following names:

    ○ **Winword.exe** for Word
    ○ **Powerpnt.exe** for PowerPoint
    ○ **Excel.exe** for Excel
    ○ **Msaccess.exe** for Access

3. Right-drag the program icon down to the Quick Launch toolbar, as you see in Figure 33.

4. On the menu that appears, choose **Create Shortcut Here**.

Figure 33   Find the Word program

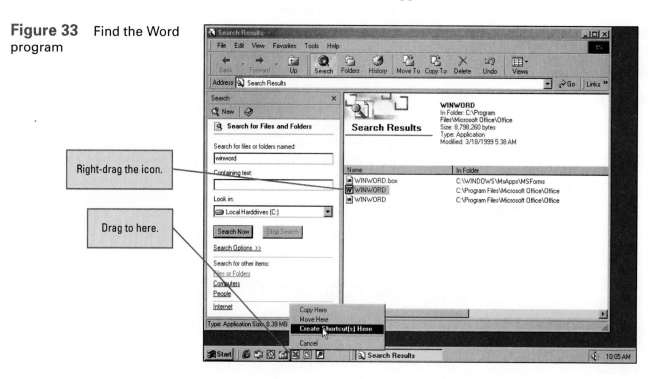

FOR WINDOWS 98

1. Click **Start**, choose **Find**, and click **Files or Folders**.

2. In the Find window, type the name of the program you want (same as above) and press **Enter**. In the bottom of the dialog box, you'll see the results.

3. Right-drag the program icon down to the Quick Launch toolbar, as you see in Figure 33.

4. On the menu that appears, choose **Create Shortcut Here**.

What: At the end of the workday, before you turn off your computer, you must exit Windows properly.

Why: If you don't exit before turning off the computer, Windows doesn't have a chance to store everything in its proper place. Sometimes files or programs are still in *RAM*, (Random Access Memory, the temporary storage place a computer uses for processing), and when you turn the power off, RAM evaporates. The next time you turn on your computer, Windows will have to do lots of checking and cleaning up to get everything put into place—or worse, some files may be damaged.

How: Follow these steps to shut down your computer safely.

1. Close all open windows by clicking their **Close** buttons.
2. Click the **Start** button and choose **Shut Down**.
3. A dialog box similar to that of Figure 34 asks what you want to do. Choose **Shut Down** and click **OK**.

Figure 34 Shut Down Windows dialog box for Windows 2000

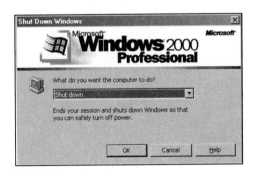

Result: Windows takes a few moments to put everything away and then either turns off your computer for you or gives you permission to turn it off yourself.

TIPS FROM A PRO: Does your computer seem to keep locking up or having trouble? Sometimes you can fix it by restarting it. Choose **Shut Down** from the Start menu, but this time, choose **Restart**. This will force Windows to clear everything up and start over, so you can continue to work.

Key Terms

Note: you can find definitions for these words in this chapter:

Active window	Menu bar
Backup	Minimize
Boot up	Mouse pointer
Buttons	Multitasking
Check box	My Briefcase
Clipboard	My Computer
Clock	My Documents
Collapse	My Network Places
Command button	Operating system
Control panel	Option button
Context-sensitive	Parent folder
Current drive	Quick Launch toolbar
Current folder	RAM
Desktop	Recycle Bin
Details view	Restore
Dialog box	Scroll bars
Disk drives	Select
Drop-down list	Shortcut icon
Expand	Shortcut menu
File	Small Icons view
Folder	Spin box
Folders pane	Start button
Icons	Start menu
Large Icons view	Subfolder
List box	Tab
List view	Taskbar
Log in	Text box
Maximize	Window

Review Questions

You can use the following review questions and exercises to test your knowledge and skills. Answers are given in Appendix D.

True/False

Indicate whether each statement is true (T) or false (F).

____ 1. An operating system is a special type of software you use to type a document.

____ 2. When the computer is busy, such as when it's booting up, the mouse pointer resembles an hourglass.

____ 3. The rectangular strip containing the Start button is called the taskbar.

____ 4. When you want to access a context-sensitive shortcut menu, double-click something.

____ 5. When you click the **Start** menu, you can see the files and folders contained in your computer.

___ 6. When one window is maximized and another is minimized, you can access the minimized one by choosing from the Start menu.

___ 7. To make a dialog box go away without making any changes, click **Cancel**.

___ 8. The main difference between My Computer and Windows Explorer is the Folders pane.

___ 9. To create a folder, click the **File** menu and choose **New** and then **Folder**.

___ 10. When you select a file on the hard disk of your computer and press the **Delete** key or **Delete** button, it is permanently deleted.

Multiple Choice

Select the letter that best completes the statement.

___ 1. A word for the entire windows screen that contains the taskbar and icons is:
   a. Background.
   b. Desktop.
   c. Explorer.
   d. My Computer.
   e. Operating system.

___ 2. When you choose a command on a menu that is followed by ellipses (...):
   a. A dialog box appears.
   b. A window appears.
   c. The menu disappears and the command is immediately put into effect.
   d. The window is minimized.
   e. Nothing happens, because the command is not currently available.

___ 3. Several documents or programs may be organized and stored together in a:
   a. Button.
   b. Desktop.
   c. File.
   d. Folder.
   e. Shortcut.

___ 4. The main hard disk on your computer is usually named:
   a. Drive A.
   b. Drive C.
   c. Drive 0.
   d. Drive 1.
   e. the Parent drive.

___ 5. The view to use when you want to sort the files in order by the date they were created is:
   a. Details view.
   b. Large icons view.
   c. List view.
   d. Small icons view.
   e. Sort view.

____ 6. A copy of an important file or folder stored on a separate disk in case something happens to the original is called a:
   a. Backup.
   b. Bootup.
   c. Keeper.
   d. Safety.
   e. Subfile or Subfolder.

____ 7. To copy a file or folder, first select it and then:
   a. Right-drag it to the destination in the Folders pane.
   b. Click the **Copy To** button and choose the destination.
   c. Right-click and choose **Send To.**
   d. All of the above.
   e. Either a or b.

____ 8. The temporary storage place for items deleted from the hard disk is called the:
   a. Desktop.
   b. Keeper.
   c. Trashcan.
   d. Wastepaper Basket.
   e. None of the above.

____ 9. To change the color or design of the desktop:
   a. Right-click the desktop and choose **Properties.**
   b. Double-click **My Computer.**
   c. Scroll up or down in the window.
   d. Click the **OK** button on the Quick Launch portion of the taskbar.
   e. Click the **Maximize** button on the window.

____ 10. To use PinPoint software, you must make sure these settings for your taskbar *do not* have a check mark:
   a. Always on Top and Auto Hide.
   b. Auto Hide and Show Clock.
   c. Always on Top and Minimize.
   d. Auto Clock and Quick Launch.
   e. Minimize and Start.

Screen Review

Match the letters in Figure 35 with the correct items in the list.

Figure 35

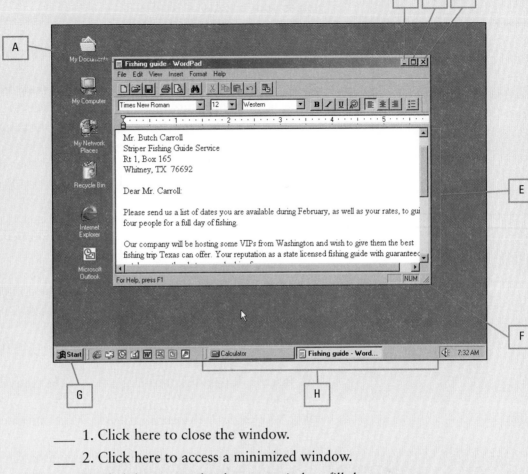

___ 1. Click here to close the window.

___ 2. Click here to access a minimized window.

___ 3. Click here to make the open window fill the screen.

___ 4. Drag here to move the window to the right.

___ 5. Click here to see a menu of the available programs.

___ 6. Drag here to make the window slightly smaller or larger.

___ 7. Click or drag here to see the contents of the window that are not currently in view.

___ 8. Click here so the open window will disappear and show only as a button on the toolbar.

Exercise and Project

Follow these step-by-step instructions to practice using your Windows skills. If you are working in a computer lab, ask your instructor how to log in and exit Windows.

Note: This exercise requires you to use a floppy disk and the CD that accompanies your book.

---

1. With your computer on, make a quick sketch of your desktop. Label several icons.

2. Open **My Computer**. On your paper, write down whether or not the window is maximized.

3. Make a list of the drives available on your computer. Write down both the drive name and the type of drive.

4. Insert the PinPoint CD from the back of your book into the CD drive. View the contents of the CD. Write down the names of the first four folders you see.

5. Change the view to see all of the views. Use Details view to find the date that one of the files or folders was last modified. Write the date on your paper.

6. Turn on the Folders pane (Windows 98 users: choose **View**, then **Explorer Bar** and click **Folders**). View the contents of the PinPoint CD. In the Folders pane, expand all the folders and subfolders. Make a sketch of their organization on your paper.

7. View the contents of the Chapter 2 folder. Write down the name of a file contained in it.

8. Insert a floppy disk into Drive A. Use the **Copy** or **Send To** command to place a copy of the file you viewed in Step 7 onto the floppy disk.

9. Make drive A the current drive. Write on your paper how much free space the disk has available.

10. Delete the file you copied to the floppy disk. On your paper, write down whether it is sent to the Recycle Bin or permanently deleted.

Project

Try out the features of both Web-style Windows and classic Windows. Compare the way you interact with Windows in the two styles. Use the Help feature to find out more about these two options; learn about the Active Desktop as well. Explain the benefits of these features, which style you prefer, and why.

Get Started with PowerPoint

Dust off your suit, shine up your shoes, and get ready to give the most dazzling presentation of your life. Well, before you head off to the cleaners to pick up your favorite suit, maybe you'd better create something first. Even if you've never given an oral presentation the following chapters show you how to design and format visual aids, and to deliver your message using PowerPoint.

PowerPoint 2000 is a graphics software package designed to help produce professional-looking visual aids to accompany a presentation. Whether you're using the World Wide Web (the Web) to solicit funds from a venture capitalist in Singapore or presenting fire-making techniques to your son's local Boy Scout troop, you can enhance your presentation and increase its effectiveness by using PowerPoint. This is good news whether you will be speaking to a group or to just one person. Why? Because studies have shown that speakers who support their message with visual aids are considered to be more professional, more effective, and more organized. More importantly, research indicates that audiences remember significantly more of what they hear when spoken words are supported in some way with graphical images. This chapter introduces you to the elements of the PowerPoint window and shows you how to create, save, and print your first presentation.

At the end of this chapter you will be able to:

*

C **E**

- ☑ ❑ Create a presentation using the AutoContent Wizard
- ☑ ❑ Navigate in the PowerPoint views
- ☑ ❑ Save a presentation
- ☑ ❑ Create a new presentation from an existing file
- ☑ ❑ Get help with PowerPoint

*Whenever you see this icon, you know that this is a skill you have to perform on the certification exam to become a Microsoft Office User Specialist. The C and E stand for Core and Expert objectives respectively.

What: Start the PowerPoint 2000 program.

Why: You can use PowerPoint to create one or all of these eye-catching visual aids:

- ❍ Electronic slide shows
- ❍ Overhead transparencies
- ❍ Self-running kiosk displays
- ❍ Web presentations
- ❍ Handouts
- ❍ 35mm slides

How: Several ways to open PowerPoint are:

- ❍ Click the **Start** button, point to **Programs** with the mouse, and then click **Microsoft PowerPoint** as shown in Figure 1.1.
- ❍ Click the PowerPoint icon on the Quick Launch bar or the PowerPoint shortcut on the desktop if they are available.
- ❍ Double-click the name of an existing PowerPoint presentation—this automatically opens the file in the program. (You can see saved files by looking in My Computer and Windows Explorer).

Note: You should have a general knowledge of Windows before you start this chapter. If you would like to get help using Windows, see the introductory chapter, "Start with Windows", in this book.

Figure 1.1
Launching PowerPoint

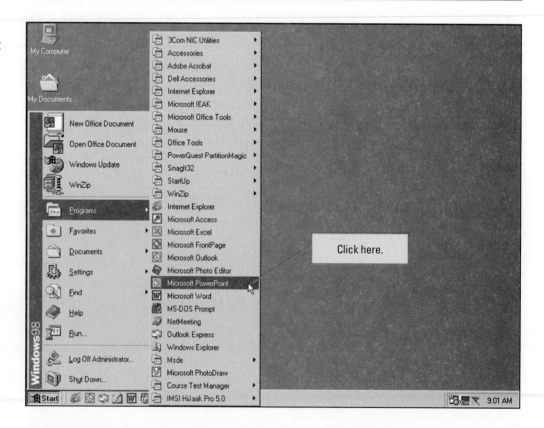

TIPS FROM A PRO: You can also open PowerPoint by clicking the **Start** button, clicking **New Office Document**, and then selecting one of the available methods for creating a PowerPoint Presentation.

Note: Though in common speech 'presentation' is generally used to refer to a delivered speech, in PowerPoint and throughout this book it refers to the various forms of PowerPoint output.

Result: When you open PowerPoint, the dialog box shown in Figure 1.2 appears. To continue you must pick one of the four options that are shown in the figure and that are described as follows:

○ **AutoContent Wizard** leads you step-by-step to create the text for a typical presentation.
○ **Design Template** gives you choices for attractive (but empty) slides.
○ **Blank presentation** gives you a blank slide with neither color nor text.
○ **Open an existing presentation** enables you to open files that have already been created and saved in PowerPoint.

If it is beginning to sound like we have lapsed into a foreign language, don't worry. Each of these choices is thoroughly explained in a later section of this book.

Figure 1.2
PowerPoint opening dialog box

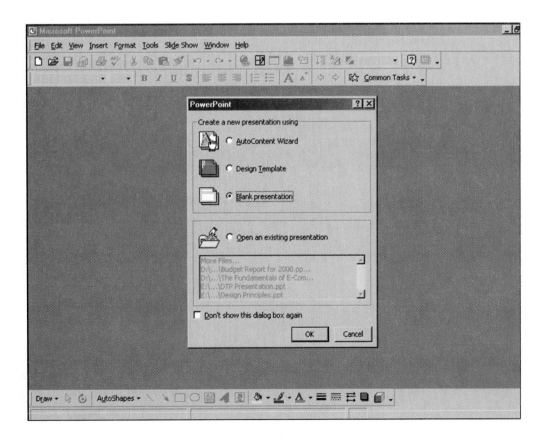

TIPS FROM A PRO: Did you know that . . .
we remember about 15% of what we hear,
we remember about 80% of what we see and hear,
without visual aids, comprehension is around 20%, and
with visual aids, comprehension jumps up to approximately 60%?

 THOUGHT QUESTION: Why do you suppose we remember more of the verbal messages that we hear if they are supported with graphical images?

TASK 2 · *Use the AutoContent Wizard*

 CORE OBJECTIVE: Create a presentation using the AutoContent Wizard

 CORE OBJECTIVE: Create a presentation from a Template and/or a Wizard

What: The creators of PowerPoint have supplied a handy tool for creating 24 typical slide shows with a minimum of thought or preparation via the AutoContent Wizard. A *wizard* is a feature of PowerPoint (as well as the other Microsoft Office products) that offers a step-by-step, guided approach to creating some common presentation types. You are led through the process with a series of questions, and then your answers are used to create the basic model for your visual aids.

Why: By providing suggestions for the content and design of common presentation themes, like selling a product or communicating bad news, the AutoContent Wizard makes it easy for you to painlessly organize your thoughts and build a slide show. Whether you're new to PowerPoint, need to create a presentation quickly, or just want some suggestions to stimulate your thinking (even the most experienced writers get stuck occasionally), the AutoContent Wizard is for you. Even if you are a professional speechwriter, why spend time and energy re-creating from scratch what has already been done for you?

How: You can start the AutoContent Wizard two ways:

- ❍ From the opening dialog box, choose **AutoContent Wizard** and press **Enter** or click **OK**.
- ❍ Click **File|New**. (When you see commands written this way, it means to click **File** on the menu bar, and then click **New** on the submenu that is subsequently displayed.) Click the **General** tab in the New Presentation dialog box, and then double-click the **AutoContent Wizard** (Figure 1.3).

Once you see the first screen of the wizard, follow these steps:

1. The first screen introduces you to the AutoContent Wizard. Press **Enter** or click **Next** to continue.

Note: The alternative command, "press Enter," is generally omitted for the remainder of this book. Remember, however, that you can use it to move to the next step after you have selected your choice in a dialog box.

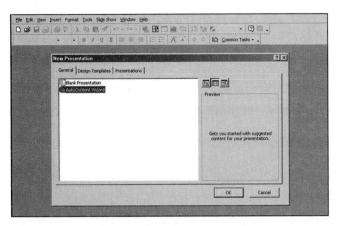

Figure 1.3 AutoContent Wizard's New Presentation dialog box

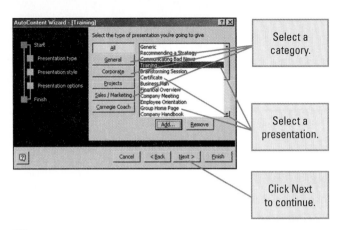

Figure 1.4 Choosing presentation type in the AutoContent Wizard

2. The second screen enables you to browse through six categories of predefined presentations to find the topic that most closely matches your requirements (Figure 1.4). If you don't make a selection, PowerPoint uses the default presentation, Generic. *Default* just means the setting or choice that is made by PowerPoint if there is no input from you. Click **Next** to continue.

3. Designate the type of output that you want on the third screen (Figure 1.5), and then click **Next** to continue.

4. The fourth screen (Figure 1.6) enables you to add a title and to include the date, slide number, and some text—such as the name of the organization you will be speaking to—at the bottom of each slide. Click **Finish** when you have added all of the information that you want to include.

Figure 1.5 Choosing output type in the AutoContent Wizard

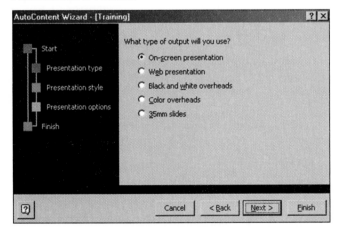

Figure 1.6 Customizing your presentation in the AutoContent Wizard

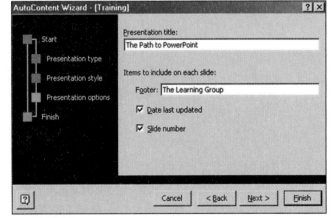

TIPS FROM A PRO: If you frequently find yourself delivering the same or similar information, you can create a template of your own and add it to the predefined set that is contained in the AutoContent Wizard. A *template* is just an outline or blueprint for creating a specific type of document. To get started, create the model for your presentation, save it, and then follow these steps:

1. Choose **File,** click **New,** and then click the **General** tab.
2. Double-click **AutoContent Wizard.**
3. Click the **Next** button.
4. Select the category where you want to incorporate your template and click **Add.** (You can't add to the All or Carnegie Coach categories.)
5. Locate the template you have created and click **OK.**

Result: The first slide of your new presentation, like the one in Figure 1.7, appears in the PowerPoint window.

Figure 1.7
Presentation created from AutoContent Wizard

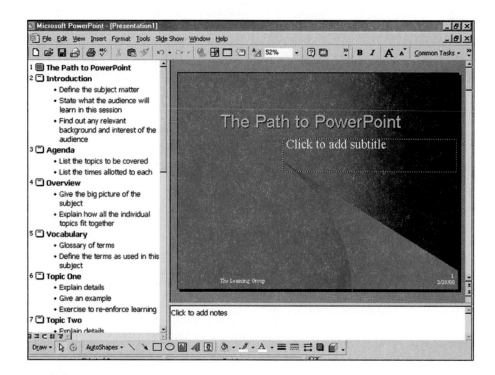

 TIPS FROM A PRO: Even if you are using the wizard, every PowerPoint presentation should begin with some advance planning. Think about the purpose of your work: What message are you trying to communicate? Whether you are soliciting a new client, conveying this month's sales projections to management, or creating overhead transparencies for next week's Sunday school class, you should begin with a goal in mind to ensure an effective outcome.

 THOUGHT QUESTION: When is it better to build your own presentation from scratch rather than to use the AutoContent Wizard?

 TIPS FROM A PRO: You can also use one of the presentation outlines included in the AutoContent Wizard by choosing **File|New.** Click the **Presentations** tab, and then double-click the desired presentation name. Modify the content as necessary to tailor it to your specific requirements.

What: Figure 1.8 shows the PowerPoint window. Study it so that you become familiar with the screen elements. The slide in the figure is shown in the default, Normal view. This view has three distinct *panes* that enable you to view different aspects of your work. Panes are sections of the active PowerPoint window that are separated from the other portions of the window by variable-width frames. These frames can be easily adjusted to enlarge or decrease the size of each pane.

○ On the left is the **Outline pane**. The outline shows the organization of the text in the presentation. Here you can see the content that the AutoContent Wizard suggests as a starting point for your presentation. As the name implies, your typing appears as a text-only outline without the visual aspects of your slides. You can add or edit text; and add, rearrange, and delete slides. You can also print the outline if you want to work with a paper copy. Still, when you want to integrate graphical features or objects into your work, or to format text, you must go to the slide pane or to a Slide Sorter view.

○ On the right is the **Slide pane**. Here you can see a single slide with the same text as shown in the outline. In contrast to the all-text view of the outline pane, the slide pane displays the graphical components of each slide as they will appear when you use them as your visual aid. In this pane you can also add or edit all aspects of your slides (such as art, charts, and sound). Your slides can be printed to produce transparencies or handouts for your audience.

○ On the bottom is a narrow **Notes pane** where you can type speaker notes to remind yourself of items, such as information that you want to share with your audience. Since this information is not visible to you or your audience when the slide show is in progress, you may want to print these pages beforehand. That way you can reference them while speaking.

Though the example in Figure 1.8 is shown in Normal view, these three panes are also components of Outline view and Slide view. You can easily change the view by using the View buttons on the lower-left corner of the screen.

Why: You will be better prepared to use the features of PowerPoint, to use this book, and to successfully take the MOUS exam, if you know the names of, and purposes for, common screen elements.

How: Many of the PowerPoint screen elements can be identified with the help of the mouse.

1. Choose **Help|What's This?** The mouse pointer changes to a big question mark.
2. Click on the screen element that you want more information about.
3. To find information about additional items, repeat steps 1 and 2.

Menu bar presents categories of command lists where you can click and display commands. Click commands to select.

Standard toolbar shows typical commands. More buttons are available when you click the arrows that appear on the row.

Outline pane shows the text of the presentation.

Placeholder guides the placement of text, graphics, and other items.

Scroll buttons enable you to jump quickly from one location to another.

Speaker Notes area enables you to type notes for yourself.

View buttons enable you to change views.

Normal view shows three panes, as in this figure.

Outline view has three panes. The outline pane is the largest.

Slide view presents a three-pane view with a large slide pane.

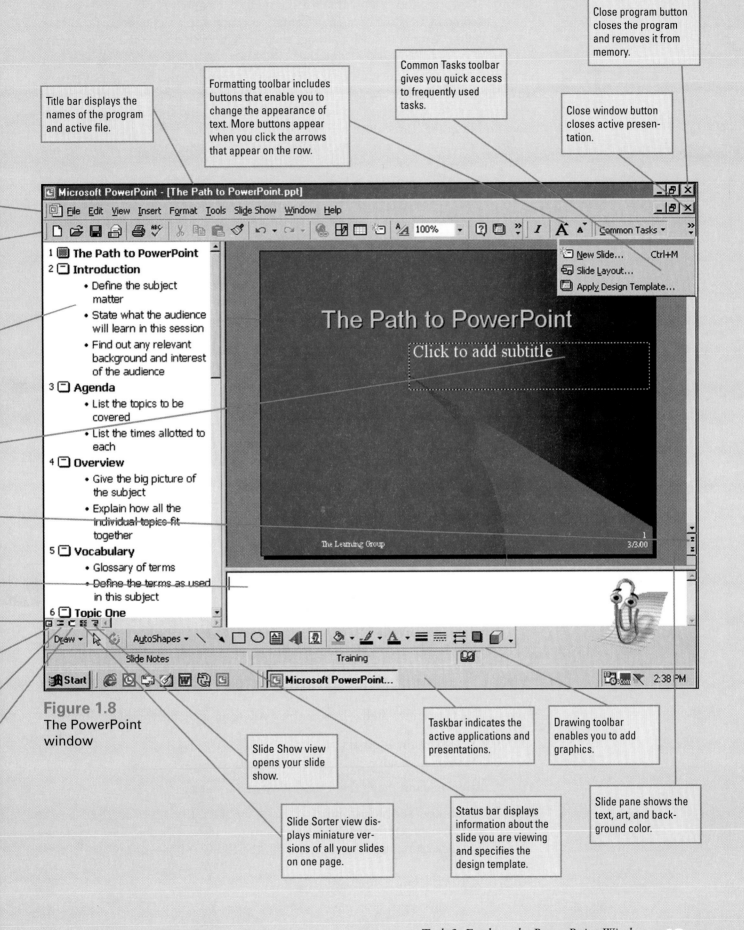

Close program button closes the program and removes it from memory.

Common Tasks toolbar gives you quick access to frequently used tasks.

Formatting toolbar includes buttons that enable you to change the appearance of text. More buttons appear when you click the arrows that appear on the row.

Close window button closes active presentation.

Title bar displays the names of the program and active file.

Taskbar indicates the active applications and presentations.

Drawing toolbar enables you to add graphics.

Slide Show view opens your slide show.

Slide pane shows the text, art, and background color.

Slide Sorter view displays miniature versions of all your slides on one page.

Status bar displays information about the slide you are viewing and specifies the design template.

Figure 1.8
The PowerPoint window

Result: If information is available for the item that you chose, it appears on the screen in a yellow box. (If information is not available, refer to Task 9 for help.) After you finish reading, click anywhere to make the box go away.

 It's easy to change the position of the frames that separate the PowerPoint panes. Move the mouse pointer over the frame that you want to resize until it changes to a small line with two arrows on each side. Press and hold the left mouse button down and drag the frame until it is the size that you require. Because the window you are working with is a set size, when you resize one pane, the visible size of the other panes will change as well.

TASK 4 *Customize PowerPoint*

What: The default PowerPoint window, which you have just seen in Figure 1.8, contains a menu bar and single row of buttons to provide you with quick access to common tasks. As you work, PowerPoint automatically customizes the toolbar to display the buttons that you use most frequently.

In addition, when you start PowerPoint, you only see the commands that you regularly use on the menus. Other commands appear after a short pause, or when you click the double down-arrows at the bottom of the menus or on the toolbars. If the buttons that you see don't suit your particular work habits, you can customize many of the visible screen elements of the screen to satisfy your individual preferences.

Why: Some people like the way PowerPoint personalizes the screen. Others want to see the same toolbars and buttons each time they turn on their computer.

TO TURN THE RULER OFF AND ON

How: Choose **View|Ruler**.

Result: When you first click the **View** menu, you only see a short menu (Figure 1.9). Be patient though because the other commands appear after a pause. To turn the **Ruler** off or on again, choose **View|Ruler**. This operation is called a *toggle*; the same thing that turns it 'on' also turns it 'off.'

TO SHOW FULL MENUS AND ALL THE BUTTONS

How: The Customize dialog box enables you to modify the following items:

○ Display the toolbars on two rows
○ Show all menu selections immediately without pausing

After opening the dialog box, follow these steps:

1. Choose **Tools|Customize**.
2. Click the **Options** tab.
3. Click to remove the checks from the top two boxes shown in Figure 1.10.
4. Click **Close**.

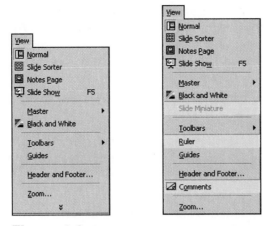

Figure 1.9 Short menus and full menus

Result: PowerPoint immediately displays two rows of buttons, with the Standard toolbar on top, followed by the Formatting toolbar (Figure 1.11). In addition, when you click the menu items, all the commands immediately appear. You learn how to add and delete buttons from these toolbars in Chapter 11, "Use Advanced Features." Modifications will remain in effect until you change them again by reversing the process.

Figure 1.10
Customize dialog box,
Options tab

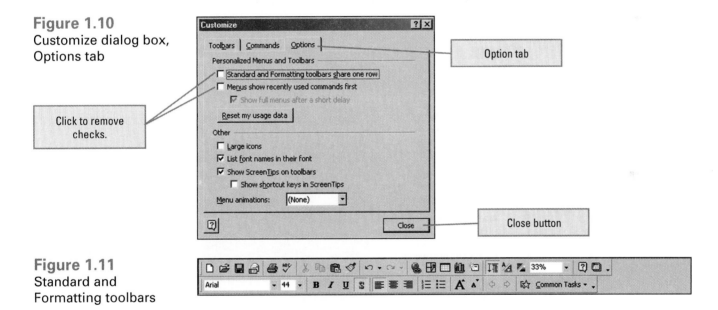

Figure 1.11
Standard and
Formatting toolbars

Note: For consistency, the figures in the remainder of the book show PowerPoint with the Standard and Formatting toolbars on different rows and the full menus displayed. It may make it easier for you to follow the examples given in this book if you set up your toolbars that way as well.

TIP FROM A PRO: It is convenient to have quick access to the menus, various toolbars, and ruler. Unfortunately, the more of these options that are visible on your screen (which means they are turned on), the less space you have to view your presentation.

CORE OBJECTIVE: Navigate among different views
(slide, outline, sorter, tri-pane)

What: An active PowerPoint window can be viewed in six different window layouts or *views*. You can quickly change these views anytime during the preparation of your visual aids.

Why: Each view provides a different visual perspective and, as such, enables you to check and work on varying aspects of your presentation. By utilizing the advantages associated with the various views, you can work more efficiently and thereby shorten the process of creating PowerPoint output.

Figure 1.12
PowerPoint window
in Normal view

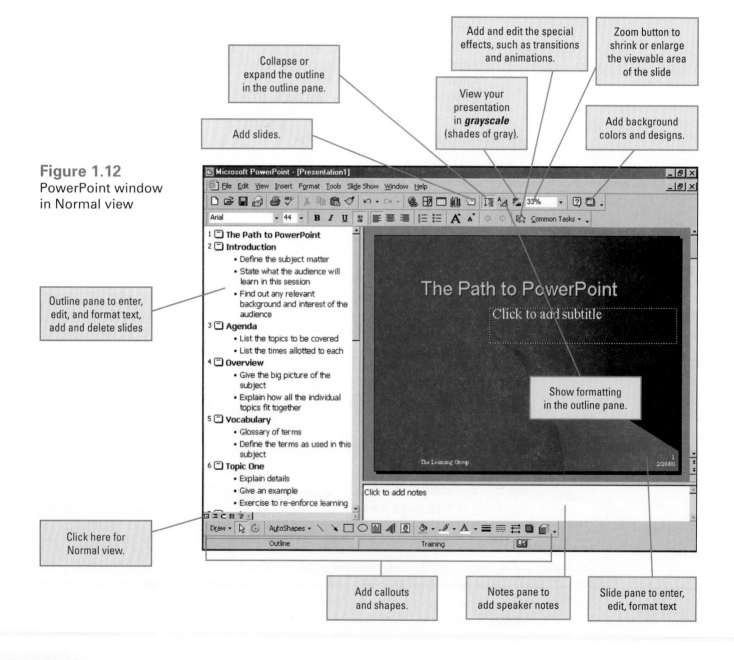

How: With the exception of the Notes Page view, you can switch back and forth between the views by clicking the view buttons at the lower-left corner of your screen. To view your presentation in Notes Page view, choose **View|Notes Page**.

Result: As you move from one view to another, the appearance of the window that you see changes. In some cases you can perform different operations as well.

- **Normal view** enables you to read the text in outline form and at the same time, see its layout on the slide. The three panes shown in Figure 1.12 are also components of Outline and Slide views. Unlike the other two views, however, resizing is not required to enter text into any of the panes in Normal view.
- **Outline view** also consists of three panes, but here the outline pane dominates. Each slide is numbered and appears next to its text in the outline pane (Figure 1.13). You can carry out all the same tasks as in Normal view, although the slide pane is too small to work on unless you enlarge it.

Figure 1.13
Outline view

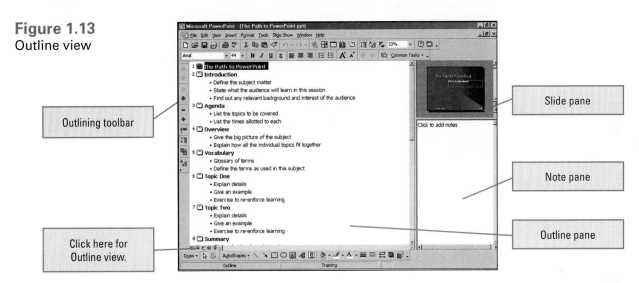

Outlining toolbar

Click here for Outline view.

Slide pane

Note pane

Outline pane

- **Slide view** shows a smaller outline pane and larger slide pane, as you see in Figure 1.14. This way you can add background color, pictures, and then see the result of changes that you make to the slide.

Figure 1.14
Slide view

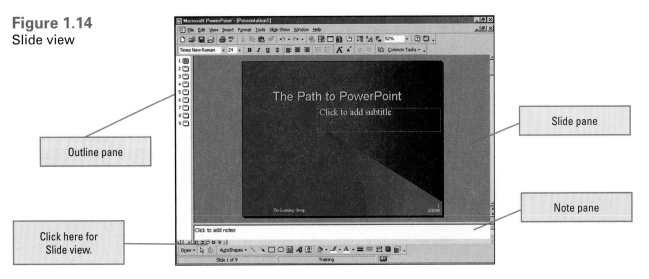

Outline pane

Click here for Slide view.

Slide pane

Note pane

- **Slide Sorter view** simultaneously displays miniature versions of several neatly organized slides (Figure 1.15). Unlike the previous three views, you can see the overall appearance of the presentation as well as add, delete, rearrange, or add special effects to individual or multiple slides in one location.

Figure 1.15
Slide Sorter view

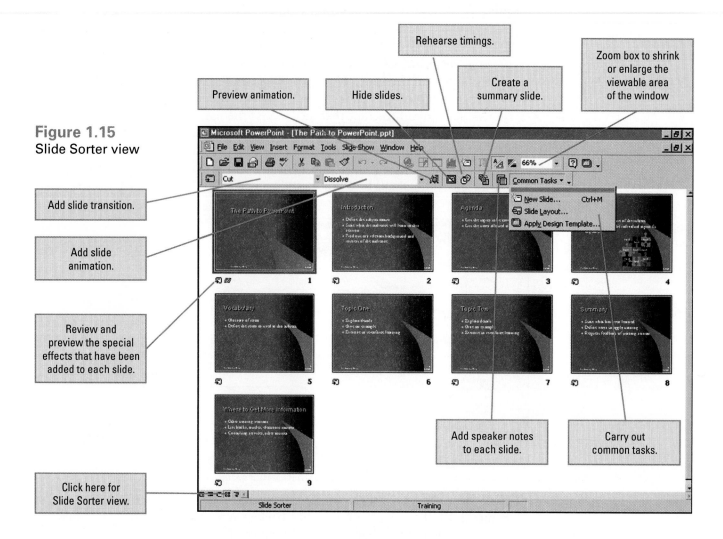

- **Slide show view** is used when you deliver your presentation. As you can see in Figure 1.16, all the menus and toolbars are removed from the screen, showing only your beautiful slide show. Press **Esc** to return to the PowerPoint program. You learn more about using this view in Chapter 6, "Elements of Sight and Sound."
- **Notes Page view** enables you to see the full notes area below the slide (Figure 1.17). Here you can add speaker notes as well as graphics. To facilitate your work, the viewable notes area and the actual size of the notes placeholder, can be enlarged or shrunk as required. (You learn how to resize objects in a later chapter.)

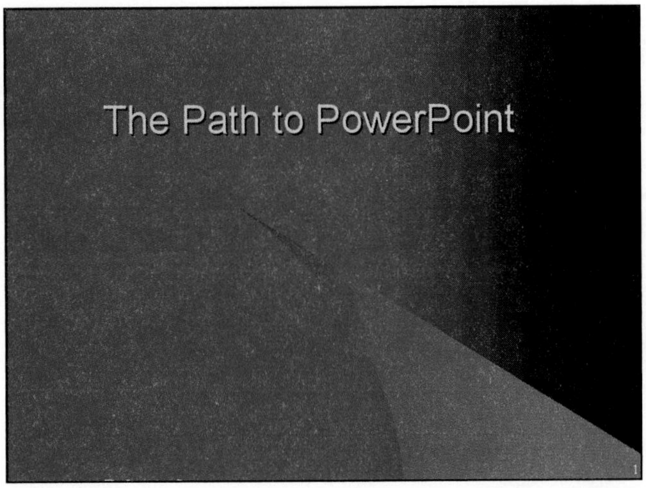
The Path to PowerPoint

Figure 1.16 Slide Show view

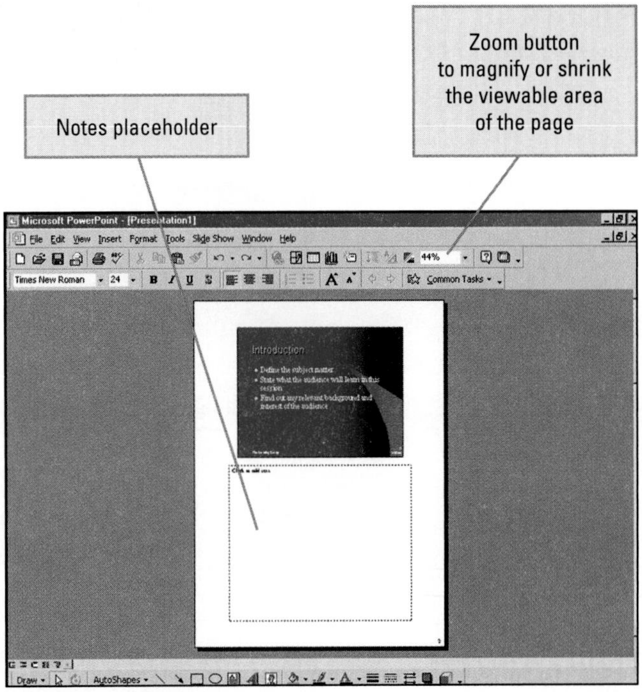
Zoom button
to magnify or shrink
the viewable area
of the page
Notes placeholder
Introduction

Figure 1.17 Notes Page view

TASK 6 *Save a Presentation*

C

CORE OBJECTIVE: Save changes to a presentation

What: When you begin a new presentation or make changes to an existing one, you will want to save it to a disk.

Why: If you don't save, all your hard work will be lost when you exit PowerPoint. Unfortunately, computers don't "remember" information. Instead, presentation files must be stored on a disk if you want to have access to them later. Saving frequently may also prevent the panic that occurs when your work disappears before your eyes as the system crashes, when you experience an electrical outage, or when your pet Doberman chews through the computer's power supply.

SAVE FOR THE FIRST TIME

How: You can begin the save process for a new presentation in any of three ways:

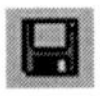

- Click the **Save** button.
- Choose **File|Save**.
- Hold down the **Ctrl** key and press **S**. (From now on, shortcut keys like this are referred to with the following notation: **Ctrl+S**.)

When the Save As dialog box appears (Figure 1.18):

1. Choose the desired save location from the **Save In** drop-down list.
2. Enter a name for your presentation in the **File name** box.
3. Click **Save**.

Figure 1.18
Save As dialog box

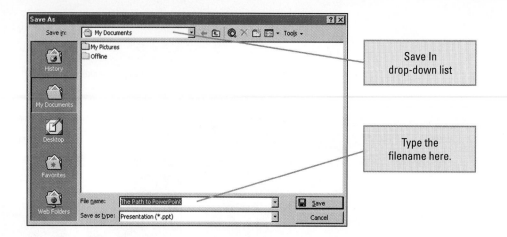

Save In
drop-down list

Type the
filename here.

Result: Your presentation is now saved; the name you have given it appears as a
button on the taskbar and on the title bar at the top of the PowerPoint
window (Figure 1.19).

Figure 1.19
Saved PowerPoint
presentation

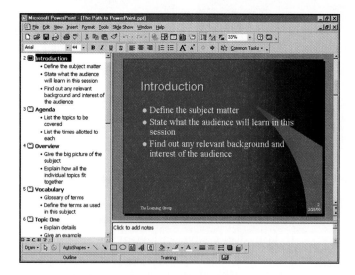

SUBSEQUENT SAVES

How: After saving a presentation the first time, you can quickly resave your
work in the same folder and disk location, and with the same file name,
using any one of the following three ways.

○ Click the **Save** button.
○ Choose **File|Save**.
○ Press **Ctrl+S**.

Result: A new copy of your file, complete with any changes that you have made
since the last time you saved, is now stored on your disk in place of the
preceding version.

 TIPS FROM A PRO: PowerPoint is set up to automatically save your work as a
recovered document in the event that you lose power or the system goes down.
You can designate how often you want PowerPoint to save recovery information

in the **Tools|Options|Save** dialog box. When power is restored, your recovered document should appear in the application window when the program is first reopened.

CORE OBJECTIVE: Save as new presentation

CORE OBJECTIVE: Create a new presentation from an existing file

What: Sometimes you will want to save an existing presentation under a new file name or in a separate location.

Why: Perhaps you are going to address two similar groups and want to provide each with subtly different information. Or, while editing one version you decide that it is a good idea to save a backup copy of your original work just in case you make some irreversible error. With a little thought, I am sure that you could come up with some excellent reasons of your own for this activity. Unfortunately, if you use one of the save methods that you learned in the last task, you just copy over the existing version, and with the click of a button, you have lost your original work.

TIPS FROM A PRO: The easiest way to open a recently used file is to choose **File** and then look at the recently used file list (at the bottom of the menu). The number of files that you see listed can be increased or decreased. Choose **Tools|Options**, click the **General** tab, and then type the desired number in the **entries** box, or click the up and down arrows.

How: To create a new file from an existing presentation, follow these steps:

1. Choose **File|Save As** to open the Save As dialog box.
2. If you want to save the file in a different drive, disk, or folder location (as in Figure 1.20), click the arrow beside the **Save In** drop-down list and select the desired save location.
3. To rename the file, type the new file name in the **File Name** text box.
4. Click **Save**.

TIPS FROM A PRO: You can create a new folder to organize and save your work from the Save As dialog box. Click the **Create a New Folder** button. Enter the new folder name and click **OK**.

Result: The file name appears on the title bar—if you renamed the presentation you see the new name—and there are now two copies of the file. If you were only creating a backup, you are done! On the other hand, if you plan to revise the presentation in some way, you learn how to do just that in subsequent chapters.

Figure 1.20
Saving a presentation to a new location

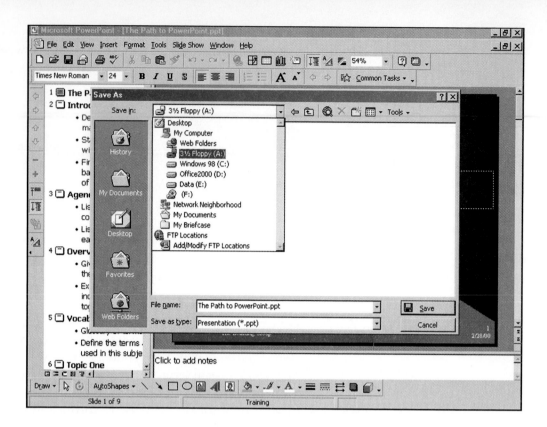

  TIPS FROM A PRO: If you make a mistake and save over your original file, don't panic—just click the **Undo** button until you have restored the file, and then use **Save As** to save it under a different name or location. You learn more about Undo in Chapter 3, "Edit Text."

TASK 8   *Print a Presentation*

What: Although PowerPoint primarily focuses on the creation of electronic output in the form of a slide show, the program provides you with the flexibility to create different kinds of printed materials as well.

Click the Print button to print a single copy of the entire presentation at once, or use the Print dialog box to get more control over the printing process.

Why: At times, you will want to print your product, even if you intend to use PowerPoint to deliver an on-screen slide show. There are four different types of output that you can print:

○ **Slides** to produce transparencies from slide copies for use on an overhead projector.

○ **Speaker notes** to jog your memory while you are speaking—after all, everyone loses his or her train of thought from time to time.

○ **Outlines** so that you can proofread the written portions of your slide show.

○ **Handouts** so that your audience can follow along or take notes.

USE THE PRINT BUTTON

How: Click the **Print** button.

Result: The printer turns out a number of pages, one for each slide in the presentation.

TIPS FROM A PRO: Although mistakes can often be seen as you stare at the computer screen, frequently they just seem to be invisible. For this reason, it is always a good idea to print your document and proofread it from paper.

THOUGHT QUESTION: When it is necessary to print one slide per sheet of paper?

USE THE PRINT DIALOG BOX

How: To control the printing process, access the Print dialog box using either of the following two methods.

❍ Choose **File|Print**.
❍ Press **Ctrl+P**.

The Print dialog box enables you to make choices about the type, quantity, and appearance of your output. Before you can print, however, you must first specify what portion of the presentation that you want to print. Figure 1.21 shows the choices that are available.

In this dialog box you can also specify:

❍ Whether to print all the slide show or choose specific slides.
❍ Whether to print in color, black and white, or grayscale.
❍ How many copies to print.

Figure 1.21
Print dialog box

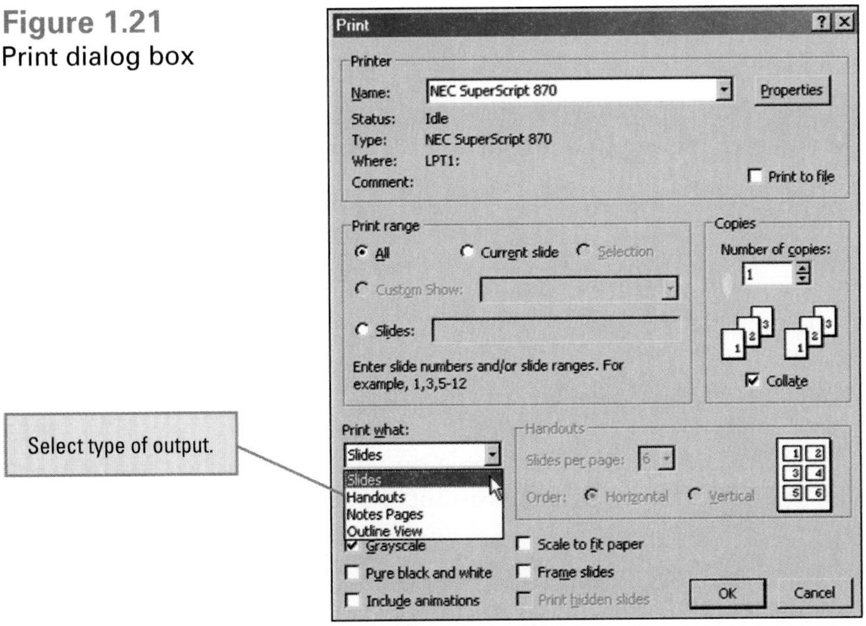

Select type of output.

Result: Depending on what choices you select in the dialog box, the printer produces one of the types of hard copies shown in Table 1.1. You learn more about printing in Chapter 8, "Print and Deliver."

Table 1.1 Printing Options

If You Choose to Print This	Each Page Will Contain
Slides	A single slide as in Slide view
Handouts	Two to six small slides on each page
Notes pages	A single slide with any speaker notes you have typed beneath it
Outline	The text of the presentation as an outline

TIPS FROM A PRO: As you have just learned, if you click the Print button, each slide in your presentation prints on a single sheet of paper. Though this is a quick way to print, it can be very time-consuming, use a great deal of ink and paper, and, if you are working in a busy office or public lab, can generate extreme displeasure in your colleagues.

TASK **9**	*Get Help with PowerPoint*

CORE OBJECTIVE: Use Office Assistant

What: When you need help with PowerPoint, the Office Assistant is only a mouse click away. The *Office Assistant* is an animated device that hangs around on your computer screen, ready to offer help when you have one of the Microsoft Office programs open. It offers suggestions and advice, often before you know that you even have a question.

Why: This process is often much easier than searching through a complicated manual or taking the time to ask someone for help. You can get help in PowerPoint in four different ways:

- ○ Press the **F1** key.
- ○ Click the **Help** button.
- ○ Click the **Help** menu (see Figure 1.22) and select one of the available choices.
- ○ Click the **Office Assistant**.

How: If the Office Assistant is not visible on your screen, click **Help** on the menu and select **Show Office Assistant**. To get help, follow these steps:

1. Click the **Office Assistant** (Figure 1.23). A yellow balloon appears—it may include answers that relate to what you are working on.
2. If you don't see the subject you are looking for, type your question or keyword(s) in the assistant balloon and then Click **Search** (Figure 1.24).

Figure 1.22
Help menu

Figure 1.23
Office Assistant

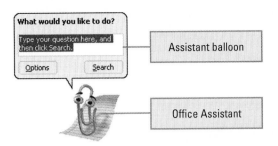

Figure 1.24 Asking the Office Assistant for help

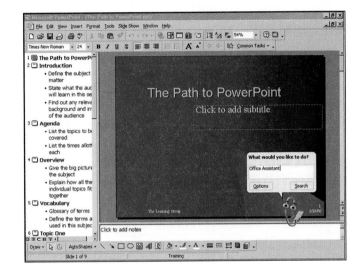

3. Click the answer that the assistant balloon returns that most closely answers your question. Or, if none of the suggestions are relevant, type another question.

 TIPS FROM A PRO: You can easily change the form that the Office Assistant takes—maybe you like dogs, so you want to get rid of that purring "furry friend." To shop for a new assistant, right-click the current assistant, click **Choose Assistant**, select the assistant that you want from the Gallery, and click **OK**.

Result: After you have chosen a Help topic, Microsoft PowerPoint Help opens in a window next to your presentation (Figure 1.25). From here you can:

❍ See the contents of Help.
❍ Ask additional questions.
❍ Browse through an index.
❍ Print subjects.
❍ Link to related topics by clicking on the underlined text.
❍ Click the Help button.

If you see a light bulb on a slide or the assistant balloon, don't be concerned. This is the Style Checker and was devised to work hand-in-hand with the Office Assistant. Chapter 2, "Work with Text," discusses this feature.

Figure 1.25
Microsoft PowerPoint
Help window

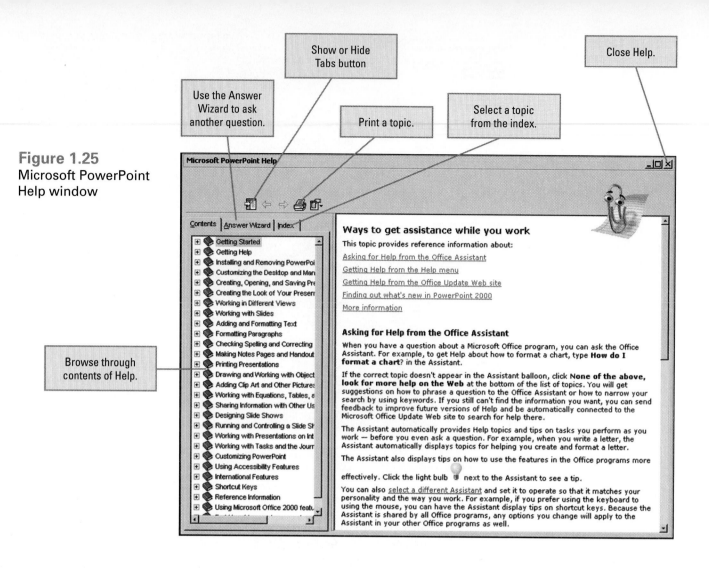

Use the Answer
Wizard to ask
another question.

Show or Hide
Tabs button

Print a topic.

Select a topic
from the index.

Close Help.

Browse through
contents of Help.

TASK 10 Close a Presentation

What: Close an active presentation.

Why: When you are finished working on a presentation, you will want to close it. If you are using an up-to-date operating system, you can probably have several presentations open at once, but this unnecessarily uses your computer's memory.

How: You can close a presentation in either of the following ways:

○ Click the **Close** window button on the upper-right corner of the window just below the Close program button (Figure 1.26).
○ Choose **File|Close**.

Result: If the file has not been saved, you are prompted to do so. The window closes and its associated button is removed from the taskbar. If no other PowerPoint files are open, your screen resembles Figure 1.27.

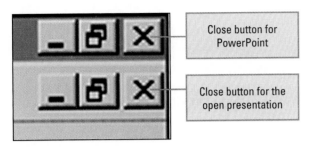

Close button for
PowerPoint

Close button for the
open presentation

Figure 1.26 Window controls

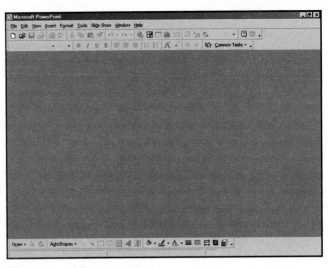

Figure 1.27 PowerPoint application window

TASK 11   *Exit PowerPoint*

What: When you've finished working in PowerPoint or are shutting down your computer, you will want to close the program.

Why: Even if you are currently working in a different program, PowerPoint uses a great deal of your computer's RAM when it is open. If you close the program, you will free resources for use in other applications. Your computer's performance improves as a result.

How: PowerPoint closes when you:
  ○ Click the **Close** program button on the upper-right corner of the window.
  ○ Choose **File|Exit**.

Result: If you have any open PowerPoint files that haven't been saved, you are prompted to do so. The PowerPoint window closes and all PowerPoint buttons are removed from the taskbar. If no other applications are open, you return to the Windows desktop.

Use PinPoint

After gaining the skills included in this chapter, you can start PowerPoint, create a presentation with the AutoContent Wizard, save your work, create a new presentation from an existing slide show, move around the PowerPoint views, get help, print, and finally, recognize many of the PowerPoint screen elements. Now it's time to see what you can do with the PinPoint software. Remember, whenever you are unsure of what to do next, you can reread the relevant portion of the chapter or you can click Show Me for a live demonstration.

Try the following skills in PinPoint:

- AutoContent Wizard
- Change view
- Save a presentation
- Save as
- New presentation from slides
- Close a presentation
- Print a presentation

Key Terms

You can find definitions for these words in this chapter:

Default

Grayscale

Office Assistant

Panes

Template

Toggle

Views

Wizard

Review Questions

You can use the following review questions and exercises to test your knowledge and skills. The answers are given in Appendix D, "Answers to Review Questions."

True/False

Indicate whether each statement is true (T) or false (F).

___ 1. PowerPoint can only be used to create slide shows.

___ 2. Handouts, slide shows, and overhead transparencies can all be produced using PowerPoint.

___ 3. When you exit PowerPoint, the computer automatically saves your work.

___ 4. A wizard is a sample PowerPoint presentation.

___ 5. Be careful when you close PowerPoint; if you click the Close application button, you automatically lose any unsaved work.

___ 6. If you click the Print button, an outline of your slide show prints.

___ 7. To access the AutoContent Wizard, start PowerPoint and choose it from the opening menu.

___ 8. To get help creating the content for a presentation, you can use the Office Assistant.

___ 9. The Office Assistant answers questions through a little recorded message you can hear through the speakers.

___ 10. When you're through using PowerPoint, to exit from the program, click the Close button on the upper-right corner of the window.

Multiple Choice

Select the letter that best completes the statement.

___ 1. To start PowerPoint:
   a. Double-click the Start button.
   b. Click Start and choose Programs, and then select Microsoft Word.
   c. Hold down the Ctrl key and press P.
   d. Choose Start|Programs|PowerPoint.
   e. All of the above.

___ 2. The best use for PowerPoint is to:
   a. Type a sales letter.
   b. Add income from sales.
   c. Make visual aids for a sales presentation.
   d. Keep records of customers.
   e. Balance a checkbook.

___ 3. When PowerPoint first opens, what you see is:
   a. A dialog box asking whether you want to use AutoContent Wizard.
   b. A blank screen ready for you to begin typing.
   c. A three-paned window with a sample PowerPoint presentation.
   d. A three-paned window without a sample PowerPoint presentation.
   e. A colorful slide ready for your text to be typed.

___ 4. The AutoContent wizard is useful because it:
   a. Provides sample text for typical presentations.
   b. Enables you to add your own name and title.
   c. Creates an attractive and colorful appearance for your presentation.
   d. Leads you step-by-step through the process of creating a presentation.
   e. All of the above.

___ 5. After you finish using the AutoContent wizard, what you see is:
   a. A dialog box asking whether you want to save.
   b. A blank screen ready for you to begin typing.
   c. A three-paned window with a sample presentation.
   d. A colorful slide ready for your text to be typed.
   e. A Sample outline of a typical presentation.

___ 6. To save a presentation:
   a. Click the Save button.
   b. Choose File|Save.
   c. Press Ctrl+S.
   d. All of the above.
   e. Both a and b.

___ 7. When you save a file the first time, you must specify:
   a. The name of the file.
   b. The save location of the file.
   c. The contents of the title bar.
   d. All of the above.
   e. Both a and b.

___ 8. To save another copy of the presentation with a different name:
   a. Click the Save button and type the new name.
   b. Choose File|Save As and type the new name.
   c. Double-click the title bar and type the new name and then click Save.
   d. Press Ctrl+N (for New Name).
   e. None of the above.

___ 9. When you click the Print button, what comes out of the printer is:

   a. Six small slides on each page.

   b. The text of the presentation in outline format.

   c. One slide on each page.

   d. A three-pane view of each page of the presentation.

   e. None of the above.

___ 10. If you close a presentation that has not been saved:

   a. The window flashes or beeps.

   b. The computer asks whether you want to save.

   c. The computer automatically saves it for you.

   d. Your presentation is lost.

   e. PowerPoint closes.

Screen Review

Match the letters in Figure 1.28 with the correct items in the list.

Figure 1.28

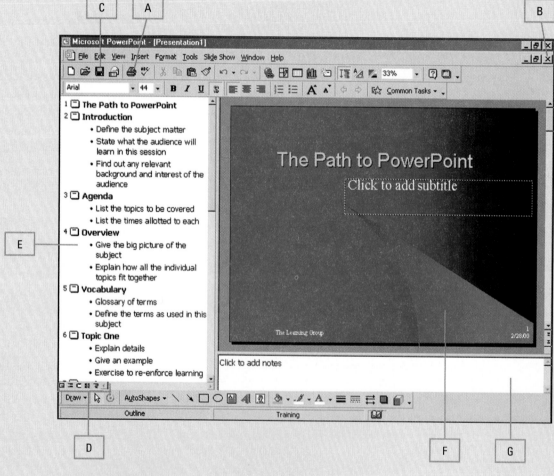

___ 1. Click here to save the presentation.

___ 2. Click here to close the PowerPoint window.

___ 3. Click here to change the view.

___ 4. Click here to print the slides one on each page.

___ 5. Click here to type notes for the presenter.

___ 6. Look here to read the text of the presentation.

___ 7. Look here to see how the slide will appear on screen.

Exercise and Project

The exercise and project in this and subsequent chapters may require you to access files provided on the CD-ROM that came with the text. If you are working in a computer lab, you may have to ask your instructor where to save or print.

Follow these step-by-step instructions to practice the skills that are included in this chapter. If you are working in a computer lab, you may have to ask your instructor where to save or print your work.

Exercise

1. Start PowerPoint.
2. Select the **AutoContent Wizard** from the PowerPoint dialog box and press **Enter** or click **OK**. Then click **Next**.
3. Click **Carnegie Coach** and select **Introducing and Thanking a Speaker**. Click **Next**.
4. Select **On-screen Presentation** as the type of output and click **Next**.
5. Type **The Path to PowerPoint** as the presentation title and **The Learning Group** as the footer. Remove the date, but leave the slide number field. Click **Finish**.
6. Create a folder in the disk location of your choice called **PowerPoint 2000**. Save your slide show in the folder with the name **Exercise 1A**.
7. Print the slides.
8. Next click **File|New**, choose the **General** tab, and double-click **AutoContent Wizard**.
9. Repeat the steps given in the preceding exercise, *but* choose **Color Overheads** as the output type. Remove the date, but leave the slide number field.
10. Save your presentation in the folder that you created in step 6 with the name **Exercise 1B**. Print your slides.
11. Exit PowerPoint.

Project

To put your newly learned PowerPoint skills to work, modify the slide show from the preceding exercise. Your task is to introduce your PowerPoint instructor to your classmates. Because you probably don't know most of this information, use your imagination. (This is a terrific opportunity for you to earn some great brownie points; don't blow it!) Save the presentation in your folder as Project 1 and print the slides. *Hint:* Just press the Print button on the toolbar.

Work with Text

In the last chapter you got a glimpse of the high-quality visual aids that you can create with PowerPoint. Now it's time to continue gathering the tools to help you create a presentation that is both attractive and compelling. Before you try to incorporate any dramatic effects (such as colorful charts or dancing monkeys), you should concentrate on the content of your text. Your words and what they say supply the motivation for your presentation, and like any foundation, they should be strong before you build the rest of the show. In this chapter you learn how to begin your own custom presentation and then how to add slides and text.

At the end of this chapter you will be able to:

C E

C	E	
☑	❑	Create a new presentation from scratch
☑	❑	Enter text in the three panes
☑	❑	Promote and demote text
☑	❑	Add speaker notes
❑	❑	Add a slide
☑	❑	Choose a slide layout
☑	❑	Check the spelling
❑	❑	Check your writing for style
☑	❑	Create and work with text boxes
❑	☑	Use the wrap text in AutoShape feature
☑	❑	Place text inside of a shape using a text box

Core Objective: **Create a blank presentation**

What: You can build a uniquely customized slide show from scratch using blank slides, and your own original content and slide design. This approach requires that you make decisions about the kinds of slides that you will use in your presentation. Because you probably won't be using the same format for each slide, PowerPoint provides 24 different predefined slide types, or *AutoLayouts*, to choose from.

Each AutoLayout is characterized by its own distinct arrangement of *placeholders*, the dotted-line boxes that determine how text, graphics, charts, and the like are positioned on the slide. Because the layout of each slide was designed with a specific purpose in mind (such as creating the title slide or building an organizational chart), selecting the right layout simplifies the process of building your presentation. (And, who doesn't want to simplify his or her life?) Adding text and other objects is easy; just click in the area inside the dotted lines as instructed.

Why: The AutoContent Wizard that you learned about in Chapter 1, "Get Started with PowerPoint," is a great way to begin and also an excellent tool to create presentations around typical situations. Sometimes you will want to take a more personalized approach, however, and not be distracted by someone else's structure.

How: You can begin a new blank presentation in three ways:

❍ From the opening dialog box, choose **Blank Presentation** and click **OK.**
❍ Click the **New** button on the Standard toolbar.
❍ Choose **File|New**, click the **General** tab, and double-click **Blank Presentation.**

When the New Slide dialog box appears (Figure 2.1), follow these steps to choose an autolayout:

1. Click to select the desired AutoLayout and then click **OK.** *Note:* Because most presentations begin with a title slide, PowerPoint uses this layout as the default selection for a new presentation.
2. A blank slide appears in Normal view.
3. Click in the placeholders and begin typing the slide text (Figure 2.2).

Tips from a Pro: If you are typing in a placeholder and suddenly see your text size shrink, don't worry! Contrary to what you may have heard, your computer is not possessed by devilish little fiends waiting to seize any opportunity to manipulate and modify your work. This is just PowerPoint's *auto-fit* feature resizing your text so that it all fits into the placeholder. For this to happen your text must contain too many words or the font size is too large for the available space. If you want to turn off Auto-Fit, choose **Tools|Options**, click the **Edit** tab, and then clear the check next to **Auto-fit text to text placeholder.**

Figure 2.1
New Slide dialog box

Click to select layout.

Click **OK** to add a slide with the layout.

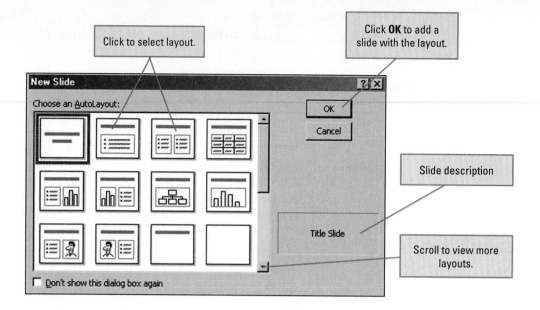

Slide description

Scroll to view more layouts.

Figure 2.2
Blank presentation slide

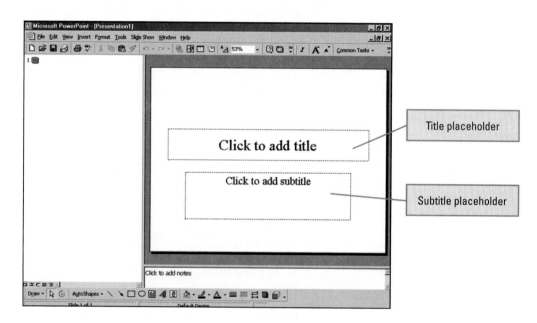

Title placeholder

Subtitle placeholder

THOUGHT QUESTION: Why is it usually best to put slide text in bulleted points rather than in paragraph form?

Result: You have just created the first slide of your new presentation. Clearly, you have a long way to go before you can unveil your handiwork, but it's a start, and an important one. In subsequent chapters you learn how to add interest with color, clip art, sound and the like. For now, however, let's concentrate on your words—the most important part of your presentation.

TIPS FROM A PRO: The average person's attention span is only 20 minutes (and for some of us, even less), so put the important stuff first. Get your point across quickly, before your audience starts to daydream about lunch, work they've left on their desks, or worse yet, about the wisdom you've shown by pairing that shirt and suit together. Some tips to help you with slide content are as follows:

- Always have a title slide.

- Try to put one main idea on each slide.

- Think of ways to use the ideas represented on the slides to foster interaction with your audience.

- Use important dollar figures, percentages, and numbers, but limit them to five or six per slide.

- Know your audience! You can fit the content and style of your presentation to their requirements if you are aware of their needs.

- Focus on the message! As you develop the content, check to see that it supports that message.

 THOUGHT QUESTION: Do you think that there is any particular order of information that is most likely to grab and keep the attention of your audience?

TASK 2   *Enter Text in Normal View*

 CORE OBJECTIVE: Enter text in tri-pane view

What: You can enter text onto your slides in several ways. Remember from the preceding task that Outline, Slide, and Normal views all have a three-pane window and, therefore, all allow for the addition of text. Still, Normal view is most frequently used for this purpose and although the information provided within this task is applicable to all of the three-pane views, it is from the Normal view perspective.

When you indent text on a slide in both the outline and slide panes, the words not only move to the right, but the size of text characters, or *font* size, also decreases. This is because PowerPoint assumes that you want to move the text to the next lower heading level (to *demote* it). Conversely, when you un-indent text (to *promote* it), the text size increases. Each slide has five possible levels of text, but you will usually use only the first two or three levels.

Why: The panes are conveniently sized to enable you to add slide text without resizing. You can add text in the outline and instantly see how it looks on the slide and vice versa. Further, you can add notes to yourself as soon as you think of them.

ENTER TEXT IN THE OUTLINE PANE

 CORE OBJECTIVE: Promote and demote text in slide and outline panes

How: The quickest way to enter text in the outline pane is to click the cursor in the pane and start typing the content of your presentation. That is, first enter the text and worry about the order and formatting later. The following suggestions will help you simplify the process. These commands are also summarized for you in Table 2.1.

Table 2.1 Entering Text in the Outline Pane

Press This Key	Or Click This Button	To Affect the Outline Like This
Enter		Creates a new line at the same level as the preceding line in the outline. When you press Enter in the title placeholder, a new slide is added.
Tab	Demote button	Indent or demote a line to a subheading under the preceding line.
Shift+Tab	Promote button	Un-indent or promote a line to a heading above the preceding line. This may result in a new slide being added.

1. Click in the outline pane and type. Assuming that you are working with a new blank presentation, this will add the text for the title of the first slide.
2. Press **Enter**. This adds a new slide and if you enter text, it will be in the title placeholder of Slide 2.

3. Press **Tab** or click the **Demote** button. This indents, or demotes, the line that you just added one level. In this case that means that the line is in the subtitle position on Slide 1. Now you can add a subtitle on Slide 1.
4. Press **Enter** from the subtitle. This adds a new line at the same level in the outline—in other words, another subtitle below the first on Slide 1.
5. Press **Shift+Tab** or click the **Promote** button. This un-indents, or promotes, the line one level from the preceding line. Here it forms the title for Slide 2, like the example you see in Figure 2.3. At the same time, a new slide appears in the slide pane.
6. Press **Backspace** or **Delete** or correct any typing mistakes that you make.

TIPS FROM A PRO: If you prefer to have all the outlining buttons close at hand, turn on the Outlining toolbar. Choose **View|Toolbars|Outlining**. The toolbar appears at the left edge of the outline pane.

TIPS FROM A PRO: If you want to see the formatting that you have applied to your text in the outline pane, click the Show Formatting button on the Standard or Outline toolbars.

THOUGHT QUESTION: What are some ways that you can check your content to see whether the message that you are trying to convey is the one being received?

Result: The text that you've just added can be seen in both the outline and slide panes. You can easily review the content to make sure that it flows smoothly and is in a logical progression. If it doesn't, don't backspace and retype just yet; you learn some useful ways to edit text in the next chapter.

Figure 2.3
Working in the outline pane

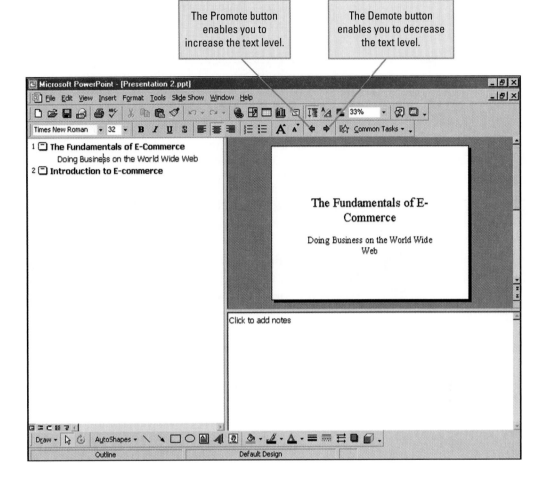

TIPS FROM A PRO: Do you want to keep your audience's attention? If so, don't put too much information on each slide! If you do, you may experience the following:

- Audience retention will decrease.

- Boredom will increase if slides last too long.

- Legibility will suffer if your typeface is small.

ENTER TEXT IN THE SLIDE PANE

CORE OBJECTIVE: Promote and demote text in slide and outline panes

How: You can use the slide pane to enter text for a single slide. The following instructions will help guide you when you want to add text in the slide pane:

1. Click in the title placeholders and type the title text. As you type, notice that when your words reach the end of a line, you don't have to press the Enter key; the words just continue onto the next line. This is called *word wrap*.

2. Click in the subtitle placeholder to enter the subtitle. You can also move to the next placeholder by pressing **Ctrl+Enter**. If you are working in the bottom placeholder of the last slide in your presentation this action adds a new slide.

3. Press **Page down** to move forward one slide. Of course if you are already on the last slide, this action has no effect.

4. Press **Page up** to move back one slide.

5. Press **Enter** to add a new line. Your cursor moves to another line or bullet point, depending on the slide's layout.

6. Press **Tab** or use the **Demote** button. This demotes the bullet and the text that you type will be indented.

7. Press **Shift+Tab** or use the **Promote** button. This promotes the line one level higher than the preceding line.

Result: You have just added text to your slide in the slide pane. Both the text and any formatting that is present are visible. To correct any mistakes, press the **Backspace** or **Delete** keys. Chapter 3, "Edit Text," provides more sophisticated ways to edit your text.

 TIPS FROM A PRO: As you add text to your slides, try to use parallel construction. For example, use a series of verb phrases or a list of nouns. Just don't mix them together. Look at the examples shown in Figure 2.4.

ADD TEXT IN NOTES PANE

 CORE OBJECTIVE: **Add speaker notes**

How: Click in the notes pane to type comments. Notice that as you type previous lines of text are not visible. If you want to see a larger section of your notes, just resize the pane.

Result: You now have notes at the bottom of your slide to help you remember when you want to give the audience handouts, when to add that relevant anecdote, or when to ask a question of the audience (Figure 2.5). Your listeners cannot see them; they are only to help you. You learn how to print your notes in Chapter 8, "Print and Deliver."

Keep Grammar Parallel

Not Parallel	Parallel
Goals for 2001	Goals for 2001
• Increase R&D sending by 50%	• Increase R&D sending by 50%
• Compensation program redesign	• Redesign compensation program
• Decrease waste by 25%	• Decrease waste by 25%
• Unprofitable unit divestiture	• Divest unprofitable unit

Figure 2.4 Parallel grammar

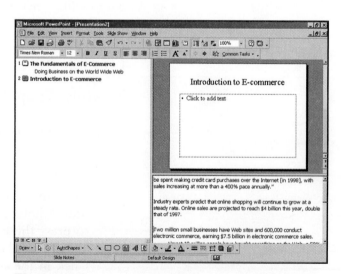

Figure 2.5 Normal view with notes in the notes pane

67% ▼

Tips from a Pro: If you want to make the text in any of the panes appear larger, use the Zoom button on the Standard toolbar. Click in the pane that you want to enlarge, click the drop-down arrow next to the button, and select the desired percentage.

TASK **3** | *Add Speaker Notes*

C

Core Objective: Add speaker notes

What: In Task 2 you learned how to enter notes in the notes pane, but PowerPoint offers two additional methods for entering speaker notes.

Why: More options means greater flexibility. You aren't limited to one view to enter notes—add them in every view!

ENTER NOTES IN SLIDE SORTER VIEW

How: Here you don't need to page from slide to slide; you can enter notes for all your slides in one convenient location.

1. Use the mouse to select the slide.
2. Click the **Speaker Notes** button.
3. Enter your notes in the Speaker Notes dialog box, as shown in Figure 2.6.
4. Repeat steps 1-3 to type notes for additional slides.

Result: The notes appear in the space at the bottom of the slide just as those you entered in the notes pane but you can't see them unless you go to one of the other PowerPoint views.

Figure 2.6
Entering speaker notes in Slide Sorter view

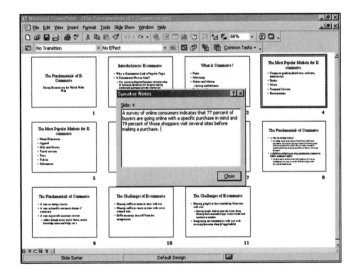

ENTER NOTES IN NOTES PAGE VIEW

How: Entering speaker notes in Notes Page view is similar to entering them in the notes pane. One obvious difference is that you can see the notes placeholder and therefore, there is a larger visible area where you can type.

1. Choose **View|Notes Page**.
2. Click in the notes placeholder and enter your text as in Figure 2.7.
3. To move to another slide, press **Page Up** or **Page Down**.

Figure 2.7
Adding speaker notes in Notes Page view

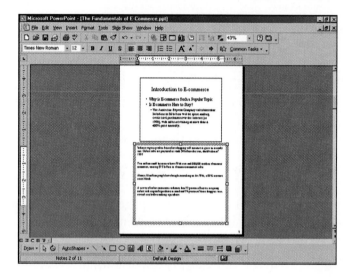

Result: The notes that you entered appear in the space at the bottom of the slide just as those that you enter in the notes pane. And, although you can see the slide pane you can't enter text in it when you are in Notes Page view. Remember, if you want to change the visible size of the notes placeholder (and therefore, the size of the text that you see) use the Zoom button.

TIPS FROM A PRO: Unfortunately, you can't put everything that you want to say on your slides. You can't even put everything that you want to say in your notes. Choose your words wisely! Here are some ideas for making effective speaker notes:

- Make sure each page is numbered—imagine dropping your notes in front your audience and not being able to rearrange them.

- Add a title to each so that you can easily find your place.

- Use bullet points or short phrases; this is to jog your memory not substitute for practice.

- Make your notes large enough to read at a glance. Too many notes will have you with your head down reading instead of making eye contact with your audience. Don't forget that you—the entire package—are the focus of the presentation, not just your words.

- Use your notes when you practice so that you know them and your material.

What: Now that you know how to begin building a slide show from scratch, you need to know how to add slides. Of course, if you're typing in the outline pane, you may be adding slides as you go. In the outline pane, however, each slide that you add after the first slide is a bulleted list by default unless you change the layout. (You learn how to do this in Task 5.) If you select a different layout, the *next* slide that you add matches that layout, and so on. When you work in the slide pane you get to choose the layout of each new slide.

Why: It is unlikely that you'll have a one-slide presentation. (Wouldn't it be great if your instructor or boss had only one slide of information to cover and then you could leave?) Even if you are using the wizard, you will need to add slides from time to time.

USE THE SLIDE LAYOUT DIALOG BOX

How: You can access the **New Slide** dialog box, and control the type of slide that you add, in several ways:

- ❍ Choose **Insert|New Slide**.
- ❍ Click the **New Slide** button on the Standard toolbar.
- ❍ Choose **Common Task|New Slide**.
- ❍ Press **Ctrl+M**.

When the New Slide dialog box appears, select the desired AutoLayout and click **OK**.

Tips from a Pro: It might help to remember the shortcut for adding slides by thinking of *M* for *more* slides.

Result: You have successfully added a new blank slide to your presentation. Click in the title placeholder and begin typing your text.

USE KEYBOARD SHORTCUTS

How: You can add slides to your presentation without accessing the menus or the New Slide dialog box. Although this is quick—you don't even have to take your hand off the keyboard—it doesn't enable you to choose the slide's layout.

1. In the outline pane, place the insertion point to the right of the title text and press **Enter** to add a slide. The slide's layout will be the same as the slide directly below it.
2. In the outline and slide panes, press **Ctrl+Enter** to move to the next lower placeholder. If the insertion point is in the bottom placeholder of a slide show, a new blank slide is added.
3. As discussed in Task 2, when you are working the outline pane, and have entered at least one line of text, and your insertion point is anywhere other than at a title text level, press **Shift+Tab** to add a slide.

TIPS FROM A PRO: Although you can change the layout of any slide (you learn how to do this in the next task), you can speed up the process of creating a slide show if you have a general idea of the material that you are going to put on a slide. That way you can choose the correct layout as you go.

Result: A new slide has been added to your presentation. If the slide falls directly after the title slide, by default it has a bulleted list layout. In all other cases, the layout mirrors that of the preceding slide.

TASK 5 *Choose the Slide Layout*

 CORE OBJECTIVE: Create a specified type of slide

 CORE OBJECTIVE: Change the layout for one or more slides

What: Sometimes you will want to change a slide's layout or reapply the original.

Why: If you're working in the outline pane or use the keyboard shortcuts to create a new slide, any slide you add is formatted with a bulleted list layout. This may not be the layout that you want to use. When you select the wrong layout or decide to change the layout of a particular slide, it's easy to switch styles or reapply the original AutoLayout.

How: You can change individual slides in the slide and outline panes, or select multiple slides in Slide Sorter view:

1. Use the mouse to select the slide or slides that you want to modify. If you are in Slide Sorter view, you can choose several slides at once by pressing and holding down **Ctrl** while you select your slides.
2. Access the Slide Layout dialog box in one of the following ways:
   * Choose **Common Tasks|Slide Layout**.
   * Choose **Format|Slide Layout**.
   * Place the cursor anywhere outside of the placeholders and right-click on the slide that you want to change to reveal the shortcut menu and choose **Slide Layout**.
3. The Slide Layout dialog box appears. If you have selected a single slide to change, the **Slide Layout** automatically defaults to that slide's original layout as in Figure 2.8. You can choose to reapply the original layout or select a new layout (Figure 2.9). Click **OK** to apply the layout and close the dialog box.

 TIPS FROM A PRO: Varying the placement of text, art, and other visual elements can add interest to your presentation. Staring at bulleted lists for the entire length of a presentation can be tedious. Don't give your audience a reason to lose interest.

 THOUGHT QUESTION: Can you have too much variation of text layout on your slides?

Result: The new slide layout is applied. If you have already added text on the slide, it is now inside the placeholders of the new layout.

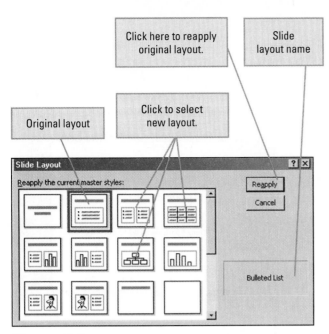

Figure 2.8 Slide Layout dialog box

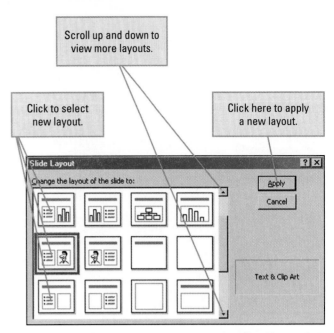

Figure 2.9 Applying a new slide layout

TASK 6 | *Use Automatic Spell Check*

CORE OBJECTIVE: Check spelling

What: Have you noticed those wavy red underlines under certain words in your slide show? That let's you know that PowerPoint's automatic spell checker is at work. PowerPoint has flagged these items as possible mistakes, enabling you to see at a glance where spelling errors are.

Why: Proofreading your visual aids is time-consuming and it's easy to miss mistakes in your own writing. Nevertheless, finding and correcting spelling errors is important if you want to have a good quality presentation. When your visual aids have misspelled words, it communicates that either you are don't care about the quality of your work or that you are unqualified. Is this the message you are trying to convey?

HOW TO TURN ON AUTOMATIC SPELL CHECK

How: To use the automatic spelling checker, you first have to make sure that it's turned on. If you see any red underlines, you know that it's on and you probably have errors in your presentation. If you don't see any red squiggly lines, follow these steps:

1. Choose **Tools|Options**, and click the **Spelling** tab. The dialog box shown in Figure 2.10 is displayed.
2. Click the top check box to turn on the automatic spelling checker.

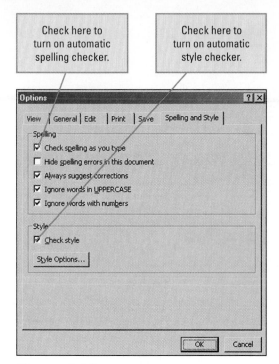

Figure 2.10 Spelling & Style dialog box

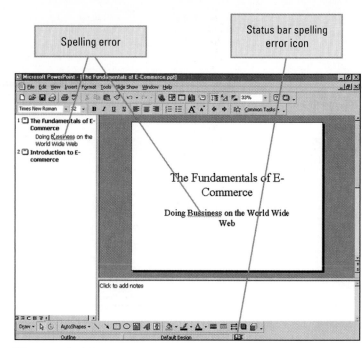

Figure 2.11 Automatic spelling checker finds an error

Result: PowerPoint places an icon of a book on the status bar and begins checking the document. If any errors are found, the icon shows a red X, as you see in Figure 2.11.

CORRECT FLAGGED ITEMS

How: To make corrections, to a flagged word or phrase, follow these steps:

1. Right-click the misspelled word to access the shortcut menu shown in Figure 2.12.
2. Choose one of the following options from the menu:
   - The word's correct spelling from the list of possible suggestions.
   - **Ignore All** to remove the wavy underlining; use this when you don't want to make a change, such as for a proper noun that is not in the dictionary.
   - **Add** to add the current spelling of the word to the dictionary, so it'll never be flagged again. Use this for your name, company name, and other words that are not in the dictionary but that you use frequently.
   - **Check Spelling** to open the Spelling dialog box to check the entire document at once. You learn more about this option in Chapter 3.
3. When you are ready to move to the next flagged item, double-click the **Spelling Status** button on the status bar.
4. Repeat steps 1-3 until all of the flagged words have been addressed.

Result: As soon as you choose one of the alternatives on the menu, the wavy underlining goes away. When you've corrected or clicked to ignore all the errors on your visual aids, the icon on the status bar shows a red check (Figure 2.13).

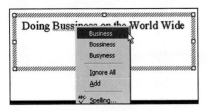

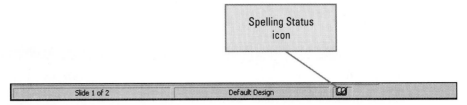

Figure 2.12 Correcting errors with a right-click

Figure 2.13 Status bar icon shows no flagged errors

Tips from a Pro: Don't assume that there are no spelling mistakes in your presentation just because none are flagged. If you mistype a word, such as *dog* rather than *God*, it won't be flagged. There is no substitute for careful proofreading.

TASK **7**	*Use the Style Checker*

What: The style checker, denoted by a yellow light bulb, is a feature of PowerPoint that checks your text to see whether you are following certain rules of thumb for writing style. It is designed to work in partnership with the Office Assistant; so if the Assistant is visible, the style checker will be hard at work.

Why: Just like getting help to decorate your home, sometimes you need help with your words. Even if you've got style, it's nice to have a second opinion. The style checker helps retain visual clarity and consistency throughout your slide show. (Wouldn't you like to have one of these bounce out of your closet each morning and say something like, "Great pair of shoes, but you might rethink wearing them with that suit!")

How: If you can see the Office Assistant, but not the style checker, follow these steps:

1. Choose **Tools|Options** and click on the **Spelling and Style** tab. Make sure that the **Check Style** check box is marked and click **Style Options** in the Options dialog box (refer back to Figure 2.10).
2. In the Style Options dialog box, select the items that you want to check for style, as illustrated in Figures 2.14 and 2.15.
3. When you see the light bulb, click it and the yellow assistant balloon appears to reveal your style faux pas and to offer suggestions to improve your slide content (Figure 2.16).
4. Click to implement or to ignore the recommended tip.

Tips from a Pro: The suggestions given by the style checker are useful as rules of thumb, but they aren't carved in stone. If you are trying to make a critical point, why not consider putting that one point on a slide by itself. "Keep it simple; keep it short!" Here are some other useful tips and rules of thumb to help make your slide show effective and professional:

- Six-by-six rule: Maximum six lines per slide, six words in each line.

- No more than two lines per title or two lines per bullet point.

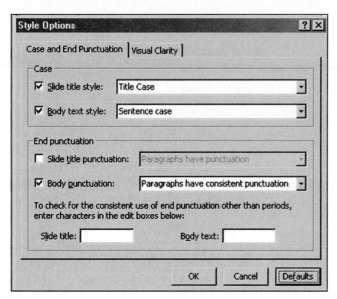

Figure 2.14 Setting up style checker to check case and end punctuation

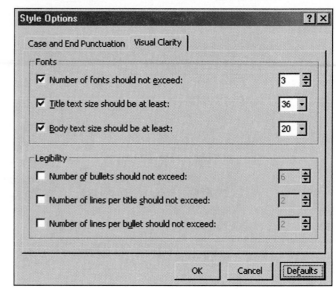

Figure 2.15 Setting up style checker to check visual clarity

 THOUGHT QUESTION: How *should* you decide what information to put on each slide?

Result: If you accept the suggested modifications, the changes are carried out. The balloon goes away, and takes the light bulb with it—that is, unless the style checker has located another perceived mistake. In that case, repeat Steps 3 and 4 until the light bulb disappears. (No matter how many mistakes you make, the style checker never gets tired or rundown; it faithfully toils away, night and day.)

Figure 2.16
Suggestions from the style checker

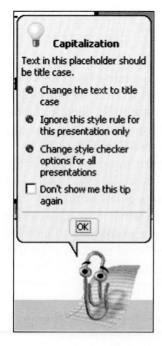

CORE OBJECTIVE: **Create a text box for entering text**

What: Text boxes are similar to placeholders; they provide a resizable area to hold text. Unlike the text in a placeholder, however, characters entered in text boxes can't be seen in the outline pane. Additionally, text boxes can only be added to your visual aids in the slide pane.

Why: Sometimes you might want to add text in an area outside of a placeholder (such as placing text on a piece of art or adding a caption to a picture). In these instances, you can insert a text box onto your slide and then type the desired text.

TO ADD A TEXT BOX WITH WORD WRAP

How: The quickest way to add a text box is to use the Drawing toolbar (Figure 2.17), but it must be turned on first. If you don't see the toolbar, choose **View|Toolbars** and click **Drawing** or choose **Insert|Text Box**.

Figure 2.17
Drawing toolbar

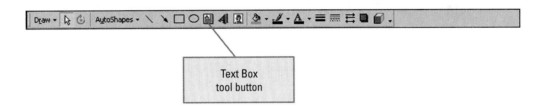

To place a text box *with* word wrap anywhere on your slide, follow these steps.

1. Designate that you want to insert a text box using one of these methods:
   - Choose **Insert|Text Box**.
   - Click the **Text Box** button on the Drawing toolbar.
2. Click the slide at the point where you want to insert the text box and, while holding down the left mouse button, drag on the slide until it is the width that you want. As you do this, the mouse pointer turns to crossbars.
3. Enter your text into the text box. The insertion point should be blinking inside the box surrounded by a diagonal-line border. As you continue to add text, the width of the box remains the size that you dragged it, but the length of the text box increases to hold additional lines.

Result: You've successfully added a text box and text to your slide (Figure 2.18). Neither the box nor the text is visible in the outline pane. The eight small squares located at even intervals on the border are called *sizing handles*. These handles, which you will learn more about in Chapter 6, "Elements of Sight and Sound," enable you to resize the box.

TO ADD A TEXT BOX WITHOUT WORD WRAP

How: To add a text box without word wrap, follow these steps:

1. Choose **Insert|Text Box** or click the **Text Box** button on the Drawing toolbar.
2. Click (do not drag) on the slide at the spot where you want to insert the text box. A small box appears with the mouse pointer flashing inside. Type your text or if you are using text that you have placed on the clipboard, click **Paste**.
3. The text box increases in width to accommodate the characters that you're typing, but the text will not wrap to a second line. That is, it will just get longer and longer as you type.

Result: Your slide now includes a text box that is long enough to accommodate the full length of your text (Figure 2.18). Word wrapping can be added anytime by double-clicking on the dotted lines of the border or choosing **Format|Text Box** and then selecting the **Text Box** tab. If you want to format your text box or any other object that you add from the Drawing toolbar, flip ahead to Chapter 6.

Figure 2.18
Inserting text boxes

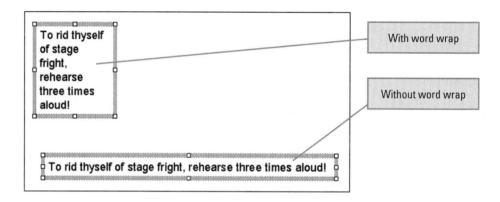

TO REPOSITION A TEXT BOX

CORE OBJECTIVE: **Place text inside of a shape using a text box**

How: To move the text box, first click anywhere in the text box to display the diagonal-line border. Then:

1. Place the mouse pointer anywhere on the border until you see it become a four-headed arrow.
2. Press down the left mouse button and drag to arrange the text box on the slide. As you drag, you will see the border change from a series of diagonal lines to dotted lines (Figure 2.19).

Result: The text box has been successful moved. It you don't like its new home, just relocate it again. You can place a text box anywhere on a slide, including on a graphical object or shape. Then you can add text to add a bit of interest or touch of humor to your slide. Chapter 6 shows you how to add many types of graphics to your visual aids.

Figure 2.19
Repositioning a text box

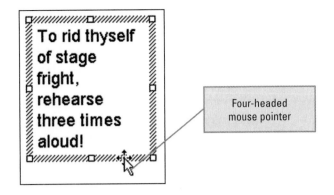

To rid thyself of stage fright, rehearse three times aloud!

Four-headed mouse pointer

TO MODIFY A TEXT BOX

 CORE OBJECTIVE: **Use the wrap text in text box feature**

 EXPERT OBJECTIVE: **Use the wrap text in AutoShape feature**

How: After you have inserted a text box on a slide—with or without word wrap—you can change many of its features. Some of these are described as follows:

❍ **To add or remove word wrap,** first click to select it. Then:
  1. Double-click on the border with the four-headed mouse pointer. When the Format|Text Box dialog box appears, click the **Text Box** tab.
  2. Click to remove the check from the **Word wrap text in AutoShape** check box (Figure 2.20). Click **OK** to close the box.

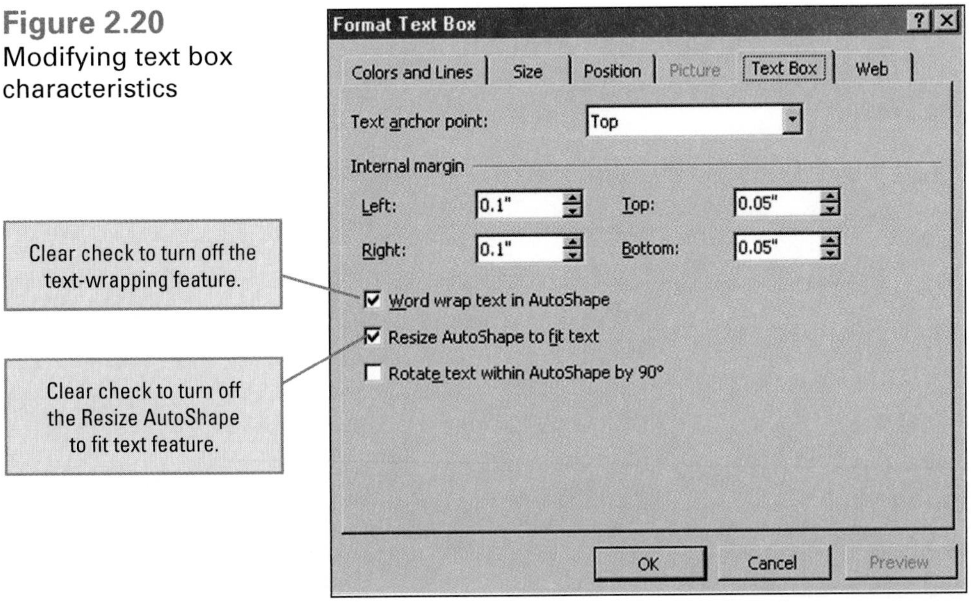

Figure 2.20
Modifying text box characteristics

Clear check to turn off the text-wrapping feature.

Clear check to turn off the Resize AutoShape to fit text feature.

Format Text Box

| Colors and Lines | Size | Position | Picture | Text Box | Web |

Text anchor point: Top

Internal margin
Left: 0.1"   Top: 0.05"
Right: 0.1"   Bottom: 0.05"

☑ Word wrap text in AutoShape
☑ Resize AutoShape to fit text
☐ Rotate text within AutoShape by 90°

OK   Cancel   Preview

○ **To size the text box,** first click to show the sizing handles. Then:

1. Double-click on the border with the four-headed mouse pointer or choose **Format|Text Box** and then click the **Text Box** tab.
2. Click in the box to remove the check from the **Resize AutoShape to fit text** check box and then click **OK**.
3. Place your mouse pointer anywhere on the sizing handles so that it turns into a two-headed arrow. Drag the sizing handle in or out to change the size of the text box.

○ **To delete a text box,** click once on the border to select it (diagonal lines should be replaced with dots). Press **Delete** or **Backspace**.

Result: The text box has been moved or deleted, or its characteristics modified.

Use PinPoint

After gaining the skills in this chapter, you can start PowerPoint, you can create a presentation from blank slides, add slides, change the slide layout, add text in the three normal view panes, promote and demote text, create speaker notes, use the automatic spell checker, add and format a text box, and use the style checker. Now it's time to see what you can do with the PinPoint software. Remember, whenever you are unsure of what to do next, you can reread the relevant portion of the chapter or you can click Show Me for a live demonstration. Try the following skills in PinPoint:

• Create a blank presentation
• Text in normal view
• Change indent level
• Speaker notes
• Add a new slide
• Change slide layout
• Word wrap in a text box

Key Terms

You can find definitions for these words in this chapter:

AutoLayout
Auto-Fit
Demote
Font
Placeholder
Promote
Sizing handle
Word wrap

Review Questions

You can use the following review questions and exercises to test your knowledge and skills. Answers are given in Appendix D, "Answers to Review Questions."

True/False

Indicate whether each statement is true (T) or false (F).

___ 1. You can enter text in all three panes in Normal view.

___ 2. The text you type in the slide pane automatically appears in the outline pane.

___ 3. Text that you type in the notes pane automatically appears in the slide pane.

___ 4. You can add a slide from the outline pane or the slide pane in Normal view.

___ 5. By default, new slides you add without accessing the New Slide dialog box have a bulleted list layout.

___ 6. Wavy red underlines under certain words means PowerPoint has flagged them as possible spelling mistakes.

___ 7. Text you type in a text box automatically appears in the outline.

___ 8. When you type in a text box, it automatically enlarges vertically or horizontally to fit your text.

___ 9. When you see a yellow light bulb on your slide, it means PowerPoint has a suggestion for a way to spell an incorrect word.

___ 10. PowerPoint enables you to have up to five different levels of indentation, so you should try to use all of them.

Multiple Choice

Select the letter that best completes the statement.

___ 1. When you are working in Slide view and click the New Slide button, you must choose the new slide's:
   a. AutoFit.
   b. AutoLayout.
   c. Font.
   d. Text box.
   e. View.

___ 2. When you are entering text in the outline and want to demote to a lower level:
   a. Press Enter.
   b. Press Tab.
   c. Press Shift+Tab.
   d. Click the Promote button.
   e. Click the Undo button.

___ 3. To be able to specify the AutoLayout of a new slide when you add one:
   a. Press Ctrl+Enter in Slide view.
   b. Click the New Slide button.
   c. Work in Outline view.
   d. Use Notes Page view.
   e. Any of the above.

___ 4. To change the slide layout of an existing slide:
   a. Press Tab on the slide in Outline view.
   b. Click Common Tasks and choose Slide Layout.
   c. Click the Slide Sorter View button.
   d. Right-click the red, wavy underlines.
   e. Double-click the text box.

___ 5. The advantage of using a text box to contain some text is:
   a. The text is automatically formatted attractively.
   b. The text can appear anywhere on the slide.
   c. The text is surrounded by an attractive border.
   d. Placeholders are difficult to use.
   e. All of the above.

___ 6. When text automatically starts a new line when it needs more room, this is:
   a. Text boxing.
   b. Text drawing.
   c. Text alignment.
   d. Word lining.
   e. Word wrapping.

___ 7. To move a text box to a different location on the slide:
   a. Change the slide layout.
   b. Click the Normal View button.
   c. Drag the diagonal-line border.
   d. Drag the sizing handles.
   e. Press Enter inside the text box.

___ 8. Obeying the six-by-six rule is important because it:
   a. Prevents you from talking too long.
   b. Limits the number of slides you will use.
   c. Helps you remember what you wanted to say next.
   d. Limits the amount of text on the slide.
   e. Grabs the audience's attention.

___ 9. The style checker is useful for checking whether:
   a. The capitalization is correct.
   b. The punctuation is consistent.
   c. The number of lines is limited.
   d. The size of the title and bullet points is large enough.
   e. All of the above.

___ 10. The place on a slide where it says "Click to add text" is called:
   a. An AutoLayout.
   b. An AutoText.
   c. A bullet.
   d. A placeholder.
   e. A text box.

Match the letters in Figure 2.20 with the correct items in the list.

Figure 2.21

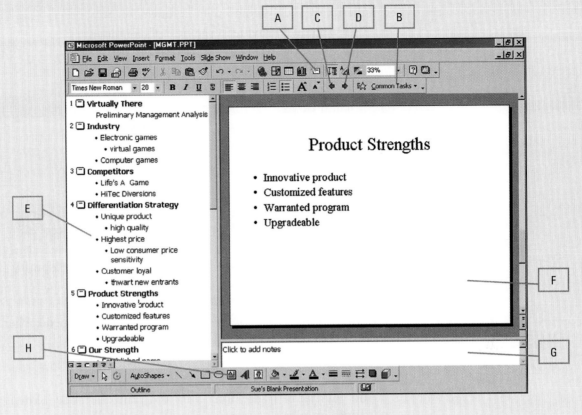

___ 1. Click here to create a new slide in Slide view.

___ 2. Click here to change the layout of an existing slide.

___ 3. Click here to indent some text to a lower level.

___ 4. Type here to add notes to yourself.

___ 5. Click here to begin creating a text box.

___ 6. Text in a text box shows in this pane.

___ 7. Click here to un-indent the text and promote it to a higher level.

Exercise and Project

Follow these step-by-step instructions to practice the skills that are included in this chapter. If you are working in a computer lab, you may have to ask your instructor where to save or print your work.

Exercise

1. Open PowerPoint.
2. Select **Blank Presentation** from the PowerPoint dialog box and press **Enter** or click **OK**.
3. Select the **Title Slide** layout for your first slide and press **Enter**.
4. Choose **Tools|Options** and click the **Spelling and Style** tab. Click **Style Options** and the **Visual Clarity** tab. Add check marks to each of the three boxes under Legibility.

5. Click in the title placeholder and type **Great Beginnings**.
6. Press **Enter** and on the second line of the title, type **Welcome to the Locker**.
7. Click in the subtitle placeholder and type **New Employee Tour**.
8. Add a new slide with a bullet layout.
9. Type **What We Provide** in the title placeholder.
10. Type the following bulleted list
    - **Performance-based pay increase**
    - **Comprehensive health care**
    - **Dental care**
    - **Two weeks paid vacation years 1 through 3**
    - **Three weeks paid vacation after third year**
    - **Two weeks sick leave**
    - **IRA**
    - **Retirement fund fully vested after 5 years**
11. Add a text box without word wrap in the lower left corner of the title slide. Type your name in it. Save your file in the PowerPoint 2000 folder as **Exercise 2A**.
12. Print this as handouts—three per page, in Pure Black and White.
13. You should see the style checker appear. Click the yellow bulb and choose **Split this slide into two slides**. You should see a second bulleted slide appear in the outline pane. Some of the points that you typed earlier should now be on this slide.
14. Select **Slide 3**. Change the layout to **Object and Text**.
15. Click in the notes area and type **Insert clip art later**.
16. Add your name in the notes area and print this slide (Slide 3) as notes pages (should only be one page) in Pure Black and White.
17. Save the file in your folder as **Exercise 2B**.
18. Exit PowerPoint.

Project

You have the good fortune of being courted by several firms that are highly respected in your field. The salaries being presented by each are comparable and all offer desirable working conditions, so you must make your job choice based on company benefits. Create a four-slide presentation (Slide 1 is the title slide) to present to your prospective future employers outlining the benefits—both tangible (such as salary and paid leave) and intangible (such as flexible hours and casual Friday)—that would help them add you to their firm.

Choose a relevant and intelligent title for each slide and the title page.

- A title slide with the company name. Subtitle should have your name in it.
- Relevant titles on each page.
- At least one bulleted list layout.
- At least two-column text layout.
- One slide with your choice of layout.
- A text box at the bottom of the title slide with the date added.

Add speaker notes for yourself on at least two of the slides. Remember that you can add notes in both Normal and Slide Sorter views. Save as **Project 2** in your PowerPoint folder and print the presentation as notes pages—six slides to a page.

Chapter 3

Edit Your Work

ow that you've learned how to create slides, add content, and save a slide show, it's time to edit your work. Editing may be one of the less glamorous aspects of creating a presentation, but it's also one of the most important. Your words make a statement about you and your capabilities. Choose those words carefully, organize your ideas, and eliminate extra verbiage. Meticulous polishing up front will ensure that your visual aids project a professional and persuasive message. After you've finished writing, you can use the skills covered in this chapter to reorganize, duplicate, remove large chunks of your text, or even delete entire slides. Then you can complete the process by checking your spelling.

At the end of this chapter you will be able to:

C E

C	E	
❑	❑	Select text
❑	❑	Rearrange and duplicate text
☑	❑	Use the Office Clipboard
❑	❑	Undo and Redo operations
☑	❑	Use the Office Clipboard
☑	❑	Copy a slide
☑	❑	Delete a slide
☑	❑	Rearrange slides
☑	❑	Find and replace text
☑	❑	Use the automatic spelling feature

TASK **1** *Select Text*

What: Before you can make changes to blocks of text, you must first designate or *select* the text. After you've selected text, it's easy to identify because it has a different appearance or exhibits different characteristics than its unselected counterparts. The text that you select will then be included in whatever operations that you perform.

Why: The Delete and Backspace keys are handy to use when you are typing, but sometimes you want to edit and format blocks of text. In those instances, it's more efficient to select the text and then delete, rearrange, or duplicate the section.

How: You can select text with either the mouse or the keyboard. The mouse is faster, but you have less control; the keyboard is slower, but more exact.

WITH THE MOUSE

1. Place the mouse pointer (I-beam) to the left of the text that you want to select.
2. Press and hold the left mouse button to drag across or down to cover the entire section of text.

WITH THE KEYBOARD

1. Place the cursor to the left of the text that you want to select.
2. Hold down the **Shift** key and press the arrow keys to cover the entire section of text.

Table 3.1 shows other ways to select various amounts of text quickly, using either the mouse or a combination of the mouse and keyboard.

Table 3.1 Ways to Select Text

To Select This	Do This	In This Pane
One word	Double-click in the word.	Outline and Slide
A bullet point and all subpoints	Click the top-level bullet. Triple-click in first level of text.	Outline and Slide Outline and Slide
Bullet subpoints	Click the topmost bullet that you want to select.	Outline and Slide
A block of text	Click at beginning of section, hold down **Shift**, click at end.	Outline and Slide
Placeholder	Click in placeholder to display border, and then click border to change it from a diagonal to a dotted line.	Slide
	Press the **Tab** key.	Slide
Slide	Click the slide icon.	Outline pane
	Click the slide miniture.	Slide Sorter view
Nonadjacent slides	Press **Ctrl** and click the individual slides.	Slide Sorter view
Entire slide show	Press **Ctrl+A**.	Outline or Slide Sorter view

Result: The text that you've selected appears in one of the ways shown in Figures 3.1–3.4. Selected placeholders have a heavy dotted border around them rather than borders formed from many short diagonal lines. Individually selected bits or blocks of text display distinct font and background colors. As you continue editing, you can be confident that any selected text will be included in whatever procedures you perform.

Figure 3.1 Selecting a slide in outline pane

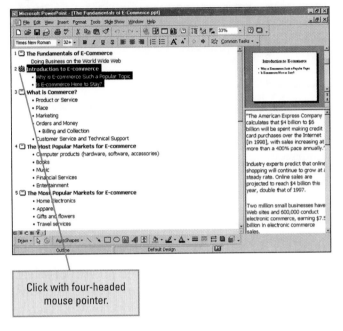

Click with four-headed mouse pointer.

Figure 3.2 Selecting a placeholder in slide pane

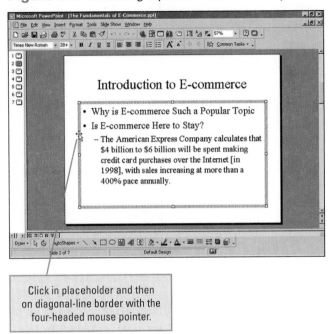

Click in placeholder and then on diagonal-line border with the four-headed mouse pointer.

Figure 3.3 Selecting a bullet point and subpoints

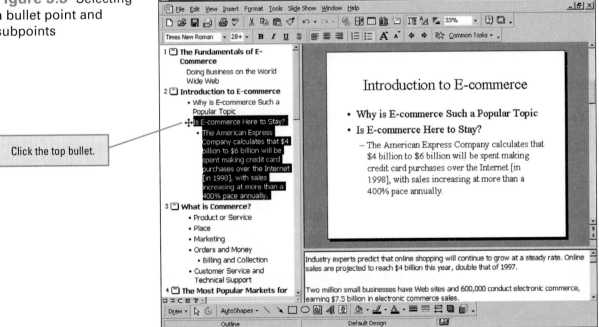

Click the top bullet.

Figure 3.4 Selecting slides in Slide Sorter view

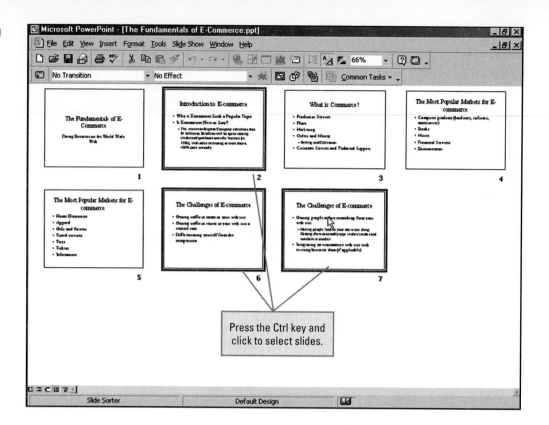

Press the Ctrl key and click to select slides.

 TIPS FROM A PRO: This chapter focuses on editing; therefore the process of selecting text is primarily discussed in relation to the cut, copy, and paste functions. However, text must be selected to be included in other operations as well, such as formatting or adding animation.

Note: Because the terminology can get confusing—remember that placeholders without text in them have a dashed-line border—for simplicity, selected and unselected borders are called *dotted-line* and *diagonal-line* respectively in the rest of this book.

TASK 2   *Rearrange and Duplicate Text*

What: As soon as you select a block of text, it can be deleted, rearranged, and duplicated. The copy-and-paste process is used to copy a block of text or graphical object and place the copy in another location. When you want to remove the text or object from its current position and put it somewhere else, you can use the cut-and-paste or drag-and-drop methods.

Processes that involve cut, copy, and paste are used in conjunction with the Clipboard. Just like a clipboard that you use to carry around your papers, the **Clipboard** serves as a temporary storage area for blocks of text that you cut or copy until you decide to paste. Another feature of PowerPoint, the **Office Clipboard**, lets you store multiple blocks of text or objects. You learn more about this feature in the next task.

Why: During the editing process, you often want to move a block of text to another location, or to duplicate text and then make a few changes to it. It would be inefficient to delete and then retype the text from scratch—particularly if the selection is a long one.

The procedures for duplicating or moving text are similar and begin with selecting the text. Table 3.2 summarizes the related commands and results of each.

Table 3.2 Cut, Copy, and Paste Commands

Command	Button	Shortcut Key	Effect
Edit|Cut	✂	Ctrl+X	Removes selected text, puts it on the Clipboard
Edit|Copy	📋	Ctrl+C	Puts duplicate of selected text on the Clipboard
Edit|Paste	📋	Ctrl+V	Inserts contents of Clipboard wherever the cursor is

Note: These commands don't just apply to text; they pertain to anything that you can select, such as graphical objects and placeholders.

DUPLICATE TEXT (COPY AND PASTE)

How: To duplicate text, follow these steps:

1. Select the text you want to copy using techniques you learned in Task 1.
2. Click the **Copy** button or choose **Edit\|Copy** or press **Ctrl+C**.
3. Move the insertion point to the location where you want the text inserted.
4. Click the **Paste** button or choose **Edit\|Paste** or press **Ctrl+V**.
5. Repeat Steps 3 and 4 to insert the text multiple times.

 TIPS FROM A PRO: If you copy information from another Office program to paste into PowerPoint, control the format of the information to be pasted by choosing **Edit\|Paste Special**.

Result: The copied text appears in two locations. Using the Copy command makes a duplicate of the text without removing it from the original location, as you see in Figure 3.5.

MOVE TEXT (CUT AND PASTE)

How: As with the copy-and-paste process, follow these steps:
1. Select the text that you want to move.
2. Click the **Cut** button or choose **Edit\|Cut** or press **Ctrl+X**.
3. Move the insertion point to the location where you want the text inserted.
4. Click the **Paste** button or choose **Edit\|Paste** or press **Ctrl+V**.

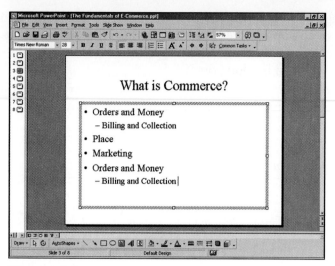

Figure 3.5 Using Copy and Paste functions

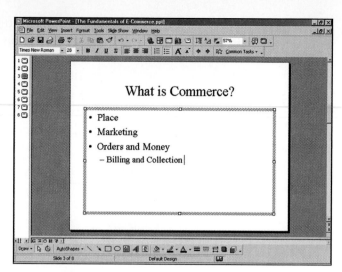

Figure 3.6 Using Cut and Paste functions

 Tips from a Pro: Do you sometimes want to delete a block of text? Just select the section to be deleted and press **Backspace** or **Delete**.

Result: The text has been removed from the first location and placed in the second, as you see in Figure 3.6.

MOVE TEXT (DRAG AND DROP)

How: Another way to move text that is perhaps even easier than cut-and-paste, is the drag-and-drop method. This method requires nothing in the way of choosing menus, clicking buttons, or pressing keys. All you have to do is select and drag with the mouse. This technique is fast, but it can be tricky. You must use your mouse expertly and exercise patience to get the results that you intend. In Outline or Slide view, follow these steps:

1. Select the text that you want to move.
2. Hold down the left mouse button. As you begin to drag, you will see that a small rectangular box with a "fuzzy" border now accompanies the mouse pointer. Notice that there is now an insertion point to the left of the selected text.
3. Drag the mouse pointer until you have the insertion point in the position where you would like to insert the text (Figure 3.7). Release the mouse button.

Result: As soon as you release the mouse button, the text is dropped into the new location—that is, unless your mouse and its delivery got away from you. If that happens, you can hunt down, recapture your prey, and try again, or use the slower but more precise cut-and-paste approach. If you made a mistake, you will learn how to reverse it in Task 4.

 Tips from a Pro: If you press and hold the **Ctrl** key while using drag-and-drop, you copy rather than move the text.

Figure 3.7 Using drag and drop

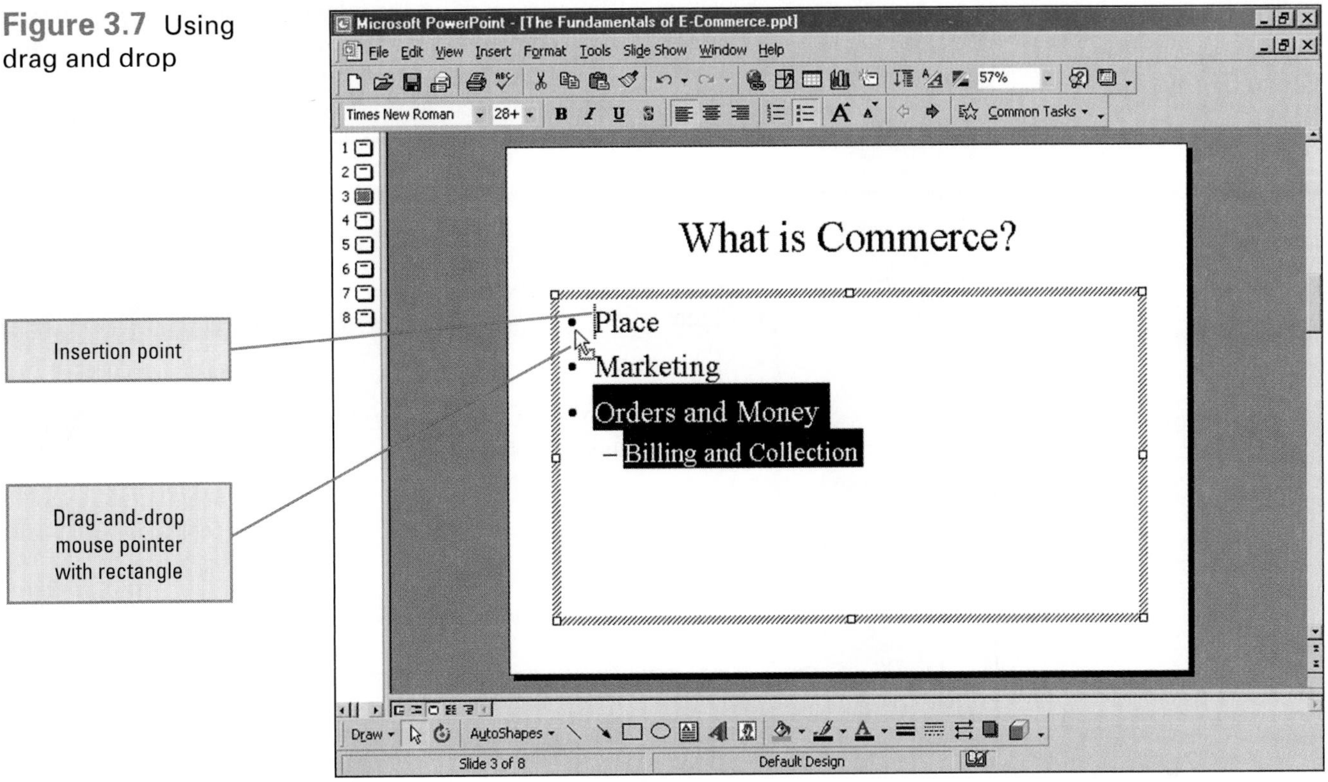

Insertion point

Drag-and-drop mouse pointer with rectangle

THOUGHT QUESTION: Where does your text go if you "lose" it while you are attempting to drag and drop?

TASK 3 — Use the Office Clipboard to Collect and Paste

C

CORE OBJECTIVE: **Use the Office Clipboard**

What: Windows provides a temporary storage place called the Clipboard to store a folder, a file, or, in this case, a block of text. Still, the Office Clipboard offers an advantage over the Windows version because it lets you to store up to 12 different items (you can store graphical objects here as well) from any of the Office programs at one time. Before you can use this feature, however, you must turn it on. To turn on the Clipboard toolbar, shown in Figure 3.8, choose **View|Toolbars|Clipboard**, or cut or copy the same thing twice in succession, without carrying out any other operations in between. When the toolbar is on and you click Copy, you will see an icon—that represents what you have copied—added to the toolbar.

Why: Not only can you collect several items and paste them one at a time, or all at once, but you can temporarily store items for use a little later in your work.

How: The process of using the Office Clipboard to collect and paste multiple items is similar to the copy-and-cut processes.

Figure 3.8
Collecting with the
Office Clipboard

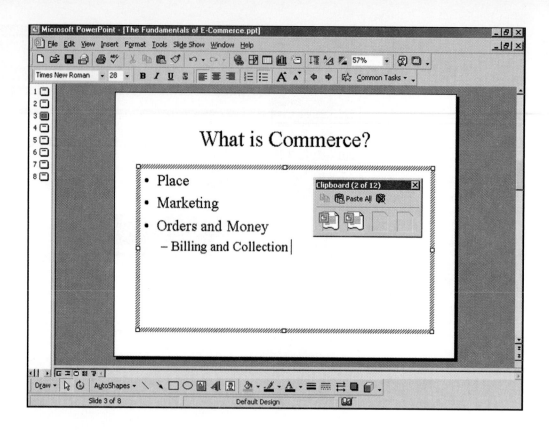

TO COLLECT ITEMS

1. Select the first bit of text or object that you want to collect.
2. Choose **Copy**.
3. Select the second item.
4. Choose **Copy** again. At this point, the Clipboard toolbar should appear.
5. If it doesn't, you must activate the feature. To do this, copy the same thing twice without pausing or choose **View|Toolbars|Clipboard**. Then repeat Steps 1 and 2.
6. Check the Clipboard toolbar to ensure that each item is being collected. Place the mouse pointer over each icon in the Clipboard toolbar and pause—don't click—to see the contents of the item (Figure 3.9).

 TIPS FROM A PRO: As soon as you have collected the 13th item, the yellow assistant balloon appears to tell you that the Clipboard is full. Now you must decide whether to copy the selected item, in which case the first item drops off the Clipboard, or to cancel your operation.

TO PASTE ITEMS

1. Move the insertion point to the destination where you want to paste.
2. To insert a single item, click its icon. To insert all the items at once in the order that they were collected, click **Paste All** (Figure 3.9).
3. When you are done with this series of edits, empty the Clipboard so that you can begin a new operation. To do this, click the **Clear** button.
4. To remove the toolbar from the screen, click its **Close** button.

Figure 3.9
Using the Office
Clipboard

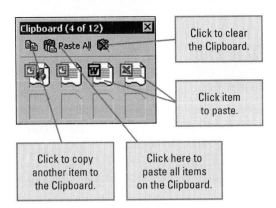

Click to clear
the Clipboard.

Click item
to paste.

Click to copy
another item to
the Clipboard.

Click here to
paste all items
on the Clipboard.

Result: If you click the individual Clipboard icons, the selected text or object is pasted wherever you've designated. When you choose **Paste All**, the blocks of text that you've collected are pasted into your presentation one by one in the same order that you collected them. Even if this isn't quite what you intended, you can test out your newly acquired skills and rearrange the pasted items.

TIPS FROM A PRO: When the Clipboard toolbar gets in your way, you can move it or close it by clicking the **Close** button. If you close the Office Clipboard three times in a row without pasting, however, it will no longer appear automatically or be collecting information for you.

TASK 4 *Undo and Redo Operations*

What: When you're typing and make a small mistake, you can easily backspace; for a large error (such as accidentally deleting an entire block of text), however, you need to use the Undo feature. This brings back what you thought was gone. (Wouldn't you love to have one of these for your checking account?) And, if you change your mind and want to delete it again, you can just click Redo.

Why: If you make a mistake, you don't have to start over; just reverse the damage.

How: Use the Undo and Redo buttons for single or multiple operations as follows:

○ To reverse the last action, click the **Undo** button.
○ To undo several actions, click **Undo** multiple times or click the down arrow next to the Undo button and drag downward to select as many functions as you want to reverse (Figure 3.10).
○ To redo the last item that you just used Undo on, click the **Redo** button.
○ To redo several actions you just used Undo on, click **Redo** until your work is fully restored or click the down arrow next to Redo and drag downward to select as many operations as you want to restore.

Table 3.3 summarizes the methods for the Undo and Redo features.

Figure 3.10
The Undo button

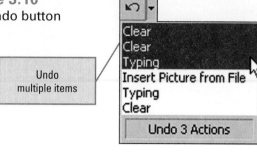

Undo
multiple items

Table 3.3 Undo and Redo Commands

Command	Button	Shortcut Key
Edit|Undo		Ctrl+Z
Edit|Redo		Ctrl+Y

Result: The mistake you made is reversed! You learn to fully appreciate this feature as you continue to work with PowerPoint and the other Office products.

 TIPS FROM A PRO: PowerPoint keeps a record of your operations, and you can choose to undo the last one, or multiple incorrect moves in reverse order. In default, PowerPoint is set to allow you to Undo 20 times in a row. You can increase this number up to 150 operations. Choose **Tools|Options**, click the **Edit** tab, and then click the spin box next to Undo.

TASK **5** *Copy a Slide*

C CORE OBJECTIVE: Copy a slide from one presentation into another

What: Now you know how to copy blocks of text, but sometimes it's more efficient to make a copy of the entire slide. It's easy to duplicate slides in an active slide show or to insert slides from an existing, saved presentation.

Why: Copying a previously prepared slide that contains related material, and then making some minor modifications, more practical than starting from scratch.

MAKE A DUPLICATE SLIDE NEXT TO THE ORIGINAL

How: To duplicate a slide in the active presentation, and to place the copy next to the original slide, follow these steps:

1. Select the slide that you want to copy in the slide pane, in the outline pane or in Slide Sorter view (in this view you can use the Ctrl key to select multiple slides to duplicate).
2. Choose **Insert|Duplicate Slide.**

Result: Your presentation now includes an exact copy (including formatting) of the selected slide (or slides) next to the original. You may want to move it, however; you learn how to rearrange slides in Task 7.

MAKE A DUPLICATE SLIDE ANYWHERE IN THE PRESENTATION

How: To copy a slide in the outline pane or Slide Sorter view, and control where you place the copy, follow these steps:

1. Select the slide (or slides in the Slide Sorter view) that you want to copy.
2. Click the **Copy** button.
3. Select the slide that is directly before the position where you want to place the duplicate slide and click the **Paste** button.

Result: Your presentation includes two copies of the slide that you selected. The new slide is located directly *after* the slide that you selected in Step 3.

COPY A SLIDE FROM ANOTHER PRESENTATION

How: To insert one or more slides from another saved presentation without having to open the second presentation, follow these steps:

1. Select the slide that will precede the slide(s) that you are going to insert. (Use the outline or slide panes, or Slide Sorter view).
2. Choose **Insert|Slides from Files**.
3. When the Slide Finder dialog box appears (Figure 3.11), click **Browse** to locate the saved PowerPoint file (Figure 3.12). Select the presentation and click **Open**.
4. Scroll through the slide show and use the mouse to select the slide(s) (press and hold **Ctrl** to select multiple slides).
5. Click **Insert** to add individually selected slides or **Insert All** to add the entire presentation, as shown in Figure 3.13. Click **Close** to the dialog box when you finish adding slides.

Click Browse to find presentation file.

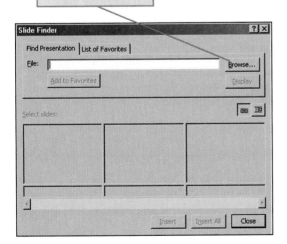

Figure 3.11 Slide Finder dialog box

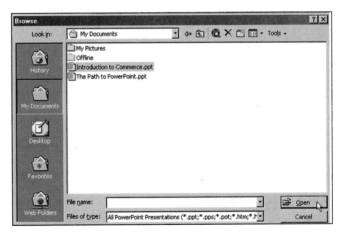

Figure 3.12 Browsing for a saved file

Result: You have added a single slide or multiple slides from another presentation to your slide show. As you can see in the slide pane, the new slide displays the design and formatting characteristics of the active show. You learn more about a presentation within a presentation in Chapter 7, "Get Ready for an Electronic Slide Show."

Figure 3.13
Inserting slides from a file

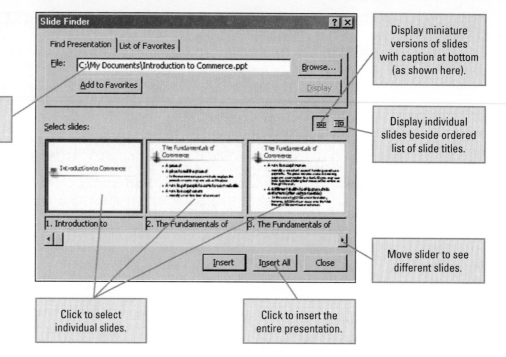

Name and location of selected file

Display miniature versions of slides with caption at bottom (as shown here).

Display individual slides beside ordered list of slide titles.

Move slider to see different slides.

Click to select individual slides.

Click to insert the entire presentation.

 TIPS FROM A PRO: You can also copy a slide from one presentation to another using the select, copy, and paste procedure described previously. Open the saved presentation, and then select, copy, and paste.

 THOUGHT QUESTION: What happens when you copy a slide using **Ctrl+A**, and then paste it onto a new slide?

| TASK **6** | *Delete a Slide* |

C

CORE OBJECTIVE: Delete slides

What: Sometimes you will want to delete an entire slide or even multiple slides from your presentation.

Why: It's easy to add too many slides when you're working in the outline pane, or discover while editing that the points covered on a particular slide aren't necessary after all.

How: In contrast to the sometimes-lengthy process required to create them, deleting slides is easy. In the blink of an eye, you can banish your slides forever. Slides can be deleted in several different ways.

TO DELETE ONE SLIDE AT A TIME

○ Select the slide that you want to delete in the outline pane or Slide Sorter view, and then choose **Edit|Delete Slide**.

○ Select the slide in the outline pane or Slide Sorter view and press **Delete**.

Figure 3.14
Deleting slides
in Slide Sorter view

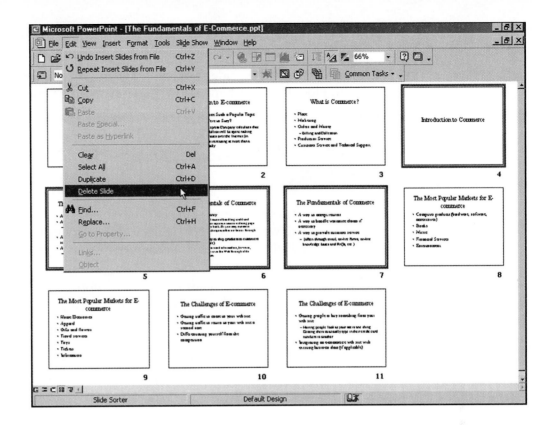

 TIPS FROM A PRO: If you think that you might use a slide later on in your preparations, you can place it on the Clipboard for a short time instead of deleting it. Once your computer is shut down, however, everything is cleared off the Clipboard.

 THOUGHT QUESTION: How can you tell what slide number you are viewing in the slide pane?

TO DELETE MULTIPLE SLIDES AT ONCE

1. Select the slides in the Slide Sorter view or in Outline view, if the slides are adjacent to each other.
2. Choose **Edit|Delete Slide** or press **Delete**.

Result: The slides that you have deleted are no longer part of your presentation. If this was not your intention, don't do anything rash. Remember that you can use Undo to return your beautiful slides from the dead.

 TIPS FROM A PRO: How many slides are too many? Its crucial to keep your audience engaged in your presentation. If you have too many slides, they may lose interest; too few, and you won't be able to cover your points adequately. Here are some hints to keep your message profound yet succinct:

- Plan on changing slides every 30 seconds to 2 minutes, not including discussion time or extra examples that you might have.

- Don't put down every idea—your slides are to show your listeners the basic structure so that they stay on track, not substitute for you.

- Practice the timing so that you have a fairly reliable estimation of the time required to present your material.

- Add extra slides, hide them, and then use them *if* time permits. You learn how to hide slides in Chapter 11, "Use Advanced Features."

TASK 7   *Rearrange Slides*

What: You know how to delete slides, but sometimes rather than removing, you want to reorganize instead (like trying to decide whether to toss out the clothes that you haven't worn in three years or just move them into the spare room).

Why: As you review your outline, you notice that the material included on a particular slide would probably have a greater impact if it were closer to the beginning of the presentation. Just as there's logic in placing tall items at the back of a cabinet rather than at the front, there should be logic in the order that information is included in your visual aids.

USE SLIDE SORTER VIEW

CORE OBJECTIVE: **Change the order of slides using Slide Sorter view**

How: The easiest way to rearrange slides in this view is to use the drag-and-drop method. If you don't care for that approach, use cut-and-paste instead.

Note: Slide Sorter view enables you can move multiple slides at once, but make certain that you select slides carefully; noncontiguous slides that you select are placed together in a group after they are moved.

To use cut-and-paste, follow these steps:

1. Select the slide and click the **Cut** button to place the slide on the Clipboard.
2. Select the slide that you want to come directly ahead of the slide that you are moving and click the **Paste** button.

To use drag-and-drop, follow these steps:

1. With the mouse pointer positioned on the slide miniature, hold down the left mouse button and drag. You see the "fuzzy" border rectangle joins the bottom of the mouse pointer. As you guide the pointer to the right or left of any slide, a horizontal line also appears (on the right or left, depending on which way you drag).
2. Drag the mouse pointer and rectangle until you see the horizontal line in the position where you want to place the slide that you're relocating (Figure 3.15). Release the mouse button to complete the operation.

Result: The slides that you selected have been rearranged. You can look at the thumbnail view of each slide to ensure that the new placement is logical. If you accidentally drop a slide in the wrong location, grab it and move it again, or click **Undo** and start over.

Figure 3.15
Rearranging slides
in Slide Sorter view

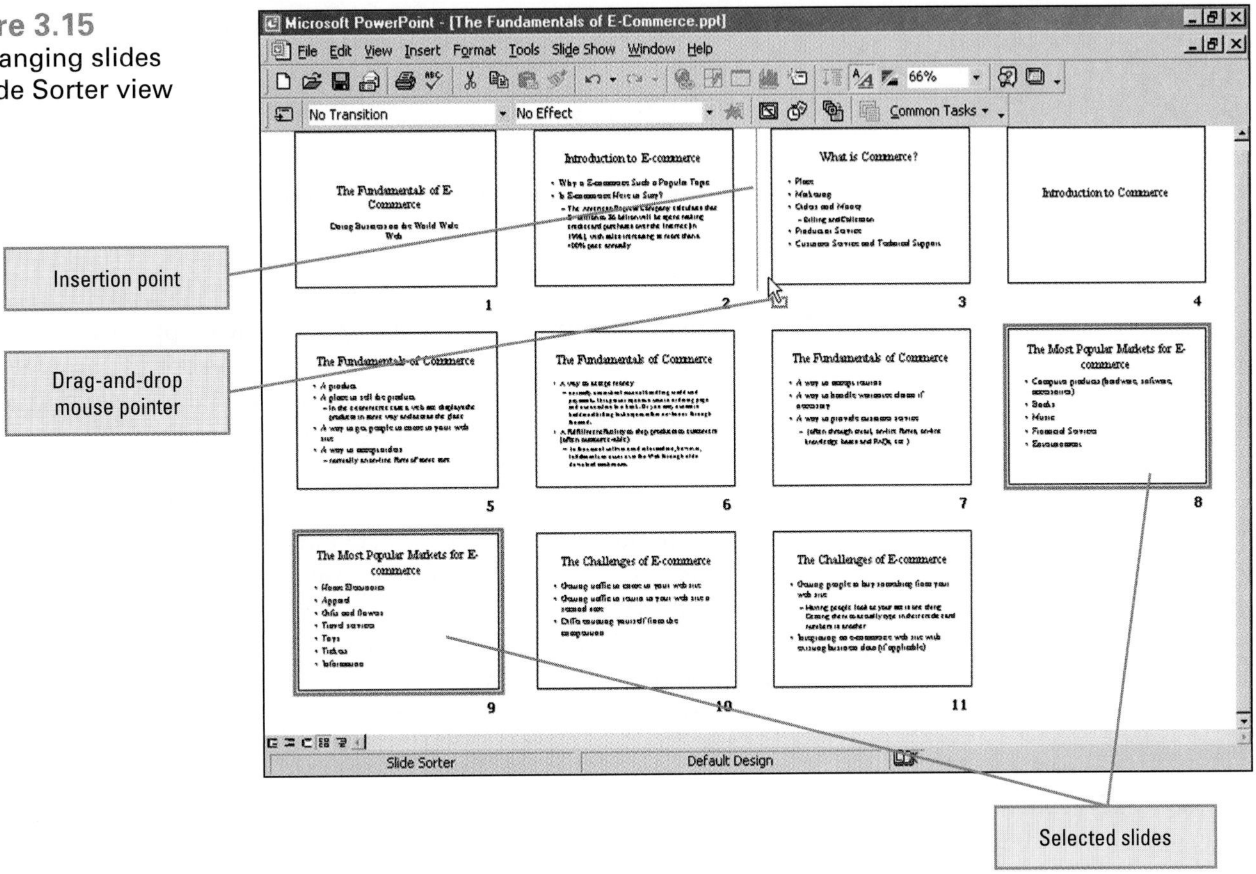

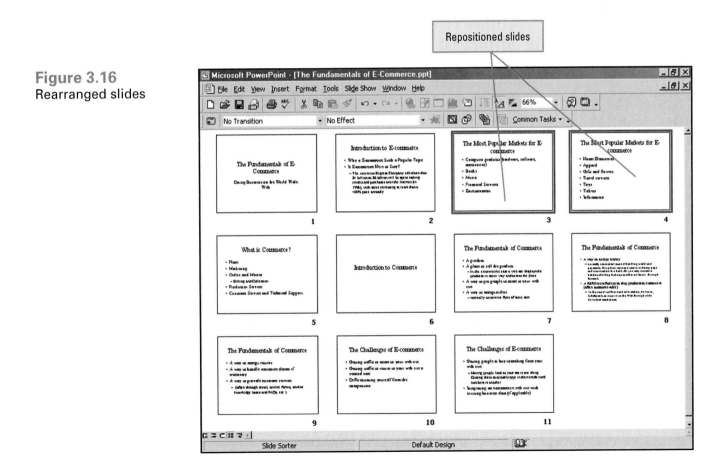

Figure 3.16
Rearranged slides

CORE OBJECTIVE: Modify slide sequence in the outline pane

How: You can move single or multiple adjoining slides in the outline pane. Click the slide icon to select the slide or slides, and then use either of the following methods to move them.

To use cut-and-paste, follow these steps:

1. Click the **Cut** button to place the slide on the Clipboard.
2. Select the slide that is positioned directly in front of the space that you want the selected slide to occupy and click the **Paste** button.

To use drag and drop, follow these steps:

1. Move the mouse pointer over the slide icon until it turns to a four-headed arrow. Hold down the left mouse button and drag. As you drag, the mouse pointer becomes a two-headed arrow. A handy horizontal leader bar also materializes and moves along in front of the pointer to indicate where the slide will be placed.
2. When you reach the place where you want to put your slide (Figure 3.17), release the mouse button.

Result: As soon as you release the mouse button, your slide is repositioned. The outline pane clearly shows you its new position in relation to the other slides.

Figure 3.17
Rearranging slides in the outline pane

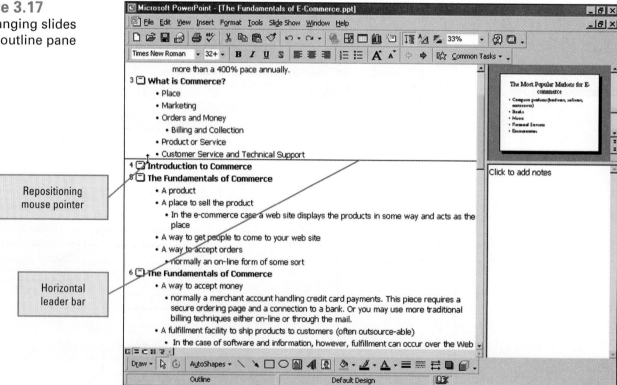

 THOUGHT QUESTION: What happens when you select a bullet point and drag to the left or to the right?

C CORE OBJECTIVE: **Find and replace text**

What: When you are editing text, you sometimes find that certain characters need to be changed every time they occur. For example, you have opened the presentation that you used for last year's budget report; you want to update the data and use it again this year. This means that each time there is a reference to the year, it will need to be changed from 2000 to 2001. PowerPoint's Find and Replace feature helps you quickly accomplish this job.

Why: Making these sorts of changes one by one may lead to errors. It would be easy to miss one occurrence of the item, or you might transpose some of the text if you have to type the same thing over and over. That's why automating the process is a good idea—not only to keep you from tiresome, repetitive tasks, but also to ensure that it's done accurately.

FIND TEXT

How: To use the Find command, follow these steps:

1. Choose **Edit|Find** or press **Ctrl+F** to open the dialog box shown in Figure 3.18.
2. Type the characters that you want to find in the **Find what** box.
3. Check **Whole Words Only** to restrict your search to the exact character set that you type. (If you leave this box empty, PowerPoint finds

Figure 3.18
Finding text

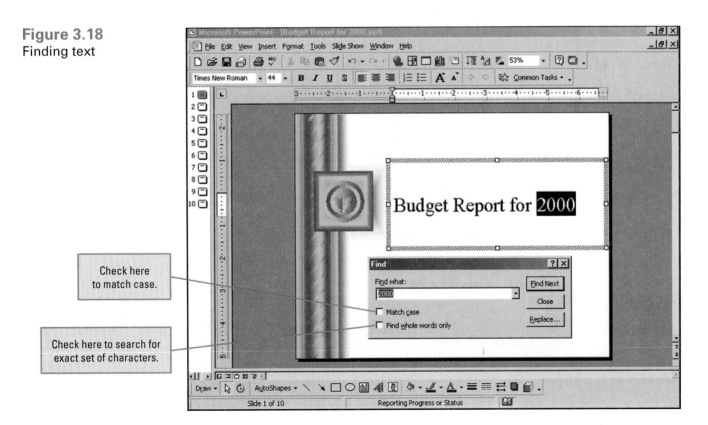

Check here to match case.

Check here to search for exact set of characters.

partial words or characters that are included within other words as well. If you want to find *pose*, for example, any word that includes this group of letters, such as pur*pose* or pro*pose*, are found as well.)

    4. Check **Match Case** to find only those words or phrases with the same combination of lower or uppercase letters as those that you enter.

    5. Click **Find Next** to move from instance to instance.

Result: When you use the Find command, PowerPoint reads ahead and jumps to the next instance of the word or phrase you were seeking. To make changes manually, click **Cancel** to remove the dialog box. Now you can make the change right in the presentation.

FIND AND REPLACE TEXT

How: To find text and then replace the "found" items with alternate text in one location, follow these steps:

    1. Choose **Edit|Replace** or press **Ctrl+H** to display the dialog box shown in Figure 3.19 (if the Find dialog box is visible, click **Replace**).

    2. Type the text to find in the **Find what** box.

    3. Enter the text to use as a replacement in the **Replace with** box and click **Find** to locate the first instance of the text.

Figure 3.19
Replacing text

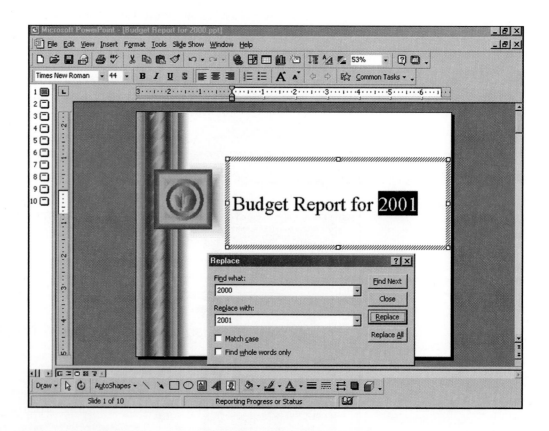

Result: What happens after you choose Find depends on which button you click next:

    ○ To step through the entire document, deciding each time whether to make the replacement, use the **Find Next** command and then **Replace**.

❍ To replace all occurrences at once without having to confirm each change, click **Replace All**. (This option is certainly the fastest; however, it can also be imprecise. For example, if you want to replace the year 2000 but your budget includes a reference to "2000 units of product xyz," this text is replaced as well, though this is clearly not your intention.)

 TIPS FROM A PRO: You can also use the Replace feature to remove text throughout the document. To do this, type the text you want to remove in the **Find What** box, but leave the **Replace With** box empty. Click **Find**, then click **Replace all**, and just like magic, all of the unwanted text is gone!

TASK 9 — *Use the Automatic Spelling Feature*

 C   *CORE OBJECTIVE:* **Check spelling**

What: Right-clicking the wavy underlines of automatic spell check is a simple way to correct spelling mistakes. Still, you may actually find that those lines distract you from getting your thoughts down. If this is the case, turn off the automatic spell checker and check your entire presentation at once, after you've finished entering your text.

To remove the red wavy underlines, reverse the process that you used to turn them on. Choose **Tools|Options**, click the **Spelling and Style** tab, and click to remove the check from the box next to **Check spelling as you type** (refer back to Figure 2.9 in Chapter 2, "Work with Text").

Why: When you use this spell check technique, the red wavy lines won't distract you while you're trying to concentrate on your writing—they seem to cry out for immediate attention as soon as you see them.

How: To perform the all-at-once spelling check, follow these steps:

1. Press **Ctrl+Home** to move the cursor to the beginning of the presentation.
 2. Choose **Tools|Spelling** or click the **Spelling** button to open the dialog box shown in Figure 3.20. PowerPoint checks its dictionary, finds the first possible error, and shows one or more possible correct spellings for word.

Figure 3.20
Spelling dialog box

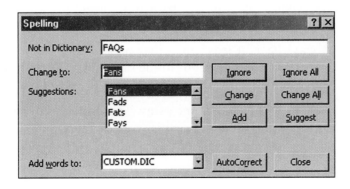

3. Respond to the Spelling dialog box in one of these ways:
   - Click **Ignore,** if you want to leave the item as it is (this only affects this word).
   - Chose **Ignore All** to skip all instances of this word.
   - Click **Add** if you want this item included in PowerPoint's dictionary. (If you choose this option, this item will never again be flagged as a possible error in *any* presentation.)
   - Select a correction from one or more possible accurate spellings, and then click **Change**.
   - Click **Change All** if you want to correct the item every time it occurs in this presentation.
   - Click **AutoCorrect** to add this mistake and its correct spelling to the list of items that PowerPoint corrects as you type.
   - Click **Suggest** if you don't have **Always suggest corrections** marked in the **Options|Spelling and Style** dialog box.
   - Click **Close** to exit the spell checker.

Result: Each time you respond to a spelling error, PowerPoint searches for the next problem and displays it in the dialog box for you to act on. If you mistakenly pick Ignore or Change, you can always choose Undo to back up a step. When the entire presentation has been checked, the Office Assistant and balloon or a dialog box will appear to inform you that the spelling check is complete (Figure 3.21).

Figure 3.21
Assistant notifying you that the spelling check is complete

 TIPS FROM A PRO: Even if you know that you have superior spelling abilities, you should still proofread your work. One tiny mistake can negate your entire message.

- Always check your own work. It's your reputation at stake. (Imagine the following mistake: "We will be suing Brown, Murnion, MacDonald and Associates," instead of "We will be using Brown, Murnion, MacDonald and Associates.")

- Always have at least one other pair of eyes examine your work for spelling errors and contradictions in the material.

- Always try to complete your work far enough in advance to allow you to come back to it after some time away. This will give you a renewed focus on the big picture rather than the details.

Use PinPoint

After gaining the skills in this chapter, you can select text; cut, copy, and paste; use the Office Clipboard; use Undo and Redo; delete a slide; copy a slide; modify the slide sequence; find and replace text; and check your spelling. Now it's time to see what you can do with the PinPoint software. Remember, whenever you are unsure of what to do next, you can reread the relevant portion of the chapter or you can click Show Me for a live demonstration. Try these skills in PinPoint:

- Reorder an outline
- Use the Office Clipboard
- Insert a slide from file
- Delete a slide
- Change slide sequence
- Replace text
- Spell check

Key Terms

You can find definitions for these words in this chapter:

Clipboard
Office Clipboard
Select

Review Questions

You can use the following review questions and exercises to test your knowledge and skills. Answers are given in Appendix D, "Answers to Review Questions."

True/False

Indicate whether each statement is true (T) or false (F).

___ 1. You must select text and slides before you can delete them.

___ 2. To select an entire slide, click the slide icon in Slide view.

___ 3. If you make a mistake, reverse its effect by clicking the Redo button.

___ 4. If you want to undo several operations, click the Undo button repeatedly.

___ 5. Cut and Paste is the same as drag and drop.

___ 6. To duplicate text, use the Edit|Cut and Edit|Paste commands.

___ 7. The Clipboard toolbar contains up to 100 items.

___ 8. You can paste several items at one time when you use the Clipboard toolbar.

___ 9. You can duplicate a slide by choosing Insert|Duplicate Slide.

___ 10. You can copy slides within a single presentation, but not from one presentation to another.

Multiple Choice

Select the letter that best completes the statement.

___ 1. To select an entire slide:
   a. Click the slide icon in Outline view.
   b. Click the slide in Slide Sorter view.
   c. Drag the mouse across the placeholder in Slide view.
   d. All of the above.
   e. Both a and b.

___ 2. If you are using drag and drop and you drop the slide in the wrong place by mistake:
   a. Click Undo and try it again.
   b. Click Redo and start over.
   c. Click Rearrange and click where you want it to go.
   d. Choose Insert|Duplicate slide.
   e. Select the slide and press Delete.

___ 3. The Office Clipboard is activated when you:
   a. Cut.
   b. Cut or copy two times without pasting.
   c. Copy an entire slide.
   d. Run the Spelling Checker.
   e. Double-click the Cut or Copy button.

___ 4. To copy slides from another presentation without having to open it first, choose:
   a. Insert|Slides from Files.
   b. Edit|Copy from Elsewhere.
   c. File|Open and select the presentation, and click the Cancel button.
   d. Tools|Slide Importer.
   e. Slide Sorter view.

___ 5. To rearrange a slide:
   a. Click the slide and drag it in Slide Sorter view.
   b. Click the slide icon and drag it in Outline view.
   c. Click the slide placeholder and drag it in Slide view.
   d. All of the above.
   e. Both a and b.

___ 6. When you want to make the same change throughout your presentation, choose:
   a. Edit|Find.
   b. Edit|Replace.
   c. Edit|Copy.
   d. Edit|Change.
   e. Edit|Redo.

___ 7. When you're checking the spelling of the entire presentation at once:
   a. Click Ignore to leave the item as is.
   b. Click Add to add the flagged spelling to the dictionary, so it won't be flagged ever again.
   c. Select a correction and click Change to fix the mistake.
   d. Click Change All to fix the mistake throughout the presentation.
   e. All of the above.

___ 8. You can move a slide by dragging it in this view:
   a. Outline.
   b. Slide Sorter.
   c. Print Preview.
   d. All of the above.
   e. Only a and b.

___ 9. When you delete a slide, you can always get it back by clicking the:
   a. Paste button.
   b. Duplicate button.
   c. New Slide button.
   d. Undo button.
   e. Redo button.

___ 10. A temporary storage place for items that have been cut or copied is the:
   a. Clipboard.
   b. Envelope.
   c. Placeholder.
   d. Recycle Bin.
   e. Template.

Match the letters in Figure 3.22 with the correct items in the list.

Figure 3.22

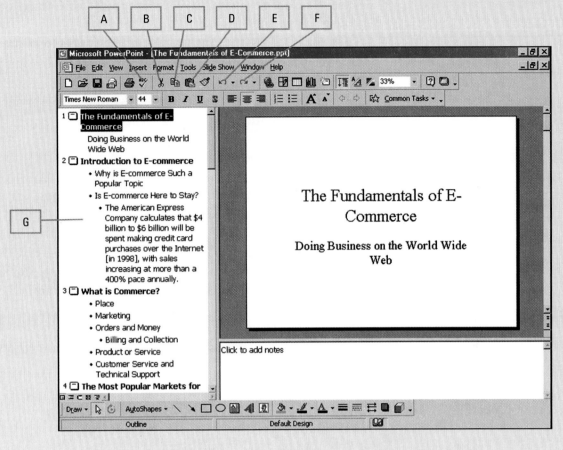

___ 1. Click this button to insert a duplicate of a copied slide.

___ 2. Click here to check the spelling of the entire presentation all at once.

___ 3. Click here to reverse the last operation.

___ 4. Click here to change your mind and restore the last operation you just reversed.

___ 5. Look here to see whether an entire slide is selected.

___ 6. Click this to delete the selected slide.

___ 7. Click this to make a copy of the selected slide.

Exercise and Project

Follow these step-by-step instructions to practice the skills that are included in this chapter. If you are working in a computer lab, you may have to ask your instructor where to save or print your work.

Exercise

1. Start PowerPoint and open **PPT3** from the Student\Chapter3 folder of the PinPoint CD-ROM that came with this book.

2. Select the first-level title on the title page (Joy Young's). Using one of the methods shown in this chapter (drag-and-drop or cut-and-paste), move the title into the subtitle placeholder.

3. Select the subtitle text and move it into the title placeholder. Replace 'Joy Young's' with your name.

4. Select Slide 4 (Proofreading) in the outline pane and create a duplicate slide.

5. Delete the last two bullet points and any related subpoints from Slide 4.

6. Modify the title on Slide 5 (this is the copy that you created in Step 5) to read 'More Proofreading Tips'. Delete the first four bullet points.

7. Edit the presentation for spelling and grammatical errors.

8. Save the file in your PowerPoint 2000 folder as **Exercise 3A**. Print the file as handouts—six slides per page.

9. In Slide Sorter view, move Slides 4 and 5 (Proofreading and More Proofreading) to the number two and three positions.

10. In the outline pane, reorganize the slide that is now Slide 4 (Spelling) so that it is the last slide.

11. Use Find and Replace to find the word Get. Replace it with Have.

12. Open the presentation "Parallel Grammar.ppt" from the Student\Chapter 3 folder and insert the slide titled "Keep Grammar Parallel" into your presentation as Slide 3.

13. Delete Slide 2 (Keep a Good Grammar . . .).

14. Read through the slides and make sure that there are no other mistakes.

15. Save the file in your PowerPoint 2000 folder as **Exercise 3B** and exit PowerPoint.

16. Print your slide show as handouts—six to a page.

Project

Your boss has just met with you regarding the Strategic Planning Committee meeting next week. The subject of your discussion is the extreme sports software game currently being developed within your division. The product has only recently moved from the concept stage to final design; however, because the high-tech industry moves at light-speed, it will be ready for market introduction in six months. Your job is to sift through three slide shows that pertain to the software and compile them into one presentation that your boss can use at the meeting. Create a new presentation titled "Introducing Virtually There" and subtitled "Challenge Corporation." Use the following three presentations (that are stored on the Student/Chapter 3 folder) for your project:

- MKT.ppt
- Mgmt.ppt
- Launch.ppt

It's your job to organize the presentations into a logical format—use whatever slides are necessary. Copy, delete, and rearrange as necessary. You notice that some of the writers used the first name that was assigned to the product, "Virtual Extremes," so you need to change that throughout to "Virtually There." Proofread for grammatical and spelling errors. Add your name to the title page in a small text box, save your presentation in your folder as Project 3 and print handouts—six to a page.

Chapter 4

Format Text

fter you perfect the content of your slide show, it's time to turn your attention to the nonverbal aspects of your presentation—the appearance. You can enhance the look and consequently the impact of your visual aids in many different ways but text formatting offers the simplest and subtlest way to change the look and feel of your work.

You can apply text formats at several levels within your presentation—the entire presentation, a single slide, a placeholder, or even single words and characters. In this chapter you learn how to format many types of text.

At the end of this chapter you will be able to:

C **E**

- ☑ ☐ Align text
- ☑ ☐ Apply simple font formats
- ☑ ☐ Apply complex font formats
- ☑ ☐ Replace fonts
- ☑ ☐ Copy font formatting
- ☑ ☐ Add bullets and numbering
- ☐ ☑ Use tabs

CORE OBJECTIVE: Change text alignment

What: The way that text is positioned between the margins of a placeholder or text box is called *alignment*. Sometimes you may want to change the alignment of text on your slides. PowerPoint offers four possible ways to align text, but you will most likely use one of the following first three options.

         Left alignment, the normal default text alignment, positions the selected paragraph to the left side of the paper with the right edge of the paragraph ending wherever the lines run out of room for the next word.

         Center alignment centers a paragraph horizontally between the left and right edge of the placeholder or text box. This is frequently used for title placeholders.

         Right alignment, the opposite of left alignment, places the straight edge of the paragraph against the right margin. Because it is difficult to read, this alignment style should generally be used only for titles.

         Justified alignment makes both the left and right edges of the paragraph even against the respective margins. This is accomplished by adding extra spaces between words wherever necessary. Justified text is normally reserved for formal documents; it is seldom used in the preparation of slides. For this reason it isn't included as one of the button options on the Formatting toolbar. (To justify text, select the text and choose **Format|Alignment|Justify**.)

Why: Imagine your slide show if all text on each slide was left aligned. Okay, so this isn't such a dreary prospect because PowerPoint offers so many other ways to make your presentation visually appealing. Still, it's nice to have the flexibility to vary the alignment if you choose to do so. Text alignment is just one of the subtle ways that you can add interest to your presentation.

How: Aligning text is easy, but the procedure for changing alignment depends on the type of text to be aligned. Though you learned how to select text in Chapter 3, "Edit Text," Table 4.1 provides some additional tips for selecting text when you want to change the alignment.

Table 4.1   Designate text to align

To *align this*	Select this
A paragraph (bullet point or subpoint)	Place the insertion point anywhere in the paragraph or bullet point.
A text placeholder or text box	Placeholder or box.
A title placeholder	Place the insertion point anywhere in the title text.

Note: Even if you have placed a paragraph break inside of the placeholder, title placeholders recognize only one alignment style.

You can change the text alignment using the menus or buttons.

1. Select the text to be aligned.
2. Click one of the alignment buttons, choose **Format|Alignment**, or use the applicable shortcut key. Table 4.2 summarizes these.

Table 4.2 Align Text

Alignment	Button	Shortcut Key
Left		Ctrl+L
Center		Ctrl+E
Right		Ctrl+R

Result: The moment you click the button or use the shortcut key, the designated text moves to its new alignment position. If you place the insertion point in text, you can see the alignment of that text by looking for the "pushed-in" button on the Formatting toolbar (refer to Figure 4.2). (This applies to all font and paragraph formatting.) Figure 4.1 shows some sample text alignments.

THOUGHT QUESTION: Can you think of an occasion when it would be appropriate to use justified text in a slide show?

Figure 4.1
Sample text alignments

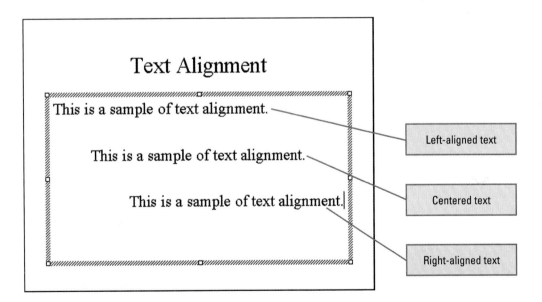

CORE OBJECTIVE: Change and replace text fonts (individual slide and entire presentation)

What: Another quick way to change the look of your slides is to vary the text characteristics. You can make text bold, italic, underlined, or shadowed; change the font style; increase or decrease the font size (or *points*); or alter the font colors.

Why: The primary reasons to modify text characteristics are to add contrast, emphasize words, and increase readability. The type of font that you use can actually determine how your audience reacts to your message. You can add emphasis to words and phrases, or force your listeners to slow down and read carefully by just choosing a particular font. The following information will help you choose the best font for your presentation.

○ Use fonts to give your presentation a distinct personality. What image are you trying to communicate? A serious business presentation may warrant a conservative font, whereas a jazzy modern font may be perfect for a frivolous social group.

○ Use fonts to promote readability. The font you use affects the audience's ability to read your text. The easiest kinds of fonts to read are *serif* fonts. Serif fonts, such as Times New Roman, Bookman, and Century, have small, horizontal lines that lead the eye across the page. They are best used for body text. On the other hand to slow the eye, and consequently slow reading, use a *sans serif* font. These block fonts, such as Arial, Franklin, and Tahoma, should be used for titles or anywhere that you want people to read carefully.

○ Use fonts to provide contrast or emphasis. If the body of the text is in a serif font, add contrast to headings by choosing a sans serif font. Make it **bold**, *italic*, or colored to further emphasize the contrast, or make the headings larger by changing the number of points.

○ Use fonts that display well with the equipment that you are using. If you plan to publish your presentation online or use overhead transparencies and a slide projector, consider applying Verdana, Tahoma, or Georgia fonts.

CHANGE FONT FORMATS

How: You can change the font after text is entered, or execute the font command before you type to set the text format from that point forward. To change the font format, follow these steps:

1. Select the text that you want to format. (If the insertion point is blinking in a word, the format will be applied to the whole word.)
2. Click the applicable button or press the shortcut keys shown in Table 4.3.
3. To remove the format, select the text, click the applicable button again, or press the shortcut keys again.

Table 4.3 Simple Font Formatting

Format	Button	Shortcut Key
Bold	**B**	Ctrl+B
Italic	*I*	Ctrl+I
<u>Underline</u>	<u>U</u>	Ctrl+U

Result: Like other formatting options, the command is immediately executed as soon as you click a button or press the shortcut keys. Figure 4.2 provides some examples of font formats that you can apply to your slides.

Figure 4.2
Sample font formats

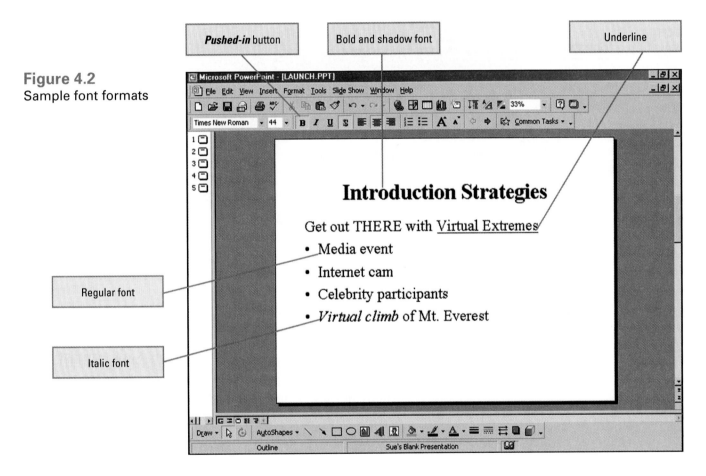

 TIPS FROM A PRO: All templates, including the blank presentation have default font formatting. When you want to change the default formatting of the blank presentation, follow these steps:

1. Open a new blank presentation and modify the fonts.
2. Choose **File|Save As** to access the Save As dialog box.
3. Drop-down the **Save as type** box and click **Design Template**.
4. Type **Blank Presentation File name** box, and then click **Save**.
5. If prompted to replace the existing blank presentation, click **Yes**.

CHANGE FONT TYPE

How: To change the font style, follow these steps:

1. Select the text, placeholder, or slide to be formatted (You can change multiple contiguous slides in the outline pane, but this results in *all* the font styles on these slides being changed at once to a single font.)
2. Click the **Font box** drop-down list (Figure 4.3). Scroll up or down to examine the various font choices. (Fonts are listed alphabetically, with the most recently used styles repeated at the top of the list.)
3. Click the font name to select and apply a style.

Figure 4.3
Selecting a font style

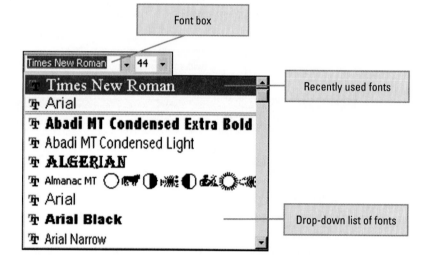

Result: The text that you selected has been changed to the new font. If you don't like its appearance, you can always use Undo to return it to the preceding style.

TIPS FROM A PRO: The following points offer some suggestions for selecting fonts:

- Three or four font styles per presentation are enough. More can actually detract and distract from your message.

- Script fonts are usually not a judicious choice for PowerPoint slides because they are difficult to read.

- Slide text should all be in the same font type unless you are emphasizing a word.

CHANGE THE FONT SIZE

How: You can change the font size two ways—use the Font Size box and manage the process or use the buttons on the Formatting toolbar.

   O To use the Font Size box:
   1. Select the text, placeholder, or slide that contains the text that you want to change.
   2. Click the **Font Size** drop-down list and choose one of the specified sizes (Figure 4.4).
   3. If you don't see the size that you want, click in the box and type the desired number of points in the box (Figure 4.5) and press **Enter**.

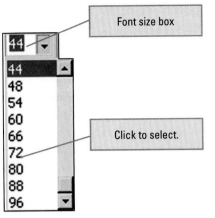

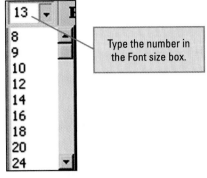

Figure 4.4 Changing the font size   **Figure 4.5** Changing the font size

○ To use the buttons
 1. Select the text that you want to change.

 2. Click the **Increase Font Size** or **Decrease Font Size** buttons until the font is the desired size.

Result: The font size of the selected text has been increased or decreased.

Tɪᴘs ꜰʀᴏᴍ ᴀ Pʀᴏ: Know your audience! Reasonable research may help you determine whether any of your group has special needs. For example, though a general rule of thumb states that a 20-point font for the body of your text is large enough, if you are presenting to a group of individuals who are in the author's age bracket, a 20-point font may be *too* small.

In general, you should vary font size to increase readability. The following points are general rules of thumb to safeguard against readability problems:

• The title text should be at least 36 points.

• The body text should be at least 20 points.

CHANGE THE FONT COLOR

How: The easiest way to change the font color is to use the Font Color button on the Drawing toolbar. If you don't see the toolbar, choose **View|Toolbars|Drawing**. To modify the font color, follow these steps:

 1. Select the text that you want to recolor.
 2. Click the Font Color button to apply the color that you see, or click the drop-down arrow next to the Font Color dialog box to display the choices of colors (Figure 4.6).

Note: The colors that you see on the palette are associated with the color scheme of the Design Template that is applied to this presentation (even if it's just the blank presentation). You learn about Design Templates and color schemes in Chapter 5, "Format Slide Characteristics."

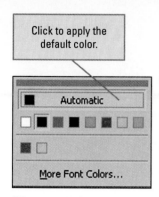

Figure 4.6
Font color palette

3. Click to choose one of the visible colors or click **More Font Colors** to see additional shades (Figure 4.7).

- To apply one of the colors from the Standard color chart, click to select it with the mouse and click **OK**.
- To create your own, custom color, click the **Custom** tab. Click in the colors and drag the mouse pointer across the box until you have the color that you want, or change the various aspects of each shade in the boxes. You change the *luminance* (brightness) directly by dragging the slider that is to the right of the Color box, up or down. When you have created the perfect shade, click **OK** to apply.

Result: Your presentation now includes colored fonts. When you add a design, or color to the background, make sure that there is a sharp contrast between the background and the font colors. (You learn how to change the background in Chapter 5, Format Slide Characteristics.) Also, check to see that the overall appearance is not too "busy."

TIPS FROM A PRO: Colored fonts can provide contrast to your slides, but too many colors can be distracting and unprofessional.

THOUGHT QUESTION: When you place the insertion point within the text of a word without selecting it and press **Ctrl+B**, the text is bolded. What happens when you select one or two letters of a word and then press **Ctrl+B**?

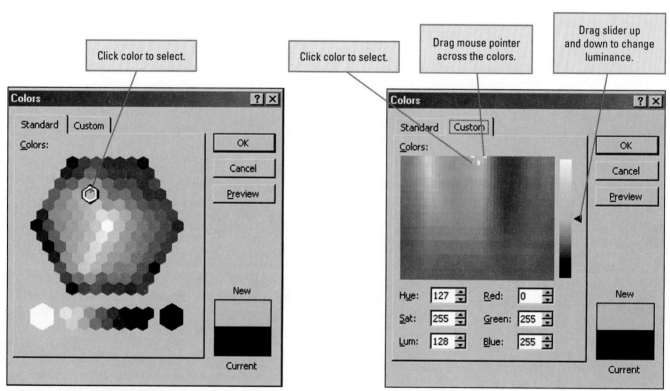

Figure 4.7 Changing the font color   **Figure 4.8** Creating a custom color

C   *CORE OBJECTIVE:* Change and replace text fonts
(individual slide and entire presentation)

What: When you want to make two or more changes to font characteristics at the same time, or to change a bit of text or a character in some specialized way, the Font dialog box is the best place to go.

Why: The dialog box not only gives you most control over the formatting process but you also have access to commands, such as Subscript or Emboss, that are not available on the toolbar. Clearly, it's also more efficient to change several attributes at one time.

How: To access the **Font** format dialog box, follow these steps:

1. Select the text or slide that you want to format.
2. Choose **Format|Font** or press **Ctrl+T**. This opens the dialog box shown in Figure 4.9.
3. Select all the text features that you would like to apply to your text.
4. Click **OK**.

Result: The dialog box closes and you can see the font modifications that you have selected. Because you performed these changes in one operation, if you choose to select Undo, all will be reversed.

Figure 4.9
Modifying font
characteristics

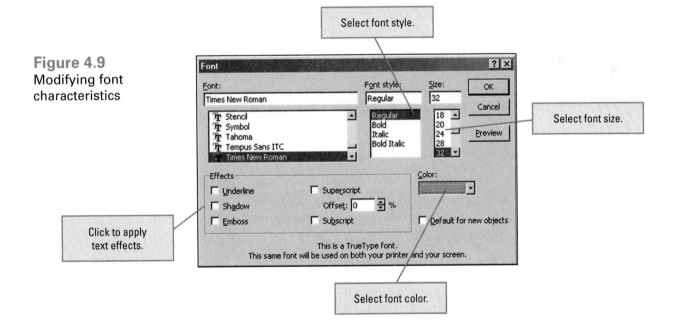

CORE OBJECTIVE: **Change and replace text fonts (individual slides and entire presentation)**

What: Sometimes when you're creating a presentation, you want to replace one font style with another throughout the entire presentation. It's an easy task to modify the font style and size of bits of text or individual slides; when you want to make the same change on every slide, however, you can use PowerPoint's Replace Fonts feature.

Why: If you've used too many fonts or just don't like a particular font style, you don't have to worry about searching through your show for the font that you want to replace. It's quicker and more accurate to make one global change than to flip from slide to slide.

How: To replace a font type throughout your presentation, follow these steps:

1. Choose **Format|Replace Fonts**. This opens the dialog box shown in Figure 4.10.
2. Click the drop-down **Replace** list and select the font that you want to replace.
3. Click the drop-down **With** list and select the font that you want to use instead.
4. Click **Replace**.

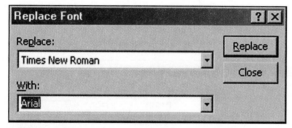

Figure 4.10 Replacing fonts with the dialog box

Result: The selected font has been replaced on each slide of your presentation. You can now choose to replace another font or click Close to close the dialog box.

TIPS FROM A PRO: Another, perhaps more efficient way to replace font styles throughout a presentation, is to change them in one quick step on the Slide Master. However, this method only works on those slides that you haven't formatted directly. You learn more about this technique in Chapter 5.

CORE OBJECTIVE: Use the format painter

What: After you have gotten one portion of text just right, you may want to duplicate this formatting in other sections of your slide show. The *Format Painter* copies the formatting of one portion of text and pastes it onto another.

Why: It can be a lengthy process to apply text formatting, especially if you employ several different font attributes. Using the Painter, you can reproduce the perfect text combination that you've devised and finish the task in one move.

How: To copy font formatting from once place to another, follow these steps:

1. Select the text that contains the formatting that you want to copy.
2. Click the **Format Painter** button. Click once if you want to copy this formatting to one section of text. Click twice to use the Format Painter more than once on multiple selections of text.
3. Drag the Format Painter mouse pointer across the text that you want to modify. When you have selected the entire section that you want to format, release the mouse button.
4. If you clicked the Format Painter button twice in Step 2, you can repeat Step 3 as many times as you like. In this case, you must click the button again to turn it off when you are finished or press **Esc** (the escape key).

Result: The text format that you have copied is applied to the text that you select as soon as you release the mouse button.

TIPS FROM A PRO: It's painless to duplicate the formatting of individual paragraphs or bits of text, but you can copy the format of placeholders as well. However, a word of caution is in order: This procedure is tricky! The difficulty arises when you try to "grab" the border of the target placeholder so that the formatting gets copied. Another, less problematic way to format a placeholder is to double-click the object's border to bring up the Format AutoShape dialog box. Then you can use that method of formatting. You learn more about formatting objects, including placeholders, in Chapter 6, "Elements of Sight and Sound."

THOUGHT QUESTION: What happens if you forget to press **Esc** after you have finished copying formats?

CORE OBJECTIVE: Add AutoNumber bullets

CORE OBJECTIVE: Add graphical bullets

What: Presentations primarily consist of summarized data, so lists are generally the most suitable format for slide text. For this reason, text placeholders are preformatted to include bulleted lists. Each text placeholder allows for five levels of text, and hence, each slide has five default bullet styles—one for each level. Sometimes you'll want to change these bullet styles, replace the bullets with numbers, or remove the bullets entirely.

Why: When the occasion calls for something showy, take your simple bulleted list and turn it into an eye-catcher by changing the bullet style or color. On the more practical side, when you need to demonstrate a certain relationship between points or between a sequence of events, you'll want to swap bullets for numbers.

ADD BULLETS OR NUMBERING

How: You can use either the buttons on the Formatting toolbar or the keyboard to add bullets or numbering but the buttons are quicker.

❍ Use the buttons:
  1. Place the insertion point in the paragraph where you want the bullet or number, or select multiple paragraphs.
  2. Click the **Bullets** or **Numbering** button.

❍ Use the keyboard
  1. With the insertion point to the right of a bullet, press **Backspace** to delete the current bullet.
  2. Type a number or letter followed by a period or closed parenthesis, press **Tab**, and type your text.
  3. When you finish adding text, press **Enter**.

Result: If you used the buttons, the paragraphs that you selected include bullets or numbering. In either case, when you press Enter, a bullet or number is automatically added to the next line (technically a paragraph). If you find that one of your points is unnecessary or is in the wrong order, just delete that point (as described later in this task) or move the text. If it was a number, PowerPoint renumbers and automatically reorders the list for you.

TIPS FROM A PRO: You can start a numbered list by typing any of the following choices at the beginning of a line: 1., (1), A., a., i., I., or any other letter, number, or roman numeral followed by a closed parenthesis or a period. If you do not start the list with a logical number one (that is, 1, A, or I, you must tab before you enter text).

ADD OR CUSTOMIZE BULLETED LISTS USING THE DIALOG BOX

How: You can add bullets to your slides using the menus as well. With this method you have more control and can also change the bullet style and certain characteristics. Follow these steps:

1. Select the text where you want to add bullets or change the bullet style.
2. Choose **Format|Bullets and Numbering** and click the **Bulleted** tab. The dialog box shown in Figure 4.11 appears. Select one of the styles

Figure 4.11
Modifying bullet styles

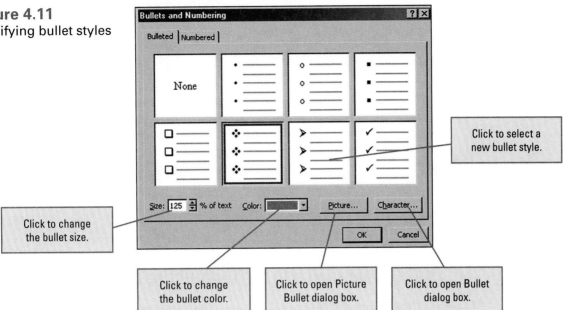

that you see and click **OK**, or pick one of the following options instead.

- Click **Character** to open the Bullet dialog box shown in Figure 4.12. Now you can choose from hundreds of possible bullet styles.
- Click **Picture** to add graphical bullets. You learn more about this feature in Task 1 of Chapter 6.
- Click the **Color** list to change the bullet color.
- Change the **Size** spin box to modify the size of the bullets in relation to the text size.

3. When you have finished modifying bullet characteristics, click **OK** to apply the styles that you have chosen.

Figure 4.12
Bullet dialog box

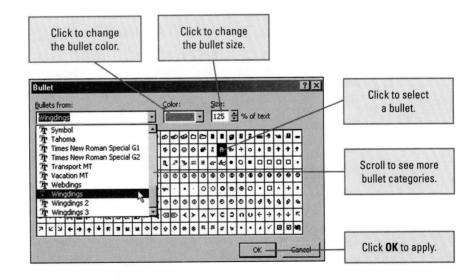

Result: The new bullet style immediately appears at the beginning of the paragraph. Figure 4.13 shows some examples of bullet styles that you can create.

Figure 4.13
Sample bullet styles

ADD OR CUSTOMIZE NUMBERED LISTS USING THE DIALOG BOX

How: Like bulleted lists, when you want to customize a numbering, you must use the dialog box. To add or modify numbering using the menus, follow these steps:

1. Select the text where you want to add numbers or to modify the current styles.
2. Choose **Format|Bullets and Numbering,** and click the **Numbered** tab to access the dialog box shown in Figure 4.14.

Figure 4.14
Modifying numbering
in the dialog box

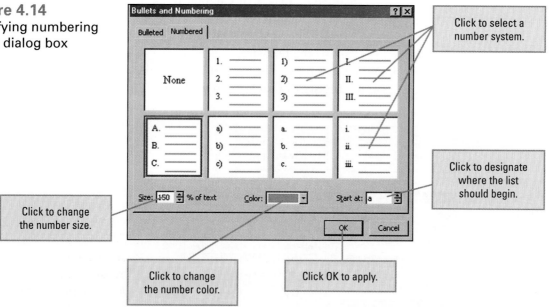

3. Click to select one of the available numbering systems. You can change the physical characteristics of the numbers, as well as designate the number that you would like to begin the list.
4. After you have finished making the desired style changes, click **OK** to apply.

Result: The new style of numbering appears at the beginning of the paragraph. Figure 4.15 shows one example.

Figure 4.15
Complex automatic
numbering

Other Promotion

★ Early adopters
  ❖ Amy special training unit
  ❖ Blue Sky Wilderness Experience
  ❖ Rocky Mountain High Adventures
    1) Used special promotion program
      a. Highly successful
      b. Will repeat next year

REMOVE BULLETS OR NUMBERING

How: To remove bullets or numbering, use one of the following methods:

○ Select the paragraph or placeholder and click the **Bullets** or **Numbering** button.
○ With the insertion point to the right of the bullet or number, press **Backspace**.

Result: The bullet or number is removed. When you press Enter, the new line that is added won't include bullets or numbers. If you want to change the styles on every slide, you should change the Slide Master. You learn how to work with the Slide Master in Chapter 5.

TIPS FROM A PRO: Many of the buttons on the formatting toolbar are toggles, so turn them off the same way that you turn them on—just select the text and click the button.

TASK **7**	*Change Tab Formatting*

EXPERT OBJECTIVE: Change tab formatting

What: Tabs allow the text to align to a given point, or *tab stop*, on a line. In PowerPoint, default tab stops are set every inch on each text placeholder (Figure 4.16). If you begin a new presentation and remove the bullet, when you press the Tab button, the insertion point moves forward in one-inch increments. PowerPoint offers you the means to customize tabs and move tab stops if this is required by your work.

There are four kinds of tabs:

○ **Left tab** lines text up with a straight left edge.
○ **Right tab** lines text up with a straight right edge.
○ **Center tab** centers text over a specific point on your slide.
○ **Decimal tab** lines numbers up over the decimal point.

Figure 4.16
Ruler and default
tab stops

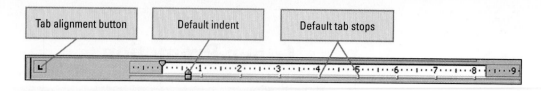

Why: Specific tabs were designed with specific tasks in mind, so utilizing the special features of each type can simplify your work. If you want to line up a few numbers over the decimal points, for instance, set a decimal tab instead of trying to get the placement right with the spacebar. Not only is this an ineffective use of time, but also what you view on the screen is not necessarily what you will get in your show. Of course, you could try to just tab, tab, tab, and so on, until you get to the right location (or get really frustrated) but this is also an unpredictable exercise.

 THOUGHT QUESTION: Why can't you just use the alignment buttons when you want to center a section of text over another block of text?

How: Tab stops in PowerPoint have a couple of unique features: First, when you change one of the preset tab stops, they all change by the same proportion. Second, if you set a tab, it affects the entire placeholder.

To change the tab formatting, you must use the ruler. If the ruler is not visible above the slide pane, choose **View|Ruler** to turn it on. Although it's not required, the least persnickety way to set tabs is to first remove any bullets. Then use the following steps to set or modify tabs:

1. Place the insertion point into the text placeholder and repeatedly click the **Tab** button until you see the tab style that you require. (Until you repeat this process to change the tab style again, each tab that you set will be this type.) Table 4.2 provides an illustration of tab types and what each one does.

Table 4.2 Types of Tab Stops

To Align Like This	Use This Button
Left edge of text	**L**
Center of text	**⊥**
Right edge of text	**⅃**
Line up decimal points	**⊥·**

2. Click on the ruler at the point where you want to set the tab (Figure 4.17). This places a tab where you click.

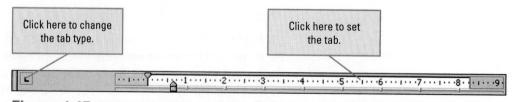

Figure 4.17 Setting tab stops on the ruler

3. To move a tab stop, click it and drag it left or right.
4. To remove a tab stop, click it and while holding down the left mouse button, drag downward.

Result: The ruler displays the tabs that you added. When you press Tab to move to a tab stop and then enter text, your text aligns under the stop. Figure 4.18 shows various types of tabs and the resulting text alignments.

Figure 4.18
Using tab stops to enter text

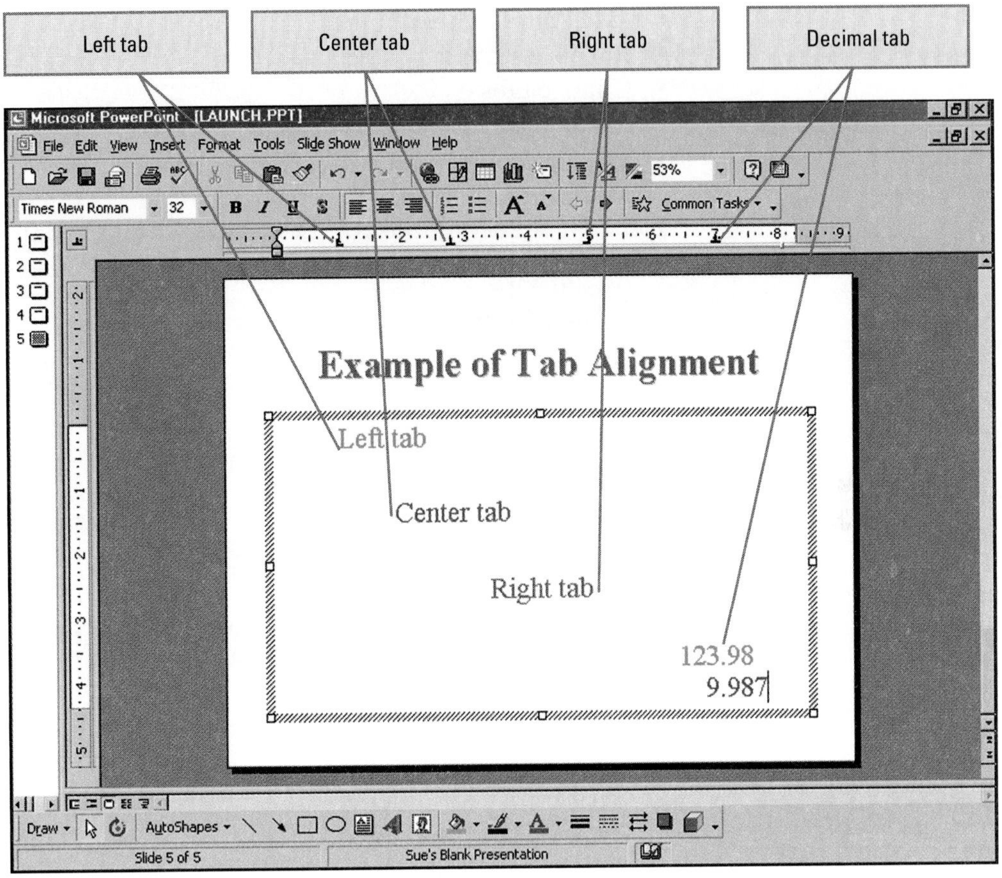

TIPS FROM A PRO: Tabs work great for short lists or to professionally display a few numbers, but tables work better for organizing longer items (and some people think that they are easier to use). You learn how to use tables for this purpose in Chapter 9, "Integrate Charts and Tables."

TIPS FROM A PRO: Sometimes it is easier to remove all the default tab stops before you begin adding additional tabs. You can do this by dragging the leftmost tab along the ruler, toward the right side of the placeholder.

Use PinPoint

After gaining the skills included in this chapter, you can change the text alignment, apply font formats, copy text formats, replace the fonts in a slide show, add bullets and numbering, and apply the tab settings. Now it's time to see what you can do with the PinPoint software. Remember, whenever you are unsure of what to do next, you can reread the relevant portion of the chapter or you can click Show Me for a live demonstration.

Try these skills in PinPoint:

- Text alignment
- Enhance text
- Format Painter
- Replace fonts
- Add AutoNumber bullets
- Bullets on and off
- Change tabs

Key Terms

You can find definitions for these words in this chapter:

Alignment
Format Painter
Points
San serif fonts
Serif fonts
Tab stop

Review Questions

You can use the following review questions and exercises to test your knowledge and skills. The answers are given in Appendix D, "Answers to Review Questions."

True/False

____ 1. You can set different tab types on different lines of a place-holder.

____ 2. Right-aligned text is perfect for bulleted lists.

____ 3. When you place the insertion point in a word and press Ctrl+B, the text becomes bold.

____ 4. If you double-click the Format Painter, you can paste the format of infinite blocks or bits of text.

____ 5. Slide text is often bold and centered.

____ 6. If you have used more than three fonts in a presentation, the Replace Fonts feature will not work.

____ 7. Colored fonts can have a big impact but can be applied in a short period of time.

____ 8. If you have added AutoNumber bullets, when you press Enter, the next line begins with a number.

____ 9. To make sure that your fonts are legible, they should be no smaller than 20 points.

____ 10. You can't have too many font colors; the more the merrier!

___ 1. Formatting text refers to:

   a. The process of bolding text.

   b. Changing the font style.

   c. Applying colored fonts.

   d. Underlining a title.

   e. All of the above.

___ 2. Title placeholders accept only one form of:

   a. Formatting.

   b. Alignment.

   c. Bullet style.

   d. Both b and c.

   e. All of the above.

___ 3. Tab stops can be used to:

   a. Center text over a point on the slide.

   b. Line up decimal points.

   c. Right-align text.

   d. Left-align text.

   e. All of the above.

___ 4. Bullet styles can be changed by:

   a. Selecting the text and then clicking the Bullet button.

   b. Typing a bullet and pressing Enter.

   c. Choosing Format|Bullets and Numbering.

   d. Choosing Insert|Bullets and Numbering.

   e. Selecting text and clicking the Format Painter.

___ 5. To increase the readability of body text, use:

   a. Many different font colors.

   b. A serif font.

   c. Bold text.

   d. A large font.

   e. Both b and d.

___ 6. The Format Painter:

   a. Looks like a moving paint brush after it is activated.

   b. Can be used to copy one style of bullet to another location.

   c. Can change left-aligned text to centered text.

   d. Can copy formatting to infinite blocks of text if double-clicked.

   e. All of the above.

___ 7. When you want to replace one font with another throughout a presentation:

   a. Select all the slides in Slide Sorter view and use the Font box.

   b. Choose Edit|Replace Fonts.

   c. Choose Format|Replace Fonts.

   d. Page from slide to slide, changing as you go.

   e. All of the above.

___ 8. When you want to add change several font characteristics at once:

   a. Select the text to be changed click the various buttons.

   b. Access the Font dialog box.

   c. Choose Format|Font.

   d. Both b and c.

   e. Press Ctrl+T.

___ 9. To add AutoNumber bullets:

   a. Backspace to delete the bullet and press the Numbering button.

   b. Select text and press the Numbering button.

   c. Choose Insert|Bullets and Numbering.

   d. Choose Format|AutoNumber bullets.

   e. a, b, and d.

____ 10. You can apply certain text formatting by:
 a. Selecting text and clicking
    the appropriate buttons.
 b. Clicking the appropriate
    format button and typing
    the text.
 c. Putting the insertion point
    inside of a word and click-
    ing the appropriate format-
    ting button.
 d. All of the above.
 e. None of the above.

Screen Review

Match the letters in Figure 4.19 with the correct items in the list.

Figure 4.19

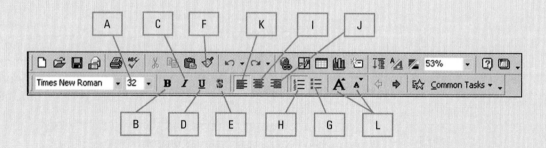

____ 1. Click here to make text bold.

____ 2. Click here to copy formatting from one bit of text to another.

____ 3. Click here to apply shadows to your text.

____ 4. Click here to underline text.

____ 5. Click here to add bullets to a paragraph.

____ 6. Click here to italicize your text.

____ 7. Click here to increase or decrease the size of your text.

____ 8. This is the default alignment for paragraphs.

____ 9. Click here to manually change the font size.

Exercise and Project

Follow these step-by-step instructions to practice the skills that are included in this chapter. If you are working in a computer lab, you may have to ask your instructor where you should save or print your work.

Exercise

1. Start PowerPoint and open the file titled **PPT4** Student\Chapter 4 folder of the PinPoint CD-ROM that came with this book.

2. Realign both the title and subtitle placeholders on the title page to show left alignment.

3. Change the title font size to 44 points.

4. Make the body text on each slide **California FB Bold**. If this font is not available, choose another bold serif font.

5. The titles look a little sleepy—modify the title color to be a darker shade of yellow.

6. What happened to the bullets on Slide 2? Select the text in the text placeholder and add bullets.

7. Upon reflection, it makes sense to order the items on Slide 4 sequentially. Add numbers to the four bullet points at the bottom of the list.

8. The default number style looks terrible! Choose **Format|Bullets and Numbering** and reduce the bullet size to 75% of the text size.

9. That doesn't look right either; change the size back and press the Indent button to indent the three bullets. (Make sure that the numbers are 100% of the text size.)

10. Change the name, **A. Reagan Artz,** on the title page to your name, and then save the file in your PowerPoint 2000 folder as **Exercise 4A**.

11. Print your slide show as handouts—six to a page.

12. Select the three sub-bullet points on Slide 2, choose **Format|Bullets and Numbering,** click the **Bullets** tab, and then click **Character**.

13. Click the **Bullets from** drop-down list, choose **Wingdings 2**, and click to select the fifth bullet from the left on the bottom row. (If you don't have this options, choose an appropriate character from the Wingdings list.) Click **OK**.

14. Using the Format Painter, copy the new bullet style to the subbullet points on Slide 3.

15. Use the Replace Fonts feature to replace the Britannic Bold font with Verdana throughout the presentation.

16. Finished! Save the presentation in your folder as **Exercise 4B**.

17. Print handouts—six to a page and exit PowerPoint.

Project

Only three days until your annual review. Has a year really gone by since the last time you were forced to take an inventory of your contributions to the firm? Well, no use putting it off. You know the drill. In three days, you will be standing in front of the corporate executives relaying how you have added value to the firm over the past year. Further, you must explain how you plan to carry these first-class contributions into the next year. Create a presentation that includes the following:

- A title slide.
- At least one slide of your value-adding activities over the past year. Include some measurable results. Use tabs to organize the information and, specifically, use decimal tabs to line up any numbers.

- At least one slide of your past continuing-education endeavors (those that pertain to your work), such as classes and seminars.
- At least one slide dedicated to future objectives.

Use your knowledge of text alignment, font formatting, bullets, and numbering, to increase the visual appeal of your slide show. When you are finished save the file in your folder as Project 4, add your name to the title slide, and print it as handouts—three to a page.

Format Slide Characteristics

Now that you know how to format text, it's time to learn some other, important nonverbal communication techniques. When you stand in front of an audience, the way you are dressed immediately conveys a message about you. The way your slides are dressed does too! Warm and friendly, cool and professional—what message are you trying to communicate? In this chapter you learn how to use color to help create the atmosphere that surrounds your presentation as you advance to the next phase of building a slide show—adding background color.

At the end of this chapter you will be able to:

C   E

C	E	
☑	☐	Apply a Design Template
☐	☑	Apply a template from a saved file
☐	☑	Customize the slide color scheme
☐	☑	Add a custom background
☐	☑	Apply a textured background
☑	☐	Add headers and footers
☑	☐	Modify the Slide Master
☐	☑	Create a custom design template

What: After you've polished the content of your presentation, you will want to polish its visual aspects. The designers of PowerPoint have simplified this process by including themed *Design Templates* that you can apply to new or existing presentations. Each template includes a comprehensive *color scheme* that defines the colors of various slide characteristics, such as *background* color and artwork (the blank area of the slide that you see behind the text), and text formatting.

Though PowerPoint 2000 comes with 44 beautiful template designs, you aren't restricted to using them when you want to add a template. You can apply templates styles that you've saved from previous versions of Office or you can create and apply your own unique variations.

Why: Tailoring the formatting and background details of your visual aids can take hours. In contrast, it only takes a few "clicks" to apply a design template! Moreover, when you use one of these beautiful coverings, each slide has the same consistent formatting, and thus helps promote a consistent message.

APPLY A DESIGN TEMPLATE TO AN EXISTING PRESENTATION

C *CORE OBJECTIVE:* Apply a design template

E *EXPERT OBJECTIVE:* Apply a template from another presentation

How: With your presentation open, access the Apply Design Template dialog box in one of the following three ways:

- ○ Choose **Format|Apply Design Template.**
- ○ Choose **Common Tasks|Apply Design Template.**
- ○ Place the cursor anywhere on the slide surface outside of a placeholder and right-click. Choose **Apply Design Template** from the shortcut menu that appears.

To apply one of the PowerPoint 2000 templates, follow these steps:

1. When the dialog box appears (Figure 5.1), browse through the predefined template designs. Preview a design by clicking once on its name.

Note: For you to be able to "Preview" each design, the **View** menu in the Apply Design Template dialog box must be set on **Preview**. Access the dialog box and choose **View|Preview**.

---

2. After you find the template that you want to use, double-click the template name or click **Apply** to close the dialog box and use it in your active presentation.

Figure 5.1
Selecting a design
template

Click to preview or
select a design.

Drop-down list to
select Preview

Scroll to view
more designs.

Click to apply.

To apply a template from a previously saved presentation, or one that you've designed, follow these steps:

1. Search through the Files of type drop-down list and select **All PowerPoint Presentations**.
2. Click to drop down the **Save In** list and browse to locate the saved presentation that includes the template you want to apply (Figure 5.2).
3. Click to select the presentation and then click **Apply**.

Note: Though you can usually execute a command within a dialog box by double-clicking a item, such as a file name, this technique will generally be omitted for the remainder of this book.

Result: The design template that you've chosen is immediately applied to every slide in the active presentation. What were black and white are now dramatically colored visual aids! If this design doesn't communicate the impression that you're seeking, just repeat the process to apply one of the other choices. Figure 5.3 provides an example of a presentation that has a template from a saved PowerPoint file applied.

THOUGHT QUESTION: Can you think of a situation when a simple black-and-white presentation would be the most suitable?

Figure 5.2
Applying a template from an existing presentation

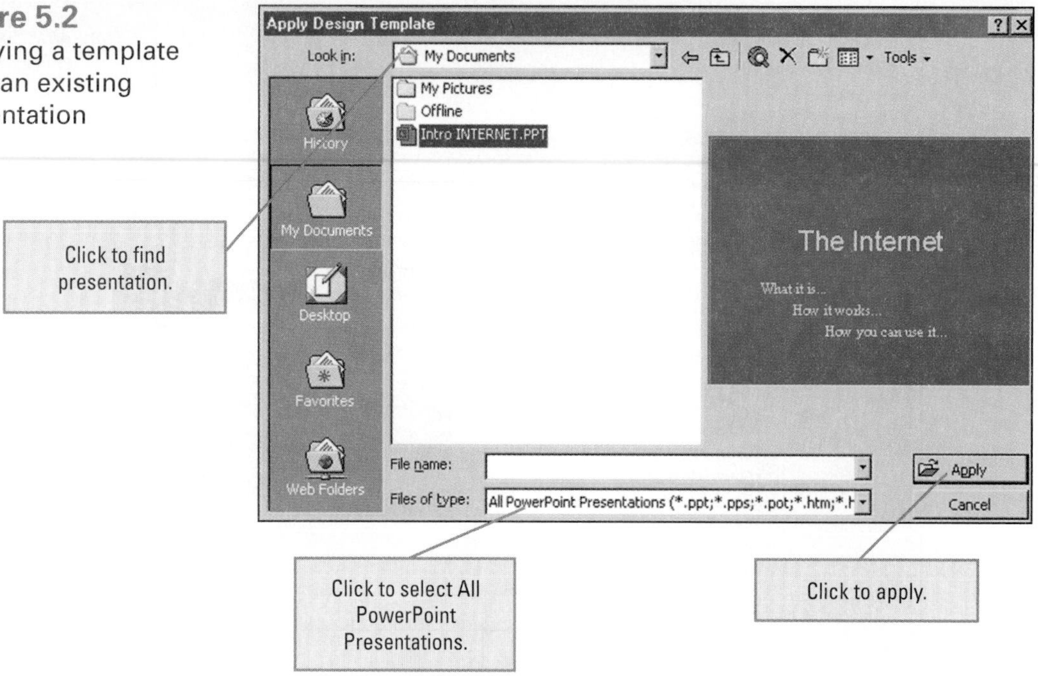

Figure 5.3
Template applied from an existing presentation

CREATE A NEW PRESENTATION USING A DESIGN TEMPLATE

CORE OBJECTIVE: Create a presentation using a template and/or a wizard

You don't have to wait until you've finished entering the contents of your slide show to add color; you can incorporate a template on your first slide.

How: To begin a new presentation with a design template, use one of the following methods:

❍ From the opening dialog box, choose **Design Template** and click **OK**.
❍ Choose **File|New**, and then click the **Design Templates** tab in the New Presentation dialog box (Figure 5.4).

Figure 5.4
Selecting a Design
Template for a new
presentation

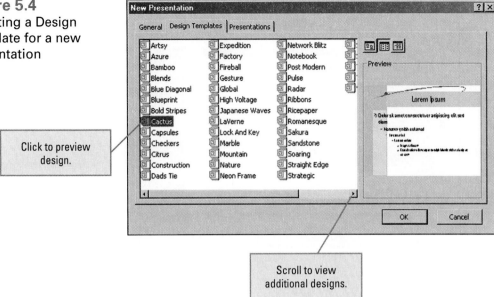

Click to preview
design.

Scroll to view
additional designs.

When the dialog box appears, follow these steps:

1. Click the template's name to select it or to preview its appearance.
   Click **OK** to apply the selected template.
2. As soon as you complete Step 1, the New Slide dialog box appears
   (Figure 5.5). Use the skills that you learned in Chapter 2, "Work with
   Text," to select the appropriate AutoLayout for your slide and click
   OK.

Figure 5.5
Selecting a slide
layout

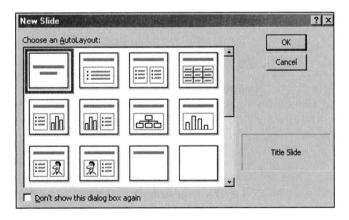

 TIPS FROM A PRO: If you are working in Slide or Normal view and you find that
after you add a template the colors and artwork are distracting, switch to Outline
view to enter or edit your text. This minimizes the effects of all of those colors
and helps to keep your attention focused on the presentation's content and not
the brightly colored fonts or background art.

 TIPS FROM A PRO: Did you know that you can open and modify the AutoContent
Wizard templates using a similar method to that described in this task? Choose
File|New and click the **Presentations** tab. Double-click the presentation name that
you want to open and then enter your own original text.

Figure 5.6
Design template
applied

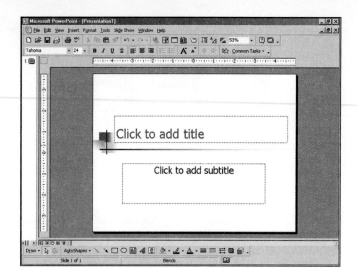

Result: As you see in Figure 5.6, the first slide in your new presentation appears, beautifully dressed in the design template that you selected. Now you can click in the placeholders and begin entering text on your slide. Each additional slide that you add will also include this design.

| TASK **2** | *Change the Slide Color Scheme* |

EXPERT OBJECTIVE: Customize a color scheme

What: Another way to alter the look of your visual aids is to change the *color scheme*. The color scheme determines what colors are assigned to eight specific slide characteristics (such as fonts, backgrounds, and bullets). Each template, even the blank presentation, comes with a set of color schemes—the default that materializes as soon as you apply it plus several others.

These predefined schemes have been specially selected to include colors that not only look good together, but that also supply a sense of balance. Still, you can choose to modify the existing schemes or create your own completely new variations. These changes can then be applied to one slide; to every slide, one at a time; or to the entire presentation via the Slide Master. (You learn how to use the Slide Master in Task 4.)

Why: Many of the visual aspects of your slides can be altered in one convenient location.

APPLY A PRESET COLOR SCHEME

How: After you have applied a design template to your presentation, you have the option of replacing the default setting with one of the other predefined color schemes.

1. Choose **Format|Slide Color Scheme** to access the Color Scheme dialog box.

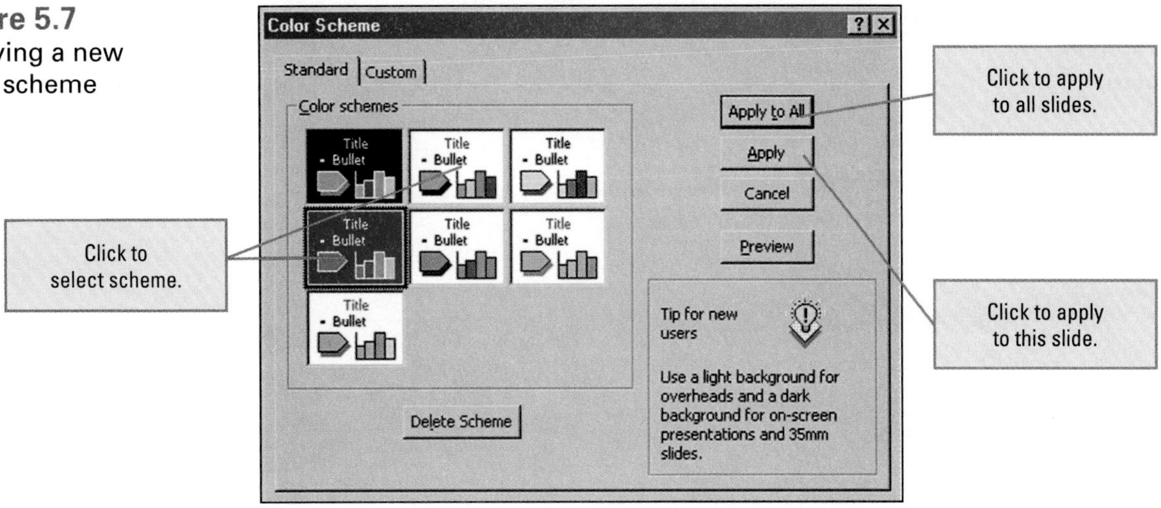

Figure 5.7
Applying a new color scheme

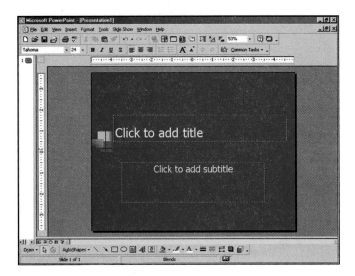

Click to select scheme.

Click to apply to all slides.

Click to apply to this slide.

2. Click to select one of the schemes associated with the template, and then click **Apply** to affect one slide, or **Apply to All** to update the entire presentation.

Result: Your slides reflect the new color scheme, as shown in Figure 5.8. The artwork and font styles associated with the template are preserved.

Figure 5.8
New color scheme applied to template

CREATE A NEW COLOR SCHEME

How: When you want to modify the existing color scheme or create your own distinctive variation, follow these steps:

1. Choose **Format|Slide Color Scheme** and click the **Standard** tab.
2. Select the color scheme most like the one that you are seeking, and then click the **Custom** tab.
3. Select the item that you want to change (click the square to the left of the element name), and then click **Change Color** (Figure 5.9) to access the Accent and Hyperlink Color dialog box. You can modify one element color, or you can change all of them, but you must make modifications one by one.

Figure 5.9
Creating a new
color scheme

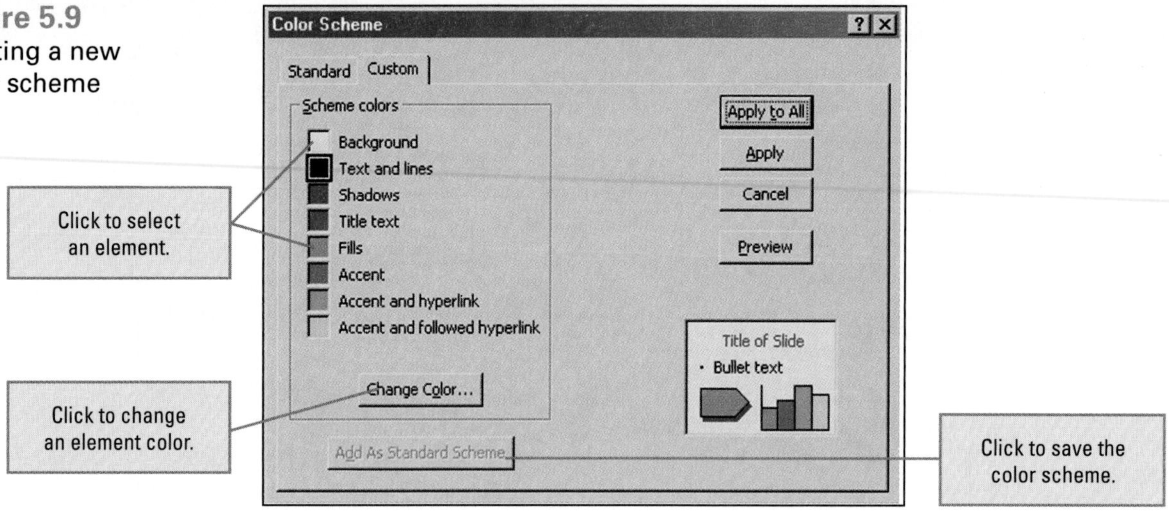

Click to select
an element.

Click to change
an element color.

Click to save the
color scheme.

4. To apply one of the colors from the palette, click the **Standard** tab, and then select a shade. Click **OK** when you are finished.
5. Click **Custom** to blend your own shade and then click **OK** to apply the chosen color.
6. Repeat Steps 4 through Step 6 until you have altered all the slide elements that you want to recolor. If you decide to save this scheme for future use, click **Add as Standard Scheme**. The scheme will be added to the "*Color Schemes*" that are associated with the particular template that you have applied, as you see in Figure 5.10.
7. Click **Apply** to use this color scheme on the slide in the viewing screen or click **Apply to All** to change the entire presentation.

Figure 5.10 Saved
custom color scheme

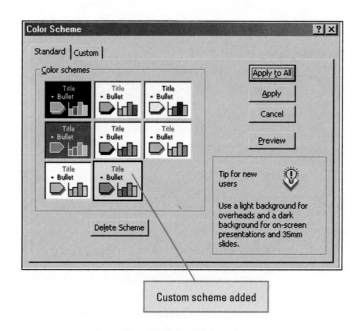

Custom scheme added

Result: The color scheme that you created is applied to one or all of your slides. Figure 5.11 illustrates one possible example of a custom color scheme that has been applied to a slide.

Figure 5.11
Custom color scheme
applied to design
template

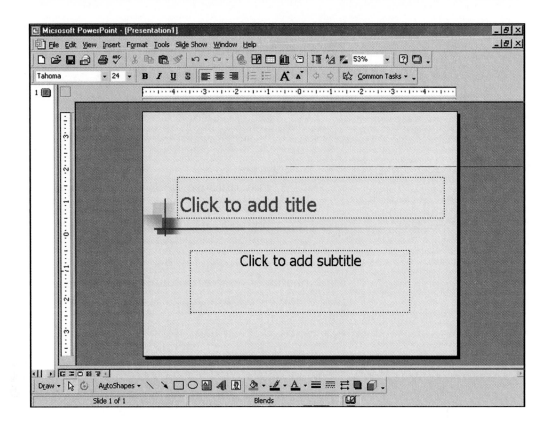

 Tips from a Pro: Check your visual aids in the room or in similar lighting and other conditions to those that you will be using to ensure that the elements on your slides are clearly visible. Pay special attention to the font and background combinations. Some text colors are difficult to read when combined with certain fill effects.

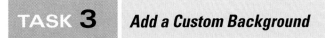

| TASK **3** | ***Add a Custom Background*** |

 Expert Objective: Create a custom background

 Expert Objective: Add textured backgrounds

What: Design templates are striking to look at and straightforward to use, but you're not limited to the use of templates when choosing colors and designs for slide backgrounds. By utilizing one of PowerPoint's other background features, you can choose from dozens of possible colors, patterns, or even your own photographs to create a completely unique and individualized look. You can use any of the following options as a slide background.

❍ Apply a solid color. Choose a solid standard color or custom shade to enhance your slides.

○ Apply one of four background types, or *fill effects*, that utilize combinations of color, texture, patterns, or pictures. Each fill effect alternative is described as follows.

- *Gradients* utilize one or two colors to add shading that gradually transition between light and dark variations of the single color or the two colors.
- *Textures* apply a 3D-like effect to the surface of your slides. This option enables you to import an outside graphic to use for a background.
- **Patterns** cover your slide background with colored or black-and-white designs, made up of lines, dots, and squares.
- **Pictures** enables you to select a saved photograph or a piece of clip art to enhance your slide backgrounds.

Why: You can create and refine an exclusively customized background. Even photos of last year's family reunion or company picnic can be used to form a backdrop for your text.

APPLY A SOLID BACKGROUND COLOR

How: To select a solid background color, use these steps:

1. Choose **Format|Background** to open the **Background** dialog box (Figure 5.12). Click the **Background fill** drop-down list to continue.
2. Select one of the visible colors (colors associated with the presentation's color scheme), or click **More Colors** to pick a color from the standard pallet or to create your own custom shade.
3. After you select a color, you can click **Preview** to see what it will look like when applied to your slides. Click **OK** and **Apply** to apply to one slide, or click **Apply to All** to use throughout the presentation.

Result: As soon as you complete Step 3, the color is applied to the slide or slides that you have designated. Figure 5.13 illustrates one example of a slide that has a solid-color background.

Figure 5.12 Selecting a solid color background

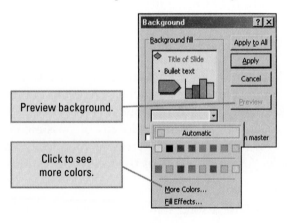

Figure 5.13 Solid color background

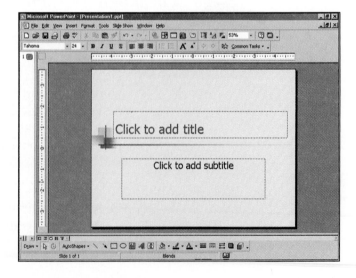

TIPS FROM A PRO: Although each of us has certain color preferences, just liking a color isn't a good reason to use it in a background or color scheme. Professional graphic designers know that certain color combinations *work* together and that others don't. The following points offer some tips for those of us who aren't professionals:

- Use only two of three colors per visual—more might distract.
- Use a consistent color scheme throughout your presentation.
- When in doubt, use one of the design templates.
- Use red and green with caution because some people have difficulty with these colors.
- Know your room. Is it light or dark? Light backgrounds work best in rooms that aren't completely dark, and dark backgrounds work best in dark rooms.
- Know your equipment. As a general rule of thumb, overheads are more effective with light backgrounds and on-screen slide shows with dark backgrounds.
- Test your color scheme before the big day . . . using people other than you if possible.

THOUGHT QUESTION: If you've already applied a design template, what happens when you apply a fill effect?

APPLY A FILL EFFECTS BACKGROUND

How: To use one of the fill effects options, choose **Format|Background**, click the drop-down list, and then click **Fill Effects**. When the dialog box shown in Figure 5.14 appears, you can choose between four possible background types.

To apply a gradient background, follow these steps:

1. Click the **Gradient** tab. The Fill Effects dialog box now includes the options shown in Figure 5.15 that are available for applying a gradient background. You can now select one of the options that are described and illustrated after Step 2.

Figure 5.14
Fill Effects dialog box

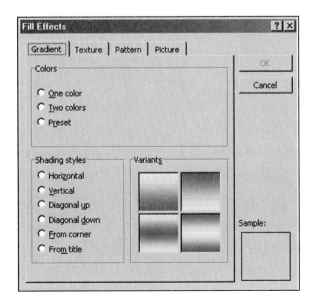

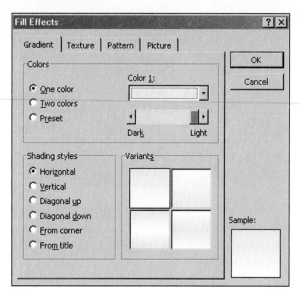
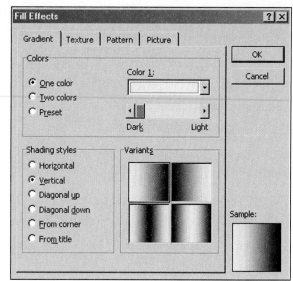

Figure 5.15 One-color gradient fill

2. After you have chosen a fill option for your presentation, click **OK** to return to the Background dialog box.

- **Apply a one-color gradient fill** and see colors fade slowly from dark to light. You can select the fill color by dropping down the **Color 1** list. Change the intensity of the color by dragging the slider left or right as shown in Figure 5.15.
- **Apply a two-color gradient fill** where colors gradually fade from one shade to the next. Click the drop-down lists associated with Color 1 and Color 2 to select each color (Figure 5.16).
- **Apply a preset gradient fill** that utilizes distinctive color or style combinations. Figure 5.17 shows an example of one of the gradient fills that are included with PowerPoint.

Figure 5.16 Two-color gradient fill

Figure 5.17 Preset gradient fill

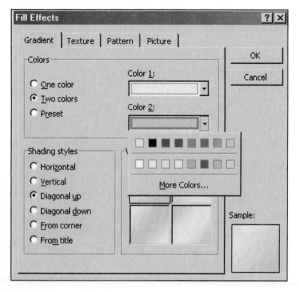
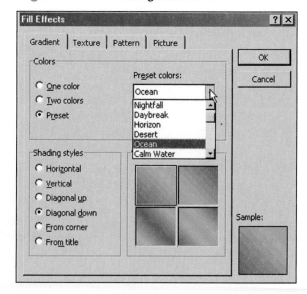

- **Select a shading style and variant** to further enhance your gradient choice. The shading style refers to the way the colors are applied to the slide (for example, horizontally versus vertically). After choosing a style, you can select additional variations of that style, or variants, that will work best for your particular situation (Figure 5.18).

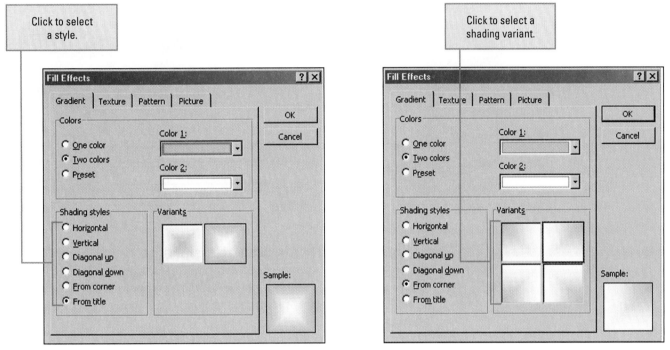

Figure 5.18 Choosing a shading style and variant

To apply a textured fill background, follow these steps:

1. Click the **Texture** tab. The Fill Effects dialog now looks like the one shown in Figure 5.19.
2. Select one of the 24 options or click **Other Texture** to import a file from another location. You can use any type of graphics file as long

Figure 5.19
Choosing a textured fill background

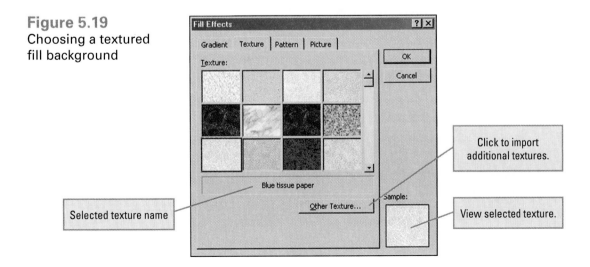

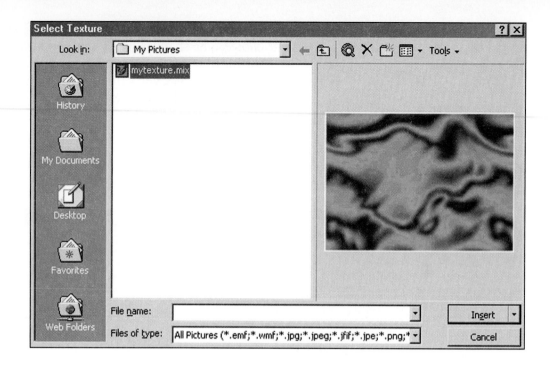

Figure 5.20
Importing a texture

as your computer has the applicable import filter installed (see Figure 5.20). (How will you know if the graphic can be applied? It will be obvious from the message prompt that you receive after you select the picture.) The Sample area lets you know which texture is currently selected.

3. Double-click a box or click **OK** to choose a texture and return to the Background dialog box.

To apply a fill pattern background, follow these steps:

1. Click the **Pattern** tab to see the 48 possible choices (Figure 5.21).
2. Click a pattern miniature to select, or to preview a choice. Selected patterns have a darker border but you can see at a glance which pattern you've selected because it displays in the Sample area.

Figure 5.21
Choosing a fill pattern background

Selected pattern name

Click to change foreground color.

Click to change background color.

View selected pattern.

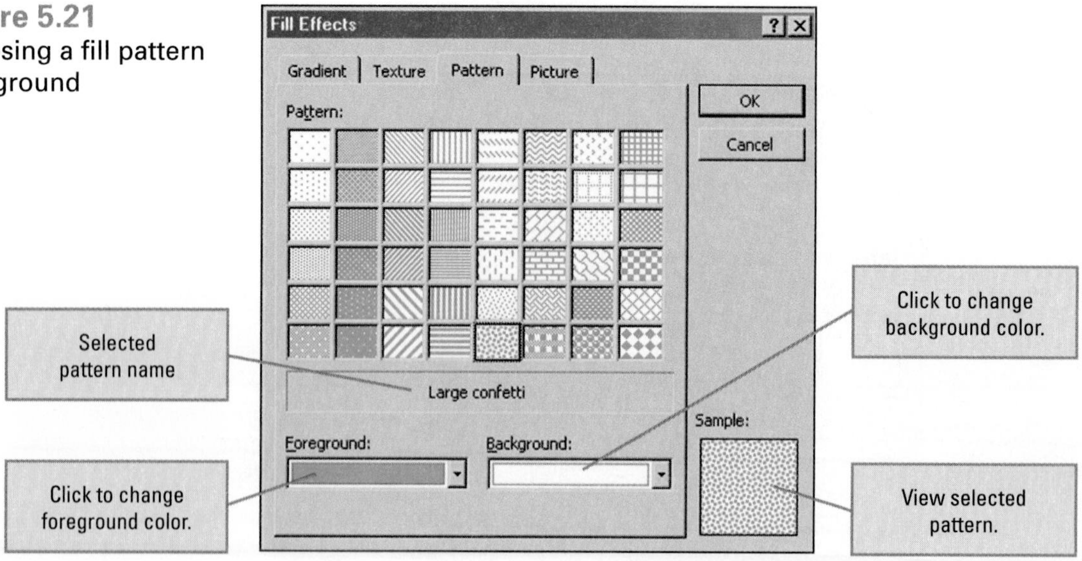

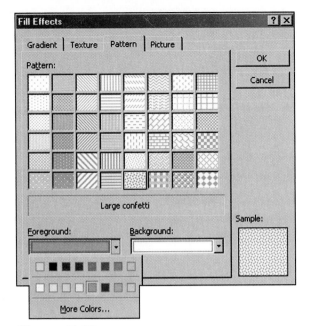
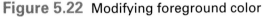
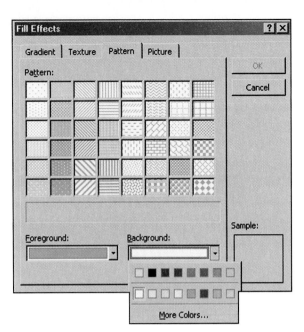

Figure 5.22 Modifying foreground color

Modifying background color

3. To change the foreground color, the color that appears to be closest to the front, or the background color, the color that appears to be behind the foreground color (Figure 5.22), click the applicable drop-down list and select a shade.
4. Click **OK** to choose a pattern and return to the Background dialog box.

To apply a picture as a background, follow these steps:

1. Click the **Picture** tab. The Fill Effects dialog box, like the one shown in Figure 5.23, is displayed.

Figure 5.23
Choosing a picture
for a background

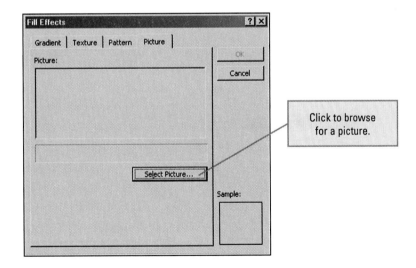

2. Click **Select a Picture** to access the dialog box shown in Figure 5.24. You can now browse for the disk and folder location of the image that you want to apply.
3. When you find the graphic, select it by clicking the file name. The picture appears in the view area (if View is set to Preview).

Figure 5.24
Selecting a picture
as a background fill

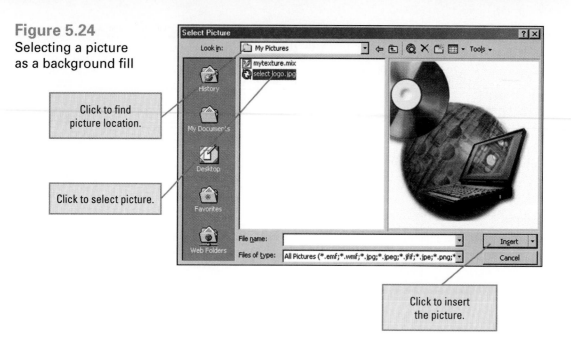

Click to find
picture location.

Click to select picture.

Click to insert
the picture.

4. Click **Insert** to return to the Fill Effects dialog box. The picture that you have chosen is now visible in the viewing window.
5. Click **OK** to return to the Background dialog box or click **Select a Picture** to search for a different graphic.

Result: After you complete the last step in each of the four fill-type procedures, the Background dialog box appears. Your background choice is displayed in the Background fill area. You can now:

○ Click **Preview** to see this choice as it will look when applied to your slides (Figure 5.25).
○ Repeat Step 2 to select a different option.
○ Click **Cancel** to end the procedure and return to the slide.
○ Click **Apply** or **Apply to All**.

Figures 5.26–5.29 display an example of each fill option.

Figure 5.25
Previewing a fill
background

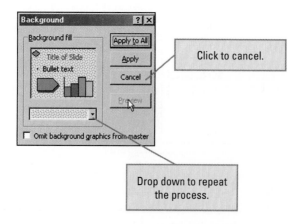

Click to cancel.

Drop down to repeat
the process.

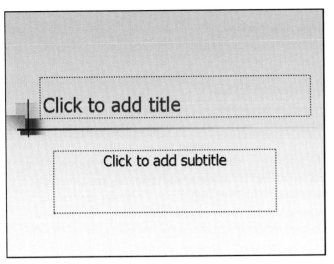

Figure 5.26 Gradient fill applied as a background

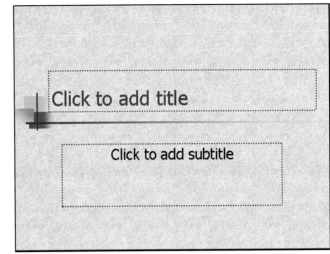

Figure 5.27 Textured fill applied as a background

 TIPS FROM A PRO: Of course you want to build an attractive and professional presentation, but toying with the visual elements can be addictive. Do you find yourself forgoing the pleasure of lunch with friends, choosing instead to stay hunched in front of your computer terminal, tinkering with an ever-increasing list of color schemes and font combinations. If so, consider joining a support group or better yet, set a time limit for the completion of your work.

Figure 5.28 Fill pattern applied as a background

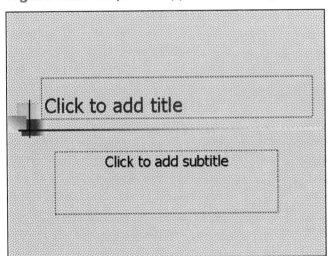

Figure 5.29 Picture applied as a background

C **CORE OBJECTIVE:** Insert headers and footers

What: A *footer* enables you to add a small piece of text at the bottom of slides, note pages, or handouts. A *header,* on the other hand, is found at the top of the page. Unlike footers, they can't be added to slides—only to notes pages and handouts. Both headers and footers are positioned in small text boxes that are positioned beneath the regular text placeholders, and that can't be seen or accessed unless you use the View menu.

Because both headers and footers are outside of the normal text placement position, they are unaffected when you add text to the slide placeholders (unless you reposition or resize the placeholders).

Why: Adding specific information (such as the name of your company, the date, or the page number) not only serves a useful purpose, but it also personalizes the slide show for your listeners. Using this method ensures that the information is consistently formatted on each page and that you have to type it only once. When applied to notes pages and handouts, it also helps organize the materials for you and for your audience.

How: Choose **View|Header and Footer** to access the Header and Footer dialog box shown in Figure 5.30.

1. To add to, or to edit the slide footer, click the **Slide** tab (Figure 5.30). Now you can implement one or all of the following options:
   - Display an automatically updating date and time each time you open the presentation.
   - Enter a fixed date and time.
   - Add a footer—such as a company or departmental name.
   - Add a page number to each slide.
   - Omit footer from the title page.
   - Apply to all slides or apply to a selected slide (or slides if you are using Slide Sorter view).

Figure 5.30
Inserting a slide footer

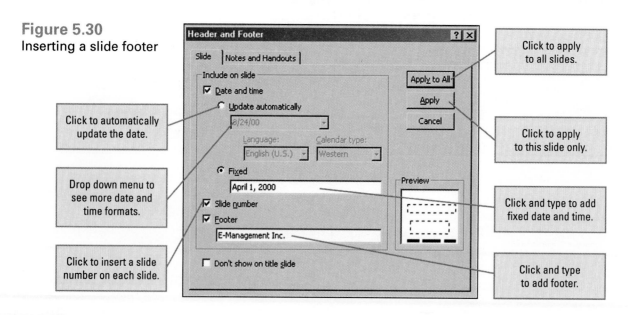

2. To add to, or to edit the header and footer area of notes and handouts, click the **Notes and Handouts** tab (Figure 5.31). You can then:
   - Click to display the current date and time automatically each time you open the presentation.
   - Decide between various types of date formatting.
   - Type in a fixed date and time.
   - Add a footer—such as a company or departmental name.
   - Add a page number to each slide.
   - Click to apply to all note and handout pages.

Figure 5.31
Inserting Header and Footer on Notes and Handouts

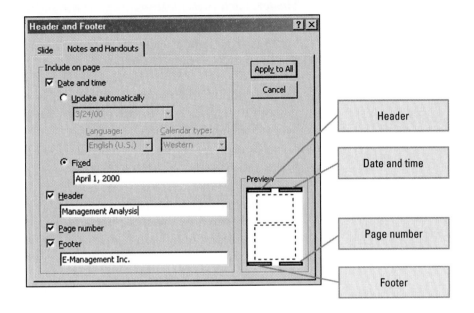

Result: Your slides and notes pages display the headers and footers that you added (Figures 5.32 and 5.33). When you print notes pages or audience handouts, they will include the data that you entered.

Figure 5.32 Slide with footer

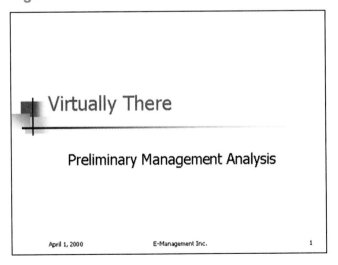

Figure 5.33 Notes page with header and footer

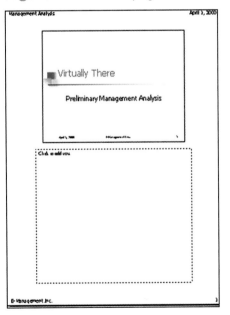

CORE OBJECTIVE: Change slide layout (modify the Slide Master)

What: Sometimes you want to change font and bullet formatting, the slide color scheme, or other aspects of slide layout and design throughout an entire presentation. For these types of global changes, you can modify the *Slide Master*. Each presentation has a master slide, a slide that defines the formatting that you see on individual slides (except the title slide).

Why: You could page from slide to slide and implement the desired changes one by one. Not only is this inefficient, it also opens the door for mistakes to creep in. With the Slide Master you can make modifications (such as adding the company logo or changing the font style) on one slide and then apply it to the entire presentation. (And, have time left over to catch the next big wave.)

How: To make changes to the Slide Master, follow these steps:

1. Choose **View|Master|Slide Master** (Figure 5.34). The Slide Master, shown in Figure 5.35, appears.
   - To make changes to text formatting in the title placeholder, click in the text or select the placeholder.
   - To make changes to text formatting in the text placeholder, click anywhere in the paragraph; or to change the entire placeholder, select the placeholder.
   - To resize a placeholder, select the placeholder and drag one of the eight sizing handles.

Figure 5.34 Accessing the Slide Master

Figure 5.35 The Slide Master

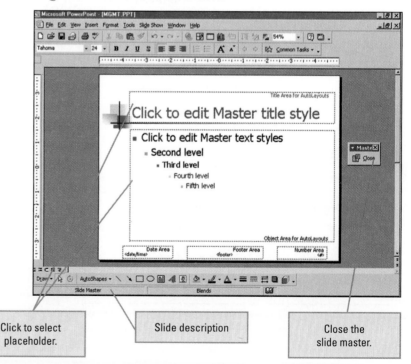

- To move a placeholder, select the placeholder and drag it with the four-headed mouse pointer to the new location.
- To remove or edit the date or footer, click in the applicable placeholder and enter changes. If you have previously added date or footer information under View|Header and Footer, you must remove the text that is in the placeholder (for example, <footer>). If you don't, your slides display both entries.
- To replace a placeholder that has been deleted, choose **Common Tasks|Master Layout**. Check the applicable box to return the placeholder to its original position.
- To format a placeholder, double-click its border or choose **Format|Placeholder**. You learn more about formatting placeholders and other objects in Chapter 6, "Elements of Sight and Sound."

2. When you finish making changes, click **Close** on the Master toolbar (if it is visible) to return to Normal view, or click one of the **View** buttons or choose a view option from the **View** menu.

Result: As soon as the Slide Master closes, the modifications that you made are reflected on your slides. If you don't like what you see, click **Undo** and begin again.

TIPS FROM A PRO: Some changes that you make on the Slide Master are reflected on the title slide; others are not. You can make changes to the *Title Master*, the master for the title slide, using the guidelines included in this skill. If you choose **View|Master** and the Title Master is not available, choose the **Slide Master**. Then choose **Common Tasks|New Title Master**.

TIPS FROM A PRO: If you have made changes to individual slides, modifications to the Slide Master won't affect these changes. That is because direct formatting applied to slide characteristics always overrides formatting applied to the Slide Master. For this reason it is best to change the Slide Master first and then make any additional changes to specific slides.

Still, even if you've applied direct formatting to slides, you can use the Slide Master. Before you do, however, select each slide individually and reapply the original slide layout by accessing the Slide Layout dialog box as you learned to do in Chapter 2. Now you can make global changes to the master slide and not worry about some slides not being changed.

TASK 6   *Create a Custom Design Template*

EXPERT OBJECTIVE: Design a template

What: It's easy to customize the appearance of an individual slide show using Design Templates and their color schemes, PowerPoint's background options, or the Slide Master. Once you create your masterpiece, you can save it as a template and use it again.

Figure 5.36
Saving a custom design as a template

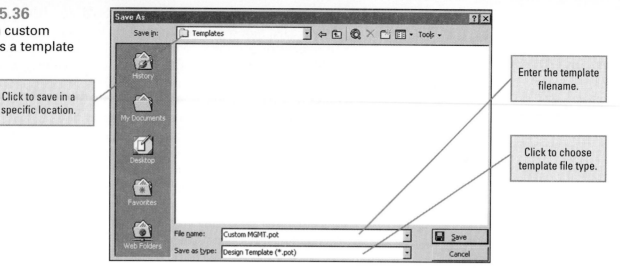

Click to save in a specific location.

Enter the template filename.

Click to choose template file type.

Why: It may take hours to create the perfect look for a presentation. After all that work, why use it only once? Instead, you can store it away to use over and over.

How: Use these steps to save a template that you create:

1. Delete all slides except the title slide and remove any text from the slide and click the **Save** button to open the Save As dialog box. (You don't have to do this, but why take up extra space on a disk; you are saving the template and empty placeholders, not the text.)
2. Type the new template name in the **File Name** box as shown in Figure 5.36.
3. Click the **Save as type** drop-down list and scroll until you see Design Template (*.ppt).
4. If you want to save the template in a location other than PowerPoint's "Templates" folder, click the **Save In** drop-down menu to locate and select the desired "save" location. Click **Save** to finish the process.

Result: The template that you carefully designed is saved for future use. Use the steps provided in Task 1 to apply it to a new presentation. Figure 5.37 provides an example of a custom template that has been added to a slide.

Figure 5.37
Custom design template applied to a slide

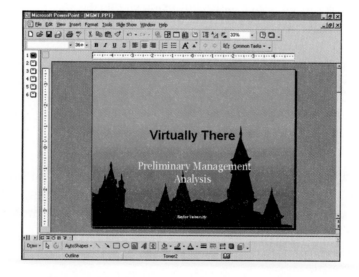

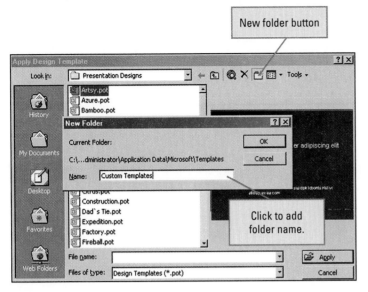

New folder button

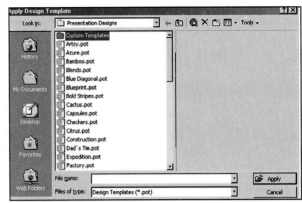

Figure 5.38 Adding a folder to the Presentation Design location

Figure 5.39 Folder added to the Presentation Design location

TIPS FROM A PRO: PowerPoint design templates are located in Program Files\Microsoft Office\Templates\Presentation Designs. If you want to save your custom models in the same folder location (like the example shown in Figure 5.39), it is a good idea to create a subfolder so that it's easy to distinguish between your designs and the PowerPoint designs. To accomplish this, follow these steps:

1. Choose **Program Files\Microsoft Office\Templates\Presentation Designs**.
2. Click the **New Folder** button, type a name for your new folder (refer to Figure 5.38), click **OK**; and if you have a template open that you want to save, click **Save**.

THOUGHT QUESTION: What is the difference between applying a template from a saved presentation and saving a custom template?

Use PinPoint

After gaining the skills in this chapter, you can apply a design template, customize the slide color scheme, design and save a custom design template or background, modify the Slide Master, and insert a footer or header. Now it's time to see what you can do with the PinPoint software. Remember, anytime you are unsure about what to do next, reread the relevant portion of the chapter or you can click Show Me for a live demonstration. Try these skills in PinPoint:

- Use a template
- Apply a design
- Master Layout
- Apply template from a presentation
- Design a template
- Customize a background

- Change a background
- Customize a color scheme
- Headers and footers

Key Terms

You can find definitions for these words in this chapter:

Background
Color scheme
Design template
Fill effects
Foreground
Gradients
Headers
Footer
Slide Master
Textures
Title Master
Variant

Review Questions

You can use the following review questions and exercises to test your knowledge and skills. The answers are given in Appendix D, "Answers to Review Questions".

True/False

Indicate whether each statement is true (T) or false (F).

___ 1. To change the font style on a single slide, change the Slide Master.

___ 2. When you make changes to individual slides, these changes are not affected by changes made later on the Slide Master.

___ 3. Footers can only be inserted onto notes pages.

___ 4. You can create your own template design and save it for future use.

___ 5. After you've applied a design template, you are stuck with it; it can't be changed.

___ 6. To begin a presentation from scratch with a design template, click the Common Tasks toolbar.

___ 7. The Slide Master controls many of the visual elements of a presentation.

___ 8. Using patterned backgrounds, you can add dots, grids, and block patterns to the background of your slides.

___ 9. It might be distracting to add visual elements to slides before you have entered the text.

___ 10. To access the master slide, right-click any slide.

Multiple Choice

Select the letter that best completes the statement.

____ 1. To use a template from a saved presentation, you must first:
   a. Choose Format|Apply Design Template.
   b. Click the New presentation button.
   c. Choose Common Tasks|Apply Design Template.
   d. Open the saved presentation.
   e. Only a and c.

____ 2. Format the master slide before making changes to individual slides because:
   a. You can't change the Slide Master after you make changes to one of the slides.
   b. The changes you have made will be overridden by the Slide Master.
   c. It easier to make changes in one location.
   d. All of the above.
   e. Only a and b.

____ 3. To add a corporate logo to each text slide:
   a. Choose View|Footer.
   b. Choose View|Master|Slide Master and add it to the master slide.
   c. Copy the logo and paste it on every slide.
   d. All of the above will work.
   e. None of the above.

____ 4. When you choose Format|Background, you can:
   a. Change the background color of your slides.
   b. Add a textured background.
   c. Select a saved photograph and apply it as a background.
   d. All of the above.
   e. Only a and b.

____ 5. To replace a template that you've applied to your slides with another:
   a. Right-click the slide and choose Background.
   b. Choose Common Tasks|Apply Design Template.
   c. Choose Format|Slide Layout.
   d. All of the above.
   e. None of the above

____ 6. To add a date to your slides that updates every time you open the presentation:
   a. Choose View|Header Footer and check Update Automatically.
   b. Choose Format|Header Footer and check Date and Time.
   c. Access the Slide Master and add the information in the date area.
   d. Make a text box on the title slide and type in the information.
   e. Only a and b.

____ 7. To change the font style of the title placeholder on every slide:
   a. Choose View|Slide Master, select the text in the title placeholder and choose a font.
   b. Close the Slide Master and change each slide, one by one.
   c. Choose View|Slide Master, select the placeholder, and then choose the font style.
   d. Click anywhere in the title placeholder of Slide 1 and choose the font style.
   e. Both a and c.

___ 8. Which of the following
enables you to insert a picture
as a background?
  a. Slide color scheme.
  b. Design template.
  c. Background fill effects.
  d. The Slide Master.
  e. None of the above.

___ 9. Design templates offer an
advantage over custom backgrounds because:
  a. They are more attractive.
  b. There are more available
     choices.
  c. They can be applied very
     quickly.
  d. They can be customized
     and still take a short period
     of time to complete.
  e. Both c and d.

___ 10. When you change the default
color scheme for a design template:
  a. The presentation's font col-
     ors may change.
  b. The presentation's bullets
     styles may change.
  c. The background colors may
     change.
  d. The fill color may change.
  e. All of the above.

Screen Review

Match the letters in Figure 5.40 with the correct items in the list.

Figure 5.40

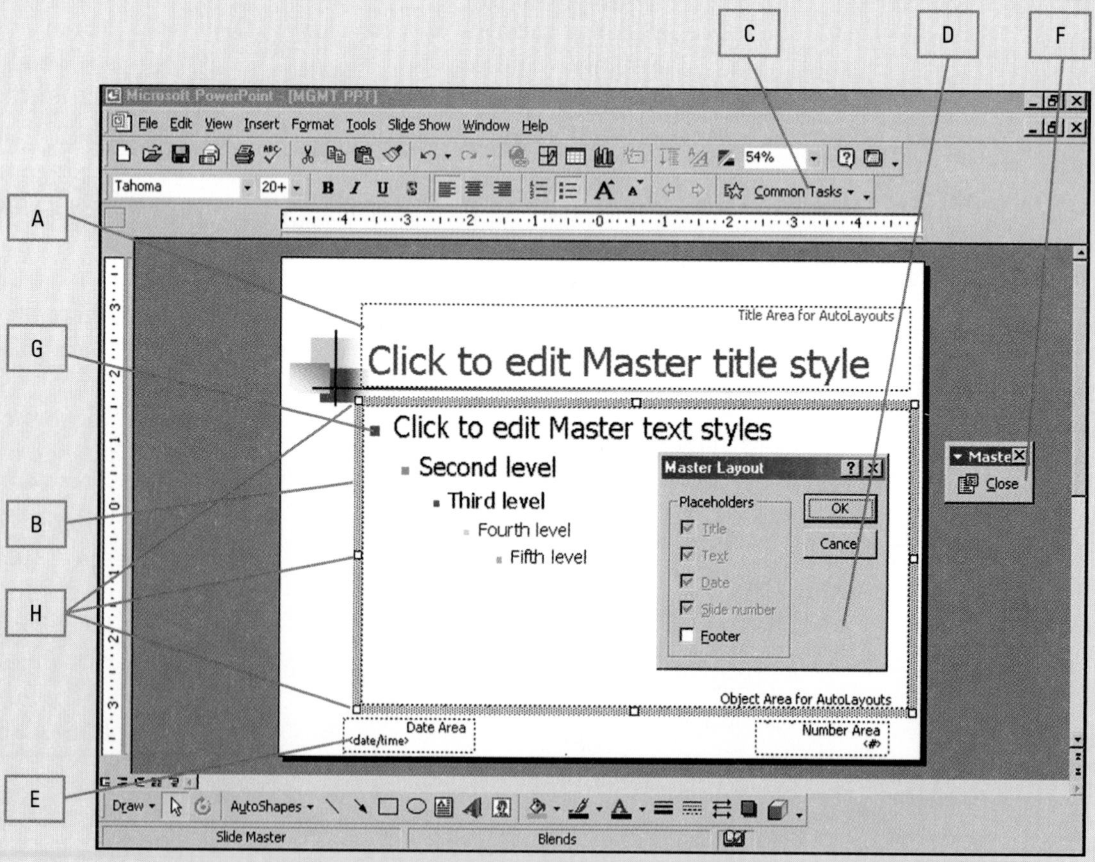

____ 1. Click here to change the title font.

____ 2. Click here to insert a footer.

____ 3. Click here to change the first-level bullet style.

____ 4. Click here to restore missing placeholders.

____ 5. Click here to access the Master Layout dialog box.

____ 6. Click here to resize text placeholder.

____ 7. Click this to close the Slide Master and return to the presentation.

Exercise and Project

Follow these step-by-step instructions to practice the skills that are included in this chapter. If you are working in a computer lab, you may have to ask your instructor where to save or print your work.

Exercise

1. Start PowerPoint and open the file named **PPT5** from the Students\Chapter 5 folder of your PinPoint CD-ROM.
2. It needs some color, so find and apply the design template **Azure**.
3. Now apply the design template from the saved presentation Serenity.
4. Azure looks better, so use **Undo**.
5. Time to change the Slide Master. Go to the master and change the title text to Britannic Bold, 40 point font; the body text to Calisto MT.
6. Replace Austin V. Artz on the title page with your name. Save your file in the PowerPoint 2000 folder as **Exercise 5A**.
7. Print your slides as handouts—six slides one a page.
8. Find the Pattern Fill Effect background called Shingle. Apply it to your presentation. Change the slide color scheme to the middle of the three options. Those colors don't work, so change it back.
9. Add the date to the footer area using the View menu.
10. Save the file in your folder as **Exercise 5B**.
11. Print your slides as handouts—six slides one a page.
12. Exit PowerPoint.

Project

You've just had a flash of brilliance. As you were in lying bed last night listening to your favorite MP3s, you started thinking about all the old computers that your friends and you have laying around collecting dust bunnies. When you consider the other obsolete computer "stuff" that must be out there in cyber junk heaps in the United States, it's staggering! Why not gather it all up (it must be nearly free) and send it off to some the third world countries that don't have our level of computer sophistication. After all, if you're only learning computer basics and sending email, you don't need the very latest model. What a great way to make a bunch of money and to help lesser-developed countries advance! Maybe you could even sell this stuff to some government agency that provides aid to foreign countries.

Make a short presentation (a minimum of three text slides) so that you can present your fledgling ideas to a few of your entrepreneurial buddies. Include custom fonts, background fill effects, a custom color scheme, and a footer with an automatically updating date. Also, add numbers and headers on the notes pages. Add your name to the title page, then save and print your assignment as notes pages.

Elements of Sight and Sound

It is time to polish the non-verbal aspects of your presentation, so have some *fun*. Add clip art and your favorite music, play a video clip during the show, or animate text. Remember, your product will be more visually appealing, and thus more likely to retain your audience's attention if you make your slides interesting. And, an interesting presentation increases the likelihood that your audience will remember the information that you present. Still, with all the sometimes-outrageous effects presented in this chapter, it is easy to get carried away. Don't forget that *you*, not your visual aids, are the primary component of your presentation.

At the end of this chapter, you will be able to:

C **E**

C	E	
☑	☐	Add a picture from the gallery
☐	☑	Add animated clip art
☐	☐	Insert a picture from a file
☑	☑	Modify pictures and clip art
☑	☐	Add and groups Drawing toolbar objects
☑	☐	Format objects
☑	☐	Rotate and full an object
☑	☐	Modify objects
☑	☐	Align, order and group objects
☑	☐	Place text inside a shape using a text box
☑	☐	Add WordArt
☐	☑	Use the Wrap Text in AutoShape feature
☐	☐	Reposition objects and pictures
☐	☑	Add sound
☐	☑	Add video
☑	☐	Add slide transitions
☑	☐	Apply animation
☐	☑	Animate text and objects

What: The colorful background that you added in Chapter 5, "Format Slide Characteristics," has really given your presentation personality, but you can do much more to spice up your visual aids. One vibrant and fun way is to add pictures. You can find pictures to add to your work in many different places, including the following:

○ The **ClipArt Gallery**.
  • **Pictures**. Insert one of thousands of graphical images from the PowerPoint ClipArt Gallery, including the graphical bullets discussed in Chapter 4, "Format Text."
  • **Motion clips**. The ClipArt Gallery also contains many animated pieces of art that display some special life-like movement during a slide show. Animated clips are inserted in the same fashion as motionless objects.
  • **Clips online**. Use the Internet to connect to the Microsoft network and access thousands of additional pieces or art.
  • **Sounds**. Insert sound clips at an appropriate place in your work. You learn how to do this in Task 8.
○ **Your own scanned photographs**. If you have access to a scanner, you can scan in your own photos or drawings and add them to your work.
○ **The Web**. Many of the graphical images that you see on the Web can be saved for your personal use, but be careful not to use copyrighted materials without permission.

Why: Why insert pictures into your slide show? To reinforce and enhance your message! Remember your best friend from grade school . . . the one that you haven't seen in years? As you thumb through your mom's old photo albums, pictures of your friend bring back memories of the past.

Relevant pictures inserted into your visual aids work the same way. We associate thoughts, words, and ideas with images. Pictures not only help grab and hold the attention of your audience during the presentation, but they also help them to recall your message long after you have finished.

FIND A PICTURE IN THE CLIPART GALLERY

How: There are scores of clips to choose from in the gallery, so you must narrow your search to find those that pertain to a specific topic. To find a picture, follow these steps:

1. Select the slide where you want to add clip art. Access the Insert ClipArt dialog box (Figure 6.1) using either the menus or buttons, as follows:
   • Choose **Insert|Picture|Clip Art**.

   • Click the **Insert Clip Art** button on the Drawing toolbar. (If the toolbar is not visible, turn it on.)
2. Click the **Pictures** or the **Motion Clips** tab to see categories of clips.

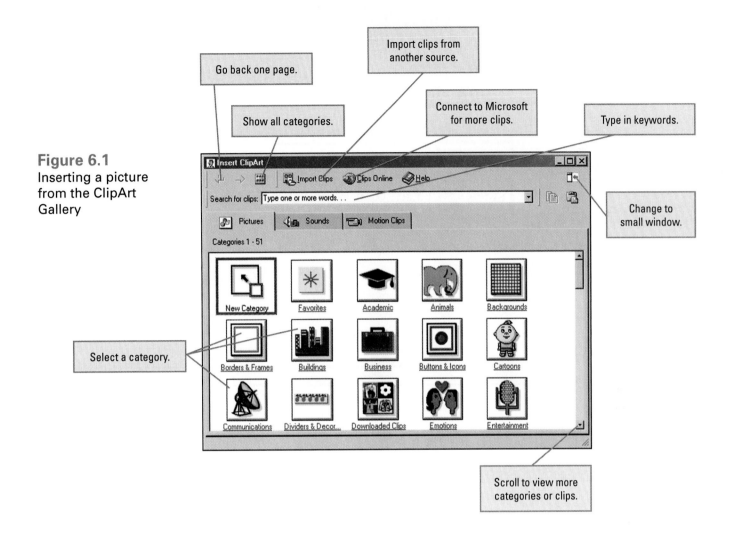

Figure 6.1
Inserting a picture from the ClipArt Gallery

Go back one page.

Show all categories.

Import clips from another source.

Connect to Microsoft for more clips.

Type in keywords.

Change to small window.

Select a category.

Scroll to view more categories or clips.

3. Click a category button to display the clips associated with that group, or type one or more keywords in the **Search for clips** box to narrow your search (Figure 6.2).

4. Page up and down to review the clips in a category. More clips are available in each category if you click in the **Keep Looking** area at the bottom center of the dialog box. (When the buttons are no longer visible, you know that you have seen all the images associated with that category or subject area).

5. Move the mouse pointer over a picture to see information about the clip, such as the subject, file size, and file type.

6. Use the buttons on the toolbar to move backward or forward one page at a time, or to show All Categories (Figure 6.1).

7. Click the *thumbnail* (miniature version) of a picture to select it.

Result: As soon as you click the picture, the pop-up menu shown in Figure 6.3 *pops up*, or appears. Now you can use the menu to:

❍ Insert the clip onto your slide.
❍ Preview a larger version of the image or review the animated aspects of a motion clip.

Figure 6.2
Searching for clips

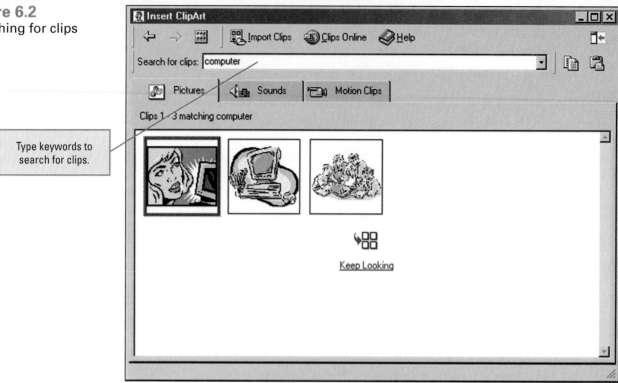

Type keywords to search for clips.

○ Add the clip to the Favorites category so that you can easily access it in the future.
○ Search through the categories to find pictures similar to the one you have selected.

 TIPS FROM A PRO: To insert an object or background into your presentation from the Web, you must first copy it. Place your cursor on the item, right-click, and choose the appropriate command from the shortcut menu that appears to save

Figure 6.3
ClipArt pop-up menu

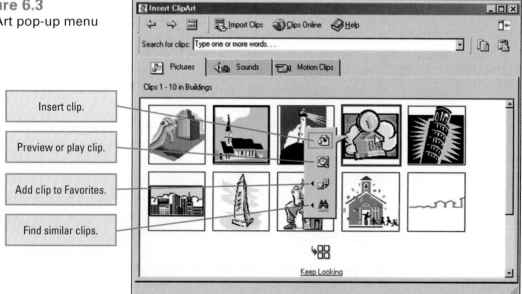

Insert clip.

Preview or play clip.

Add clip to Favorites.

Find similar clips.

the image to a folder or disk. Now you can add it to your presentation using one of the methods described later in this task.

INSERT A PICTURE FROM THE GALLERY

 CORE OBJECTIVE: **Add a picture from the ClipArt Gallery**

 EXPERT OBJECTIVE: **Add animated GIFs**

How: After you find and select a piece of art that you want to add to your slide, you can insert it using one of several techniques. Regardless of the method that you choose, you may be prompted to insert the PowerPoint or Microsoft Office CD-ROM that stores the picture.

○ **Pop-up menu.** Select a clip and click the **Insert Clip** button.
○ **Drag and drop.** This might be the easiest way to insert a picture—you can add and position the picture in one move with the following steps.
　1. Click to select the clip, and while holding down the mouse button, drag.
　2. As you begin to drag, the dialog box shrinks and moves to the left of the viewing window. The mouse cursor is joined by a small rectangle with a fuzzy border, and a dashed line placement box. When you reach the spot where you would like to place the clip, release the mouse button. The clip appears on your slide and the dialog box automatically minimizes.
○ **Copy and paste.** You can also use the copy and paste techniques that you learned in Chapter 3, "Edit Text," to insert clip art. Use these steps:
　1. Select a clip, right-click, and choose Copy.
　2. Right-click the slide where you what to place the clip and choose Paste.

Result: If the picture you've added is a motion clip, its animated aspects are visible only if you are viewing the presentation in Slide Show view.

 TIPS FROM A PRO: Pictures should be added only when they add meaning. Sometimes it's difficult to restrain yourself from inserting images onto your slides just because they're "cute," but they can actually divert attention away from your message, or add an unprofessional quality. Of course, this ignores the possibility that you are *trying* to divert attention from, say, last quarter's dismal financial report. In which case, a carefully positioned motion clip might be just the thing.

 TIPS FROM A PRO: When you save your presentation, you will notice that the file size has dramatically increased. Graphics require more file space than text files. Unfortunately just shrinking the picture doesn't affect the file size, so you won't save disk space by making a picture smaller. If storage space is an issue, add pictures with caution, or keep several disks handy. A single slide show with graphics—background design, images, and the like—can easily require more space than provided by a single 3½-inch floppy disk.

INSERT A PICTURE FROM A FILE

How: To insert a picture that you have saved in a disk location, follow these steps:

1. Select the slide where you want to add the picture and choose **Insert|Picture**, and then choose **From File** from the submenu.
2. When the Insert Picture dialog box appears (Figure 6.4), locate the drive and folder location of the file in the Look In box. Click to select the file.
3. If the dialog box View option is set on Preview, you can see a sample of the picture on the right side of the dialog box. Double-click the filename or click **Insert** to add this clip to your slide.

Figure 6.4
Inserting a picture from a file

Click to select a picture.

Preview picture.

Click to insert.

 TIPS FROM A PRO: To delete a picture from a slide, click to select it, and then press **Delete** or **backspace**.

 TIPS FROM A PRO: After you have inserted a picture, you can duplicate it by selecting the object and choosing **Edit|Duplicate**, or using **Copy** and then **Paste**.

Result: A copy of the picture that you saved has been inserted onto your slide. When you look at it, it may seem like it's too small, too big, or in the wrong location. If this is the case, you can rest in the knowledge that you'll learn how to change all these characteristics in subsequent tasks.

 TIPS FROM A PRO: Motions clips are a different file type than most of the other pieces of clip art in the gallery—they are animated GIF files rather than WMF files. Still, you aren't limited to using these two types of graphics files when you want to dress up your slides. You can use any of the following file types as images in PowerPoint without installing additional software components: EMF, PNG, BMP, JPG (scanned pictures).

 THOUGHT QUESTION: Why are many of the PowerPoint 2000 clips stored on a disk rather than loaded onto your hard drive?

C *CORE OBJECTIVE:* Scale and size an object including clip art

E *EXPERT OBJECTIVE:* Customize clip art and other objects (Resize, scale, etc.)

What: You have just inserted a picture on your slide and immediately see that although it is close to what you want, it's not exactly right either. Rather than repeating the process of searching for and inserting another picture, modify it to suit your specific requirements. You can customize pictures and clip art in several ways, including the following:

❍ Resize to smaller or larger dimensions
❍ *Scale*, or resize in proportion to the original
❍ *Crop*, or trim off one or more edges
❍ Change to black and white or grayscale
❍ Increase or reduce contrast and brightness

To modify a piece of art, the first step is to click to select the object. As soon as you do this, eight sizing handles appear at each corner and along the edges of the picture (remember these from working with text boxes in Chapter 2, "Work with Text") and the Picture toolbar appears (Figure 6.5). The second step is to decide whether to use the handy mouse and the button, or to use the slower, more precise dialog box.

Figure 6.5
A selected picture

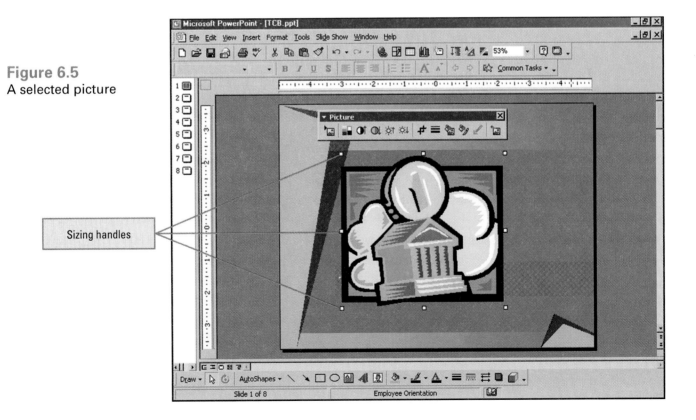

Sizing handles

Why: Wouldn't it be great if every time that you add a picture that it is the exact size that you want and its colors blend flawlessly with the slide background? A picture has to fit the document, not only in size but also in appearance. This isn't just a matter of personal preferences—often these characteristics impact the object's usefulness. If you are going to print overheads or handouts in black and white, for example, you will want to use pictures that look good in those colors.

RESIZE AND SCALE A PICTURE

How: You can change the size of a picture or scale it in relation to the original by using the mouse (quickest) or by accessing the Format Picture dialog box (most precise). (You can also use these techniques to resize the shapes and objects that you learn about in Task 3.)

To use the mouse, follow these steps:

1. Place the mouse pointer over one of the four corner sizing handles until it turns into a diagonal two-headed arrow. Grab the handle and drag in or out. The picture will change sizes but stay in the same scale as the initial piece of art.
2. Place the mouse pointer over an edge sizing handle and drag. This changes the picture's dimensions by elongating or shrinking the height or width, and results in a distortion when compared to the original picture.

To use the menus, follow these steps:

1. Select the picture to be modified and open the dialog box in one of the following ways:
   - Click the **Format Picture** button on the Picture toolbar.
   - Choose **Format|Picture** from the menu.
   - Right-click and choose **Format Picture** from the shortcut menu.
2. Click the **Size** tab to see the dialog box shown in Figure 6.6. Type the exact measurements for height and width in the respective boxes, or under **Scale**, specify a percent to increase or decrease the dimensions relative to the original picture.
3. Click **OK** to close the dialog box and implement your changes.

Result: If you drag one of the edge sizing handles, you may stretch or squash the picture out of proportion. If this wasn't your intention, and you want to restore the picture to its original size, access the Format Picture dialog box and click the **Reset** button.

Figure 6.6
Size tab of the Format Picture dialog box

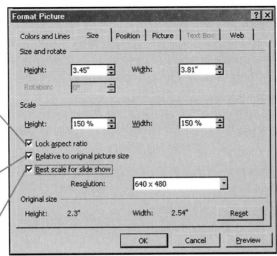

Keep the image in its original proportions of height and width.

Show the new size in relation to the original height and width.

Let PowerPoint determine the best size.

CROP A PICTURE

How: After you select a picture, you can cut, or *crop*, the edges off pictures using either of the following procedures:

To use the mouse, follow these steps:

1. Click the **Crop** button on the picture toolbar. The mouse pointer changes to indicate cropping (Figure 6.7).
2. Position the cropping pointer over one of the sizing handles, press and hold the left mouse button, and drag inward. The pointer changes again, as shown in Figure 6.8.

Figure 6.7 Getting ready to crop a picture

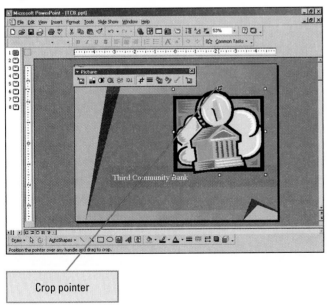

Crop pointer

Figure 6.8 Cropping a picture

To use the menus, follow these steps:

1. Access the Format Picture dialog box and click the **Picture** tab. The **Crop from** area shows the picture's current dimensions relative to an untrimmed picture (zeros in each category indicate that the picture hasn't been cropped).

2. Click the spin box arrows up or down, or click in the box that controls the side that you want to crop from and enter a number to designate an amount to crop.

 TIPS FROM A PRO: If you want to add a solid space between a graphic and its border (that is, to increase the amount of space around the graphic that is within the area defined by the picture borders), but not affect the picture itself, enter negative numbers in the **Crop from** boxes or drag out with the mouse pointer. To fill this "empty" space, refer to Task 4.

 THOUGHT QUESTION: Why would you enter "empty space" around a picture?

Result: The image is smaller and, depending on what you trimmed off, may look very different from your original picture (see Figure 6.9). If you want to return to the original picture, click the **Reset Picture** button on the Picture toolbar. If you only want to return the edges, not reverse all of the changes that you have made, click the **Undo** button.

Figure 6.9
Cropped picture

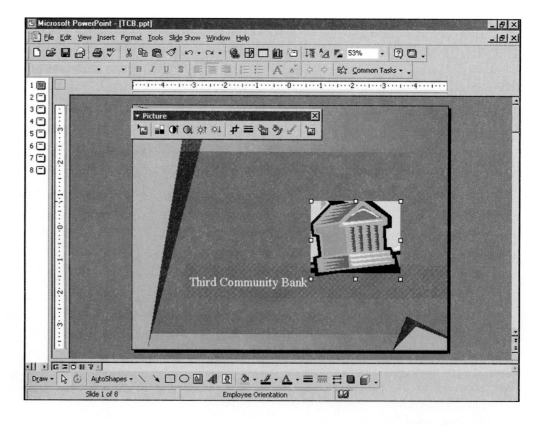

CHANGE IMAGE CONTROL SETTINGS

How: After you insert a picture and have selected it, you can change it from colored to black and white, adjust the contrast or alter the brightness of the image. Again, you can use the toolbar or access the dialog box for more control.

To use the mouse follow these steps:

1. To change a picture in one of the following four ways, click the **Image Control** button (Figure 6.10) and select one of the options:
   - **Automatic.** Restores the pictures original colors
   - **Grayscale.** Shades of gray
   - **Black and white.** Changes your image to pure black and white
   - ***Watermark.*** Converts the picture to preset levels of brightness and color contrast to create a transparent image that you might use for a task such as placing a company logo behind a presentation title
2. To increase or decrease the level of contrast, repeatedly click one of the **Contrast** buttons.
3. To increase or decrease the brightness, repeatedly click one of the **Brightness** buttons.

Figure 6.10
Image Control menu

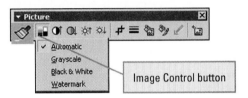

To use the menus, follow these steps:

1. Access the Format Picture dialog box and click the **Picture** tab.
2. Now you can change one or all of the following characteristics:
   - To change the Image Control color, drop down the Color list and choose a variation.
   - To change the picture's brightness, drag the slider right to lighten, left to darken, or enter an exact number in the relevant box. (The higher the number, the brighter your picture will be.)
   - To change the color contrast, drag the slider or enter a number in the box.
   - To recolor various components of the picture click **Recolor** and make the desired changed in the Recolor Picture dialog box. (This option is only available for Windows Metafiles (designated by a wmf file extension.)

TIPS FROM A PRO: Sometimes you might want to recolor a piece of clip art for use in a Word document. You can make the changes in PowerPoint and then copy and paste as follows:

- Insert the image onto a PowerPoint slide.
- Access the Recolor Picture dialog box and modify the clip.
- Copy the picture and open the Word document.
- Place the insertion point where you would like to insert the clip and choose **Edit|Paste Special** and select **Picture (Enhanced Metafile)**.

Figure 6.11
Sample image
control settings

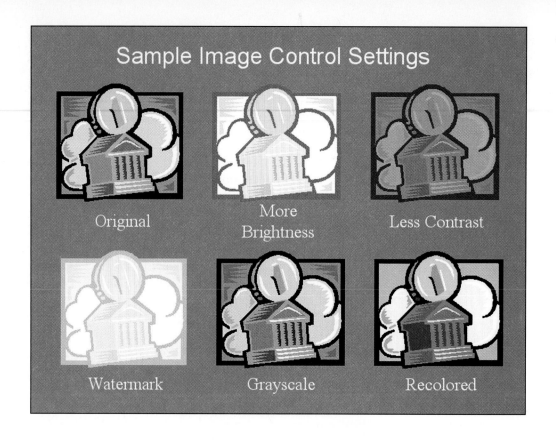

Result: Your picture has undergone minor or major modification. Look at the images shown in Figure 6.11 to see some of the possible results of making some of these changes.

TASK 3   *Add Objects and Shapes*

CORE OBJECTIVE: **Add and group objects using the Drawing toolbar**

What: The Drawing toolbar presents a handy little device for—you guessed it—drawing different kinds of objects. You can make your own drawings or insert ready-made objects (*AutoShapes*) such as squares, circles, and block arrows, from the AutoShapes Gallery (Figure 6.12).

Why: Despite all the available clip art choices, sometimes you need a different way to enhance your ideas. With the Drawing toolbar, you can use an arrow to draw attention to a particular element, or build a professional looking diagram (a flow chart, for example).

How: Use the buttons shown in Table 6.1 and the mouse to make various drawing objects (or access the menu by choosing **Insert|Picture|AutoShape**). Remember to release the mouse button after creating the object to produce the desired effect.

Figure 6.12
AutoShapes menu

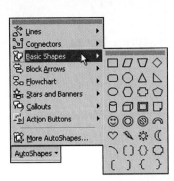

Table 6.1 Shape and Line-Drawing Buttons on the Drawing Toolbar

Button name	Button	Drawing method
Line	\	Drag on the page to draw a straight line. Ctrl+drag on the page to draw a line extending both directions from a center point. Shift+drag to constrain the line to 15-degree angles.
Arrow	↘	Drag from the tail to the head of the arrow. Shift+drag to constrain the line to 15-degree angles.
Rectangle	□	Drag from corner to corner to draw a rectangle. Click once to draw a square of set size. Shift+drag to draw a perfect square of any size. Ctrl+drag to draw a rectangle from a center point.
Oval	○	Drag to draw an oval. Click once to draw circle of set size. Shift+drag to draw a perfect circle of any size. Ctrl+drag to draw an oval from a center point.
AutoShapes	AutoShapes ▾	Click once to draw the shape a preset size. Drag to draw the shape any size. Shift+drag to keep height and width in proportion. Ctrl+drag to draw outward from a center point.

TIPS FROM A PRO: Want to make different styles of AutoShapes that are all the same size? Select the AutoShape and choose **Edit|Duplicate**. Now select the shape you just created and choose **Draw|Change AutoShape**.

Result: Your shape seems to "float" above the text, as well as any previously added objects. It is also surrounded by eight sizing handles that you can use to size, scale, or position the object, just as you did with pictures. In addition, some shapes have an ***adjustment handle***, designated by a small yellow square. This feature enables you to reshape the object by dragging the handle.

TIPS FROM A PRO: Want to add a shape or a piece of clip art to every slide? Insert the art on the master slide.

TIPS FROM A PRO: Want to change the boxy shape of your placeholders? Find and insert an attractive AutoShape, and type in some text. Select the shape and drag it to the border of an *empty* placeholder and release the mouse button. The shape immediately resizes to fit the placeholder borders. This can be a tricky process; don't give up!

CORE OBJECTIVE: **Apply formatting**

CORE OBJECTIVE: **Rotate and fill an object**

CORE OBJECTIVE: **Scale and size an object including clip art**

What: After you create a drawing object on your slides, you customize it in dozens of ways, including the following:

○ Change the fill color.
○ Restyle and recolor lines.
○ Add special effects, such as shadows and 3-D.
○ Rotate and flip the object.
○ Resize the object.

When you change any of these features you have the option of using the quick method—the mouse, or of using the menus. The menus are slower but offer you the ability to make more precise changes and to change several aspects in one place.

Why: It would be difficult for PowerPoint to include enough shapes to satisfy every user's individual needs. Instead, the basic models are incorporated, along with the tools to tailor them to fit your personal tastes and requirements.

CHANGE FILL COLOR

How: When you first draw a shape, it is a preset color (depending on the default that is set). You can change the color of a selected shape, and add fill effects, with the Drawing toolbar or the menus.

To use the mouse, follow these steps:

1. Select the object and click the **Fill Color** button to apply the default, or click the arrow beside the button to see more colors (see Figure 6.13).

Figure 6.13
Changing fill colors

Figure 6.14
Adding Fill Effects

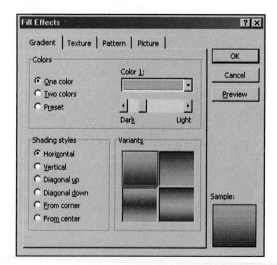

2. Choose one of the visible colors, click to see more colors or to add fill effects, as you learned in Chapter 5 (see Figure 6.14).

To use the Format AutoShape dialog box, follow these steps:.

1. Double-click the object or choose **Format|AutoShape.** When the dialog box appears, click the **Colors and Lines** tab.
2. Drop down the **Fill Color** box, and choose one of the available options.

 TIPS FROM A PRO: You can change the default object fill color. Double-click the object, click the **Colors and Lines** tab, change the fill color, and check the **Default for new objects** box.

Result: The object displays the solid or fill effect option that you selected. If you prefer that the shape have no fill, like the *no-fill* object in Figure 6.15, choose the **No Fill** option.

Figure 6.15
Sample shape fills

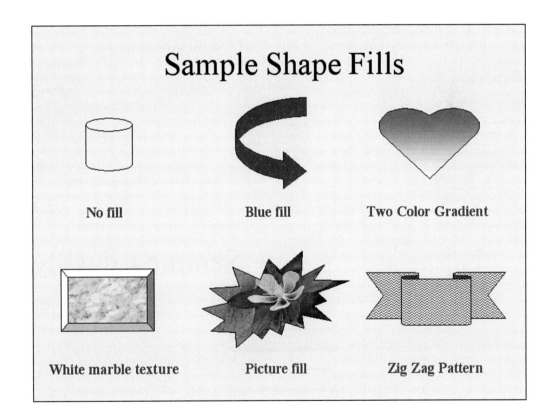

CHANGE LINE AND ARROW COLOR AND STYLE

How: You can change the color, thickness, or style of a line that you add with the Drawing toolbar. First click the object to select it.

The borders around shapes are also a form of line. Therefore, with the exception of the arrow styles, you can format them using the techniques in this task.

To use the mouse, follow these steps.

1. Click the **Line Style** button to display the varieties of lines that you can apply to the shapes and lines that you have drawn (Figure 6.16).
2. Click the **Dash Style** button to change any line styles to dotted or dashed lines (see Figure 6.17).
3. Click the **Line Color** button. The choices that you see are similar to the Fill Color button (see Figure 6.18).
4. Click the **Arrow Style** button to add or change the arrow style of a line. Figure 6.19 shows some arrow choices.

To use the dialog box, follow these steps:

1. Double-click the object, choose **Format|AutoShape**, or right-click the object, and choose **Format AutoShape** to access the Format AutoShape dialog box.
2. Click the appropriate tab and change the desired characteristics.

Figure 6.16 Line style choices

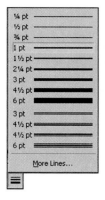

Figure 6.17 Dash Style choices

Figure 6.18 Line color choices

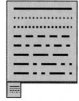

Figure 6.20 Sample line styles

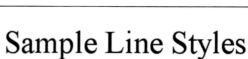
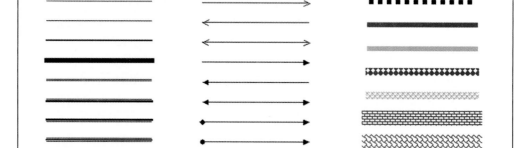

Figure 6.19
Arrow style choices

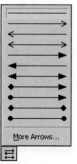

Result: You can combine the described features and make many interesting and functional lines. Figure 6.20 shows a few of the possible styles. As with fill color, when you don't want a line around an object, click the **Line Color** button and choose **No Line**.

ADD SHADOW AND 3-D EFFECTS

How: Shadow and 3-D are two of the most dramatic effects that you can add to your shapes and lines. Select an object and use these buttons to bring your flat shape to life:

To add shadow to an object, use these steps:

1. Click the **Shadow** button (Figure 6.21) to add one of PowerPoint's preset shadows to an object.
2. To customize the shadow color and *offset* (the direction and depth of the shadow) choose **Shadow Settings** to show the Shadow Settings toolbar, shown in Figure 6.22.
3. To remove a shadow, click the button and choose **No Shadow**.

To add 3-D effects to an object, use these steps:

1. Click the **3-D** button and see the variety of effects that you can add to your shape (Figure 6.23).
2. Choose **3-D Settings** to customize the color, tilt, depth, lighting, and surface texture with the 3-D toolbar, shown in Figure 6.24.
3. To remove a shadow, click the button and choose **No 3-D**.

Result: Clearly there are dozens of possible variations for adding shadows or 3-D effects to objects. Figure 6.25 illustrates a few of them.

Figure 6.21
Shadow options

Figure 6.22
Shadow Settings toolbar

Figure 6.23
3-D effects

Figure 6.24
3-D toolbar

Figure 6.25 Sample 3-D and shadow effects

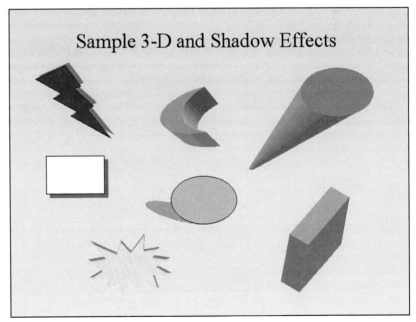

Tips from a Pro: You can add shadows, but not 3-D, to most pictures and pieces of clip art.

ROTATE AND FLIP AN OBJECT

How: To change an object's direction or its angle of position, select it, and then you can use PowerPoint's flip and rotate features.

To rotate an object using the mouse, follow these steps:

1. Click the **Free Rotate** button or click the **Draw** button on the Drawing toolbar and choose **Rotate or Flip|Free Rotate**. Now the sizing handles have changed to four green circles—one on each corner—and the mouse pointer is represented by a partial circle.
2. Drag any of the green handles in a circular direction around the shape, as you see in Figure 6.26.
3. After you have finished, press **Esc** or click away from the shape to return the mouse pointer to normal.

To flip an object upside down, sideways, or even turn it backward, select the object, click the **Draw** button, and choose one of the menu choices under Rotate or Flip (Figure 6.27).

 Tips from a Pro: You can also rotate objects using the Format Object dialog box. Access the box, click the **Size** tab and enter the number of degrees that you want to rotate the object in the **Rotation** box.

Result: When you rotate and flip a drawing object, you are moving it from side-to-side, through one-dimensional space. Conversely, if you add a 3-D effect to an object, you can tilt it right, left, up, or down like the examples in Figure 6.28. You can see samples of rotated, flipped, and tilted objects, both vertically and horizontally, in Figure 6.28.

Figure 6.26 Rotating an object

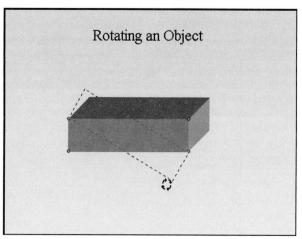

Figure 6.27 Draw menu

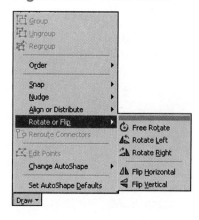

Figure 6.28
Sample objects
rotated, tilted, and
flipped

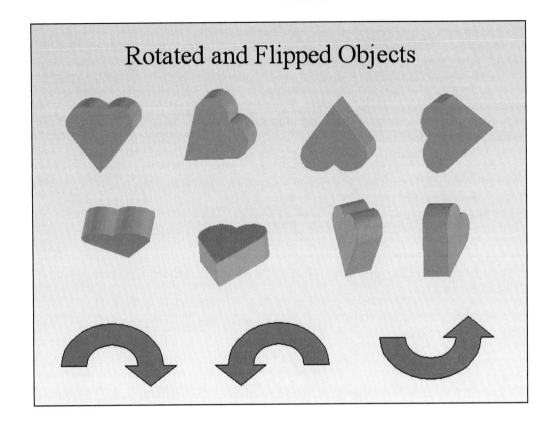

Rotated and Flipped Objects

 TIPS FROM A PRO: You can only rotate and flip drawing objects, not pictures or clip art. If the clip art image is a Windows Metafile (WMF), however, you can ungroup it to change it into a drawing object and then modify it in parts or as a whole.

SELECT MULTIPLE OBJECTS

How: If you want to apply the same effect to several objects you could select and format them one by one. It is more efficient, however, to select all the objects at one time, and then apply the formatting in one move. You can select multiple objects in either of the following ways:

○ Click the **Select Objects** button on the Drawing toolbar, click the slide, and while holding down the mouse button, drag to surround all the objects with a dotted line (Figure 6.29). When you have surrounded the objects that you were aiming for, click the **Select Objects** button again to restore the normal mouse pointer.

○ Click the first object, hold down the **Shift** key, and select additional items. If you want to remove one of the items that you have selected while keeping the other items intact, hold down the **Shift** key and click the one that you want to omit (this technique works with both options).

Result: The selected objects now include sizing handles, as you see in Figure 6.29. When you perform one of the operations that you have just learned (coloring or flipping, for example), all these objects are included.

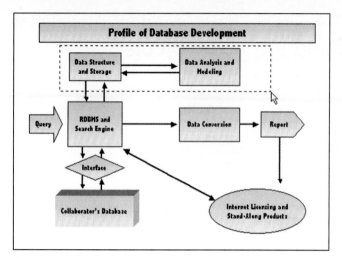

Figure 6.29 Selecting multiple objects with the
Select Objects tool

Multiple objects selected

ALIGN, ORDER, AND GROUP OBJECTS

CORE OBJECTIVE: **Add and group objects made using the Drawing toolbar**

How: After you create several drawing objects that are intended to work
together (such as the various parts of a flow chart), you may want to
align them precisely, arrange them in various layers on top of one
another, or group them together to form a single unit. The choices on
the Draw menu of the Drawing toolbar make this a simple process.

○ To align several objects simultaneously, select them and choose
Draw|Align or Distribute. Now you must specify how you want
them aligned. You can align objects relative to each other or relative
to the page (Figure 6.30).

Figure 6.30
Aligning objects

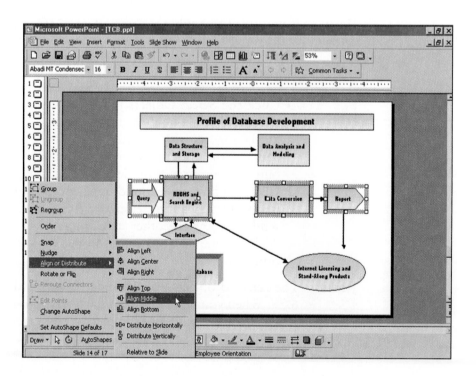

❍ To *order*, or stack objects behind your text, behind other objects, or sandwiched between two others (like the pieces of a layer cake), click to select the first object, and then choose **Draw|Order** to see the options shown in Figure 6.31.

❍ To join separate objects into a single unit, select them and then choose **Draw|Group**.

Result: After items have been grouped (Figure 6.32), they no longer have individual sizing handles—just a single set. In effect, they now form one object; therefore you can size, position, and modify them at one time. Later, if you want to ungroup them, reselect them and choose **Draw|Ungroup**. Figure 6.33 shows several objects that have been aligned, stacked, or grouped.

Figure 6.31 Ordering objects

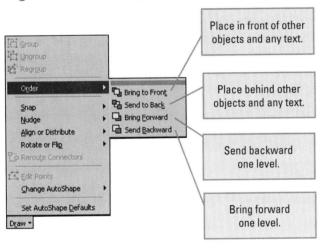

Figure 6.32 Ordering objects

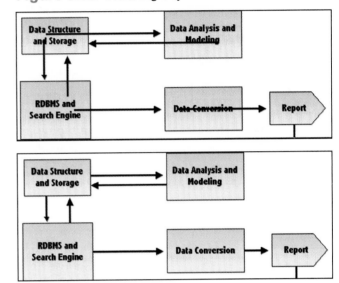

Figure 6.33 Samples of aligned, stacked, and grouped objects

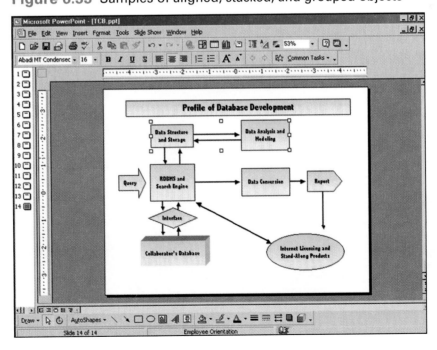

TIPS FROM A PRO: If the clip art you chose is a Windows Metafile, you can convert it to a drawing object so that you can rotate, flip, align, and the like. To convert clip art, select the picture and choose **Draw|Ungroup**; then choose **Draw|Group**.

TASK 5 | Add Text to Shapes

C

CORE OBJECTIVE: **Place text inside a shape using a text box**

What: You learned how to make text boxes in Chapter 2, and you can use them to add text in or on shapes or any other type of graphic (Figure 6.34). However, many PowerPoint shapes behave much as text boxes; they accept text and then assume many of the same characteristics.

Why: The usefulness of shapes is increased when you have the ability to add text to them. Now they can show *and* tell! Create a stop sign by adding text to a circle, announce a new product with a banner, or direct attention to the next step in a flow chart with a numbered arrow.

How: Click and type! That's the easiest way to add text to a shape. Just click the object and begin typing (Figure 6.35). You can add the object and begin typing in the text as soon as the object appears.

Result: After you add text, you can apply font formatting, or use the techniques that you learned in previous tasks to modify the shape. However, you may want to apply additional formatting after you add text to a shape. To format the object, or to modify its text box features (Figure 6.36), access the dialog box in one of the following ways:

○ Double-click the border of the object.
○ Choose **Format|AutoShape**.
○ Right-click the object and choose **Format AutoShape** from the menu.

Figure 6.34
Adding text to a shape
using a text box

Figure 6.35
Adding text to a shape

Figure 6.36
Formatting text box
features of a shape

Check to apply
Word Wrap.

Check to increase text box size
to accommodate text.

Check to rotate the
text by 90°.

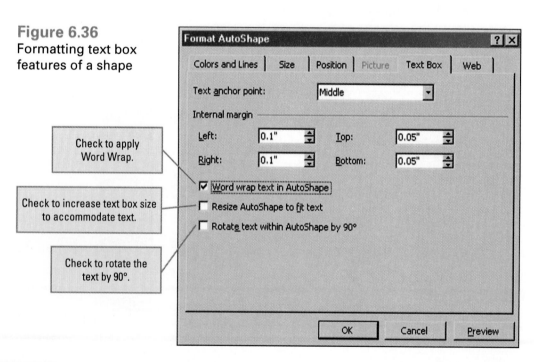

Figure 6.37
Sample text in shapes

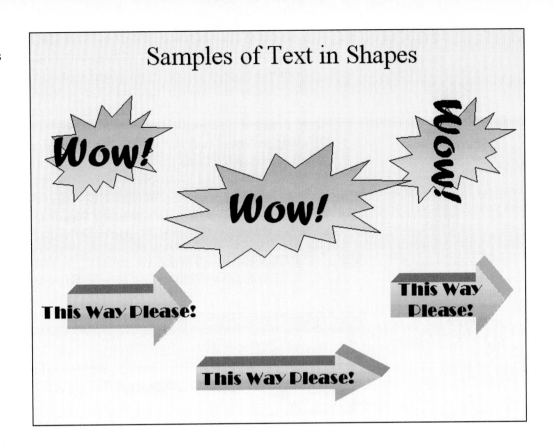

Figure 6.37 shows some examples of shapes with text added.

 TIPS FROM A PRO: The PowerPoint "click and type" feature isn't available when you create shapes in Word. You can make a shape that includes text in PowerPoint, however, and then copy it into Word.

 TIPS FROM A PRO: You can also add text to a shape by creating a text box, adding text, and then positioning it on the object.

 THOUGHT QUESTION: Why do you need text boxes if we can add text to any AutoShape?

TASK 6   *Create and Modify WordArt*

 C *CORE OBJECTIVE:* Add and group shapes made using Drawing toolbar

What: You know how to format text and insert graphics to communicate a message to your audience. Still PowerPoint offers an additional method for creating text called WordArt that includes many of the features available with shapes. *WordArt* enables you to make decorative text and then define its shape and fill characteristics. There are 25 predefined WordArt styles to choose from but each design can also be customized in many ways. You can add or increase the shadowing, add or increase the depth of the 3-D effect, adding dramatic fill effects, and the like.

Why: Sometimes font styles, even when you add fancy lettering and color, don't carry the impact that you are seeking. When you want to make one piece of text stand out from the rest, use WordArt. Or, if you want to create a designer graphic using text, use WordArt. The shape and color of letters and the words that they form are an important part of your message. Even without your spoken words, they can create a casual or a formal atmosphere or convey optimism or gloom.

How: You can turn text into WordArt by using the button on the Drawing toolbar or the menus. To access the WordArt Gallery and the predefined styles shown in Figure 6.38, use either of the following methods:

○ Click the **Insert WordArt** button.
○ Choose **Insert|Picture** and choose **WordArt** from the submenu.

Figure 6.38
WordArt Gallery

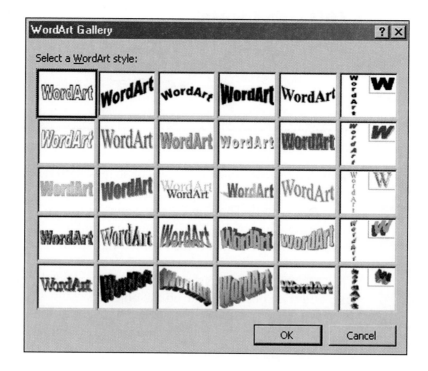

When the WordArt Gallery appears, you can change your text to a graphic as follows:

1. Click the design thumbnail to select a style and access a second dialog box (you can change the shape, color, and other properties later).
2. In the Edit WordArt Text dialog box, type your text, choose a font style and size, and then click **OK**.

 TIPS FROM A PRO: To make WordArt out of the words of existing text, select the text before you access the WordArt Gallery. The step will save you from having to retype the text. After the WordArt appears, you can delete the text that you used as your model.

Result: WordArt appears on screen with an adjustment handle and sizing handles, as you see in Figure 6.40. The WordArt toolbar (Figure 6.39) is

Figure 6.39 WordArt toolbar

Figure 6.40 A sample WordArt object

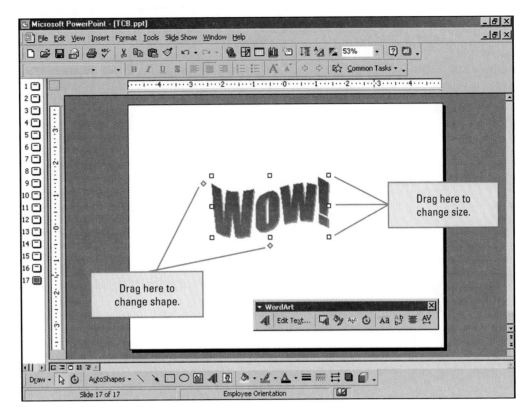

also visible. Because the art is already selected, you can make the following modification using the toolbar or by choosing **Format|WordArt** (you can make any of the changes later as well by selecting the object).

○ Size and position the WordArt as you do with pictures.
○ Drag the yellow adjustment handle to change the shape of the WordArt.
○ Group with other objects and shapes.
○ Edit the text or return to the gallery.
○ Adjust the rotation.
○ Change text alignment, and spacing
○ Change the shadow, fill, line, and 3-D effect, just as you do with any drawing object.

TASK 7 | *Reposition a Picture or Object*

What: When you insert a picture or object from the Drawing toolbar, you often find that it needs to be moved to a different location on the slide. In PowerPoint, pictures and shapes are floating objects that exist in a different layer than text or than each other. You can move them anywhere on the slide, even over text.

Why: To add to the overall attractiveness of your slides, pictures must be positioned appropriately. If randomly placed, they weaken rather than strengthen your message.

How: Repositioning a picture or a drawing object is easy!

1. Place the mouse pointer anywhere over the item until you see the four-headed mouse pointer.
2. Hold down the left mouse button and drag. As you begin to move the picture or object, a dotted line that represents the outline of the image appears.
3. When you reach the desired location, release the mouse button.

 TIPS FROM A PRO: To move or copy a graphical image to another slide, use the Cut, Copy, and Paste procedure.

Result: As soon as you release the mouse button, the picture is repositioned. If it is still not in the right spot, move it again.

 TIPS FROM A PRO: You can modify and format placeholders just as you would other objects. Select a placeholder, and then move it, resize it, or double-click the border to apply formatting.

TASK 8   *Add Sound*

 E   *EXPERT OBJECTIVE:* **Add sound**

What: Add jingles, music, or other sounds to your slide show and then program them to play at designated points in your presentation. You can get sound clips from a number of sources, including the following:

○ The Clip Gallery
○ Clip Gallery Live
○ The Windows Media folder
○ Tracks from your own CDs
○ The Web

Why: In some instances you may have a great reason to add sound to your slide show—you are presenting an advertisement and sound is integral to the product, for example. At other times it might be appropriate to add a bit of soothing music to your introductory slide and then play it as you wait for your audience to settle in before you start your presentation. Still, the self-running kiosk-style slide show, which repeats over and over, is possibly the best use for sound because it won't be competing with you.

ADD SOUND CLIPS FROM THE GALLERY

How: The gallery contains two kinds of sound files: WAV files, represented by a small speaker; and MIDI files, which appear as a musical score. Finding and inserting the file is similar to inserting a picture.

1. Click to select the first slide where you want music to play.
2. Choose **Insert|Movies and Sounds** and **Sound from Gallery** from the submenu. The Insert Sound dialog box appears (Figure 6.41).

Figure 6.41
Insert Sound dialog box

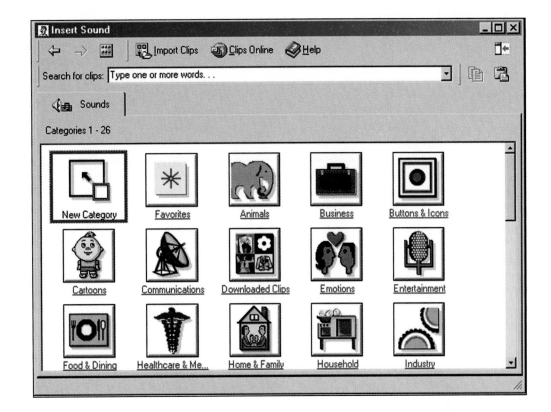

3. Click to select a category and search through the available clips. Click the **Keep Looking** area to see more clips.
4. To select a clip, click the icon. A pop-up menu, like the one shown in Figure 6.42, appears.
5. Click the **Play Clip** button to preview the clip.
6. Click the **Insert Clip** button, copy and paste or use drag and drop to add the clip to your presentation.

TIPS FROM A PRO: If you decide to use music, have a good reason to do so and choose it very carefully!

Result: A sound icon, represented by a tiny speaker, is now in the center of your slide. You are prompted by a dialog box or balloon to choose between playing the sound clip automatically when you reach this slide, or to

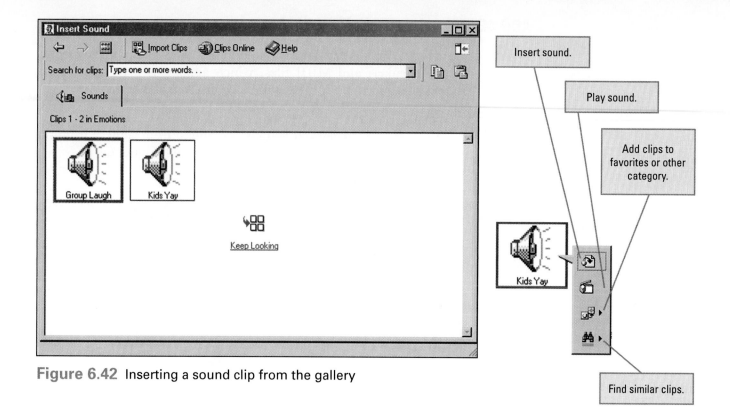

Figure 6.42 Inserting a sound clip from the gallery

play after you click the sound icon (Figure 6.43). As soon you respond to the prompt, it disappears. Now you can reposition the sound icon with the four-headed mouse pointer.

When you run your slide show, sound will only play as long as the slide show is on the slide where you inserted the sound icon. That is, when you move to the next slide, the music or other audio stops unless you revise the play specifications as described later in this task.

Figure 6.43
Choosing the
Automatic Play option

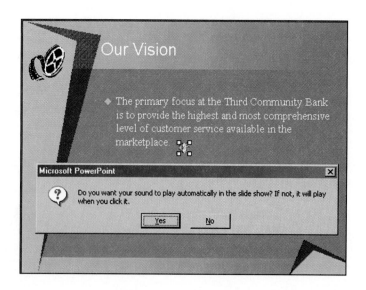

ADD CLIPS FROM A FILE

How: You can also insert sound clips that you have saved to a disk location.

1. Select the slide where you want the sound to begin.
2. Choose **Insert|Movies and Sounds**, and then choose **Sound from File** from the submenu to see the Insert Sound dialog box (Figure 6.44).
3. Click in the **Look in** box to search for the saved file. When you locate the clip, double-click the filename to add it to your slide.
4. When prompted, indicate whether you want the clip to play automatically when the show begins or to play after being clicked by the mouse.

Figure 6.44
Insert Sound dialog box

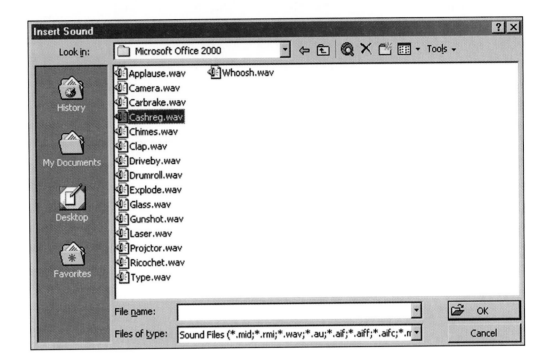

Result: Again you will see the sound icon appear on your slide. Sound insert this way can also be customized to play in one of the ways presented later in this task.

TIPS FROM A PRO: When you insert a sound clip from a file, make sure that you take the clip file with you if you are going to be showing the presentation on a computer other than the one you used to create it. Save the file in the same disk and folder location as the presentation. Then insert the sound clip onto your slide. Or, better yet, use PowerPoint's Pack and Go feature and bundle everything up to travel in one easy move. You learn how to use this feature in Chapter 7, "Get Ready for an Electronic Slide Show."

PLAY CDS

How: You don't have to listen to sound clips from the gallery or those that you have saved—program your favorite CD to play during a presentation. Select the slide where you want the CD track(s) to begin playing.

1. Choose **Insert|Movies and Sound|Play CD Audio Track**. The Movies and Sound Options dialog box appears (Figure 6.45).
2. Now you can make choices regarding play options:
   - Play the chosen track(s) over and over until the show finishes.
   - Designate the track(s) to play.
   - Enter the beginning and ending time for the track(s).
3. Click **OK** to implement and to be prompted about whether to play the CD automatically when you reach this slide or after you click the sound icon.

Figure 6.45
Movies and Sound
Options dialog box

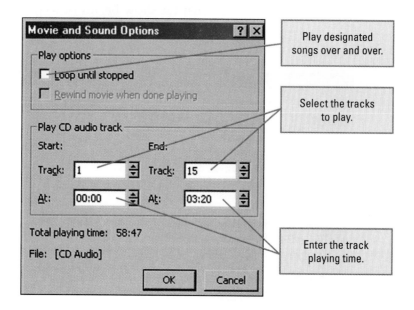

Result: A small movable, resizable CD icon is visible in the center of your slide. Now that you have programmed the CD to play, you can change or modify any of the play settings. When you begin the slide show, the CD plays as you have instructed.

 TIPS FROM A PRO: If you plan on playing music from a CD, don't forget to take it with you to the presentation.

 THOUGHT QUESTION: What happens if you add a sound clip and also insert a CD track to play on the same slide?

CUSTOMIZE PLAY OPTIONS

How: When you add any of the previously described forms of music you can customize the way that it plays. To modify sound play options: choose **Slide Show|Custom Animation** and click **Multimedia Settings**. The dialog box shown in Figure 6.46 displays and you can implement the following choices:
   - ○ Check **Hide while not playing** to conceal the sound or CD icon while the show is in progress.
   - ○ Clear the **Play Using Animation Order** check box to prevent sound from playing until all slide *animations* have occurred.

Figure 6.46
Customizing music play options

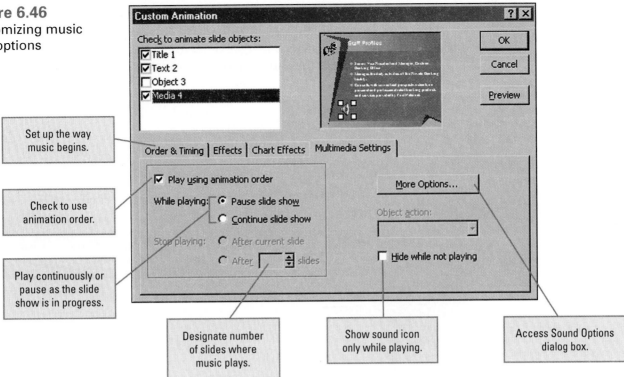

Set up the way music begins.

Check to use animation order.

Play continuously or pause as the slide show is in progress.

Designate number of slides where music plays.

Show sound icon only while playing.

Access Sound Options dialog box.

○ Elect to have the music play continuously as the slide show is in progress or to pause.

○ Change the number of slides where music plays.

○ Click **More Options** to revise other play preference, such as looping or the number of tracks to play if it is a CD.

○ Click the **Order and Timing** tab to have music play automatically when the slide show begins or on the click of a mouse. You can also specify the number of seconds that you want to elapse between events. (You learn more about this in Task 11.)

Result: When you begin the slide show, the CD or other sound clip plays as you have designated. If it is still not what you had in mind, tweak it using the same method.

TASK 9   *Add Video*

EXPERT OBJECTIVE: Add video

What: You can set up digitized movies and video clips to play at a specified point in your slide show.

Why: Sometimes your presentation will require you to show a movie or film clip—it's part of your work! By using this PowerPoint feature, you can blend it seamlessly into the presentation and provide a very professional look. There's no fooling around with those confusing VCR controls, just a smooth transition into digitized video.

How: Setting up and customizing a video to play is much like inserting sound. Click to select the slide where you want the video to begin and follow these steps:

1. Choose **Insert|Movies and Sounds|Movie from File** to access the Insert Movie dialog box (Figure 6.47).
2. Locate the drive and folder location of the file and click the filename to select it and click **OK**.
3. When prompted, indicate whether you want the movie to play automatically or to play after the movie icon is clicked.

Figure 6.47
Insert Movie
dialog box

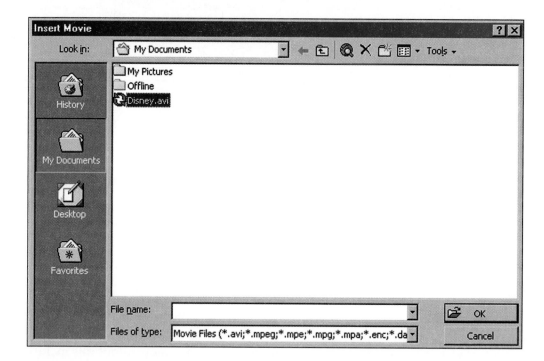

Note: When you choose **Insert|Movies and Sounds**, and then choose **Movie from Gallery**, you are not actually inserting a video; you are inserting one of the animated clips that are included in the Clip Gallery. Refer to Task 1 to insert one of these animated clips.

Result: The video plays according to the play guidelines that you have selected. To modify any of the setting, select the video icon, choose **Custom Animation**, and click the **Multimedia** tab (see Figure 6.48). Now you can specify the way that you want the video to play by choosing one or all of the following:

○ Check **Hide while not playing** to conceal the clip before and after it plays.
○ Clear the **Play using animation order** check box to keep the movie from playing until slide animations have occurred.
○ Pause the show until the video finishes, or have the video play continuously as the slide show is in progress. When you choose continuous play, you can move from slide to slide and the video will continue to

Figure 6.48
Customizing video
play options

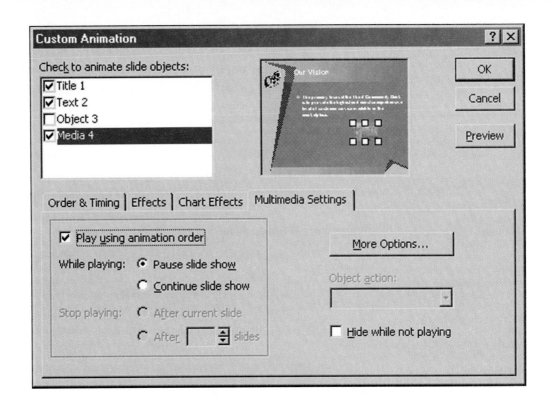

play on each of the slides that you have designated, or until it ends.
○ Designate the slide where the video will play.
○ Click **More Options** to have the video play over and over.
○ Click the **Order and Timing** tab to change whether the movie plays automatically, plays after a set period of time has elapsed, or plays on the click of a mouse. You can also specify the number of seconds that you want to pass between events. (You learn more about this in Task 11.)

TIPS FROM A PRO: Before you play a *relevant* video, briefly discuss what it is about and why you are showing it. Tell the audience what to look for—they will be more likely to pay attention. You can also stop the video briefly when a critical portion is shown to make sure that important information is not missed. If possible, show the video right after a break. Your audience will be less likely to nod off or lose interest.

TASK 10   *Use Slide Transitions*

CORE OBJECTIVE: Add slide transitions

What: The way that an electronic slide show moves from one slide to the next during the show is called a *transition*. Transitions can be as subtle—watch slide gracefully appear from black—or, they can be dramatic and include crazy sounds, such as breaking glass or skidding breaks. You can use one of PowerPoint's predefined varieties or create your own animation effects.

Why: Besides adding polish to your work, these special effects add variation and can help keep your audience alert and attentive.

How: Slide transitions can be added in the slide and outline panes or in Slide Sorter view. Still, Slide Sorter view offers an advantage because you can add transitions, preview them, and then view the overall effect in one location. To add transitions in Slide Sorter view, select the slide or slides where you want to add a transition effect and then use either of the methods described below. As usual, the dialog box offers more control and more options than the buttons.

To use the buttons, click to drop down the **Slide Transition** list and then choose a preset animation.

To use the dialog box, follow these steps:

1. Click the **Slide Transition** button or choosing **Slide Show|Slide Transition**.
2. Click to drop down the **Effects** list, shown in Figure 6.49, and select one of the available transitions. After you make a selection, you will see the option that you have chosen previewed on the thumbnail slide area.

Figure 6.49
Preset slide transitions

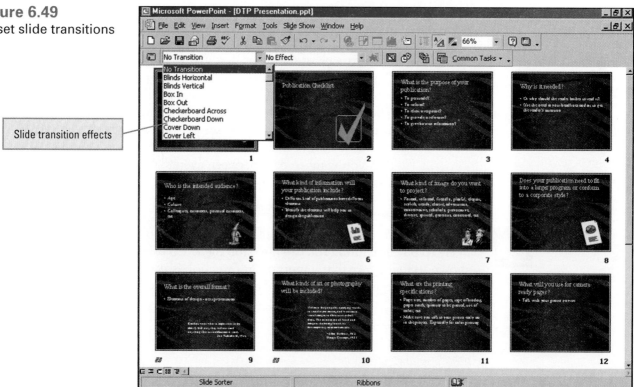

Slide transition effects

3. Click the sample picture again to repeat the preview (see Figure 6.50). You can now implement one or all of the following additional options:
   • Select the speed at which you would like the slides to transition.
   • Check whether you want the show to move to the next slide after a mouse click or automatically. (This option requires that you designate a time frame.)
   • Choose a sound to accompany each transition.
   • Apply to selected slides or to the entire presentation.

Figure 6.50
Adding slide
transitions in Slide
Sorter view

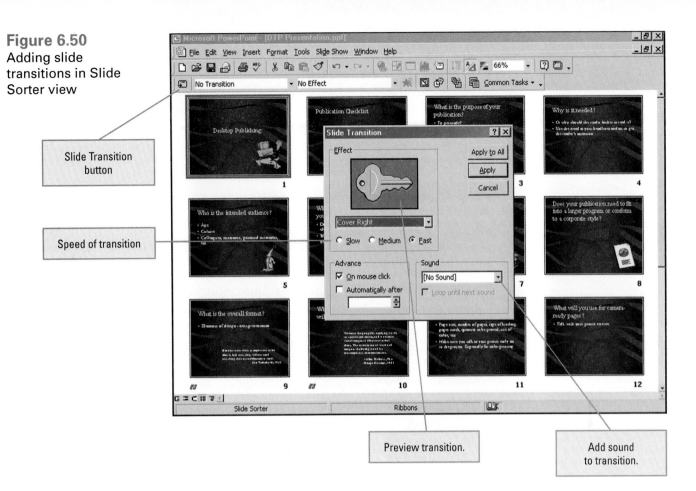

Result: When you run your show, your audience sees your professionally transitioning slides but you won't be able to see the transitions unless you are in slide show view (or you preview them). You can identify the slides that have transition effects in Slide Sorter view by the icon at the bottom of each slide miniature. Click the icon to preview the transition.

 TIPS FROM A PRO: Unless you are aiming for a wacky and wild slide show—a presentation to a class of first graders, for instance—one or two transitions styles per slide show is enough.

TASK **11** *Apply Animation*

 EXPERT OBJECTIVE: **Apply animation effects**

 CORE OBJECTIVE: **Animate text and objects**

What: You know how to add animated clip art, but you can also *animate*, or bring to life, many other items. Graphics, objects, pictures, movies, placeholders—almost anything that can be selected can also be animated. PowerPoint includes 14 different predefined animation styles that often include a special sound effect as well. Apply these effects or create your own unique variations.

Why: Why add animation? You can make goofy cartoon characters to add humor, or you can have a particular word or phrase enter with a sound (such as breaking glass) to communicate a certain meaning. (If you're at a presentation being sponsored by your firm, and see your name entering this way, it might be a great time to start a new job search.) However, the primary purpose for animating items is to focus attention by controlling the sequence in which information is presented; bullet points can be introduced one at a time.

APPLY PRESET ANIMATION EFFECTS

How: You can add predefined animation effects in Slide Sorter view or add and customize in the same location in both Slide and Outline views.

1. Select the item that you want to animate.
2. Choose **Slide Show|Preset Animation**, and without releasing the mouse button, choose one of the available alternatives (see Figure 6.51).

Figure 6.51
Adding preset animation

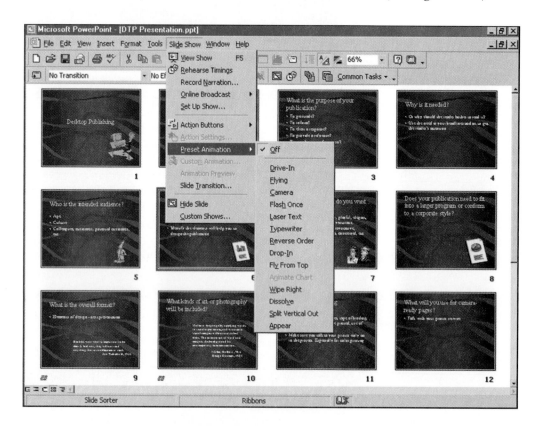

Result: You slide show has been brought to life! Each slide that you add animation to has an icon beside the transition icon in Slide Sorter view (Figure 6.52). Click the icon to preview the effect on one slide or select all the slides and choose **Slide Show|Animation** Preview to view animation in the show in the order that you set.

You can add additional effects or customize some transition characteristics. For example, words can come in from the top rather than from the right, or you can play different music during the animation. You learn how to do so in the next portion of this task.

To remove preset animation, select the slide(s), and choose **No Effect**.

Figure 6.52
Special effects

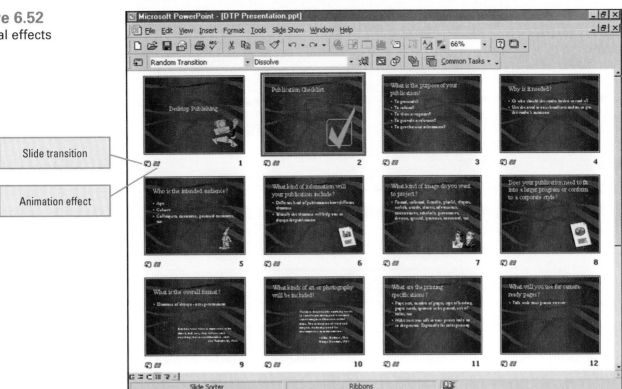

Slide transition

Animation effect

 TIPS FROM A PRO: Animations are interesting and fun. However, too much of a good thing can be overwhelming and unprofessional. Imagine a slide with transitioning slides, plus animated words being formed one letter at a time to the sound of a noisy, manual typewriter. Even if your audience doesn't run from the room, is this the image that you want to project?

APPLY CUSTOM ANIMATION EFFECTS

How: You can customize PowerPoint's preset animations or create your own special effects by combining the various options. Select the item(s) that you want to animate or modify in the slide pane or make your selections in the dialog box. Access the dialog box as follows:

❍ Choose **Slide Show|Custom Animation**.
❍ Right-click and choose **Custom Animation** from the shortcut menu.

Figure 6.53 presents the Custom Animation dialog box with the Effects tab selected. The upper-left portion of the box displays the items that can be animated. Check the items in the box to add or modify the animation effect. Conversely you can remove animation by clearing the box.

To apply custom animations:

1. Drop down the list in the first box under **Entry animation and sound**, and then select one of the animation styles.
2. To further modify the effect, click the drop-down arrow in the upper-right box in **Entry animation and sound** to display the animation options. Click to select an alternative.
3. To add sound, drop down the sound box and click an alternative, or choose **More**.

Figure 6.53
Adding custom
animation to an object

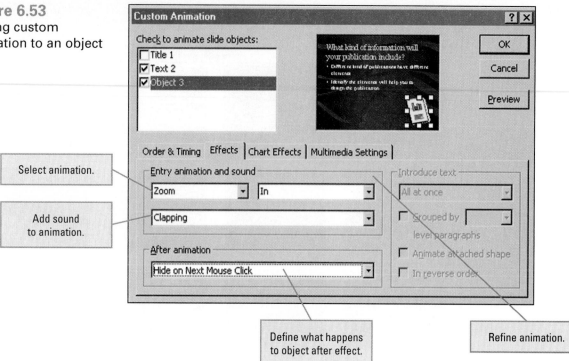

4. To determine what will take place after the animation has occurred, drop down the **After animation** list and make a selection.
5. If you are adding animation to the text in a text placeholder or in an AutoShape, you must make additional decisions, as shown in Figure 6.54.

Figure 6.54
Adding custom
animation effects
to text

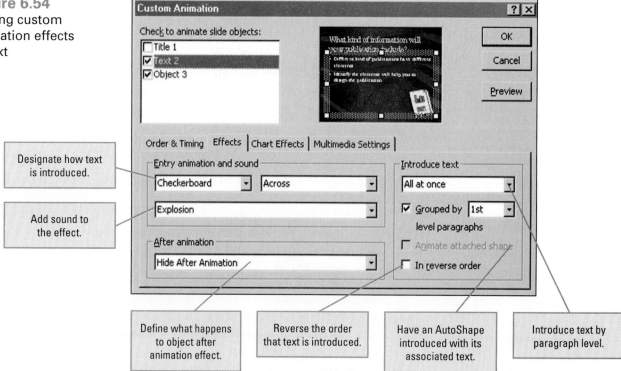

Figure 6.55
Changing the order and timing of animations

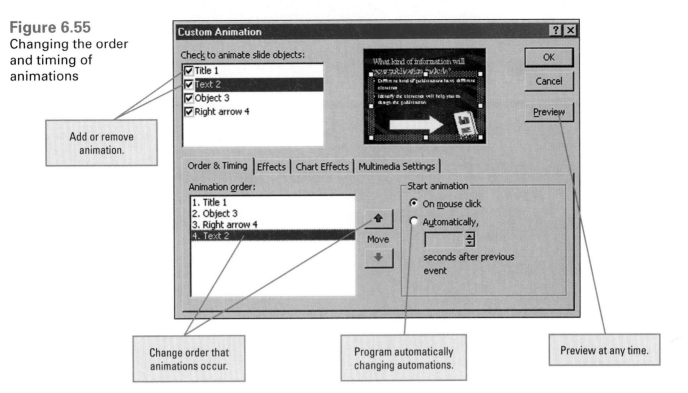

Add or remove animation.

Change order that animations occur.

Program automatically changing automations.

Preview at any time.

6. To set the order sequence in which object animations occur, click the **Order & Timing** tab. Now you can make one or all of the changes shown in Figure 6.55.
7. Choose **Slide Show|Animation Preview** to preview animations.

Result: The custom animations that you added dances across your screen while you are running the slide show. If you change your mind and want to remove them, you must select the item(s) in the slide pane, access the Custom Animations dialog box, and clear the check box beside each individual item.

Use PinPoint

After gaining the skills in this chapter, you can insert, format, and size pictures and drawing objects; add slide transitions and animation; and add video and sound. Now it's time to see what you can do with the PinPoint software. Remember, whenever you are unsure of what to do next, you can reread the relevant portion of the chapter or you can click Show Me for a live demonstration. Try these skills in PinPoint:

- Insert a clip art image
- Animated GIF
- Insert an object from a file
- Customize clip art
- Insert AutoShapes
- Scale an object
- Apply format to a shape
- Draw a master object

- Group objects
- Rotate and fill an object
- Text in a shape
- Word wrap text in an AutoShape
- Draw WordArt
- Text Animation
- Add video
- Add slide transitions
- Custom animation

Key Terms

You can find definitions for these words in this chapter.

Adjustment handle
Animation
AutoShape
Crop
Order
Scale
Slide transition
Watermark

Review Questions

You can use the following review questions and exercises to test your knowledge and skills. Answers are given in Appendix D, "Answers to Review Questions."

True/False

___ 1. You can use the same techniques to resize both scanned pictures and clip art.

___ 2. With all the "cool stuff" that can be added to your slide show, you can just stay home and let the show take care of itself.

___ 3. AutoShape is another term for a text box.

___ 4. Motion clips aren't the same thing as animated GIFs.

___ 5. You really can't have too many graphics on your slides.

___ 6. Special effects, such as 3-D and shadow, bring objects to life on the slide.

___ 7. Pictures add color to your visual aids, but serve no other useful purpose.

___ 8. After you have edited a picture, you can click Reset to return it to its original state.

___ 9. Fill effects in shapes are applied the same way as the fill effects used to create a slide background.

___ 10. The adjustment handle attached to certain shapes is designated by a small green square.

Multiple Choice

___ 1. Sizing handles enable you to:
   a. Adjust the size of a picture.
   b. Adjust the size of a shape.
   c. Reposition an object.
   d. Both a and b.
   e. None of the above.

___ 2. When you double-click a picture:
   a. It disappears.
   b. What happens depends on the file type.
   c. The Edit Picture dialog box appears.
   d. Nothing happens.
   e. Only a and b.

___ 3. The term slide transitions refers to:
   a. The order in which animations occur.
   b. The way that you switch from one view to the next.
   c. The manner in which slides change from one slide to another.
   d. What happens when you open a second presentation.
   e. The process of taking a blank slide and creating a thing of beauty.

___ 4. To reposition WordArt or another object:
   a. Click the object and drag it to a new location.
   b. Choose Edit|Cut and Edit|Paste.
   c. Right-click the object and choose Cut, move the cursor and choose Edit|Paste.
   d. Choose Edit|Duplicate.
   e. Only a and b.

___ 5. If you use this method to insert a clip from the gallery, you can control the placement at the same time.
   a. Copy and Paste.
   b. The pop-up menu.
   c. Cut and Paste.
   d. Drag and drop.
   e. Only a and b.

___ 6. When you group pictures and objects together and then select them:
   a. Any operations that you perform will include the entire group.
   b. There will be only one set of sizing handles.
   c. They automatically become the same color.
   d. They visibly merge into one object.
   e. Only a and b.

___ 7. To crop a picture, you must first:
   a. Access the Picture toolbar.
   b. Click to select the picture.
   c. Choose Format|Picture.
   d. Click the Format Picture button on the toolbar.
   e. All the above.

___ 8. AutoShapes can be:
   a. Rotated.
   b. Resized.
   c. Recolored.
   d. Repositioned.
   e. All of the above.

___ 9. To add sound to a slide show:
   a. Choose Insert|Movies and Sounds.
   b. Choose Slide Show|Movies and Sounds.
   c. Plug in a CD and it will automatically play at the desired time.
   d. Right-click the slide and search for the clip.
   e. Choose Insert|Music.

___ 10. To access the Custom Animation dialog box:
   a. Right-click and choose Custom Animation.
   b. Choose Slide Show|Preset Animation.
   c. Choose Slide Show|Custom Animation.
   d. All the above.
   e. Both a and c.

Match the letters in Figure 6.56 with the correct items in the list.

Figure 6.56

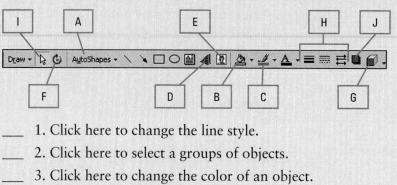

___ 1. Click here to change the line style.

___ 2. Click here to select a groups of objects.

___ 3. Click here to change the color of an object.

___ 4. Click here to add 3-D effects.

___ 5. Click here to rotate an object.

___ 6. Click here to insert clip art from the gallery.

___ 7. Click here to add shadow to an object.

___ 8. Click here to change the line color.

___ 9. Click here to create WordArt.

___ 10. Click here to add a callout.

Exercise and Project

Follow these step-by-step instructions to practice the skills that are included in this chapter. If you are working in a computer lab, you may have to ask your instructor where to save or print your work.

Exercise

1. Start PowerPoint and open the **PPT6** file in the Student\Chapter 6 folder of your PinPoint CD-ROM.
2. Add a clip from the gallery that is relevant to a day care facility and has some association with an angel.
3. Position the picture so that it is centered below the title.
4. Select the title **Miss Nicky's** and create WordArt. Select the second part of the title, and create the same type of WordArt.
5. Modify and place both WordArt objects appropriately. Delete the original text.
6. On Slide 2, create three, square shapes.
7. Add 3-D effect number 2 to each of them.
8. Add the letters A, B, and C to the block, one letter on each block. Enlarge and format the text.
9. Recolor the blocks, using three different fills, so that they look attractive with the background.
10. Reposition them so that they are touching (make them look like children's building blocks).
11. Add a piece of the clip art that includes students and a teacher to Slide 3.

12. Resize and reposition the picture. Save your file in the PowerPoint 2000 folder as **Exercise 6A**.

13. Print your slides as handouts, three to a page.

14. Add a music clip from the Windows Media folder titled **Beethoven's Fur Elsie**. Set the clip to play automatically. Drag the sound icon to the lower-left corner of the slide.

15. Program the sound to play on all three slides.

16. Select both **Miss Nicky's** and **Day Care for Darlings** together (use the draw arrow, or Shift plus the mouse) and add the Preset Animation effect, **Split Vertically Out**.

17. On Slide 2, group the three building blocks and then add the custom animation **Dissolve**.

18. In Slide Sorter view, select all the slides, and add the **Box Out** transition.

19. Save the file in your folder as **Exercise 6B**. Press **Print Screen**, open a blank PowerPoint presentation, and paste the screen onto the first slide.

20. Print the page as a slide in pure black and white.

21. Exit PowerPoint.

Project

Your music promotion firm has just gained a new client—a hot new British band. You managed to snare the account by promising to put together a first-class North American tour for them by the first of next year. No problem! Well, thanks to your contacts this really *shouldn't* be too tricky. The real dilemma is that you have a meeting with your boss, the group, and their attorneys next week. Everyone wants to see some concrete ideas for their tour, including a timeline with tentative dates and cities, and other promotional events as well.

Prepare a short presentation with a title slide, two slides with your promotional ideas, and a flow chart timeline (that utilizes AutoShapes).

Include the following:

- Clip art
- AutoShapes
- Sound
- Slide transitions
- Animations

Remember these are artists, so you don't have to be *too* professional. Make this fun! Save your presentation as Project 6 and print.

Chapter 7

Get Ready for an Electronic Slide Show

Your presentation is almost ready. Nevertheless, if your visual aids are going to be used in an electronic slide show, you need to address a few additional details. Unlike printed material, slide shows can be interactive. They can also provide access to outside resources, such as the Internet or other computer programs, and if you use these features, they require additional setup. Still further preparation is required in the likely case that you will be using a different computer to present your slide show than the one that you prepared it on—even if it is just down the hall.

At the end of this chapter, you will be able to:

C E

☑	☐	Use hyperlinks
☐	☑	Add links to slides within a presentation
☐	☑	Use action buttons
☐	☑	Create a custom show
☐	☑	Create a summary slide
☐	☑	Create an agenda slide
☐	☑	Set automatic timings
☐	☑	Use hidden slides
☐	☑	Save embedded fonts
☐	☑	Save a presentation to show on another computer

What: When you want to jump quickly from one place in your presentation to another location during your slide show, insert a link. A link provides quick access to another location by linking one item (or location) with another. Links can be to another slide, another file, or a distant location on the Web. One specific kind of link, a *hyperlink*, enables you to jump to or from a location using the power of the Internet. You learn more about PowerPoint and the Web in Chapter 10, "Prepare for an Internet or an Intranet Presentation."

Note: Hyperlinks are actually more complex than this but for the purposes of this book, the simple definition provided above is sufficient. Additionally, though a hyperlink is really a type of link, they are often used synonymously throughout this chapter.

Why: Don't waste time or diminish your professional image as you exit a slide show, minimize PowerPoint, and fumble about searching for slides, files, or Web addresses. Instead, insert a hyperlink and "click!" You'll be more effective, and your audience *will* notice.

INSERT A HYPERLINK

 CORE OBJECTIVE: Insert hyperlink

 EXPERT OBJECTIVE: Add links to slides within a presentation

How: Whether you're creating a link to another slide or a hyperlink to a source outside of the active presentation, you must first select the object or text where you want the link to begin, or be anchored. Anything that can be selected—text, pictures, placeholders, and the like—can be used to anchor a hyperlink.

     1. Select the link anchor and then access the dialog box in one of the following ways:

- Right-click and choose **Hyperlink** from the shortcut menu.
- Click the **Insert Hyperlink** button.
- Choose **Insert|Hyperlink**.
- Press **Ctrl+K**.

     2. When the Insert Hyperlink dialog box appears (Figure 7.1), you can choose from the following four options:
- Click **Existing File or Web Page** to insert a hyperlink to a location outside of the active presentation. If you know the exact address of the file or Web page that you want to link to, enter it as indicated. If you don't, browse for the address as shown in Figure 7.1.
- Click **Place in This Document** to link to a slide title, to another slide, or to a custom show, within the active presentation (Figure 7.2). (You learn how to make a Custom Show in Task 3.)

Figure 7.1
Inserting a hyperlink
to an existing file or
a Web page

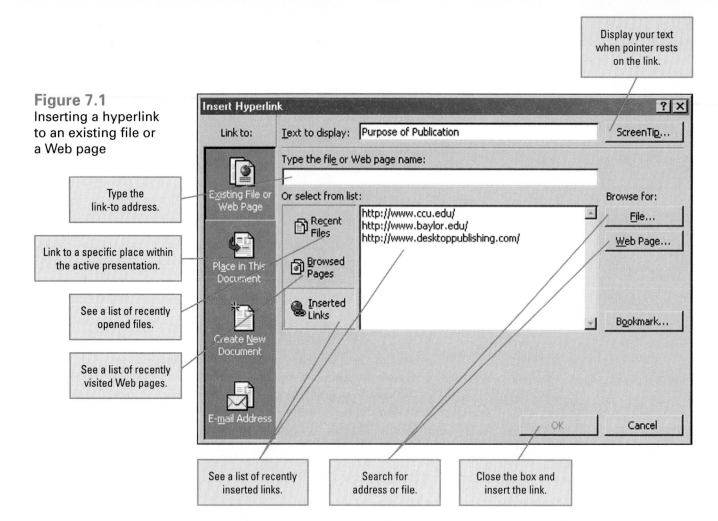

Display your text
when pointer rests
on the link.

Type the
link-to address.

Link to a specific place within
the active presentation.

See a list of recently
opened files.

See a list of recently
visited Web pages.

See a list of recently
inserted links.

Search for
address or file.

Close the box and
insert the link.

Figure 7.2
Inserting a link to
another slide

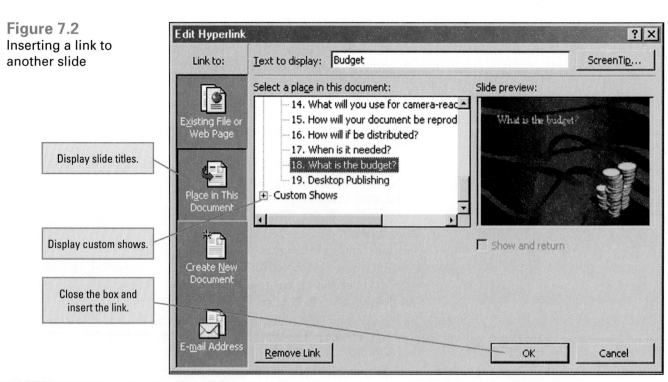

Display slide titles.

Display custom shows.

Close the box and
insert the link.

Figure 7.3
Creating a new slide show as a linked presentation

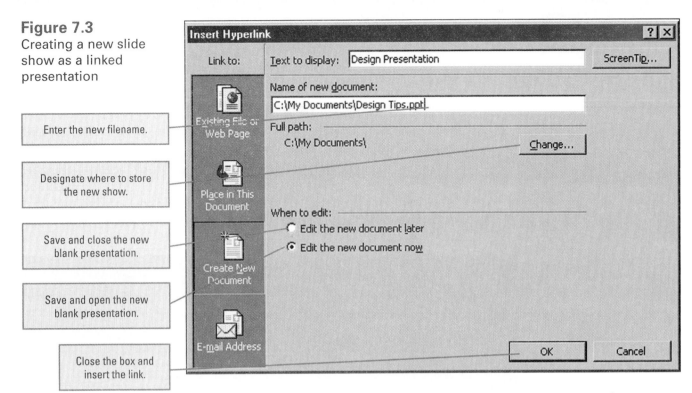

Enter the new filename.

Designate where to store the new show.

Save and close the new blank presentation.

Save and open the new blank presentation.

Close the box and insert the link.

- Click **Create New Document** to make a new PowerPoint presentation and then link it to the selected text or object in the active presentation (Figure 7.3).
- Click **E-Mail Address** to enable users to send feedback to a specified email address. When the link is activated (clicked), this address is automatically displayed in the "To" line (Figure 7.4).

Figure 7.4
Inserting a hyperlink to an email address

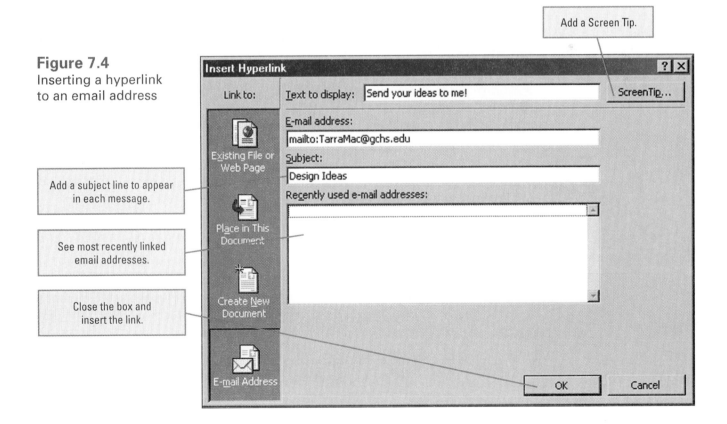

Add a Screen Tip.

Add a subject line to appear in each message.

See most recently linked email addresses.

Close the box and insert the link.

Tips from a Pro: If you want to return to the current slide after using a link, insert a return link on the destination slide.

Result: When you are in Slide Show view and move the mouse pointer over the item that anchors the link, the pointer changes to a small hand. If the link is to an external file or Web page, this address appears as you move the pointer. That is, unless you added a Screen Tip. In that case, the text associated with your tip appears instead.

        To activate the link, and therefore jump to the link-to location, click the link with the hand mouse pointer. If the link that you added is anchored to text, the font is probably a different color from the surrounding text, and is also underlined. Figure 7.5 provides two examples of hyperlinks.

Figure 7.5
Hyperlinked text

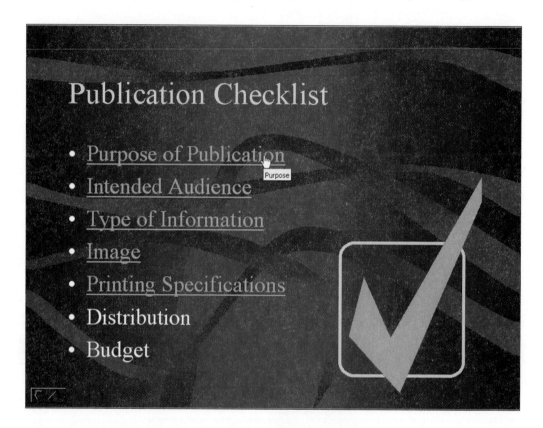

Tips from a Pro: The color of hyperlinked text is defined by the slide color scheme. You can change both the before and after hyperlink font colors by choosing **Format|Slide Color Scheme**.

MODIFY A HYPERLINK

How: After you insert a hyperlink, you can modify its characteristics or remove it completely. To change a link, reselect the text or object, and open the Edit Hyperlink dialog box by using one of the same methods that you used to access the Insert Hyperlink dialog box. When the dialog box opens, you can alter your link as follows:

      ○ **To remove a link**, click **Remove Link**.
      ○ **To modify a link**, enter the new information by repeating the steps provided in the preceding section of this task.

TIPS FROM A PRO: To add sound when the link is clicked or change the way that a link is activated, choose **Slide Show|Action Settings.** For more information about Action Settings, refer to Task 2.

Result: The hyperlink is gone or has been modified in some way.

 TIPS FROM A PRO: As soon as you add a link, check to make sure that it is working. Go to Slide Show view and activate each link. Remember that old cliché, "You can't be too careful"? Well, it's true! As you set up and run through your show and checking your equipment before your presentation, check the links again.

TASK **2** *Use Action Buttons*

 EXPERT OBJECTIVE: **Use an action button**

What: Although it's easy to insert a custom hyperlink, PowerPoint includes some 3-D AutoShapes called *Action Buttons* that include built-in links. Insert an Action Button and jump to a typical place, such as the first slide, the next slide, or the previous slide. You can also add generic buttons and add your own links, or customize the buttons to link to locations outside of the presentation, such as other files or Web pages.

Why: Action Buttons are handy because they include a link and are easily recognized as something that can be "pushed." This is especially useful when you are setting up a self-running kiosk display because they are straightforward and easy to use. Visitors can click buttons and maneuver through the show at their own pace. Not only does this hands-on approach enable them to interact with the information included in the display, but it also enables people who don't possess an intimate knowledge of computers or of PowerPoint to participate.

ADD AN ACTION BUTTON

How: To insert an Action Button use one of the following techniques:

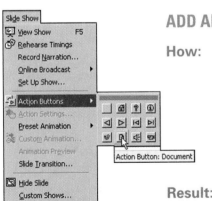

Figure 7.6 Choosing an action button

❍ Choose **Slide Show|Action Buttons,** click to select one of the buttons, and then click the slide pane. You can check a buttons function before you insert it by running the mouse pointer over it.
❍ Click **AutoShapes|Action Buttons** and then choose the button style that you want from the submenu (Figure 7.6). Click the slide where you would like the button.

Result: The button immediately appears on your slide, along with the Action Setting dialog box (pictured later in Figure 7.8). Click **OK** to implement the default link setting or modify it as discussed in the subsequent section of this task. When you click the button during a slide show, it appears to be pushed in. Figure 7.7 displays some sample action buttons.

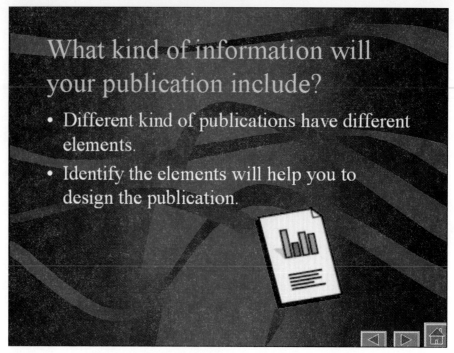

Figure 7.7   Sample action buttons

MODIFY ACTION SETTINGS

How: You can modify the characteristics of an action button as soon as you insert it (and the dialog box is visible), or you can change it later using the following techniques:

1. Select the button and then access the Action Settings dialog box in one of the following ways:
    - Choose **Slide Show|Action Settings**.
    - Click the **Insert Hyperlink** button.
    - Right-click the slide.
2. When the dialog box (Figure 7.8) appears, you can:
    - Change the link-to location.
    - Add sound.
    - Modify the way that the link is activated from a "click," to a *mouse over* action (the link is initiated by running the mouse pointer over the button).

Result: The Action Button has been modified (see Figure 7.9). When you move the mouse over the button, or click it, in Slide Show view, you jump to the link-to location. You can now customize the button in other ways, such as format, reposition, or add text using the skills that you learned in Chapter 6, "Elements of Sight and Sound."

Figure 7.8
Action Settings dialog box

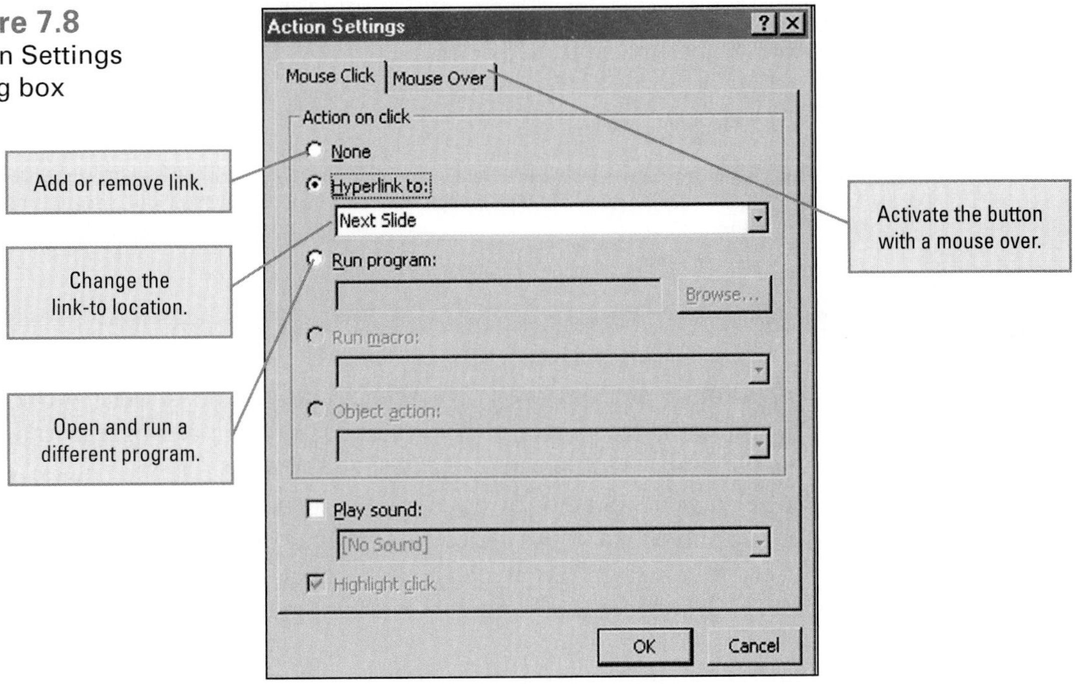

Action Settings
Mouse Click
Mouse Over
Action on click
None
Hyperlink to:
Next Slide
Run program:
Browse...
Run macro:
Object action:
Play sound:
[No Sound]
Highlight click
OK
Cancel
Add or remove link.
Change the link-to location.
Open and run a different program.
Activate the button with a mouse over.

TIPS FROM A PRO: The color palette that appears when you select an Action Button and click the **Fill Color** button or double-click the button is based on the slide's color scheme. Remember that these colors have been chosen to "work" together, but you can choose any of the other colors from the palette as well.

TIPS FROM A PRO: If you can't think of any text to add to a custom action button, consider inserting a symbol on the surface by choosing **Insert|Symbol**.

Figure 7.9
Modified action buttons

Customized Next Slide Action Buttons
Next Slide
Click for Next Slide
Next Slide
Next!

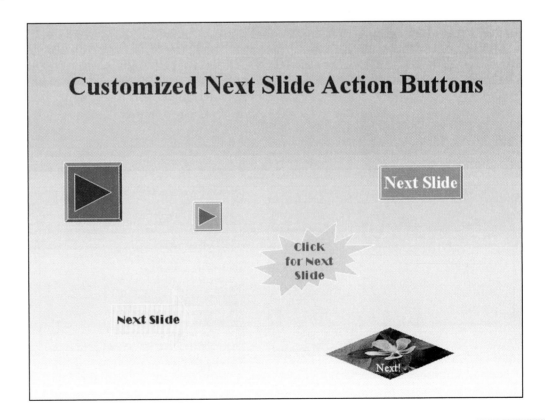

THOUGHT QUESTION: What happens when you select an action button and then click the Insert Hyperlink button?

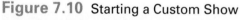

TASK **3**   *Create a Custom Show*

 E   *EXPERT OBJECTIVE:* **Add a presentation within a presentation**

What: PowerPoint enables you to select individual slides within one PowerPoint file and group them together to form a subpresentation, or ***Custom Show***, within the primary slide show.

Why: Rather that producing several similar presentation files, you can create one file and then choose slides from within the slide show to present to different groups. That way you can quickly build one show for the finance department, another for marketing, and a third for public relations.

How: You can create a Custom Show in any of the PowerPoint views; however, Slide Sorter view presents a superior choice—you can view as well as select several slides at once. To create a presentation within an active presentation, follow these steps:

1. Choose **Slide Show|Custom Show**. When the dialog box shown in Figure 7.10 appears, click **New**. A second dialog box, Define Custom Shows, is displayed (Figure 7.11). Now you can carry out the following operations:
    - **To rename the show,** click to select the default name that was assigned by PowerPoint. Now you can enter a different name of your choice.
    - **To add slides,** scroll through the Slides in Presentation list to locate the first slide that that you want to include in the custom show. Click to select the slide, or select multiple slides by holding down **Ctrl**. Click **Add** to copy the slide to the bottom of the list of Slides in Custom Show.

Figure 7.10 Starting a Custom Show

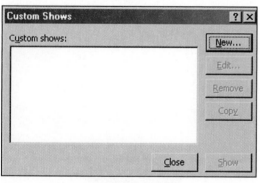

Figure 7.11 Creating a Custom Show

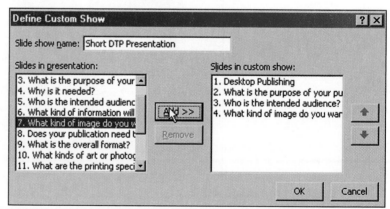

- **To rearrange a slide,** select it in Slides in Custom Show, and then move it up or down with the arrows.
- **To delete a slide,** select it in **Slides in Custom Show** and click **Remove.**

2. After you finish adding or rearranging slides, click **OK** to return to the Custom Shows dialog box (Figure 7.10). You may now:
   - Click Show to preview the presentation.
   - Click **Edit** to make additional changes.
   - Click **Copy** to make a duplicate.
   - Click **Remove** to delete the custom show (this will not affect your original presentation).
   - Click **Close** to close the dialog box.

 TIPS FROM A PRO: Are there slides in other PowerPoint files that you want to add to one of your custom shows? Use the techniques that you learned in Chapter 3, "Edit Text," for inserting slides from another saved slide show.

 TIPS FROM A PRO: You can navigate around the Define Custom Shows dialog box, as well as many other dialog boxes, with the **Tab** and arrow keys.

Result: The Custom Show that you created is contained within your original file. When you are ready to present your Custom show, open the primary PowerPoint file. The shows that you created can be displayed in either of the following ways:

❍ **To begin your presentation with a custom show,** choose **Slide Show|Set Up Show.** Check the **Custom Show** check box and select the correct show from the drop-down list displayed in Figure 7.12.

Figure 7.12
Setting up a custom show

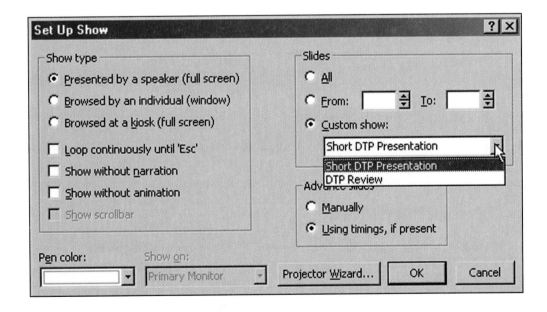

❍ **To begin a custom show during the presentation,** right-click any slide or click the onscreen **pop-up** menu button, if it is available, to reveal the shortcut menu. Choose **Go|Custom Show** and select the presentation that you want your audience to see (Figure 7.13).

Figure 7.13
Viewing a custom
show

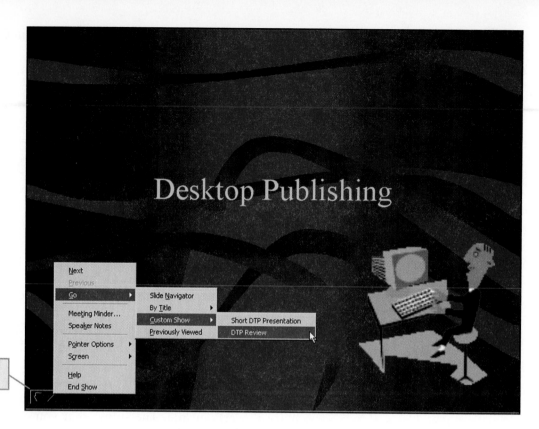

Pop-up menu button

TASK 4 — Create a Summary Slide

 E

EXPERT OBJECTIVE: **Automatically create a summary slide**

What: By utilizing the information entered in slide titles, you can automatically generate a *summary slide* that provides an outline of the points that you're going to discuss.

Why: A summary slide provides a framework to organize and tie your materials together. It shows where you've been and where you are going. Your listeners are more likely to remember the key points that you present if they are reinforced in this way.

How: Despite its importance, creating a summary slide is uncomplicated. In Slide Sorter view, follow these steps:

1. Select each slide whose title you want to be included in your summary.
2. Click the **Summary Slide** button.

Result: The summary slide that is generated is automatically placed directly before the first slide that you selected, as you can see in Figure 7.14. If you want, you can put the techniques that you learned in previous chapters to work, and edit, reposition, and format the slide.

Figure 7.14
Creating a summary
slide

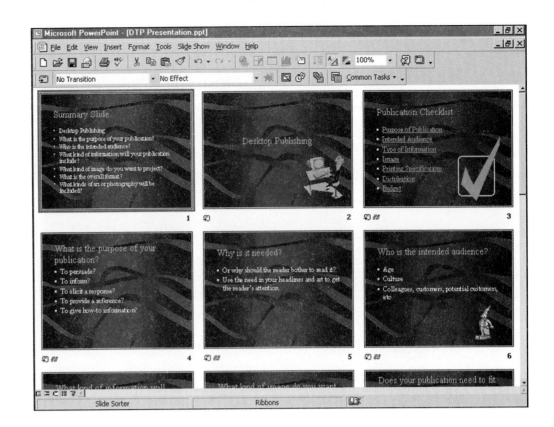

TASK **5**   *Create an Agenda Slide*

 E

EXPERT OBJECTIVE: **Automatically create an agenda slide**

What: You know how to create a summary slide but you can also create
another kind of outline, or *agenda slide*, to furnish your audience with
an overview of the material that you plan to cover. Although you might
typically think of an *agenda* as being synonymous with a *summary*, a
PowerPoint agenda slide combines the features of summary slides and
hyperlinks. Each agenda item (or summary point) is linked to its associated information in the body of the slide show. You can also set up your
show to enable you to jump back to the agenda after you present the
material included in each point.

Why: Using an agenda slide produces similar benefits to that of a summary
slide. It supplies organization to your presentation and helps engage
your listeners. Unlike a typical summary, however, it provides an ongoing reminder of your message, from the beginning until the end of your
show.

How: To create a linked agenda slide, you must utilize some of the skills that
you learned earlier in this chapter. In Slide Sorter view, follow these steps:

1. Create a custom show for each point that you will have on the agenda.
2. Select the first slide in each of the custom shows and click the **Summary Slide** button. The slide appears as the second slide in the show.
3. Double-click the slide that you've just created to go to Normal view.
4. Select the first bullet point on the slide and click **Insert Hyperlink** to access the Hyperlink dialog box. (It is not necessary to select the entire point—you could select a letter, word, or even insert an action button beside each point.)
5. Click the link type, **Place in This Document** (Figure 7.15), and locate and select the custom show. If you want to return to the agenda slide after presenting this material, check **Show and Return**. Click **OK** to close the dialog box.
6. Repeat Steps 4 and 5 until you have linked each point to its associated custom show.

 THOUGHT QUESTION: How can you remember what the first slide in each custom show is when it is time to create the agenda slide?

Result: When you click one of the agenda points, the first slide of the linked custom show immediately opens. If you checked the Show and Return feature, the presentation automatically returns to the agenda slide after you cover all the slides in the custom show.

Figure 7.15
Creating links to custom shows

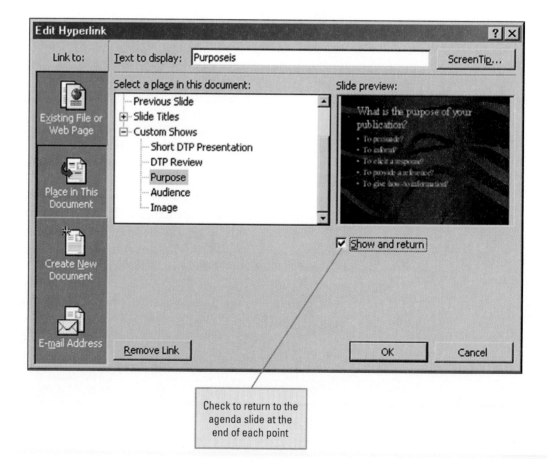

Check to return to the agenda slide at the end of each point

E

EXPERT OBJECTIVE: Set automatic slide timings

What: Did you know that your electronic slide show could be programmed to run itself? Timings can be added that instruct your presentation to automatically advance from one slide to the next after a preset period of time has elapsed.

Why: The ideal use for slides that automatically transition to the next slide is a self-running kiosk, but there are other times when you might want to use this feature. And, during those occasions, why expend energy needlessly running back and forth to the computer or lifting your arm to press an electronic device? (Even if you had a power breakfast and were Mr. or Ms. Universe last year you might want to conserve your strength.) When you set automatic timings, you are free to concentrate on your delivery or on the visitors to your kiosk and to ignore any finicky projection equipment.

SET MANUAL TIMINGS

How: One way to set transition timings is to manually specify a fixed time for each slide to run before it transitions to the next slide. To set times for individual slides or for the entire slide show, follow these steps:

1. Select the slide(s) that you want to set timings for and choose **Slide Show|Slide Transitions** or click the **Slide Transition** icon in Slide Sorter view. The familiar Slide Transitions dialog box appears (Figure 7.16).

2. Under Advance, in the **Automatically after** box, enter the number of seconds that you want to pass before the next slide appears on the screen. Click to apply these settings to the entire show or only to selected slides.

Figure 7.16
Setting slide timings

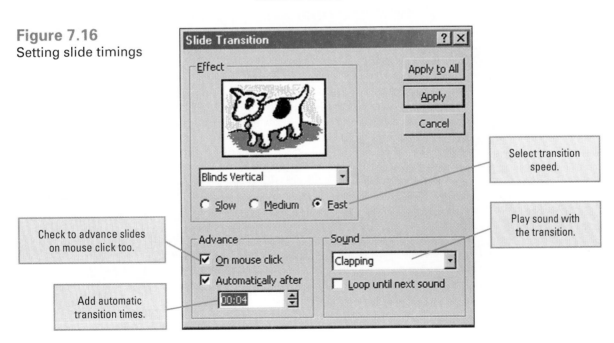

3. Check the **On mouse click** check box and clear the **Automatically after** box if you want your slide show to move ahead *only* after you click the mouse.

4. Check the **Automatically after** check box and clear the **On mouse click** box if you want your slide show to move ahead as soon as the time that you set in the Seconds box has elapsed. (Leave both boxes checked if you want to move to the next slide after either of these occurs.)

5. Repeat Steps 1 and 2 to set different transition times on any slides that weren't included in this operation.

Result: When the slide show begins, your slides will advance without any action from you. If you find that the timings need some adjustment, repeat Steps 1 and 2 or set rehearsed timings.

SET REHEARSED TIMINGS

How: When the material that you've prepared will be presented in person, there is another more accurate way to establish automatic timings. You can set the length of time that elapses between slides as you practice the slide show.

1. In Slide Sorter view, press the **Rehearse Timings** button. The presentation begins in Slide Show view and is accompanied by a small timer called the Rehearsal dialog box as shown in Figure 7.17. The clock on the dialog box immediately starts running to keep track of the time.

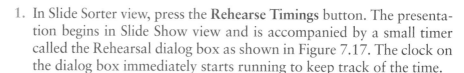

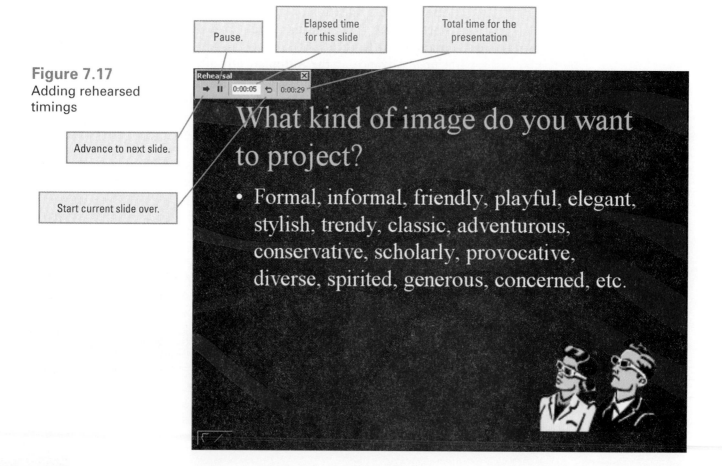

Figure 7.17
Adding rehearsed timings

2. As you practice your speech, the counter on the dialog box is working. It's keeping track of the length of time it takes you to get through the information contained on each slide. When you finish rehearsing a slide, click the **Advance** button or press **Page Down** to move to the next slide.

3. The center counter starts over and tracks the timing for the new slide. Repeat this process until you reach the end of your show. If you make a mistake, start any slide over by clicking **Repeat**.

4. After the last slide, a dialog box appears to inform you of the total time that elapsed while you rehearsed the slide show. You can accept the recorded times, or reject them and begin again. In either case, you are returned to Slide Sorter view.

Result: If you accepted the transition times, they now appear at the bottom of each slide, along with the icons for any other special effects that you have added. To clear automatic timings, select the slide(s) in Slide Sorter view, click the **Slide Transition** icon, and clear the **Advance Automatically after** check box.

TIPS FROM A PRO: It's important to rehearse your presentation at least three times, even if you aren't using timings. If you will be relying on preset timings, however, make sure that they are accurate. Who wants to look like a clown or Charlie Chaplin, first moving quickly and then slowly as you try to match the slide transition times?

| TASK **7** | ***Use Hidden Slides*** |

E   *EXPERT OBJECTIVE:* **Hide slides**

What: Did you know that you can conceal slides in your slide show and reveal them when, or if, you want to during a presentation?

Why: If you're not sure that you'll be able to get through the material that you've prepared, hide some slides! Or, create a contingency plan in case you don't have enough material—make some extra slides to fill any spare time.

HIDE SLIDES

How: Slides can be hidden in all the PowerPoint views by using the Slide Show menu; however, Slide Sorter view offers the easiest method. Select the slides that you want to hide, and then click the Hide Slide button.

Result: The slide number at the bottom of each hidden slide now includes a null sign, as shown in Figure 7.18. When you present your electronic slide show, your audience can't see these slides unless you choose to show them.

Figure 7.18
Hidden slides

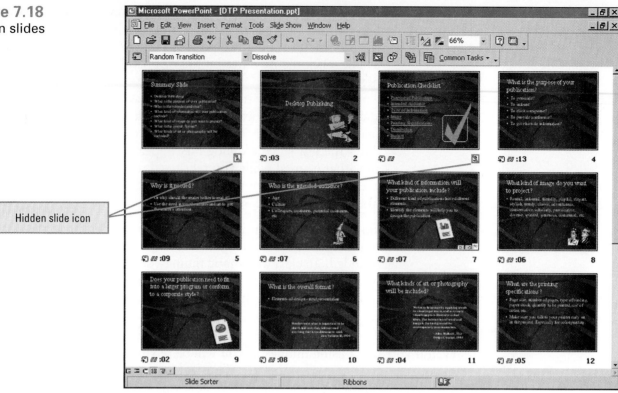

Hidden slide icon

REVEAL HIDDEN SLIDES

How: When the time arrives for you to introduce a hidden slide to your audience, follow these steps:

1. Right-click on any slide or click the onscreen **Popup menu** button to show the shortcut menu seen in Figure 7.19.

Figure 7.19
Revealing a hidden slide

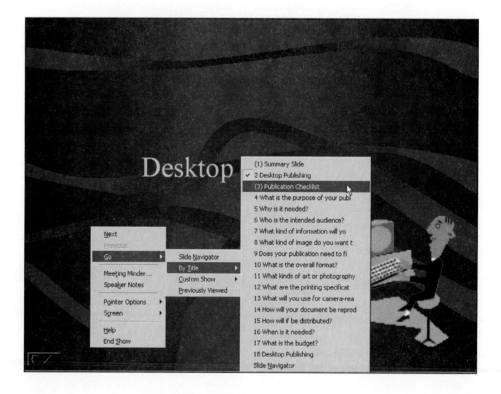

2. Choose **Go|Slide Navigator** or **Go|Slide Title** from the menu and select the slide that you want to display. (You learn more about Slide Navigator in Chapter 8, "Print and Deliver.") Hidden slides are easy to spot because their slide numbers are enclosed in parentheses.

Result: What was hidden is now revealed! You can now present its content to your listeners.

Save Embedded Fonts

EXPERT OBJECTIVE: Save embedded fonts in a presentation

What: Not every computer contains the same font styles. If you create a presentation on one computer and plan to show it on another, you can save, or *embed*, the font formatting when you save the file. Any *TrueType* fonts (fonts that come with the Windows operating system) that you used are then preserved; they become a permanent part of the presentation file. (To see whether a font is TrueType, by drop down the Font box; TrueType fonts are clearly marked with a double "T" to the right of the font name.)

Why: All the beautiful font formatting that you carefully created will be preserved when you present your slide show. Although many computers today have standard operating systems and programs, prepare for Murphy's Law and the resulting font potluck that could follow—embed your fonts!

How: To embed TrueType fonts, use the Pack and Go Wizard described in the next task or follow these steps:

1. Choose **File|Save As**. When the Save As dialog box appears, click the **Tools** drop-down list.
2. Click to select **Embed TrueType Fonts**, designate a **Save in** location, and click **Save**.

If the fonts that you used in your presentation can't be embedded, a prompt appears to tell you why. In that case, replace the offending font style and repeat Steps 1 and 2.

Result: When you're ready to give your presentation, you can open your file with confidence—your font styles are intact!

TIPS FROM A PRO: Saving embedded fonts increases your file size, so make sure that you have adequate disk space.

EXPERT OBJECTIVE: Save a presentation to use
on another computer (Pack'N Go)

What: You will frequently find yourself presenting your slide show on a different computer from the one on which you prepared it. It can be a complicated process to find and store all the files associated with a particular slide show. This is especially true if you have numerous font types, sound, motion clips, and the like. The makers of PowerPoint realized this and prepared a wizard to help you with the task. When you use the Pack and Go Wizard, all your files and text characteristics are packed and ready to travel.

Why: You could sift through various folders and disks to find all the files that you need to make your presentation a success, only to find on the big day that you missed a critical element. (Now you have no music to go with the TV commercial that you've spent weeks developing.) Or, you can click a few buttons and have all the components neatly zipped, packed, and ready to go. It's easy and no suitcase is required!

How: To compress and save your files in one convenient location, choose **File|Pack and Go.**

1. The first dialog box of the wizard appears to provide a list of the items that will be addressed in the process. Click **Next** to move to the second screen.

2. The second dialog box, shown in Figure 7.20, prompts you to pack the active presentation or browse for other presentations. (Select multiple presentations by pressing and holding **Ctrl.**) Click **Next** to continue.

Figure 7.20
Choosing the files
to pack

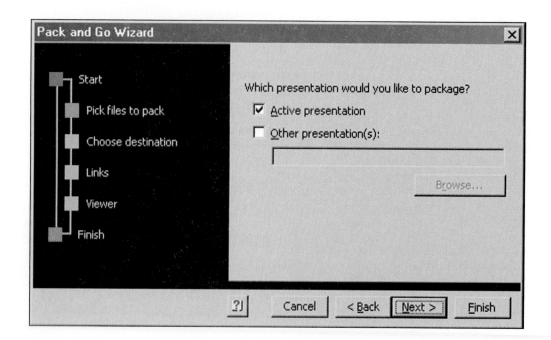

Figure 7.21
Choosing a save-to
location for packed
files

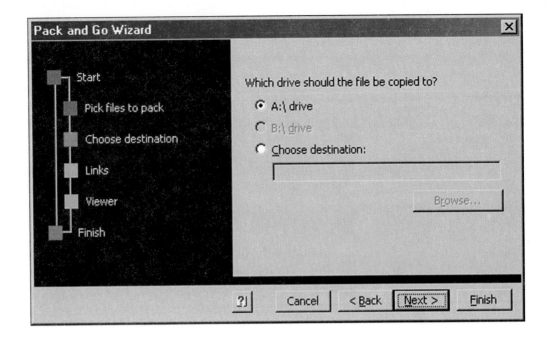

3. In the third dialog box, (Figure 7.21), choose the disk and folder location where you would like the packed file saved. Click **Next**.

4. In the fourth dialog box, shown in Figure 7.22, click to embed TrueType fonts and include linked files. Move to the next slide by clicking **Next**.

5. Last, you can choose to save the PowerPoint Viewer. The Viewer is a program that can be used to display your slide show if you are using a computer that doesn't have PowerPoint installed. Click **Finish** to pack your presentation.

Figure 7.22
Save embedded fonts
and linked files

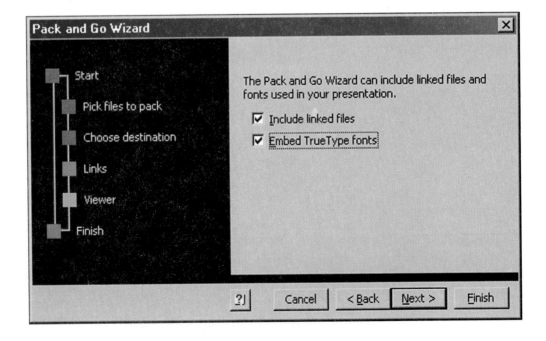

Result: As the wizard saves your files, you are prompted to insert additional disks if the one that you are using doesn't have enough free space. You'll know when the process is finished because an assistant balloon appears and displays this message: "Pack and Go has successfully packed your presentation."

The disk location where you saved your packed slide show now contains two files: an application file to unpack the files, and the zipped presentation files. If you make changes to the slide show at a later time, just rerun the program. This copies over the previous version of each file. When you want to unpack, follow these steps:

1. Open Windows Explorer and locate the Pngsetup file.
2. Double-click on the file and designate a save location.

After the files are unpacked, you can choose to start the slide show or to close the dialog box and view the show later.

 TIPS FROM A PRO: It pays to be careful, so take your slide show on a trial run as soon as you unpack it. This is especially true if you are using the Viewer. The PowerPoint Viewer is only for displaying your slides; mistakes or errors that you find can't be corrected.

 ## Use PinPoint

After gaining the skills in this chapter, you can insert different types of hyperlinks, record automatic timings, hide slides, make a summary and an agenda slide, and pack up your slide show to present on a different computer. Now it's time to see what you can do with the PinPoint software. Remember, whenever you are unsure of what to do next, you can reread the relevant portion of the chapter or you can click Show Me for a live demonstration. Try these skills in PinPoint:

- Insert a hyperlink
- Link to a slide
- Action button
- Custom Show
- Summary slide
- Agenda slide
- Slide timing
- Hide slides
- Pack and Go

Key Terms

You can find definitions for these words in this chapter:

Action button	Hyperlink
Agenda slide	Mouse over
Embed	Summary slide
Embedded fonts	True Type font

Review Questions

You can use the following review questions and exercises to test your knowledge and skills. Answers are given in Appendix D, "Answers to Review Questions."

True/False

Indicate whether each of the following statements is true (T) or false (F).

____ 1. To add a summary slide, choose Insert|Summary Show.

____ 2. Hyperlinks enable you to jump from one location to another by clicking text or objects.

____ 3. Rehearsed timings enable you to practice your slide show as you record the times for each slide transition.

____ 4. Pack and Go is one of the menu options under Slide Show view.

____ 5. You can set rehearsed slide timings in Slide Sorter view.

____ 6. Insert an action button when you want to link to various places in your slide show.

____ 7. Embedded fonts are used to insert hyperlinks.

____ 8. Hiding slides is a good idea if you don't know whether you will have enough time to get through your material.

____ 9. When you use the Pack and Go Wizard, you don't have to worry about saving your linked files separately—the wizard does it for you.

____ 10. Automatic timings won't work for a self-running kiosk display.

Multiple Choice

____ 1. Add a summary slide in:
   a. Normal view.
   b. Slide view.
   c. Outline view.
   d. Slide Sorter view.
   e. Slide show view.

____ 2. Hyperlinks are a component of:
   a. An agenda slide.
   b. A summary slide.
   c. Action buttons.
   d. Hidden slides.
   e. Both a and c.

____ 3. To create an agenda slide, you must first:
   a. Set automatic timings.
   b. Go to Slide Show view.
   c. Create custom shows.
   d. Set hyperlinks to the agenda points.
   e. Add action buttons to each point.

___ 4. A PowerPoint custom show:

    a. Enables you to show different groups customized information.

    b. Is a mini slide show within a larger presentation.

    c. Requires you to create a summary slide.

    d. Can't be made in Slide Sorter view.

    e. Both a and b.

___ 5. To save a presentation and all linked files for use on another computer:

    a. Click the Save button.

    b. Choose File|Pack and Go.

    c. Choose File|Save As|Pack and Go.

    d. Right-click the slide and choose Pack and Go.

    e. Both a and b.

___ 6. You can anchor a hyperlink to:

    a. A graphic object.

    b. A word of text.

    c. A placeholder.

    d. An action button.

    e. All of these.

___ 7. To customize the link-to location of an Action button:

    a. Choose Format|Action Button.

    b. Choose Edit|Action Settings.

    c. Choose Slide Show|Action Settings.

    d. Double-click the button.

    e. Delete the button and insert a new one.

___ 8. When you want to insert an agenda slide:

    a. Create a summary slide and link bullet points to custom shows.

    b. Create a summary slide—they are the same thing.

    c. Choose Insert|Agenda Slide.

    d. Click the Agenda Slide button.

    e. Choose Insert|Summary Slide.

___ 9. To set automatic timings:

    a. Click the Slide Transitions button in Slide Sorter view.

    b. Click the Rehearse Timings button in Slide Sorter view.

    c. Choose Slide Show|Rehearse Timings.

    d. Choose Slide Show|Slide Transition.

    e. All of the above.

___ 10. When you want to hide a slide:

    a. Choose Edit|Hide Slide.

    b. Choose Slide Show|Custom Show.

    c. Choose Insert|Hide Slide.

    d. Click the Hide Slide button.

    e. Click the Custom Show button.

Match the letters in Figure 7.23 with the correct items in the list.

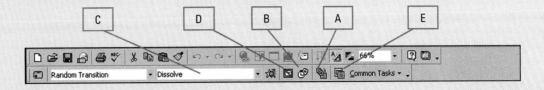

Figure 7.23
Slide Sorter view

___ 1. Click here to add rehearsed slide timings.
___ 2. Click here to create a summary slide.
___ 3. Click here to start an agenda slide.
___ 4. Click here to hide a slide.
___ 5. Click here to preview slide animations.
___ 6. Click here to add a preset animation.

Exercise and Project

Exercise

Follow these step-by-step instructions to practice the skills that are included in this chapter. If you are working in a computer lab, you may have to ask your instructor where to save or print your work.

1. Start PowerPoint and open the file named **PPT7** from the Student\Chapter 7 folder of the PinPoint CD-ROM that came with this book.
2. Create three custom shows using the following groups of slides. Change the default show names as follows:
   - Public Relations   Slides 1-4
   - Management   Slides 5-10
   - Marketing   Slides 11-16
3. Create a summary, or agenda, slide from the three title slides.
4. Link the three bulleted points on the agenda slide to its associated custom show. Select **Show and Return**.
5. Add manual timings to each slide except the summary slide. Each slide should transition after five seconds.
6. Insert a small text box at the bottom of the summary slide and add your name.
7. Add a hyperlink to your email address. Save your file in the PowerPoint 2000 folder as **Exercise 7A**.
8. Now, place a new disk in the drive that you are using and use the Pack and Go Wizard to get the slide show ready to take to another computer. Save the fonts and the viewer.
9. Close the presentation and begin a new blank presentation. Drag the title placeholder near the top of the slide, resize it to a smaller height, and enter your name.

10. Open Windows Explorer and find the disk and folder location of your slide show. Press **Print Screen**, return to the blank presentation, and **Paste** the screen that you have just copied onto the slide.
11. Press the **Print** button.
12. Exit PowerPoint.

Project

You are a member of a service organization that raises funds for disaster relief. Primarily the organization raises money, food, and clothing for people who have suffered a loss due to some type of natural disaster. The local Chamber of Commerce has recently invited your group to participate in an upcoming non-profit fair. One of the goals of the fair is to inform the community about service organizations such as yours, as well as to provide a venue for the solicitation of new membership and donations. Due to your knowledge of PowerPoint, you have volunteered to create a display for the event. The PowerPoint portion of your booth will operate as a self-running kiosk display.

The show should include at least five slides (one being the title slide) plus the following features:

- Action buttons
- Automatic timings
- A link to another file
- A link to a Web page
- A link to an email address

Save the file as **Project 7** and print.

Chapter 8

Print and Deliver

Your presentation is finished and ready to go. The big day is drawing near. Only a few final tasks remain (to print materials, and to rehearse the delivery). Being a successful speaker isn't a matter of good genes or special gifts; it just requires practice. Rehearsing your delivery beforehand not only helps build your competence, but also your confidence.

Printing the slides, notes, outline, and handouts is one way to create paper output to accompany a speech; and printing overhead transparencies gives you a great substitute for an electronic slide show when you need to go low-tech. Before, during, and after the presentation, you need to pay attention to several important tasks and techniques discussed in this chapter to help make you a successful speaker.

At the end of this chapter, you will be able to:

C E

- ☑ ☐ Print slides in a variety of formats
- ☑ ☐ Create overhead transparencies
- ☑ ☐ Preview a presentation in black and white option
- ☑ ☐ Print handouts
- ☐ ☐ Print the outline
- ☑ ☐ Print speaker notes
- ☑ ☐ Start the slide show on any slide
- ☐ ☐ Run the show manually for a live presentation
- ☐ ☐ Set up an automatic kiosk show
- ☑ ☐ Use on-screen navigation tools
- ☑ ☐ Use the pen during a presentation
- ☐ ☑ Generate meeting notes

CORE OBJECTIVE: Print slides in a variety of formats

What: Sure, you've printed before, but there's still much more you can learn about PowerPoint's print features. Now rather than just clicking buttons to choose an output type, you learn about all the options available in the Print dialog box.

Why: Printing slides can be used as a way to proofread or review the contents of your visual aids away from the computer. More importantly, you can use these print features to produce professional-quality output such as overhead transparencies, audience handouts, and speaker notes.

How: You can access the Print dialog box in two ways:
- ○ Choose **File|Print**.
- ○ Press **Ctrl+P**.

Result: When the Print dialog box appears (Figure 8.1), you have decisions to make about the type, quality, and format of your printing. Here you can designate the following:

- ○ Which printer to use. Click to see a list of all the available printers—perhaps you have the choice of printing to either a color inkjet printer or a black-and-white laser printer.
- ○ Which slides to print—all, the current slide, selected slides, or slides you designate by number.
- ○ How many copies to print.
- ○ Whether to collate the copies.

Figure 8.1
Print dialog box

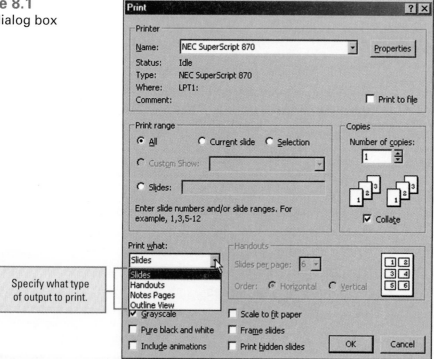

- What type of output to print—slides, handouts, notes pages, or Outline view.
- Whether to print in grayscale or pure black and white rather than color (see Task 3).
- Whether to enlarge the slide to fill the printed page (by using Scale to Fit Paper).
- Whether to include hidden slides in the printout.
- Whether to display animations by printing multiple copies of a slide (a real paper or transparency waster, in most cases).

When you have finished making your choices, press **Enter** or click **Print** to complete the process. As you go through Tasks 2, 3, and 4, you are shown exactly which options to select to get the type of output that you want.

TASK **2**	*Create Overhead Transparencies*

CORE OBJECTIVE: Print a slide as an overhead transparency

EXPERT OBJECTIVE: Change the output format (Page Setup)

What: One reason for printing slides is to create overhead transparencies for use on an overhead projector. Before you actually print a transparency, you should first set up the page and print a paper draft in black and white. When you're sure that everything is in order, print the pages in color or black and white, either on paper or directly on the transparency film.

Why: Some speakers prefer using overhead transparencies rather than an electronic slide show (so long as sound and motion are not required). Others like to use them to supplement their high-tech presentation. Using overhead transparencies as a visual aid to accompany a speech offers several benefits, including the following:

- Availability! Most conference rooms have an overhead projector; and even if they don't, the machines are lightweight and easy to transport.
- Overhead transparency slides are reusable, require less equipment, and are therefore economical.
- Overhead projectors don't crash or get viruses. A bulb may blow out, but that's easily solved.
- When using overhead transparencies, you can keep the lights on, making it much easier for you to make eye contact with the audience.
- You can alternate overheads with an electronic slide show to provide diversity in the presentation (and, to wake up that sleepy after-lunch crowd as you throw on the lights).
- You can print overhead transparencies in color to present an attractive and professional display.

How: To create great looking transparencies, follow these steps:

1. Set up the page. Choose **File|Page Setup** to see the dialog box shown in Figure 8.2. When the Page Setup dialog box appears, choose **Overhead** under **Slides Sized For**.
   - If you want to create a 10 × 7.5-inch page, appropriate for printing within the margins of a piece of paper, check **Portrait** and click **OK**. When you use Portrait orientation, you must page from slide to slide so that you can adjust the placement of text, clip art, and other objects (Figure 8.3).
   - If you want to create transparencies that are wider than long, choose the default, **Landscape** orientation.

Figure 8.2 Page Setup dialog box

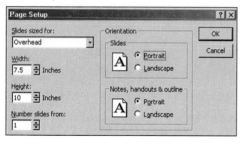

Figure 8.3 An overhead in portrait orientation

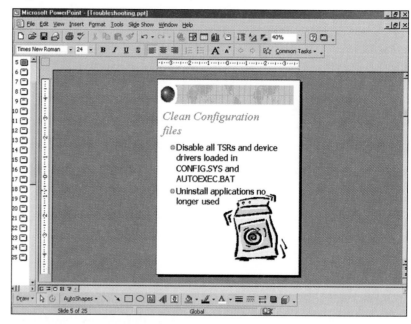

2. Adjust the colors. One of the benefits of overheads is that they can be used in bright rooms without having to turn off all the lights. To maintain this advantage, you should use a light, or better yet, a white background. (This also saves ink and speeds printing time.) To accomplish this, use one of these methods:
   - Choose **Format|Background** and change the background to **White**.
   - Apply a template that has dark text on a light background.
   - Change to black and white or grayscale to save printing costs and increase contrast (see the next section).
3. Print a draft in black and white or grayscale just to proof the overheads (see the next section).
4. Print the transparencies in color. To do this, choose **File|Print**, and click to remove the checks from Grayscale and Pure Black and White.

Result: Your colored or black and white transparencies are ready. You can use them with confidence knowing that they won't crash, talk back, or timeout.

Tips from a Pro: The following tips pertain to using overhead transparencies:

- Place transparencies in special cardboard frames, and then number them to keep them in order. You can also place them in transparent sleeves with three-hole punch edges so that you can keep them in a notebook.
- Write your speaker notes on the frames so that you can keep your hands free.
- Stack transparencies in the order you will use them, and then lay them in that same order in a separate stack as you finish with them. If someone asks you a question, you won't have to dig through a disorganized mess to find the one you need.
- Lay a pen on top of the projector to point to the item you are discussing. Never point with your finger, because when it gets projected, the size and shakiness are magnified.
- Lay a sheet of paper over the transparency and pull it down to reveal one point at a time.
- Turn off the projector when it is not being used.
- Take along a spare bulb and an extension cord, just in case.

Tips from a Pro: Because you don't know when you will be addressing people who have low vision, it is a good idea to always use highly contrasting text, such as black or very dark letters on white or very light backgrounds. You can still use color for accents and clip art, but you don't want people missing the essential part of your visual aid because they can't see it.

TASK 3 Use the Grayscale or Pure Black and White Option

CORE OBJECTIVE: Preview a presentation in black and white

What: When you are printing colored handouts or transparencies, you will want to preview how the slides look in black and white before you waste materials. PowerPoint provides Grayscale preview and Pure Black and White preview for you to see how the slides appear, and also so that you can adjust individual objects for the best appearance in black and white.

When you use these previews, various items turn black, white, or grayscale. Table 8.1 summarizes what happens.

Table 8.1 Effect of Grayscale Preview

These Items Become Black	These Items Turn White or Invisible	These Items Are Shown in Shades of Gray
Text frames	Text shadows	Colored fills (white in pure black and white)
Lines	Background	Shadows (black in pure black and white)
Black fills		Charts

Why: Color copies are very expensive, so most of the time it makes sense to print audience handouts and drafts in black and white instead. You can also use this feature to preview black-and-white overhead transparencies before you print them.

How: You can use Grayscale preview or Pure Black and White preview in any view except Notes Page view; to control how individual objects appear, however, it is easiest to use Normal view or Slide view.

1. Click the **Grayscale Preview** button to see the slides in grayscale. Click it again to see the slides in color.
2. Hold down the **Shift** key and click the **Grayscale Preview** button to see the slides in pure black and white.
3. Adjust how individual items appear. To do this, right-click an object, choose **Black and White** from the shortcut menu, and then pick one of the available options. Figure 8.4 shows the choices.
4. Click the **Grayscale Preview** button again to view the slides in color.

Figure 8.4
Black and White
options menu

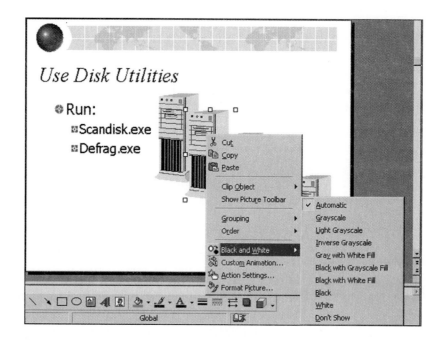

THOUGHT QUESTION: When would you want to eliminate objects from the slides completely by choosing the White option?

Result: As you adjust each object, you can optimize how your slides will appear when you print them in grayscale and black and white. Figure 8.5 provides some examples of objects in varying shades of gray, or black and white.

Figure 8.5
Black and White
options

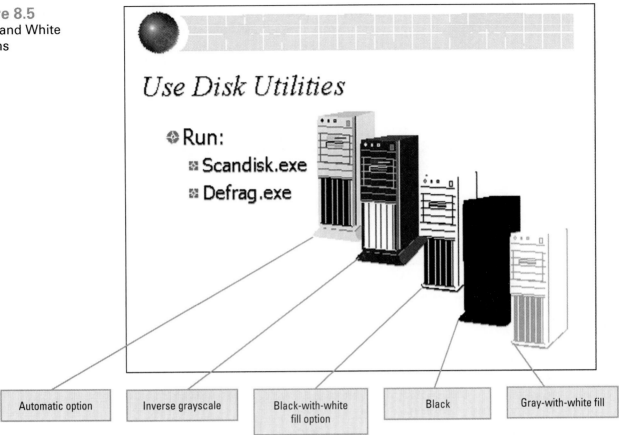

| Automatic option | Inverse grayscale | Black-with-white fill option | Black | Gray-with-white fill |

TASK **4**　*Print Handouts*

C　*CORE OBJECTIVE:* **Print audience handouts**

What:　Many presenters want to give a copy of their visual aids to members of the audience. Creating handouts in PowerPoint can be as simple as printing slides, one to a page. This may not be the best choice, however, because it requires so many pages and doesn't leave any room for people to take notes. Instead, you can print two, three, four, six, or nine slides per page, and arrange them horizontally or vertically on the page.

Why:　To help the audience remember critical points, use handouts. Handouts can also help keep your listeners involved by providing a place for them to jot down notes.

How:　To set up and then print handouts, follow these steps:

1. Choose **View|Master** and **Handout Master**. Add any text or images that you want to include on every page and close the master.
2. Choose **File|Print** and specify which slides to include.
3. Click **Print What** and choose **Handouts**.
4. Specify the number of slides that you want to show on each handout page. The dialog box shows a preview of how the slides are

arranged. Figure 8.6 shows that you get a small area for note taking when you choose three slides per handout.

5. Indicate whether you want the slides in grayscale or pure black and white rather than color, as you learned in Task 3.

6. Check the **Frame slides** option if you want each slide on your handouts to be framed by a border. Click **OK** to print.

Figure 8.6
Printing handouts,
three per page

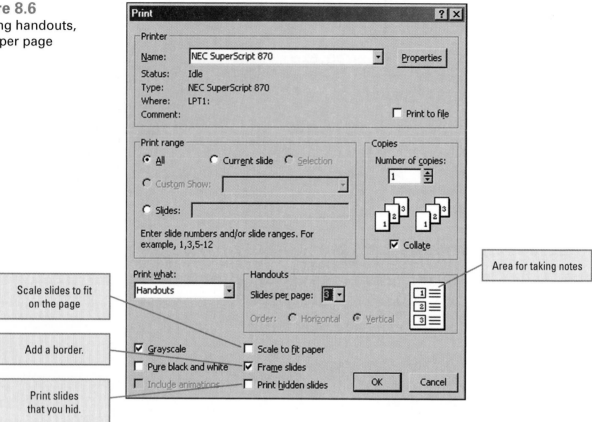

Scale slides to fit
on the page

Add a border.

Print slides
that you hid.

Area for taking notes

Result: As soon as you click OK, the handouts come rolling out of your printer. Be sure to carefully proofread each one for typos and for illegible text (black text on a black shadow, for instance, if you chose pure black and white) before you have them duplicated.

 TIPS FROM A PRO: The Handout Master, along with the other masters found in the View menu, is similar to the Slide Master that you learned about in Chapter 5, "Format Slide Characteristics." The Handout Master enables you to see the positioning of the slides when you choose to print a different number of slides on each page. That way you can carefully choose the placement of any graphics.

 TIPS FROM A PRO: If you want to create professional-quality handouts, include your name, the date of your presentation, and the name of your host organization. You may also want to add a copyright line. To add this information, access the Handout Master, add a logo or other image, and add a header and footer to contain the text.

TIPS FROM A PRO: To ensure audience participation, create handouts containing the text and images from your slides, but leave blanks for the audience to write in key words and phrases. An easy way to do this is to export the presentation to Word. You learn how to do this in Chapter 9, "Integrate Charts and Tables."

TASK **5**	*Print the Outline*

What: Whether you are in the process of building your presentation or completely finished, you can print the outline to read and edit away from the computer. PowerPoint enables you to view and print the outline two ways: *collapsed*, so that only the slide titles appear; or *expanded*, to show all the text.

Although you learned how to turn the formatting off and on while viewing the text in the outline, when you print the outline, it always shows the full formatting.

Why: A printed outline is not just for editing; it can also be useful as an aid to help the speaker during the presentation. You can keep track of which slide number you are on, and how many that you have to go, enabling you to pace yourself or find your place quickly. It is also handy to know the slide numbers so that you can quickly navigate to a certain slide, both when editing in PowerPoint and when presenting.

How: To print the outline, first collapse or expand, and then print.

 1. Click the **Expand All** button to collapse or expand the outline, whichever you prefer.

2. Choose **File|Print** and under **Print What**, choose **Outline View**. Click **OK**.

Result: The outline for your presentation is printed. This feature is nice because you can see the text for your presentation on just a couple of pages. Watch out, though: Text that you placed in tables, text boxes, org charts, WordArt, and AutoShapes isn't included in the outline.

TASK **6**	*Print Speaker Notes*

C *CORE OBJECTIVE:* **Print speaker notes in a specified format**

What: If you have taken the time to type notes in the notes pane, you will want a *hard copy*, a paper printout of your material.

Why: You can use speaker notes to practice your presentation away from the computer, or to duplicate for audience handouts.

How: To print speaker notes, follow these steps:

1. Access the Notes Master (choose **View|Master|Notes Master**) to add images and text that you want to appear on every page. Include page numbers or other text in the header and footer.
2. Choose **File|Print** and under **Print What**, choose **Notes Pages**.
3. Be sure to check the **Frame slides** option if you want to add a border around each slide, and click **OK** to print.

Result: The notes pages are printed, with one slide and its accompanying notes on each piece of paper.

 TIPS FROM A PRO: Another way to create speaker notes that you can hold in your hand is to print handouts, three per page, and cut them apart. Glue them to black, gray, or navy paper to match your suit, and they will hardly be noticeable.

TASK **7**	*Get Ready, Get Set*

 CORE OBJECTIVE: **Start a slide show on any slide**

What: On the day of your presentation, you need to take care of a few important details. If you are attending a trade show you will need to set up your display. When the event begins, start the computer, load up your PowerPoint presentation, and start it running on its own. That way some visitors to your booth can view the presentation while you greet and attract others with samples and other freebies.

On the other hand, perhaps you are presenting to a live audience. In this case, you should arrive at the room where you will be speaking at least an hour in advance to set up and test your equipment. Start the computer, make sure the projection equipment is working properly, and determine what lighting is optimal to allow the audience to see both you and the screen. Open your presentation and run through your slides and check to confirm that sound, video, and links are working. Leave Slide 1 on the screen for the audience to see when they arrive. When you leave extra time before your presentation, you can be relaxed rather than rushed; you also have plenty of time to greet the audience members as they arrive.

Whether your PowerPoint show is running as a standalone kiosk or you are using it as a visual aid to accompany a live presentation, you must use the Set Up Show dialog box to specify how you want to run it.

Why: The Set Up Show dialog box enables you to specify how you want the show to advance to the next slide. Do you want the speaker to move to the next slide or would you prefer for the show to move forward automatically and loop back to the beginning in a continuous loop (as is appropriate for a trade show booth)?

 TIPS FROM A PRO: Check out the layout of the room that you will be using to deliver your presentation before the big moment. Layout helps set a particular atmosphere and affects how you will utilize your visual aids. Make sure that everyone can see, that you have room for equipment, that the setup conveys the atmosphere that you are seeking (intimate, hierarchical, and so on).

RUN MANUALLY FOR A LIVE PRESENTATION

How: When you will be giving a live presentation and haven't previously added any transition timings, you can use the PowerPoint default settings and advance your slides manually. If you have added automatic timings or just like to be careful, however, you will want to follow these steps to set up the show before the presentation:

1. Choose **Slide Show|Set Up Show**. The dialog box shown in Figure 8.7 appears.
2. Choose **Presented by a Speaker (Full Screen)**, and **Advance Slides Manually**. (Notice that the default here is Use timings, if present.)
3. If necessary, use the **Projector Wizard** to help the computer connect properly to the projection system. Click **OK**.
4. Choose **Slide Show|View Show** to start the presentation on Slide 1 in Slide Show view. To start on a different slide in the presentation, make it the current slide, and then click the **Slide Show View** button.

Result: The slide that you have chosen to begin with, whether Slide 1 or another slide, fills the screen. The menus and toolbars are hidden, so the audience sees only the visual aid. Now everything is ready for your big moment.

RUN AUTOMATICALLY FOR A STANDALONE KIOSK

How: Before you run the show, you must first set it up.

1. Choose **Slide Show|Set Up Show**. The dialog box shown in Figure 8.7 appears.
2. Choose **Browsed at a Kiosk (Full Screen)**. The choice, **Loop Continuously Until 'Esc'**, is automatically selected. This keeps viewers from making changes to your show.

Figure 8.7
Set Up Show dialog box

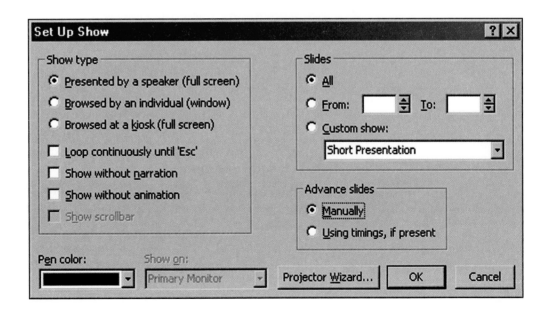

3. Choose either **Advance Slides Using Timings,** to run the show automatically using timings you have recorded, or choose **Advance Slides Manually** if you have set up action buttons for the viewer to use. (Without timings or action buttons, the slide show just sits there on Slide 1.)

4. Specify whether you want to omit narration or animation. Leave these boxes empty to use both animations and voice narration you have recorded.

5. If necessary, use the Projector Wizard to help the computer connect properly to the projection system. Click **OK.**

6. Choose **Slide Show|View Show** to start the presentation on Slide 1 in Slide Show view; or to start on any slide in the presentation, make the slide the current slide, and then click the Slide Show View button.

Result: The slide with which you have chosen to begin the show appears in Slide Show view and your presentation begins to advance according to the timings you set, or when the user clicks the action buttons. The show automatically restarts when the last slide is reached or (for manual advance) if it is left untouched for five minutes.

 TIPS FROM A PRO: The third choice in the dialog box, Browsed by an Individual (Window), starts the presentation within an individual window with a scrollbar for navigation. This can be used for a Web-based presentation, in which the user has several windows open (so the show must not take over the entire screen). You learn more about this in Chapter 10, "Prepare for an Internet or Intranet Presentation."

 TIPS FROM A PRO: Did you know that you could cause your slide show to open automatically in Slide Show view? To do this, choose **File|Save As,** and change Save As Type to PowerPoint Show (*.pps). Now you can open the file from the desktop when you are ready to use this feature. Double-click the filename from My Computer or Windows Explorer, and the show will open in Slide Show view.

TASK **8**   *Give Your Presentation*

What: You have carefully prepared your presentation's content, your visual aids, and your clothing—the time is here, and you are ready to go. When delivering your presentation, you need to know how to navigate from slide to slide, as well as how to *annotate,* or mark on, your slides.

In Slide Show view, you can navigate and control the screen by pressing keys or by accessing the shortcut menu.

During your presentation, you can use PowerPoint's Meeting Minder to take notes or list action items decided during the interaction with the audience.

Why: Navigating smoothly around your presentation, including going directly to the slide you want to show, is an important aspect of a smooth and professional delivery.

TIPS FROM A PRO: It's important to grab your audience's attention in the beginning of a presentation. Here are some ideas to help accomplish this:

- Startling fact.
- Tell a relevant (clean) joke, if you have that talent.
- Tell an anecdote or story that relates to your audience and leads into your topic.
- Use a clever acronym.
- Use a strong visual.

After you have gotten the attention of your listeners, it is important to keep it. Getting the audience involved is one way. Some techniques that might help are as follows:

- Ask a thought-provoking question.
- Present a problem.
- Ask for the causes of a situation.

NAVIGATE WITH KEYS

How: You can use the keys shown in Table 8.2 to navigate from slide to slide in Slide Show view.

Table 8.3 shows ways that you can press keys to make other things happen on screen.

Table 8.2 Navigating Using the Keyboard

To Go Here	*Press This Key*
Advance to the next slide or next animated item	Spacebar
	Enter, N, right arrow, down arrow, Page Down, or mouse click
Back up one step	Left arrow
	Backspace, P, Page Up, up arrow (or right-click, but see the next section)
Go to the first slide	Home
	Hold down both mouse buttons for two seconds
Go to any slide	Type slide number and press Enter
Go to the last side	End
Go to the next hidden slide	H
Exit Slide Show view	Esc
Stop or start an automatically advancing slide show	S

Table 8.3 Controlling the Screen

To Do This	*Press This Key*
Show a black screen (or return it to the slide show from black)	B
Show a white screen (or return it to the slide show from white)	W
Erase annotations (discussed in the next section)	E

Result: Without leaving Slide Show view, you can confidently go to the slide that you want to show. Even when you have a remote control, it is quite easy to walk over to the keyboard (if the computer is nearby) and casually tap the spacebar to advance to the next slide, or to press a key to control the presentation.

 TIPS FROM A PRO: Print the keyboard shortcuts and keep them near the computer during your presentation.

 TIPS FROM A PRO: You have spent hours and hours preparing your perfect visual aids. You open your mouth, and in a few moments you have lost your audience's attention and your credibility.

Don'ts
- Using fillers like um, ah, and like
- Pacing around and appearing generally ill at ease
- Appearing unfriendly, bored, or nervous
- Playing with anything such as change, hair, jewelry, glasses, or pens
- Turning you back on the audience

Dos
- Dress appropriately for the situation. Your audience starts forming an opinion about you as soon as they seen you.
- Be prepared and articulate—know your material and your audience.
- Be confident and enthusiastic about your subject and your audience.
- Be friendly. Use a tone that conveys these characteristics.
- Be comfortable—move around the room and be yourself.

SET UP THE POPUP MENU

 CORE OBJECTIVE: **Use on-screen navigation tools**

How: In the pressure of the moment, you may not remember the key that you need to press to cause a specific action. That is not a problem because you are not limited to using keys with PowerPoint—you can access the Popup (shortcut) menu instead. Before you can use it, however, you must first make sure that it is turned on.

1. Choose **Tools|Options** and click the **View** tab (Figure 8.8).
2. Click to check one of the Popup menu options shown under Slide show in the dialog box, and click **OK**.

Result: If you choose **Show Popup Menu Button**, when you wiggle the mouse in Slide Show view, the Popup Menu button appears on the lower-left corner of the screen. Then you can click it to see the Popup menu.

If you choose **Popup Menu on Right Mouse Click**, you will not be able to use a right-click to go to the previous slide. Instead, the popup menu appears on screen.

 TIPS FROM A PRO: The last choice in the View Options dialog box is one that you can consider using for your presentations: End your show with a blank slide or black screen. You might also consider creating a duplicate of the title slide to end with. Not only does this help the audience realize that the show is over, but also the last thing that they see is your name and company.

Any of these choices will help prevent you from getting caught up in giving your presentation and forget that you are done. You won't advance past the last slide and get thrown back into PowerPoint's with your audience staring at the menus and toolbars. That is the equivalent of letting the audience of a play see the mess backstage—it spoils the illusion.

Figure 8.8
View Options dialog box

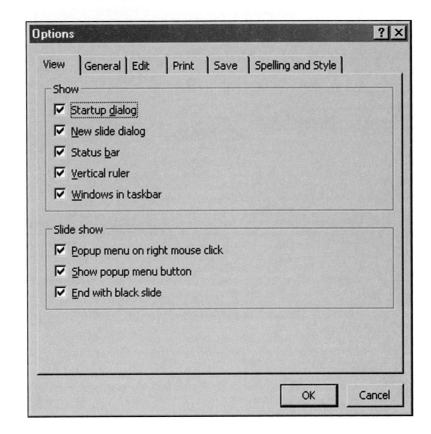

NAVIGATE USING THE SHORTCUT MENU

CORE OBJECTIVE: Use on-screen navigation tools

How: Use this option in Slide Show view.

1. Right-click or wiggle the mouse and click the **Popup Menu** button on screen to see the shortcut menu.
2. Choose **GolBy Title,** and click the slide you want to view (Figure 8.9).

TIPS FROM A PRO: As you learned in Chapter 7, "Get Ready for an Electronic Slide Show," when you are working with a custom show, you can use the Slide Navigator to open a custom show. As you see in Figure 8.9, the Slide Navigator not only lets you navigate to a different show, but also lists the slides in the current presentation as well.

Figure 8.9
Slide Show popup
menu

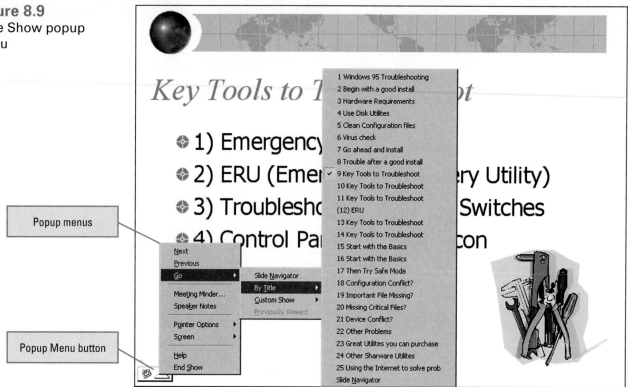

Popup menus

Popup Menu button

Result: You can also use the Popup menu to black out the screen, end the show, or navigate to the next and previous slide. With your expertise in PowerPoint, however, you probably know more convenient methods.

TIPS FROM A PRO: Be careful when using the mouse during a slide show. If you move the mouse, the arrow moves on screen and may distract the audience. Even worse, if your hand is shaky or you're nervous, you may unconsciously wiggle the mouse, causing the pointer to dance all around the screen. After the arrow mouse pointer appears, it remains on screen for about 10 seconds. To get rid of that annoying mouse pointer in a hurry, press the **A** key.

ANNOTATE

CORE OBJECTIVE: Use the pen during a presentation

How: To use the mouse pointer to draw on screen in Slide Show view, follow these steps

1. Right-click and choose **Pointer Options|Pen**.
2. Drag the mouse to draw on the screen.
3. To change to another color of pen, right-click and choose **Pointer Options|Pen Color** and click the color (Figure 8.10).
4. To erase the annotation, press **E**.
5. To remove the pen pointer, right-click and choose **Pointer Options|Automatic**.

Figure 8.10
Annotating with a
different color pen

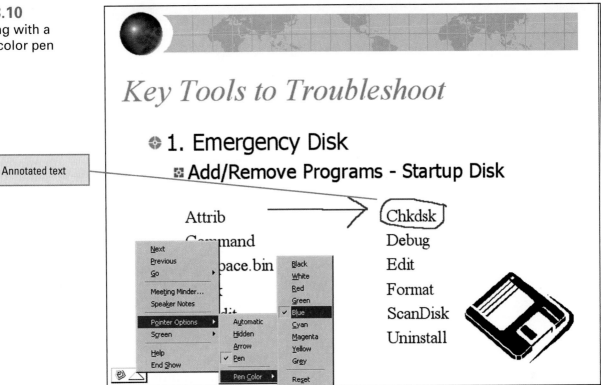

Annotated text

Result: You can mark items you want to draw attention to. Check, underline, circle, or draw an arrow to an item on screen, but keep it to a minimum. Unless you are able to write legibly, think carefully before writing on your slides.

TIPS FROM A PRO: If you are making notes to yourself, you can also right-click and choose **Speaker Notes**. That way you don't have to export the items to Word to see them. Wait for a break in the presentation and no one will even know what you are doing.

MAKE NOTES DURING THE MEETING

How: During the interactive portion of your presentation, you may come up with some ideas or conclusions you want to note, or some tasks that you want to carry out after the show. To access the applicable dialog box in Slide Show view, right-click and choose **Meeting Minder** (Figure 8.11).

To add notes using the Meeting Minder, follow these steps:

1. Click the **Meeting Minutes** tab. Enter meeting notes or minutes.
2. Click **OK** to remove the dialog box and continue with the presentation.

To add action items, click the **Action Items** tab to see the dialog box shown in Figure 8.12.

1. Click in the **Description** box, and add your text. Tab to assign the task to someone, and then tab and enter the due date.

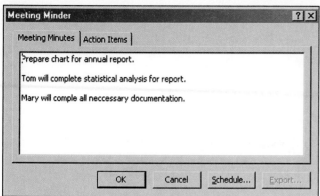

Figure 8.11 Adding meeting minutes

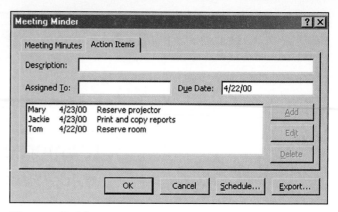

Figure 8.12 Adding action items

2. Click **Add** and the action items are added to a slide at the end of the presentation.
3. Click **OK** to remove the dialog box and continue with the presentation.

Result: Clicking Add after adding action items automatically creates a new slide at the end of the presentation, as you see in Figure 8.13. At anytime during or after the presentation, you can export a copy of these notes to Word so that you can print them. Task 10 describes exactly how to do this.

Figure 8.13
Action items slide

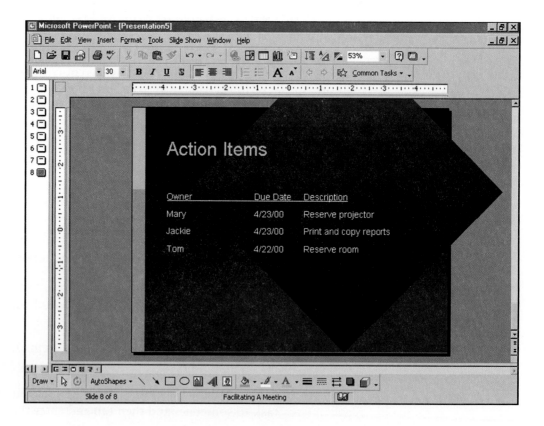

Expert Objective: **Generate meeting notes**

What: End your presentation with a big finish, and enjoy the applause. Even when it is all over, maintain your poise—you are still being observed until you are out the door. Make yourself available for audience members who want to talk with you one on one.

You can generate meeting notes from the action items and minutes you took using Meeting Minder before you go, or generate them back at the office and email them to the intended recipients.

Why: The relief of finishing is a wonderful feeling, but you have got to tie up loose ends before the thoughts are out of your mind.

How: To generate meeting notes, follow these steps:

1. Choose **Tools|Meeting Minder**, or if you're still in Slide Show view, choose **Meeting Minder** from the shortcut menu.
2. In the Meeting Minutes tab, click **Export**. (You may have to type something to activate the button.)
3. Be sure to check "Send meeting minutes and action items to Microsoft Word." Click **Export Now** (Figure 8.14).

Result: Word opens with a new document containing the notes from the Meeting Minutes tab and the action items you recorded during your presentation (Figure 8.15). Save and print them as you would any Word document.

Figure 8.14 Exporting notes and action items to Word

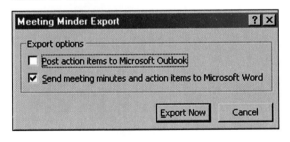

Figure 8.15 Word document created by export of meeting minutes

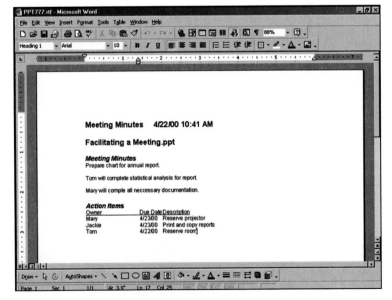

Tips from a Pro: To add dialog to a kiosk display or a Web presentation, or to add meeting notes, you can record voice narration to include with your slides.

Voices can be recorded before, during, and after the slide show. If your computer has a microphone and a sound card, choose **Slide Show Record Narration**, and follow the instructions provided.

Use PinPoint

After gaining the skills in this chapter, you can print slides, handouts, overheads, and speaker notes. You can also navigate confidently in Slide Show view, annotate the slides, and generate notes using the Meeting Minder. Now it's time to use the PinPoint software to test your skills. Remember: Anytime that you are unsure of what to do next, reread the relevant portion of the chapter or click Show Me. Check out these skills in PinPoint:

- Change output formatting
- Generate meeting notes
- Print a presentation
- Print handouts
- Print overhead transparencies
- Print speaker notes
- Run a slide show
- Slide show navigation
- Use the slide show pen

Key Terms

You can find definitions for these words in this chapter:

Annotate
Collapsed
Expanded
Hard copy

Review Questions

You can use the following review questions and exercises to test your knowledge and skills. Answers are given in Appendix D, "Answers to Review Questions."

True/False

Indicate whether each statement is true (T) or false (F).

___ 1. To print the outline, click the Print button, press Ctrl+P, or choose File|Print.

___ 2. To make overhead transparencies, choose File|Page Setup to specify the page size and orientation.

___ 3. Use Print Preview when you want to see how the handouts will look when printed.

___ 4. To preview how the slides will look in pure black and white, hold down the Shift key and click the Grayscale Preview button.

___ 5. To print handouts, you must first choose File|Page Setup.

___ 6. If you collapse an outline, when you print it, only the titles are listed.

___ 7. To run a self-running, automatic slide show, you must first have timings set.

___ 8. If you want to print only page 3, click the Print button and type p 3.

___ 9. In Slide Show view, the easiest way to advance a slide is to press the spacebar.

___ 10. In Slide Show view, when you click and drag the mouse, it draws on the slide.

Multiple Choice

Select the letter that best completes the statement.

___ 1. When creating overhead transparencies, it is a good idea to:
a. Print the final copy in black and white.
b. Change the background to white or a light color.
c. Set the margins for the page to 1 inch, at least.
d. Turn off the projector when it is not needed.
e. Purchase a laser pointer.

___ 2. Grayscale preview changes colors of elements on the slide so that:
a. Text appears black.
b. The background appears white.
c. Filled objects appear in shades of gray.
d. Charts appear in shades of gray.
e. All of the above.

___ 3. To print audience handouts that automatically include an area for note taking, choose:
a. 2 per page.
b. 3 per page.
c. Outline view.
d. Portrait orientation.
e. Expanded view.

___ 4. To add text or an image to every printed page of handouts or notes pages:
a. Use the Notes Master or Handout Master.
b. Add a header and footer.
c. Choose Frame Slides before you print.
d. Change to Grayscale preview.
e. Both a and b.

___ 5. Printing handouts saves pages because you can print this many slides per page:
a. 2, 4, 6, or 8.
b. 2, 3, 5, 7, or 9.
c. 2, 3, 4, 6, or 9.
d. 3, 4, or 6.
e. 2, 3, or 4.

___ 6. In Slide Show view, the fastest way to advance to the next slide or animated item, is to:
a. Double-click.
b. Press the spacebar.
c. Type the slide number and press Enter.
d. Right-click and choose Next.
e. Find the laser pointer, aim it at the infrared sensor, and click.

___ 7. To navigate quickly to a particular slide in Slide Show view:

    a. Type the slide number and press Enter.

    b. Right-click and choose Go and choose the slide title.

    c. Scroll down using the scrollbar until you see the correct slide in the yellow box.

    d. All of the above.

    e. Both a and b.

___ 8. When you draw on the screen using a pen-shaped mouse pointer, this is called:

    a. Annotating.

    b. Annoying.

    c. Commenting.

    d. Drawing.

    e. Noting.

___ 9. If you type action items and click Add, the action items are automatically added to:

    a. A list you can see in the Meeting Minder.

    b. A new slide at the end of the presentation.

    c. A Word document.

    d. A new PowerPoint show.

    e. A custom show.

___ 10. When you are through with the presentation, to get a printed copy of the meeting minutes and action items:

    a. Click the Print button.

    b. Choose File|Print.

    c. In the Meeting Minder, click Export.

    d. In the Meeting Minder, click Print.

    e. All of the above.

Screen Review

Match the letters in Figure 8.16 with the correct items in the list.

Figure 8.16

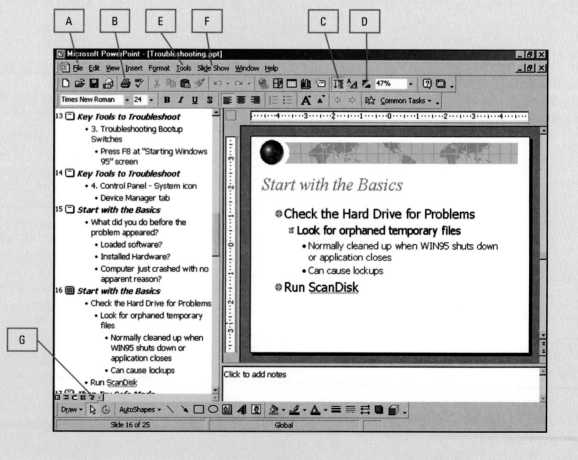

___ 1. Click here to view the current slide in Slide Show view.

___ 2. Click here to end the show with an all-black slide.

___ 3. Click here to see how the slides look in black and white.

___ 4. Click here to collapse the outline to show only titles.

___ 5. Click here to print audience handouts.

___ 6. Click here to print the outline.

___ 7. Click here to run the show at a standalone kiosk.

Exercise and Project

Follow these step-by-step instructions to practice the skills that are included in this chapter. If you are working in a computer lab, you may have to ask your instructor where to save or print your work.

Exercise

1. Start PowerPoint and open **PPT8** from the Student\Chapter 8 folder of the PinPoint CD-ROM that came with this book.
2. Collapse the outline and print it so that only the slide titles show.
3. Add your name and the page number to the Handout Master. Change the orientation of the handouts to landscape, and then print handouts, nine per page.
4. Preview Slide 2 in pure black and white. Change any objects so that all the text appears. Print the slide in pure black and white.
5. Use the Help facility under Slide Show Controls to find all the shortcuts you can use for navigating in Slide Show view. Save the file in your PowerPoint 2000 folder as **Exercise 8A** and print the page.
6. In Slide Show view, use the pen to annotate the second slide by drawing a line around External Purposes. To make a record of the annotation, press the **Print Screen** key. End Slide Show view, insert a new blank slide, and paste. Print the slide.
7. In Slide Show view, use Meeting Minder to add an action item. Remind your teacher to give you an A on this assignment, and remind yourself to study hard for the next exam. Click Add. Print the action items slide.
8. In Slide Show view, use Meeting Minder to note *who* attended the meeting (use your name and some of your friends). Export the notes and action items to a Word document and print.
9. Save your presentation as **Exercise 8B** and exit the program.

Project

Create a PowerPoint show explaining the benefits of using overhead transparencies, audience handouts, and speaker notes. Add a slide or two to explain the special steps required to run a kiosk-style automatic slide show. Last, create a slide or slides explaining when and how to annotate slides.

Format the slide show for black-and-white overhead transparencies with portrait orientation. Add your name and page number, save the file as **Project 8** and then print.

Integrate Charts and Tables

Sometimes the most effective way to communicate a particular point is to present it in a chart or table. PowerPoint includes several slide layouts particularly useful for displaying specific types of information. The first of these, Table layout, sets up a grid to display columns and rows of text or numbers side by side. On the other hand, the Chart layouts are good for showing numeric data in a graphical form. Microsoft Office also has a complementary program called MS Graph that you can use in PowerPoint to create charts from numeric data. Another program that you can access from PowerPoint, Organization Chart, can be used to display a hierarchy, such as the employees in a company.

At the end of this chapter, you will be able to:

C E

C	E	
❑	☑	Build an organization chart
❑	☑	Modify an organization chart
☑	❑	Create tables within PowerPoint
❑	☑	Add a table from Word
❑	☑	Modify PowerPoint tables
❑	❑	Format a table
❑	☑	Apply diagonal borders to a table
❑	☑	Build a chart or graph
❑	❑	Import data into the datasheet
❑	❑	Choose the appropriate chart type
❑	☑	Modify a chart or graph
☑	❑	Import text from Word
❑	☑	Export an outline to Word
❑	☑	Insert an Excel chart

What: PowerPoint offers a slide layout for a specialized type of diagram called an *organization chart*, or "org chart." These charts show the relationship between specific information, such as the hierarchy that exists between managers and subordinates, or between divisions within a company. To create an org chart, use Microsoft Organization Chart, a program with its own menus, toolbars, and help system.

Why: Although you learned in Chapter 6, "Elements of Sight and Sound," how to add shapes and lines onto a slide, think of how much work it would be to create and format all these items to make sure that they align correctly. Microsoft Organization Chart makes this process much easier.

START AN ORG CHART

How: To start an org chart, follow these steps:

1. When you want to add an org chart, insert a new slide with the Organization Chart layout shown in Figure 9.1 or change the layout of an existing slide.
2. Double-click anywhere in or on the placeholder to launch the program.

 TIPS FROM A PRO: You can also begin an org chart on an existing slide by choosing **Insert|Picture** and **Organization Chart**.

Figure 9.1 Inserting an organizational chart slide

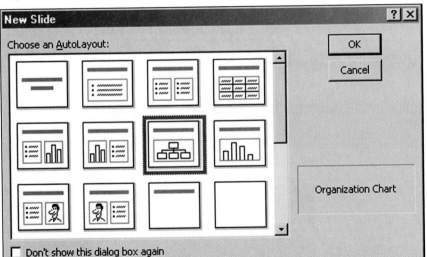

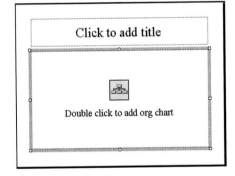

Result: The Microsoft Organization Chart program opens in a new window over the PowerPoint presentation. You can now add information to the four data boxes included with the default chart (Figure 9.2). Or, you can add additional data boxes and format the chart using the methods provided in the remainder of this task.

Figure 9.2
Microsoft
Organization Chart
window

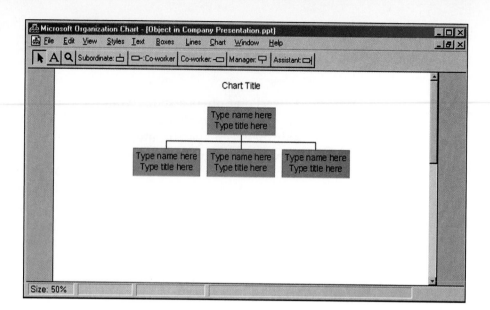

BUILD THE ORG CHART

EXPERT OBJECTIVE: **Build an organization chart**

How: After you have inserted a blank org chart, you can use the following instructions to build various aspects of the chart.

- ❍ To add information to a data box, click in the box and type the name, title, and up to two more lines. Press **Enter** or **Tab** to advance to the next line each time. The default text disappears as you type.
- ❍ To save changes as you work, choose **File|Update** [*filename*].
- ❍ To add new data boxes for additional employees, departments, and so on, follow these steps:
    1. Click the button on the toolbar for the type of data box that you want to add. The mouse pointer becomes a small replica of that box (Figure 9.3).
    2. Click the existing data box to attach the new one.

Figure 9.3
Adding a data box to
the org chart

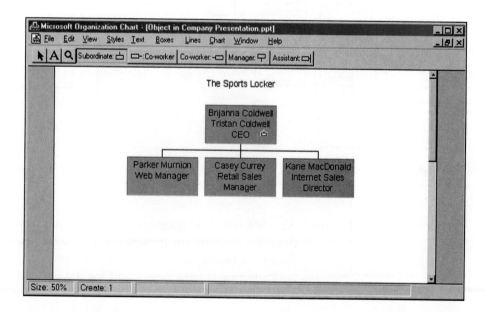

Figure 9.4
A selected data box
appears black

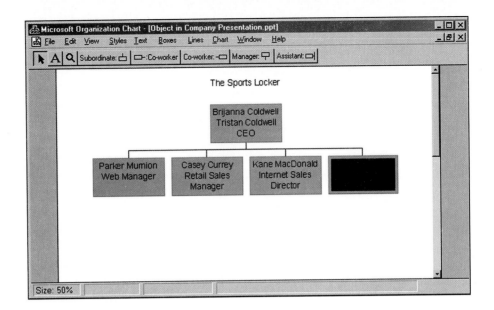

O To delete a data box, click the box to select it and press **Delete** (Figure 9.4).

O To close Microsoft Organization Chart and insert the completed org chart onto the slide, choose **File|Exit and Return**. When prompted, click **Yes**.

Result: The org charge programs closes and you are back in the PowerPoint window. Your slide displays the org chart that you just made, as you see in Figure 9.5. The sizing handles that surround it are useful to size and position the chart (like with clip art, as discussed in Chapter 6).

Figure 9.5
Slide with org chart

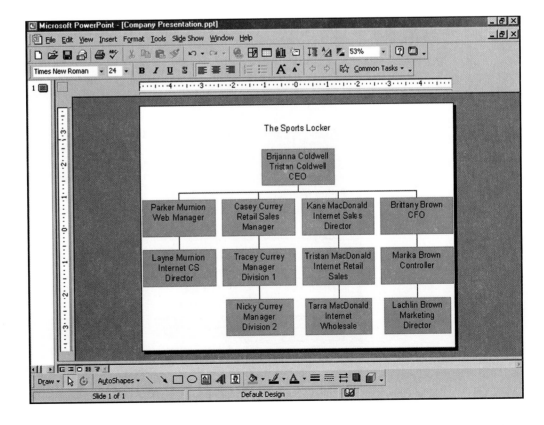

EXPERT OBJECTIVE: **Modify an organization chart**

How: As with other objects, you must double-click an org chart to make changes. This reopens the Microsoft Organization Chart program and its window.

❍ To add or delete boxes, use the methods described earlier in this task.
❍ To format the org chart, select the item that you want to change and then use the program menu. If you want to select several boxes at once for formatting, use the **Select** arrow and drag. Access the following menu items to modify various chart features.
  • **Text** controls the text font, color, and alignment.
  • **Boxes** controls the color, shadow, and borders of the boxes.
  • **Lines** controls the thickness, style, and color of the connecting lines between the boxes.
  • **Chart** controls the background color of the chart itself.
  • **Styles** changes the way the groups appear (Figure 9.6).
❍ To update the chart, and continue working in the program, choose **File|Update** [your *filename*].
❍ To close the program and return to the PowerPoint window, click the **Close** button or choose **File|Close and Return to [your file name]** or **File|Exit and Return to [your file name]**. When prompted, click **Yes** to update the org chart.

Result: Regardless of the way that you closed the program the org chart in your presentation is immediately updated to reflect the changes that you made (Figure 9.7).

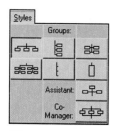

Figure 9.6
Org chart styles

Figure 9.7
Formatted org chart

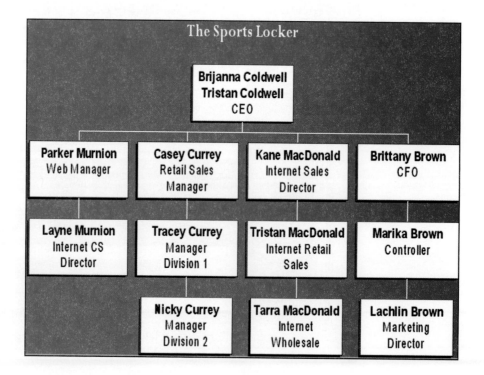

CORE OBJECTIVE: Create tables within PowerPoint

What: When you want to line up text side by side in a slide, create a *table*. This grid-like structure can contain words or numbers. A table keeps items properly aligned in columns and rows, so you don't have to fuss with setting tabs.

Why: Regardless of the particular task, tables are invaluable when you have text that must be precisely aligned. When you are creating a schedule and want days, times, and events next to each other, use a table! Or, you may want to use a table to neatly present products and sales figures for several time periods. Clearly there are many other examples of when using a table will not only present your data in an organized fashion, but will also save you time as well.

INSERT A TABLE

How: To begin a PowerPoint table on a new slide, follow these steps:

1. Add a new slide and choose **Table** layout. The new slide appears as in Figure 9.8.

Figure 9.8 Inserting a Table layout slide

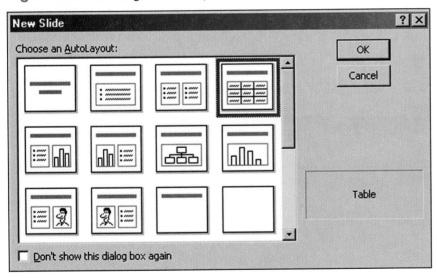

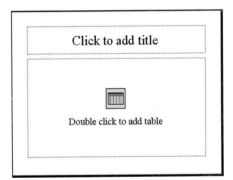

2. Double-click in the slide placeholder as indicated to begin the table. Enter the dimensions of the table in the dialog box that appears (Figure 9.9).

TIPS FROM A PRO: You can create a table on an existing slide. Click the **Insert Tables** button and drag to specify the number of columns and rows, or choose **Insert|Table**. Unlike the previously described method, these tables don't automatically replace the standard placeholder. Instead, a table becomes an additional object on the slide, along with a hatched border and sizing handles (similar to other objects). If you find that you now have too many placeholders, select any unnecessary ones and press **Delete**.

Result: A grid-like table fills the placeholder (Figure 9.10), and the Table toolbar appears, along with buttons that will help you modify the table. In addition, the mouse pointer changes into a pencil that you use to divide the table into more columns and rows.

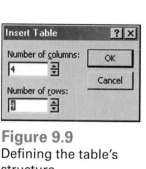

Figure 9.9
Defining the table's structure

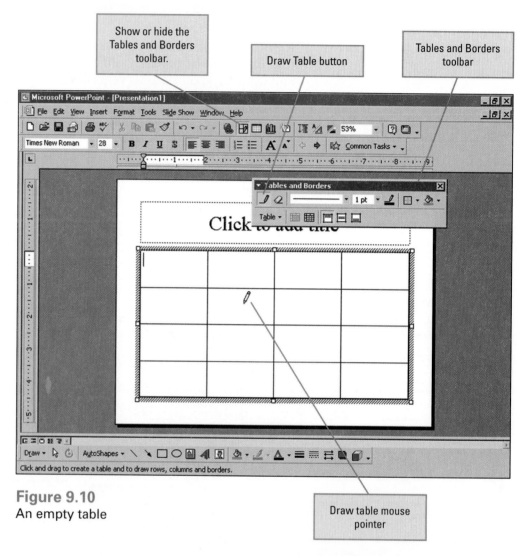

Figure 9.10
An empty table

TIPS FROM A PRO: You can also use the Draw Table button to draw a table on a slide. To begin, click the **Tables and Borders** button on the Standard toolbar to display the toolbar. Next click the **Draw Table** button to turn on a pencil-like mouse pointer (Figure 9.10). Draw to define the overall dimensions of the table, and then draw to divide it into rows and columns.

After you have finished, click the **Draw Table** button again or press **Esc** to restore the normal mouse pointer. Drawing tables this way can be a tricky process, so don't lose patience and try to break the pencil.

ENTER TEXT IN A TABLE

How: To add text to your new table, follow these steps:

1. If the insertion point isn't blinking in the first *cell*, the box formed where the column and row intersect, click in the cell and begin entering text.
2. Press **Enter** when you want to start a new paragraph *within the cell*. The height of the row expands to contain all the text that you enter.
3. Press **Tab** to advance to the next cell, and then type its contents. Press **Tab** at the last cell in a row to advance to the first cell in the next row. If you are in the bottom row in the far-right cell when you tab, a new row is added to the table.
4. Press **Shift+Tab** to go back to the preceding cell.

Result: The table keeps the text aligned side by side, as you see in Figure 9.11. You can format the fonts and paragraphs within a table using the techniques that you learned in previous chapters or that are given in Task 4. Notice that the text in the table doesn't appear in the outline pane. Like text placed in a text box, all the data that you type into a table is visible or accessible only in the slide pane.

Figure 9.11
Completed table

The Sport's Locker

2000	Qtr 1	Qtr 2	Qtr 3
Shoes	$1,375	$2,530	$3,044
Apparel	$2,585	$2,064	$3180
Equipment	$1,864	$2,905	$2,435

CREATE A WORD TABLE

EXPERT OBJECTIVE: Add a table from Word

How: Are you familiar with creating tables in Word? If you are, that's good news because you can create a Word table within your PowerPoint presentation.

1. Choose **Insert|Picture|Microsoft Word Table**.
2. Specify the number of rows and columns.

TIPS FROM A PRO: When you create table this way, you can use all of PowerPoint table features not available in PowerPoint, such as Table AutoFormat.

Result: A blank Word table is inserted into the presentation, ready for you to enter text and to format. As you can see in Figure 9.12, the Word ruler surrounds the table and Word's menus and toolbars replace the normal PowerPoint menus and toolbars. Nonetheless, you can see by your surroundings that you are still in PowerPoint. Even though you are using Word, the table is completely contained within PowerPoint. No separate Word file exists! Click outside the table to return to the presentation and restore PowerPoint's menus and toolbars.

When you want to edit or modify the table, double-click anywhere in the table.

Title bar shows
PowerPoint.

Figure 9.12 Word table inserted into slide

Menus, toolbars, and formula bar are Word's.

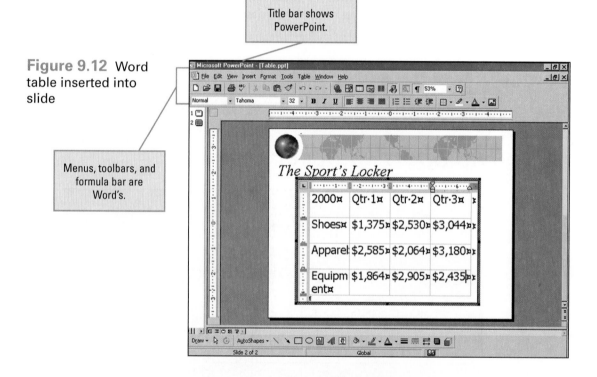

Example of formatted Word table

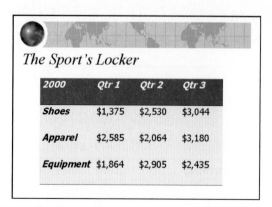

Expert Objective: Modify PowerPoint tables

What: After your text has been entered into the table, you can restructure the table.

Why: You may find that you need more or less columns or rows, or that the ones you have are the wrong size.

INSERT AND DELETE ROWS AND COLUMNS

How: To insert or delete rows and columns, follow these steps:

1. If it is not visible after you click the table, click the **Tables and Borders** button on the Standard toolbar to display the Tables and Borders toolbar.
2. Click to place the insertion point in the table where you want to insert or delete the row or column.
3. Click the **Table** button on the Tables and Borders toolbar to see the menu shown in Figure 9.13. Choose the appropriate operation to delete or insert.

Figure 9.13
The Table menu

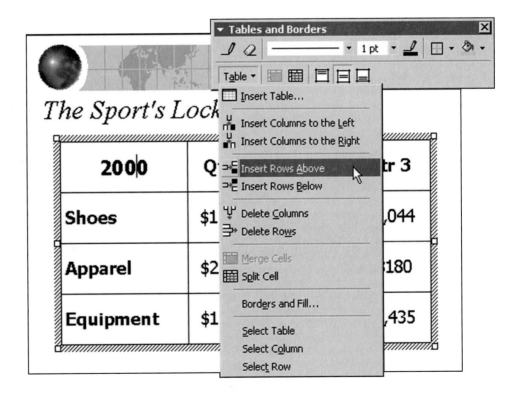

Result: The table structure now contains a different number of rows or columns. One problem may arise when you add more columns or rows this way, however. When you first create a table, it fills the placeholder; adding more rows or columns may make the table too large to fit on the slide. Also, when a column or row is deleted, the text it contains is also deleted.

TIPS FROM A PRO: You can adjust the width of columns or the height of rows. Place the mouse pointer over the gridline between rows or columns until it turns into a two-headed arrow, as you see in Figure 9.14. Now you can drag to adjust the column width or row height.

Figure 9.14
Adjusting row height

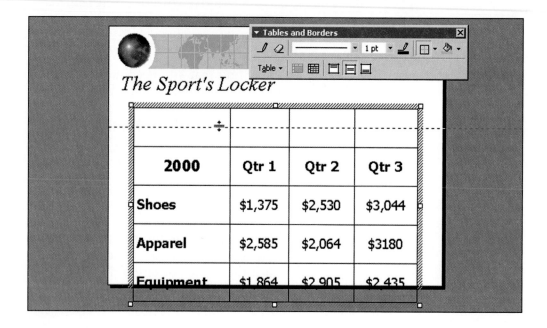

DRAW AND ERASE GRIDLINES

How: Perhaps a better way to add or remove rows and columns from a table is to use the Draw Table and Eraser buttons on the Tables and Borders toolbar. Using your mouse, you can drag the pointer to divide the table into rows and columns of varying sizes and shapes.

1. Click the table or the **Tables and Borders** button on the Standard toolbar to display the Tables and Borders toolbar. The Draw Table button is active as soon as you turn on the toolbar. The Eraser button next to it changes the structure by removing the gridlines.
2. Drag across the table to add rows; drag down to add columns (Figure 9.15).
3. Click the **Eraser** button and drag along a line to erase it and, thus, to remove a row or column.

Result: The table contains the additional rows and columns that you have drawn; and unlike the elements that you inserted using the Table button, they don't extend off the slide. When you use the Eraser button, the text is not deleted, but placed in an adjacent cell.

Figure 9.15
Drawing rows and
columns

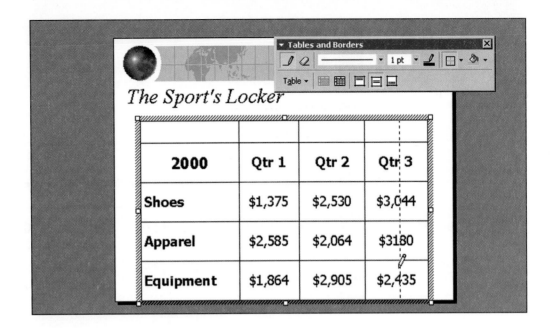

MERGE CELLS

How: You may want to *merge*, or combine, cells to make a single cell. You could use this feature when you want a title to span several columns, or a heading to be the height of several rows. Other times you will want to split a cell into two or more cells.

To merge cells, select the cells and use any of the following techniques:

1. Click the **Merge Cells** button on the Tables and Borders toolbar.
2. Choose **Table|Merge Cells**.
3. Right-click and choose **Merge Cells**.
4. Click the **Eraser** button and drag across the gridline separating the cells.

Result: What had been "cells" is now a "cell"—a single cell the same size as the total of the original cells has been formed. Any text within the individual cells is combined in the single cell that was created, as the title is in Figure 9.16.

SPLIT CELLS

How: The opposite of the Merge Cells operation, the Split Cells feature, enables you to split cells into two or more cells. Select the cell, and then follow these steps:

1. Click the **Draw Table** button and drag a line to divide the cell.
2. Click the **Split Cells** button on the Tables and Borders toolbar.
3. Choose **Table|Split Cells**.
4. Right-click and choose **Split Cells**.

Result: A cell is divided into two cells. If you want, you can select the cells and split them again. Figure 9.16 provides an example of a merged and a split cell.

Figure 9.16
Merged and split cells

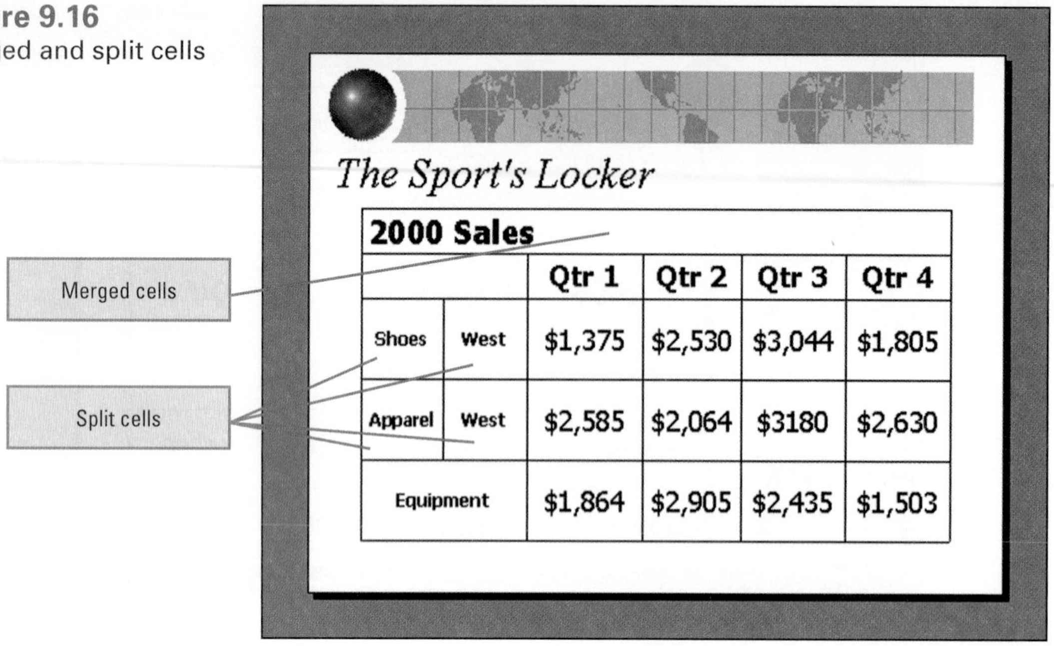

Merged cells

Split cells

The Sport's Locker

2000 Sales		Qtr 1	Qtr 2	Qtr 3	Qtr 4
Shoes	West	$1,375	$2,530	$3,044	$1,805
Apparel	West	$2,585	$2,064	$3180	$2,630
Equipment		$1,864	$2,905	$2,435	$1,503

TASK 4   *Format a Table*

What: After the table structure is just the way that you want it, you can format the table so that it looks attractive. By default, text in the table appears in the font assigned to the text placeholders in the template that you are using. It is also left aligned at the top of each cell. You can change both the horizontal and the vertical alignment of the text within the cells.

Although the default table has simple borders, you may want to remove the borders or change their color, weight, or placement. The lines that form a border can vary in width and line style, as well as color. PowerPoint gives you several ways to control the table borders and fill: a dialog box and buttons on the Tables and Borders toolbar.

Why: Choosing appropriate alignment and borders can enhance the table and help communicate the message.

CHANGE ALIGNMENT

How: To change how the text is aligned within the cell, use the alignment buttons on the Formatting toolbar, as well as the vertical alignments on the Tables and Borders toolbar.

1. Select the cell or cells you want to align.
2. Click the **Align Left, Center,** or **Align Right** buttons to change the horizontal alignment within the cell.
3. Click the **Align Top, Center Vertically,** or **Align Bottom** buttons to change the vertical alignment.

Result: Figure 9.17 shows several different possible ways to align text within the cells of a table.

Figure 9.17
Changing horizontal and vertical alignment

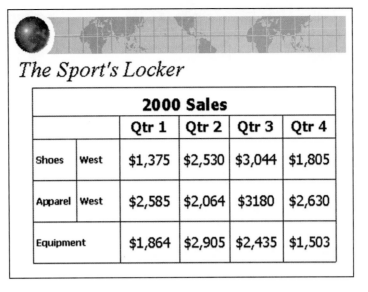

ADD BORDERS AND FILL

 C *CORE OBJECTIVE:* Apply diagonal borders to a table

How: To use a different border type, such as a heavier border around the outside of the table, or to remove the borders completely, select all or part of the table. Then use one of the following methods to modify various aspects of the border:

❍ Choose **Tables|Borders and Fill** to access the dialog box shown in Figure 9.18. Now you can specify the border style, weight, color, and placement. You can also change the fill color of the cells.

❍ Click to display the **Tables and Borders** toolbar, click the **Table** button, and choose **Borders and Fills** to access the dialog box (Figure 9.18).

Figure 9.18
Borders and Fill dialog box

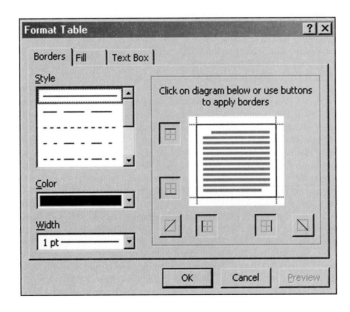

Figure 9.19
Specifying the border
style, weight, and
color

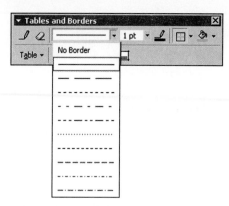

(a) Border style

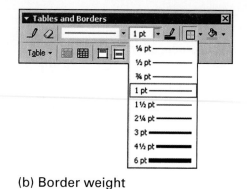

(b) Border weight

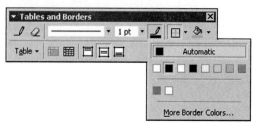

(c) Border color

○ Click to display the **Tables and Borders** toolbar.
○ Click the buttons on the toolbar to specify the border style, weight (width), and color, as in Figure 9.19.
○ Click one of the **Borders** buttons to apply that border to one or more sides of the selected cells, or click the **No Borders** button to remove the borders from the selected cells, as in Figure 9.20.
○ Click the **Fill Color** button. Now you can specify the fill color of the cell.

Figure 9.20
Borders button and
menu

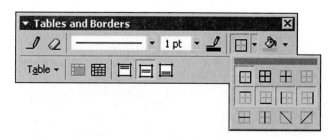

Result: When you use the Borders and Fill dialog box, or the buttons on the Tables and Borders toolbar, you can easily modify the format of a table. Figure 9.21 shows a sample table with diagonal borders.

Figure 9.21
Table with customized borders

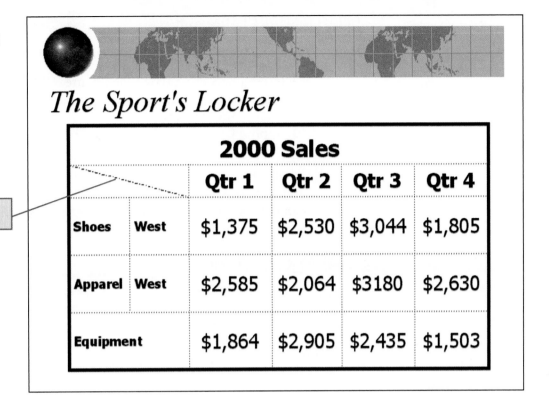

The Sport's Locker

2000 Sales		Qtr 1	Qtr 2	Qtr 3	Qtr 4
Shoes	West	$1,375	$2,530	$3,044	$1,805
Apparel	West	$2,585	$2,064	$3180	$2,630
Equipment		$1,864	$2,905	$2,435	$1,503

Diagonal border

TASK **5**   ***Use MS Graph to Create a Chart***

E   *EXPERT OBJECTIVE:* **Build a chart or graph**

What: Microsoft Office has a supplementary program called MS Graph that you can use in PowerPoint to create charts from numeric data. Excel also has a full-featured charting capability and you can also import a sophisticated Excel chart into a presentation as well.

When you access Microsoft Graph, you begin with the ***datasheet,*** a small worksheet containing the text and numbers that make up the chart.

Note: Although the words "chart" and "graph" generally mean the same thing in everyday usage, this book uses "chart" to refer to the diagram that you create and "Graph" to refer to the program that creates it.

Why: Slides dealing with numeric data can often get so bogged down in details that the audience misses the main message. A well-placed chart can show trends or relationships among numbers at a glance.

BEGIN A CHART FROM SCRATCH

How: You can begin creating a chart using any of the following methods:

     ❍ Insert a new chart type slide (Figure 9.22).
     ❍ Click the **Chart** button.
     ❍ Choose **Insert|Chart**.
     ❍ Apply a **Chart** layout to a slide and double-click the chart placeholder.

Result: As you can see in Figure 9.23, the Microsoft Graph menus and toolbars replace those of PowerPoint. The window displays a sample datasheet and a chart is formed on the slide from the data in the sheet. Now you can enter your own data into the sheet, as described in the next section of this task.

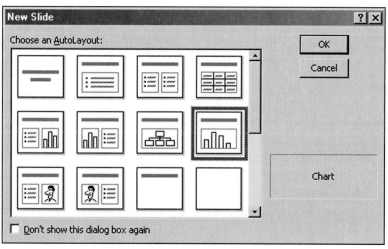

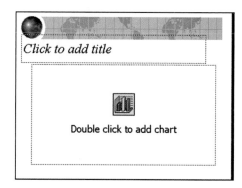

Figure 9.22   Inserting a Microsoft Graph slide

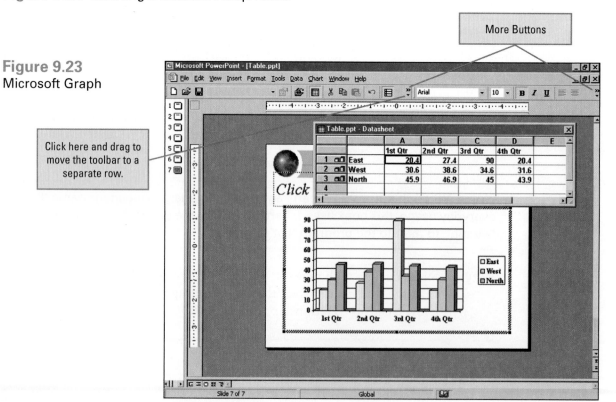

Figure 9.23
Microsoft Graph

Tips from a Pro: By default, the toolbars for Microsoft Graph appear on a single row. Click **More Buttons** to display additional buttons you can use to build and format your chart. (You can also separate the toolbars by dragging the Formatting toolbar's move handle to another row, as shown in Figure 9.24.) For information about rearranging and modifying toolbars, refer to Chapter 11, "Advanced Topics."

Figure 9.24
Chart toolbars on two rows

ENTER DATA IN GRAPH'S DATASHEET

How: The data in the sample datasheet must be changed to reflect your own information like the one shown in Figure 9.25. As soon as you make a change, it immediately appears on the sample chart. To update a datasheet, follow these steps:

Figure 9.25
Updating a chart datasheet

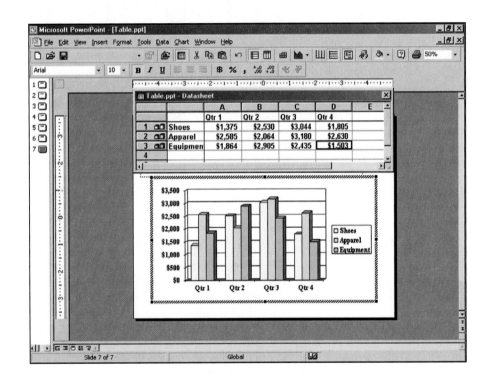

1. Click in the datasheet cells and type your text and numbers. Press **Tab** or the arrow keys to navigate from cell to cell.
2. Add more rows or columns to the chart by typing data in the datasheet.
3. Eliminate data by selecting the information and then pressing **Delete**. Alternatively, you can leave the data in the datasheet but not include it in the chart. To do this, double-click the column heading (A, B, or C) or row heading (1, 2, 3). Turn it back on by repeating this process.

4. When your datasheet is complete, click the **View Datasheet** button, click the **Close** button, or click outside of the datasheet to remove it from the screen so that you can format the chart.

Result: You can see the data values that you entered within the columns of the chart. Text appears either as categories or in the legend (Figure 9.26).

Figure 9.26
A modified chart

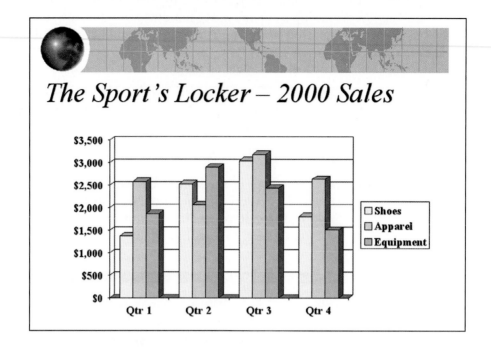

IMPORT DATA INTO THE DATASHEET

How: If the data that you want to display already exists in another file, such as an Excel worksheet or Word table, you don't have to retype it to create a chart using Microsoft Graph. Instead, you can import it directly into the datasheet. To import data into an open datasheet, follow these steps.

1. Click the **Import File** button or choose **Edit|Import File.**
2. In the dialog box, navigate to the correct drive or folder that contains the file. If necessary, change the file type.
3. Double-click the name of the file you want to import.
4. If you are importing a spreadsheet, a dialog box appears (Figure 9.27), enabling you to designate the specific range or selection of

Figure 9.27
Importing a file from
Excel

cells to import. If you are importing a text file, the Text Import Wizard appears to lead you step by step through the import process.

Result: The portions of the file that you designated are imported into the datasheet.

 TIPS FROM A PRO: You can import a Lotus 1-2-3 file, an Excel file, or any file in which tabs, commas, or spaces separate the data. Graph imports up to 4,000 rows by 4,000 columns, although this would clearly be meaningless in such a small space. (You should really limit the number of rows or columns.) Of course, if the data is contained in Excel, you can also cut and paste into the datasheet.

TASK 6 *Select Chart Types*

What: Graph offers 14 basic types of charts plus many more ways to create subtypes by modifying these. Which one you should use depends on the purpose of your chart and the data you will depict. Table 9.1 shows a sample of each chart and a possible reason for using that particular chart.

Table 9.1 Microsoft Graph Chart Types

Chart Type	Sample	Use This Type To
Column		Compare values by category or across time
Bar		Compare values by category but *not* over time
Line		Display trends over time
Pie		Show each item's contribution to the total
XY (scatter)		Show relationships between two aspects
Area		Display trend of totals over time
Doughnut		Show proportions, like several pie charts
Radar		Plot points on two intersecting axes
Surface		Display trends in three dimensions
Bubble		Show relationship, like scatter; includes a third factor
Stock		Record stock prices (high, low, close)
Cylinder		Same as column, using a unique shape
Cone		Same as column, using a unique shape
Pyramid		Same as column, using a unique shape
Stacked column (subchart)		Compare totals by category or over time
100% stacked column (subchart)		Compare proportions of a whole over time, like a series of pie charts

Why: Although the default column chart is attractive, it may not be the best way to portray your numbers. You must carefully determine which type of chart to use so that your message is presented in the most enlightening format.

For example, column charts and bar charts might seem to be used the same way because they look similar. However, column charts can be used to compare data over time, with the years represented by the horizontal axis. Bar charts, in contrast, aren't appropriate for comparing data over time, because the time would appear on the vertical axis; in our Western culture, time is always depicted from left to right, never from top to bottom.

How: Make sure to enter data correctly in the datasheet and to exclude irrelevant rows and columns, before you close the sheet. You can click the **Chart Type** button to choose a type of chart from the drop-down list, but this limits your choices. Instead, follow these steps:

1. Choose **Chart|Chart Type**. This opens the dialog box shown in Figure 9.28.
2. Designate the primary chart type on the left side of the dialog box, and then click the subtype on the right side of the dialog box.
3. Click and hold the button to preview your data with that chart type.
4. Click the **Custom Types** tab to use one of PowerPoint's jazzy, preformatted charts (Figure 9.29).

Figure 9.28 Chart Type dialog box

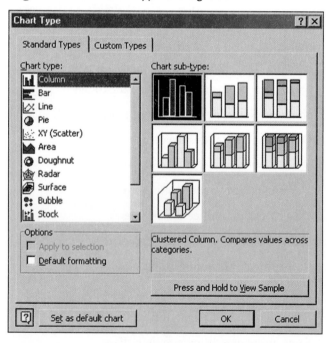

Figure 9.29 Custom Types tab

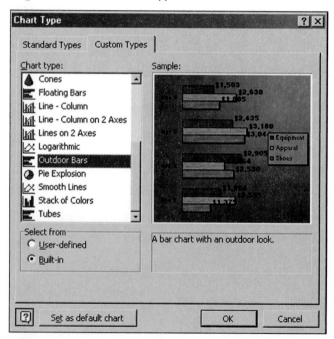

Result: The slide displays your text and numbers using the chart that you chose. Click elsewhere in the slide to return to the PowerPoint menus and toolbars.

TIPS FROM A PRO: Although they look visually attractive, 3-D charts make your charts harder to read and may even distort the numbers. Compare the two sets of charts in Figure 9.30. Notice how the 3-D chart distorts the size of the columns, making it impossible to judge the percentages. And in the column chart, it is difficult to see exactly the number represented. In general, 2-D charts present data more accurately.

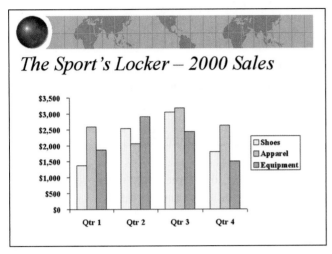

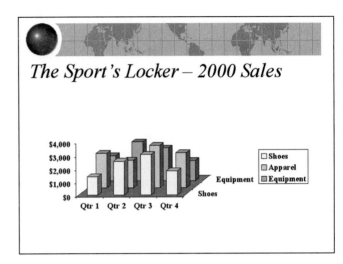

Figure 9.30 3-D charts may mislead

 E   *EXPERT OBJECTIVE:* Modify a chart or graph

What: When you use Microsoft Graph to create a chart in your presentation, you can always go back and modify the chart later.

Why: You may be completely satisfied with the appearance and the way your figures are represented, but it's more likely that you will see some refinements you want to make. Graph gives you control over the location of the legend and the colors of the lines or bars; it enables you to add gridlines and labels and to format the text and numbers appropriately. These features are identical to the charting feature used in Microsoft Excel.

How: As with other embedded objects, to make changes you must double-click the chart. This opens the Graph menus and toolbars, enabling you to make any of the following changes to the chart:

     ❍ To change the text and numbers, click the **View Datasheet** button to display the datasheet.

     ❍ To add titles and axis labels, choose **Chart|Chart Options** and click the **Titles** tab.

      ❍ To reposition the legend or delete it completely, choose **Chart|Chart Options** and click the **Legend** tab, shown in Figure 9.31. You can also click the **Legend** button on the toolbar to turn the legend off and on.

Figure 9.31
Options for a chart's
legend

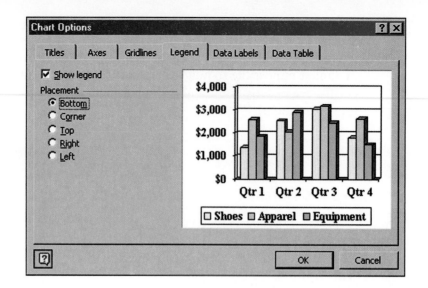

○ To place the actual numbers next to the pie slices or columns, choose **Chart|Chart Options** and click the **Data Labels** tab.
○ To format one part of a chart, click to select the item and then change its color and so on using the Format dialog box. You can access the dialog box three ways: double-click the chart element, click the **Format Chart Options** button on the Graph toolbar, or right-click and choose **Format** on the shortcut menu.

TIPS FROM A PRO: To format an individual data point, such as a single bar, column, or pie wedge, click once to select the data series, and then click it again to select the individual point.

Result: The chart is immediately updated to reflect your changes and enhancements. Click elsewhere on the slide to restore PowerPoint's menu and toolbars. Figure 9.32 displays a formatted chart.

TIPS FROM A PRO: MS Graph has its own Help system, with additional details about all the relevant techniques described in this chapter.

Figure 9.32
Formatted chart

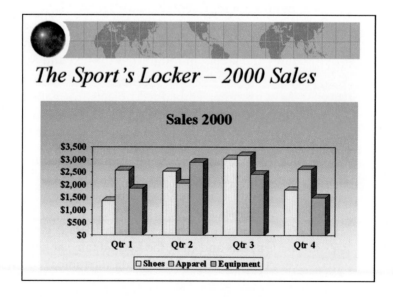

What: If the information you want to bring into PowerPoint already exists in Word or Excel, it is a simple matter to import it into your PowerPoint presentation.

You are basing your presentation on a report that you created in Word, you may be able to quickly create the outline without having to shuffle pages and retype. To do this, you must have the Word document formatted with Heading 1 and Heading 2 styles. (You probably did this if you used Word's Outline view to organize your document.) Likewise, you can export an outline from a PowerPoint presentation and use it as the basis for a Word document.

You can also create a chart using Excel without leaving PowerPoint, or you can import an existing chart from Excel.

Why: Why retype to re-create the outline or a chart if you don't have to. Save yourself the time and trouble, and avoid making those mistakes that seem to magically appear in typing.

IMPORT AN OUTLINE FROM WORD

CORE OBJECTIVE: Import text from Word

How: To create a new presentation by importing text from Word, follow these steps.

1. Open a new blank presentation or open an existing presentation.
2. Choose **Insert|Slides from Outline** to see the Insert Outline dialog box (Figure 9.33).
3. Find and select the Word file that you want to insert, and then click **Insert.**

Figure 9.33
Importing from Word to PowerPoint

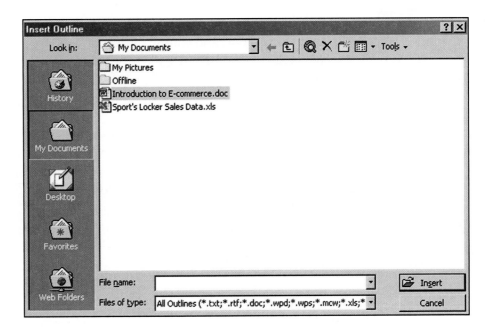

Result: The number of slides that were added depends on the number headings in the Word document with the Heading 1 style applied—one slide is created for each. That is, text formatted with a Heading 1 style becomes the slide titles and the lower-level headings form the bulleted text; normal body text is not included. The formatting of the presentation is based on your individual settings for the blank presentation (Figure 9.34).

Figure 9.34
Imported slide presentation

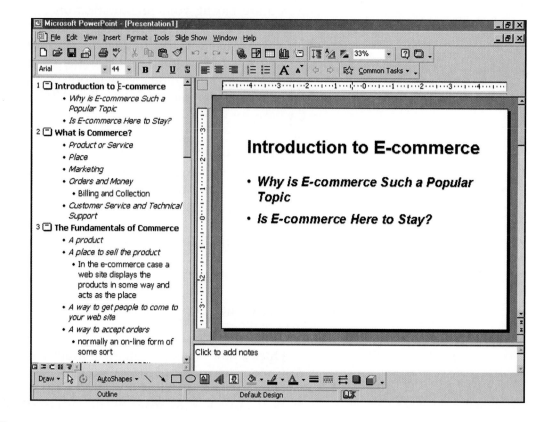

 TIPS FROM A PRO: PowerPoint offers a second way to import an outline from Word.

1. Start PowerPoint and choose **File|Open**.
2. When the dialog box appears, drop down the Files of type box and select **All Outlines**.
3. Locate and select the Word file, and then choose **Open**.

A new PowerPoint presentation opens with the imported outline. (You can't import slides into an active presentation this way.) Text designated with Heading 1 styles forms the slide titles, and lower-level styles are included as bulleted points in the text placeholders. With this method, text is imported with the same font styles as the original document.

EXPORT AN OUTLINE TO WORD

EXPERT OBJECTIVE: **Export an outline to Word**

How: In PowerPoint, choose **File|Send To|Microsoft Word**. The Write Up dialog box, shown in Figure 9.35, appears, giving you several options of what to include in the new document.

Result: Word opens and starts a new document based on the option that you chose in the dialog box. If you chose **Outline Only**, you now have an outline formatted with Heading 1 and Heading 2 styles. The font sizes are very large, similar to those used in the presentation, so you must reduce them so that the text is appropriately sized for a printed page.

If you chose one of the other available choices in the dialog box, you have created a document with a table containing thumbnail views of the slides, accompanied by your speaker notes or blank lines for notes to be added.

 TIPS FROM A PRO: You can also export an outline from Word to PowerPoint. Start Word and open the document that you want to export. Choose **File|Send To|Microsoft PowerPoint** (Figure 9.36).

PowerPoint opens with a new presentation and completes the outline for you based on the headings in the document. Text formatted with a Heading 1 style becomes the slide titles. Text formatted with a Heading 2 style becomes bulleted text. All normal body text is omitted.

Figure 9.35 Exporting an outline to Word

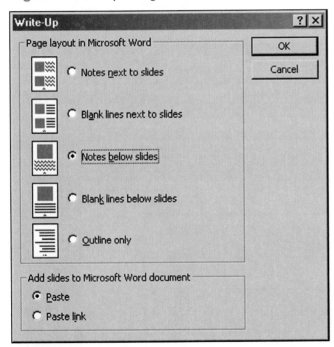

Figure 9.36 Exporting to PowerPoint from Word

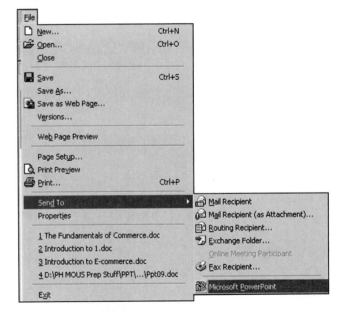

 THOUGHT QUESTION: What happens if you try to import a document that doesn't have heading styles applied?

CREATE AN EXCEL CHART FROM POWERPOINT

EXPERT OBJECTIVE: Insert an Excel chart

How: To create a new Excel chart from inside a PowerPoint presentation, follow these steps:

1. Choose **Insert|Object** to access the dialog box shown in Figure 9.37.
2. Scroll to find, and then click to select, **Microsoft Excel Chart**.

Figure 9.37
Insert Object dialog box

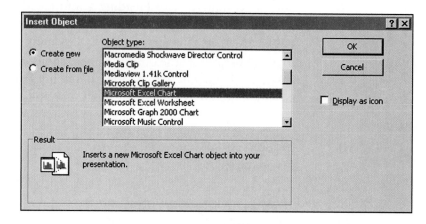

1. If you want to create a new chart (Create New is the default choice), click **OK**.
2. If you want to insert an existing file, check **Create from existing file**. Now you can browse for an existing file to use for the chart.

Result: A sample Excel chart, like the one shown in Figure 9.38, appears on the slide surrounded by a thick border. A datasheet accompanies the chart.

Figure 9.38
Default Excel chart

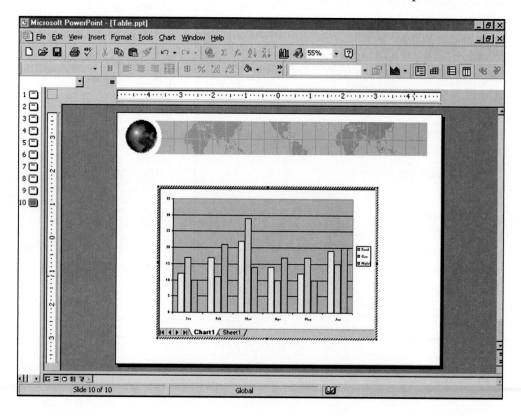

As you saw when inserting a Word table, Excel's toolbars and menus replace PowerPoint's. This means that you can modify the data in Sheet 1, as well as the chart, using all the tools available in Excel. After you have finished creating and formatting the chart, click elsewhere on the slide to exit Excel and restore PowerPoint's menus and toolbars.

INSERT AN EXCEL CHART ONTO A SLIDE

EXPERT OBJECTIVE: Insert an Excel chart

How: To link or embed an Excel chart into a presentation, follow these steps:

1. Open the relevant PowerPoint and Excel files.
2. In Excel click to select the existing chart, and then click **Copy**.
3. Switch to PowerPoint and click the slide where you want the chart to be inserted.
4. Choose **Edit|Paste Special** to see the dialog box shown in Figure 9.39.
5. Click **Paste** and **Microsoft Excel Chart Object** to embed, or click **Paste Link** to link the chart.

Figure 9.39
Embedding a chart

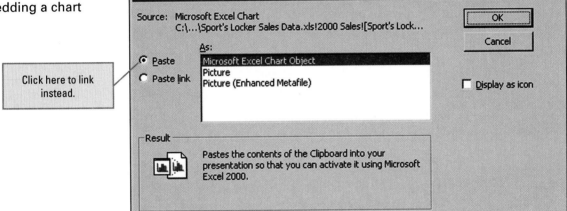

Result: The chart acts like a picture that you inserted onto the slide—it is surrounded by sizing handles. Use the handles to enlarge and position the chart on the slide. Double-click to reopen Excel's menus and modify the chart and its contents (Figure 9.40).

Figure 9.40
Embedded Microsoft
Excel chart

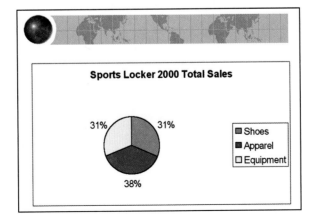

TIPS FROM A PRO: Excel charts are imported into PowerPoint with the same size font and in the same size proportions as in Excel. Although this size is appropriate for a printed page, they are much, much too small to be visible in a presentation. Forcing your audience to squint is a serious mistake; therefore, you *should* carry out one of the following operations to make the chart readable:

- Use the sizing handles to enlarge the chart in PowerPoint so that the fonts are of a readable size. (Test it in Slide Show view: If you can't read it easily standing six feet away from the monitor, try another option.)
- Before you copy the chart, change all the font sizes to 24 points or larger. Eliminate distracting details such as data labels, tick marks, and gridlines.
- Import the Excel data into the MS Graph datasheet and then create a chart in MS Graph. This creates a chart with the appropriate size fonts.
- Print the chart in Excel and make copies as handouts for your audience.

 ## Use PinPoint

After gaining the skills in this chapter, you can create and edit tables, create and edit various kinds of charts, link and embed worksheets and charts, as well as use Microsoft Graph to create a chart from scratch. Now it is time to use the PinPoint software and see what you can do. Remember: Anytime you are unsure about what to do next, reread the relevant portion of the chapter, or you can click Show Me for a live demonstration.

Check out these skills in PinPoint:

- Create an organization chart
- Edit an organization chart
- Add a table
- Modify a table
- Add a Word table
- Create a chart
- Chart a data series
- Insert an Excel chart

Key Terms

You can find definitions for these words in this chapter:

Cell
Datasheet
Merge
Organization chart
Table

Review Questions

You can use the following review questions and exercises to test your knowledge and skills. Answers are given in Appendix D, "Answers to Review Questions."

True/False

Indicate whether each statement is true (T) or false (F).

____ 1. To create an org chart, use the Organization Chart layout and double-click the place-holder.

____ 2. The trouble with Microsoft Organization Chart is that you cannot add new employ-ees to the table after you have created it.

____ 3. When you use the Microsoft Organization Chart program, its menus and toolbars appear in place of the PowerPoint menus and toolbars right over the slide pane.

____ 4. You can type up to four lines of text for each box in an org chart.

____ 5. To modify an org chart on a slide, double-click it to open a new window.

____ 6. When you select a chart, you can use sizing handles to make it larger, just as with a picture.

____ 7. When you double-click the Table placeholder to create a table, by default you get a 4-by-4 table (4 rows by 4 columns).

____ 8. You can create a table on a slide using either PowerPoint or Word.

____ 9. When you want to create a chart, and the data you want to chart is in Excel, you must still retype the data into Microsoft Graph.

____ 10. The first step for modifying a chart within a presentation is to double-click it.

Multiple Choice

Select the letter that best completes the statement.

____ 1. Use an org chart to depict:
  a. Sales of sports equipment.
  b. Increases in sales over time.
  c. Proportion of sales in shoes, equipment, and apparel.
  d. Hierarchy of employees.
  e. All of the above.

____ 2. The reason you create a table on a slide is to:
  a. Be able to chart the num-bers easily.
  b. Keep bits of text or num-bers side by side.
  c. Place borders around the data.
  d. Make the font large enough to read easily.
  e. All of the above.

___ 3. When turn on the Table toolbar, the mouse pointer turns into a pencil so that you can:
   a. Draw new rows or columns.
   b. Add text to the table.
   c. Align text within the cells.
   d. Change the color, style, thickness, or placement of the borders.
   e. All of the above.

___ 4. You can tell when you are modifying a Word table in a slide because:
   a. Word's menu and toolbars replace PowerPoint's.
   b. A heavy border surrounds the table.
   c. Rulers appear on the top and left side of the table.
   d. All of the above.
   e. Both a and b.

___ 5. The most important advantage to creating a Word table on a slide is that:
   a. You can use all of Word's functionality.
   b. You can move it around, just as if it were a picture.
   c. The numbers are updated if the Word source file changes.
   d. You can show off your Word expertise.
   e. You can edit it using Word directly within the presentation.

___ 6. When typing text in a table:
   a. Press Tab to advance to the next cell.
   b. Press Enter to advance to the next cell.
   c. The text appears in the outline pane.
   d. All of the above.
   e. Both b and c.

___ 7. When you use Microsoft Graph to create a chart, you must put figures into its:
   a. Database.
   b. Datasheet.
   c. Spreadsheet.
   d. Worksheet.
   e. Chart sheet.

___ 8. If you create a table using the Table placeholder and then add more rows or columns:
   a. The chart extends off the slide if you use the Table menu.
   b. The columns are much narrower if you use the Draw Table button.
   c. The text becomes too small to read.
   d. The alignment must be changed.
   e. The cells must be split.

___ 9. The best type of chart to use when you want to show the proportion of several items to the whole is a:
   a. Bar chart.
   b. Bubble chart.
   c. Column chart.
   d. Pie chart.
   e. Stock chart.

___ 10. To create an outline from the headings in a Word document:
   a. In Word, change to Outline view and then copy and paste.
   b. In Word, choose File|Send To and click Microsoft PowerPoint.
   c. In PowerPoint, click the Import Word Outline button.
   d. In PowerPoint, choose Insert|Outline from Word and choose the file.
   e. All of the above.

Match the letters in Figure 9.41 with the correct items in the list.

Figure 9.41

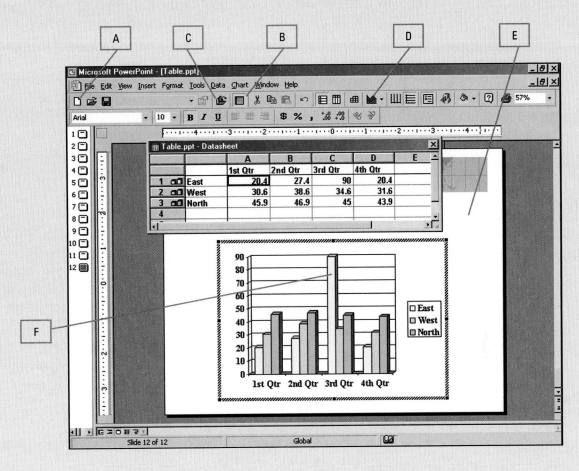

___ 1. Click here to import data into the datasheet.

___ 2. Click here to remove the datasheet from view.

___ 3. Click here to display PowerPoint's toolbars and menu again.

___ 4. Double-click here to change the color of the columns.

___ 5. Click here to change the chart to a line chart.

___ 6. Click here to add an x-axis title.

Exercise and Project

Follow these step-by-step instructions to practice the skills that are included in this chapter. If you are working in a computer lab, you may have to ask your instructor where to save or print your work.

Exercise

1. Open PowerPoint and start a blank presentation. Choose **Insert|Slides** from Outline and browse for the file **Coke Outline.doc** in your Student\Chapter 9 folder of the PinPoint CD-ROM that came with this book.

2. Correct the text on the first two slides so that there is a heading and sub-heading.

3. Change the capitalization of the bullet points, as suggested by the style checker. Edit the text to follow the 6-by-6 rule.

4. Add a design template appropriate for Coca-Cola. Add clip art where appropriate.

5. Add a new slide after Slide 3 and create an org chart. Title the slide **Coca-Cola Management**. Show your name as the CEO, and your friends as vice president of finance, marketing, and sales.

6. Add a new slide after the New Advertisements slide. Title it **US Media Spending**, and then create a table on the slide. Insert the following text in the table.

Year	1998	1999	2000
Coke	$155	$170	$182
Pepsi	$ 83	$ 94	$108

7. Change the alignment in the cells.

8. Remove borders from the inside of the table, and add a thick border around the outside of the table. Adjust other formatting appropriately.

9. Place a text box in an appropriate place to show that the numbers are in Hint: Add "Millions" to the text box.

10. On a new slide, create a chart based on the same data.

11. Choose **Chart|Chart Options** and remove all major and minor gridlines.

12. Change the color of the columns for Coke to **red**, and for Pepsi to **bright blue**.

13. Change the chart type to a cylinder chart.

14. Place a border around the chart and a title above it.

15. Save the presentation as **Exercise 9** in your PowerPoint 2000 folder and print handouts, six slides per page.

Project

Your boss just called; you need to present and explain December's sales figures to upper management tomorrow. Remembering that numeric data is often displayed most effectively in a chart, you decide to create one by importing the sales data from an Excel workbook titled **December1999.xls** (from the Student\Chapter 9 folder of your PinPoint CD-ROM). At a minimum, you know that you need to include the following:

- A title slide (of course).
- A pie chart to present net sales.
- A table of sales data on one slide.
- A description on a slide of the best-selling product.
- A bar chart to compare 1999 and 2000 sales totals in each category.
- A comparison and explanation of the changes in these categories from 1999 to 2000.
- In addition, create an org chart to show who's who in the local store.
- Add the design template and clip art to enhance the message.

Add your name to the title page, save the file as **Project 9** and print handouts, six per page.

Chapter 10

Get Ready for an Internet or Intranet Presentation

Typically you will be sharing the information included in your slide show with an audience in the traditional manner discussed in Chapter 8, "Print and Deliver." However, the Internet, that giant network of computers, offers additional channels for you to communicate your visual aids. Instead of standing before an identifiable, cloistered group, you can broadcast your message on the World Wide Web; then, anyone with access becomes a potential audience. Before you can think about publishing your handiwork on the Internet or even locally on an intranet, however, you will need to make some modifications to your slide show. This chapter shows you how to carry out a few simple changes to quickly transform your PowerPoint file into a Web presentation.

At the end of this chapter, you will be able to:

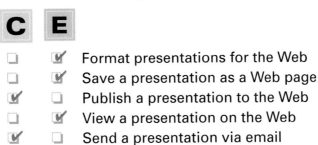

C	E	
☐	☑	Format presentations for the Web
☐	☑	Save a presentation as a Web page
☑	☐	Publish a presentation to the Web
☐	☑	View a presentation on the Web
☑	☐	Send a presentation via email

E *EXPERT OBJECTIVE:* **Format presentations for the Web**

What: You have spent hours creating a first-class slide show and handouts to present at a conference in the Bahamas next week. Now you find that you will have to electronically broadcast your presentation over the Internet instead (ghastly budget cuts!). Don't lose sleep; all your hard work won't be wasted (but you won't be lying on the beach, getting a tan in your spare time)!

Now that you won't be standing in front of an audience, passing out handouts and controlling the way your slides transition, you need to make a few formatting adjustments. You must ensure that your presentation retains its visual clarity, that your audience can easily maneuver through the show, and that various Web browsers support the features that you have used in your presentation.

Why: In the past you have generally formatted your slide show for viewing on some type of projection screen. When a presentation is seen that way, it presents a much different picture than a slide show that is seen through various sized computer monitors using a *Web browser*, the software program that enables you to interact with the Web portion of the Internet.

How: To format your PowerPoint presentation as a Web page, choose **Tools|Options**, click the **General** tab, and then click **Web Options**. The dialog box seen in Figure 10.1 appears.

○ **In the Web General dialog box**, you can make adjustments to increase the visual clarity of your Web presentation. Here you can:

1. Add slide navigational controls. This enables the outline and notes panes to be seen when the slide show is being viewed in a Web browser. It also adds on-screen controls so that viewers can click and move from slide to slide by going forward or backward. They can also jump to different slides by clicking on the slide titles that they see in the outline pane.

2. Change the background and text coloring of the outline and slide panes to draw attention to the slide pane, and thus increase the visual clarity of the slide text.

3. Designate to have any animated objects and text or slide transitions that you have added displayed on the Web.

4. Resize graphics so that they remain in proportion to the rest of the page. The size of the browser window is largely determined by the screen size of the viewing monitor. If you check this box, graphics are sized in proportion to the screen size that you set in the Picture tab. You learn more about this option later in this task.

 TIPS FROM A PRO: You can also access the Web Options dialog box by accessing the **Tools** menu in the Save As Web Page dialog box and choosing **Web Options**. Then you can format, save, and publish all in one step.

Figure 10.1
General tab of Web
Options dialog box

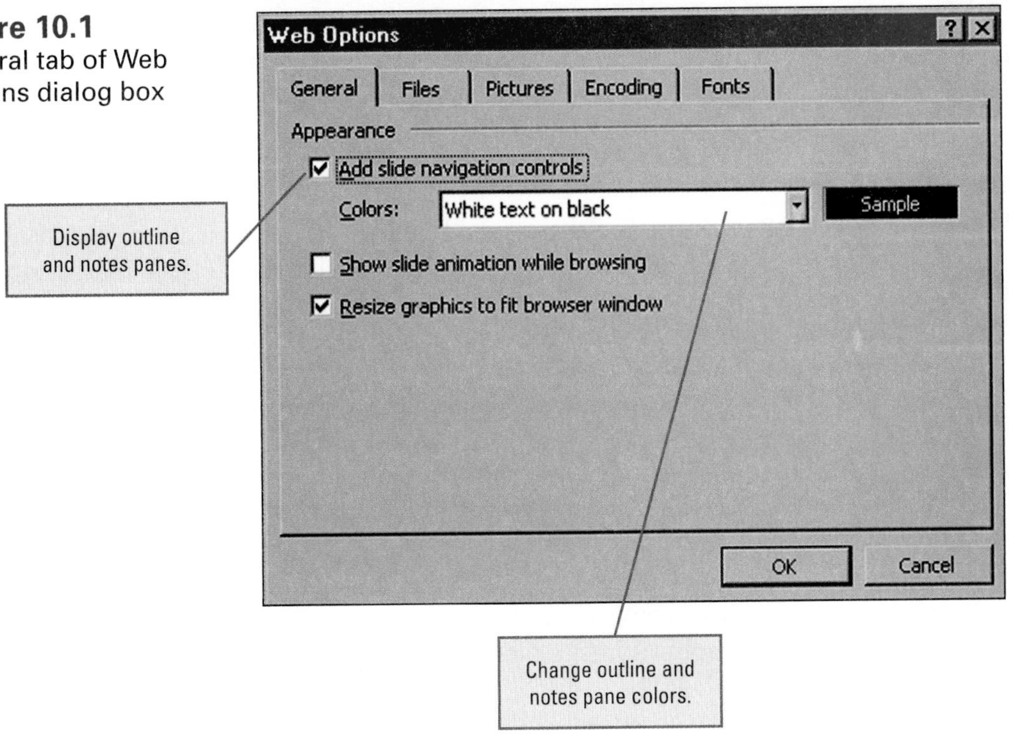

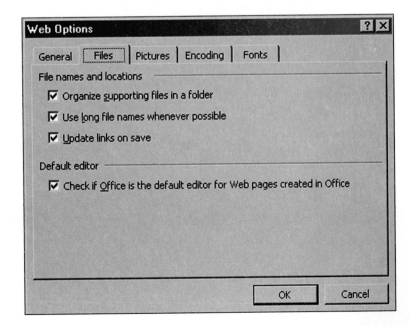

Display outline
and notes panes.

Web Options

General | Files | Pictures | Encoding | Fonts

Appearance

☑ Add slide navigation controls

Colors: White text on black ▾   Sample

☐ Show slide animation while browsing

☑ Resize graphics to fit browser window

OK   Cancel

Change outline and
notes pane colors.

○ **In the Web Files dialog box** (Figure 10.2), you can designate the following features to help you save your Web page now, as well as maintain it after it is published. Here you can:

1. Create a secondary folder to store all supporting graphics files when you save the presentation as a Web page. This is an invaluable tool to help you organize and keep your Web page updated if you plan on leaving it on the Web for a period of time.

2. Use long filenames so that you can more easily remember which files contain specific information. If you clear this box, files are saved with eight-character names.

Figure 10.2
File tab in the Web
Options dialog box

Web Options

General | Files | Pictures | Encoding | Fonts

File names and locations

☑ Organize supporting files in a folder

☑ Use long file names whenever possible

☑ Update links on save

Default editor

☑ Check if Office is the default editor for Web pages created in Office

OK   Cancel

3. Automatically update your links and hyperlinks when you save, move, or rename your Web presentation. This also help keep links unbroken when the secondary folder is created.
4. Check to see whether an Office program is registered as the default HTML editor for this Web page.

 TIPS FROM A PRO: Have you ever opened a Web site and seen a square with a red X in its center? That means that the browser can't find the graphic that is supposed to be showing in that spot. Make sure that you transfer the supporting graphics folder to the Web server where your presentation is being published—if you don't, your graphics will not be visible when your presentation is being viewed in a Web browser. This is not an issue when you save and publish in one operation.

○ **In the Web Options Pictures dialog box** shown in Figure 10.3, you can make decisions relating to the graphics included in your presentation. Here you can:

1. Save your graphics in vector markup language (VLM). Although this option requires less disk space when you save because the graphical image files are not actually saved, not all browsers support VML.
2. Save pictures in a Portable Network Graphics (PNG) format. This type of graphics formatting also takes less disk space and therefore less time to download to a server. Again, some browsers do not support a PNG format.
3. Specify the Target monitor size. Because you can't possibly specify dimensions that match the resolution of every monitor that will be used to view your presentation, consider using the 640 × 480 option.

Figure 10.3
Picture tab in the Web Option dialog box

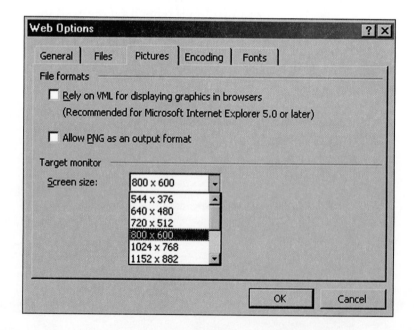

 TIPS FROM A PRO: Web pages often appear differently when viewed using different browser software. To increase the odds that your Web page will appear the way that you want it to for the greatest number of people, view it using several browsers before it is published. Open your Web page in a browser and then:

- View the graphics and fonts on each page.
- Test all your links to see that they are unbroken.
- Check all special effects; if they aren't working, and having them in your presentation will look odd, remove them.

Result: Depending on which options you have chosen, your presentation may look differently than it did before you began your Web formatting; you probably won't notice any visible changes, however, until you view it through a Web browser (Figure 10.4). Even with all this work upfront, some formatting options and special effects, such as continuously playing music or hyperlinks to custom shows, aren't available when your presentation is viewed with a browser.

Figure 10.4
Viewing a slide show in a browser

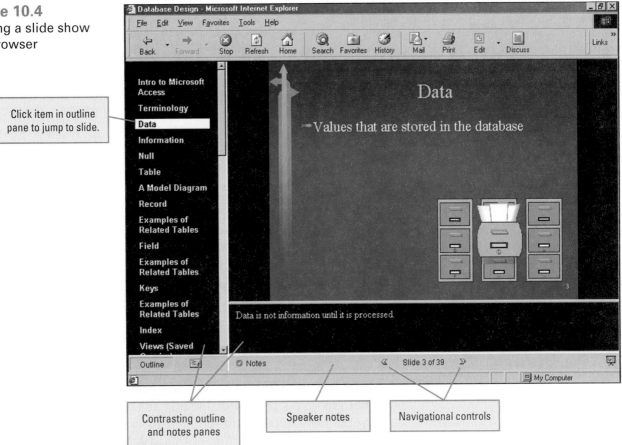

 TIPS FROM A PRO: If you choose not to use navigational controls, consider putting action buttons on your pages so that they can be accessed quickly.

What: Although you know how to create a typical presentation, PowerPoint is not limited to building files that you save locally on a disk. You can also create a Web presentation and publish it on a Web server or on your local network. Then anyone with access can view your work.

Before you can publish a presentation, however, you must convert it to a Web page or to *HyperText Markup Language (HTML)*. You must also make some additional decisions before you transfer your work to the Internet (what portion of the presentation to publish and whether to show your speaker notes to your Web audience, for example).

Why: Web browsers don't speak or read the same language as your personal computing software. Instead, they use their own special language called HTML. If you want your Web presentation to be interpreted by a browser, and thus be viewed on the Web, you must first translate it into that language. After you publish your presentation on a Web server, people anywhere in the world can view it as long as they have Internet access (and provided it's not in a secured location that requires special authorization to enter).

SAVE A PRESENTATION AS A WEB PAGE

Expert Objective: Save HTML to a specific target browser

How: To convert an existing PowerPoint presentation into a Web page, or to save a new PowerPoint file in that format, follow these steps:

1. Choose **File|Save as a Web page** to access the Save As dialog box (Figure 10.5). Notice that this is a bit different from the typical version that you have seen in previous chapters. Here you can:
   - Designate a Save in location and enter a filename.
   - Change the title of your Web page. (The title is the line that appears in the title bar of the Web browser when your page is being viewed.)
   - Choose **Web Options** from the Tools menu and use the skills that you learned in Task 1 to format your presentation for the Web.
2. After you have finished, click **Save** to save your newly created Web presentation to a disk location and to close the dialog box. Or, click **Publish** to access another dialog box and select options to publish the presentation directly onto the Web from PowerPoint. (This is fully described in the next portion of this task.)

Tips from a Pro: You can also convert a file to HTML by choosing **File|Save As** and then changing the Save As type to Web Page. As soon as you change the Save As type, the dialog box changes to the Web page version shown in Figure 10.5.

Result: A couple of things happen as soon as you save your presentation as a Web page. First, your slide show is translated into HTML. (The file now has an .htm file extension.) Second, a secondary folder now exists

Figure 10.5
Saving a file as a Web page

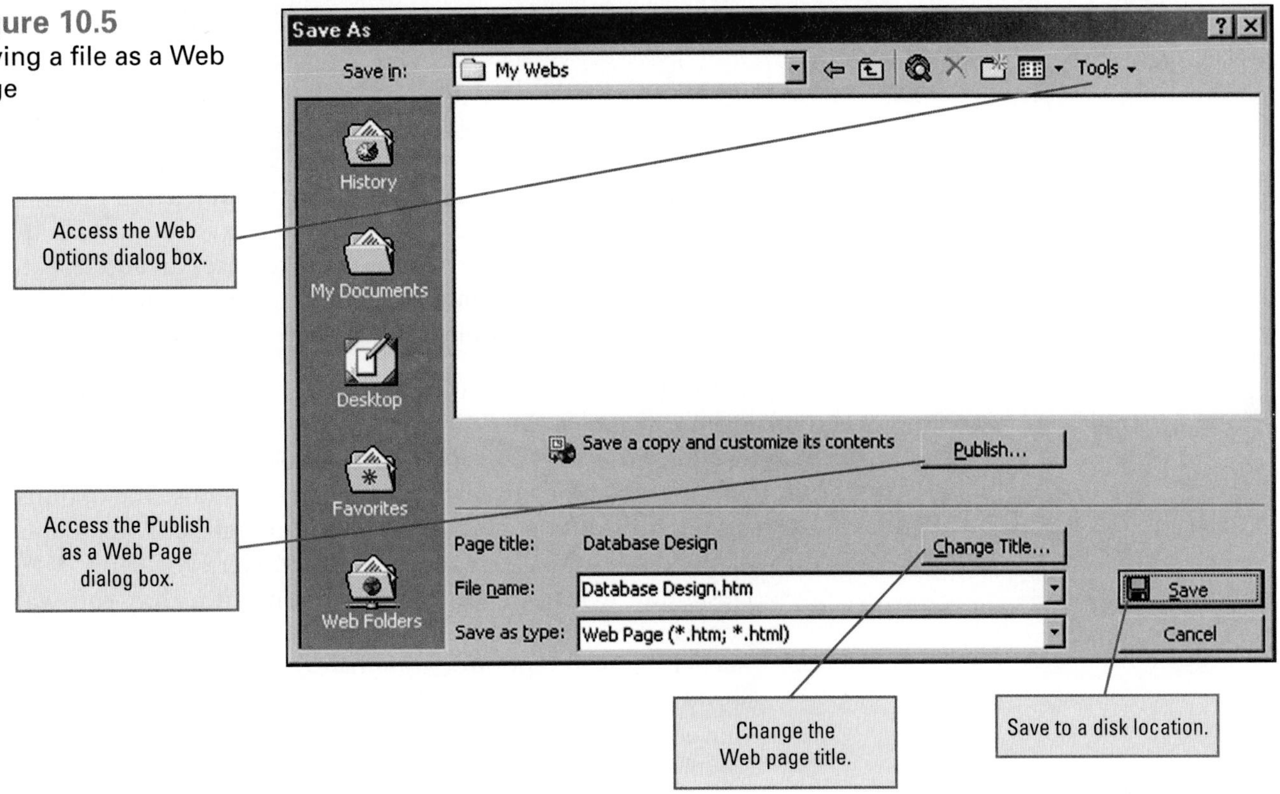

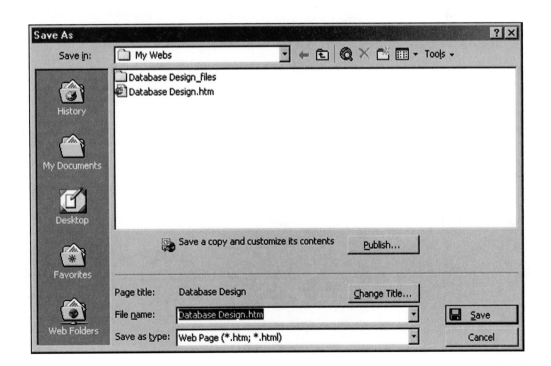

Access the Web Options dialog box.

Access the Publish as a Web Page dialog box.

Change the Web page title.

Save to a disk location.

within the save location that you chose (Figure 10.6). (That is, unless you changed the default in Task 1.) This folder organizes and stores all the supporting graphics files such as bullets, backgrounds, pictures, and the like.

You are now ready to transfer, or *upload*, your newly created Web page to a Web server.

Figure 10.6
Saved Web presentation and supporting graphics folder

CORE OBJECTIVE: Publish presentations to the Web

How: After you have saved your presentation as a Web page, you can upload or publish it to an Internet or intranet site without leaving PowerPoint. The presentation that you saved in Task 2 was saved locally on a disk, therefore, to transfer it to a Web server now requires an additional step. PowerPoint offers you the ability to be much more efficient than that— you can format, save, and publish to the Web all in one place.

1. Open the file that you want to publish on the Internet or on an intranet network, or create a new file.
2. Choose **File|Save as Web Page** to access the dialog box that you saw in the last portion or this task (Figure 10.5). Choose the options that you would like for your page. When you are finished, click **Publish** to access the Publish as Web Page dialog box. Here you can:
   * Designate what portion of the presentation that you want to publish.
   * Access the Web Options dialog box described in Task 1.
   * Show speaker notes in the notes pane when the page is being viewed.
   * Change the title of your Web page.
   * Select the Web browser that will be used to view your presentation. If you aren't sure, choose the third option (although this results in some of the more recent Web features being inoperative, because not all browsers support the same features). However, it does enable viewing on the greatest number of browsers.
   * Browse to find a Save to location. If you know the Web address, or *Uniform Resource Locator (URL),* of your Web space, type it,

Figure 10.7
Publishing a file to the Web

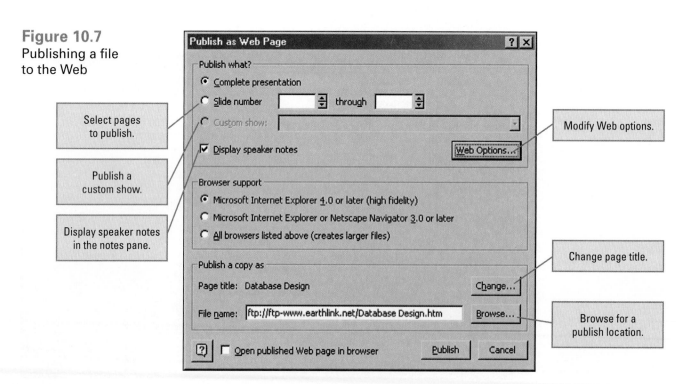

plus your filename into the **File name** box (For example; http://www.servername/your_name/home.htm). You can also use either of two Windows features to publish your page: Web Folders or FTP Locations. (If you need help with this aspect, contact your instructor or system administrator.) If you leave in the disk address, your file is saved locally.

- Open the Web presentation in your default browser after it is published.

3. When you have finished, click **Publish** again.

Note: Before you can publish a presentation on the Internet, you must have access to space on a Web server via an Internet service provider, your firm, or another organization. To publish locally on an intranet, contact your system administrator.

Result: As soon as you complete Step 3, your file begins to download to the Web location that you have chosen. If the files being transferring are large (maybe you have a lot of graphics, font styles, and the like), you may see a balloon that provides an update about the components being downloaded. When the process is complete, a prompt appears to inform you. If you checked Open in Browser, the Browser window opens and you see your Web presentation displayed.

 TIPS FROM A PRO: You can upload files to your Web server account in several different ways. You can use an FTP program, use the method described in the preceding task, or use either Windows Web Folders (if you are publishing to a server that supports this feature) or FTP Locations to publish your Web page.

To set up a Web folder, follow these steps:

1. Open **My Computer** from the Windows desktop and double-click the **Web Folders** icon.
2. Double-click the **Add Web Folders** icon to access the Add Web Folders dialog box. (If you are using Windows 2000, this will be Add Network Places.)
3. When the dialog box opens, type in the URL for the Web server where you will be publishing your page in the **Type Location to Add** field and click **Next**. If you aren't connected to the Internet, you must now connect.
4. If you like, change the default and add a folder name that is easier to recognize and click **Finish** close the dialog box and add the folder.
5. When prompted, enter your username and password. (In either case, if you are unfamiliar with these options, contact your Web administrator for help.) Then click **OK**.

To set up a *File Transfer Protocol (FTP)* location for easy Web page publishing, follow these steps:

1. Choose **File|Save as a Web page**. When the Save As dialog box appears, click to drop down the Save in box and find and select **FTP Locations** (Figure 10.8).
2. Double-click **Add/Modify FTP Locations** to access the dialog box shown in Figure 10.9.

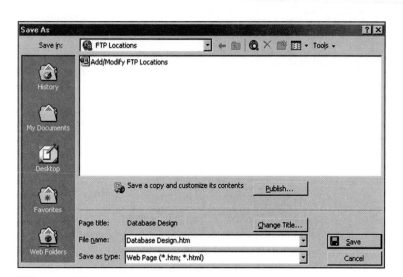

Figure 10.8 Setting up an FTP location

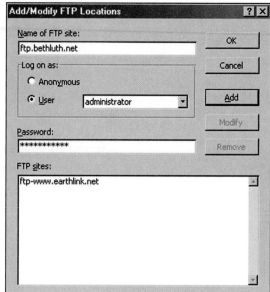

Figure 10.9 Add/Modify FTP Locations

3. Enter the name of the Web site where you would like to establish a connection.
4. Check **User** and enter your assigned username, enter your password as indicated, and click **OK**. (Ask the system administrator if you have any site-specific questions.)

 TIPS FROM A PRO: Have you ever noticed that square box that appears when your browser is trying to load a picture? You can insert text behind each of your graphical objects so that viewers can see something while they wait for the picture to appear. Double-click the picture to open the Format Picture dialog box. Click the **Web** tab and type in the text that you want to display.

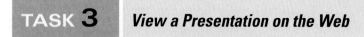

TASK **3**   *View a Presentation on the Web*

 E   *EXPERT OBJECTIVE:* View a presentation on the Web

What: Before you actually go to the trouble of sending or uploading your presentation to a Web server, take it for a test drive and view it in a browser window.

Why: No matter how thoroughly you checked the formatting of your presentation, some text, graphic, and special effect items won't translate correctly when you convert a PowerPoint file to a Web page. By checking your Web page before you publish it on the Internet, you can remove or fix any elements that are not working correctly before they are exposed to your audience.

How: To see how your saved presentation will look when viewed in a browser, open the file, and choose **File|Web Page Preview**.

Result: The Web presentation opens in the default browser window (refer back to Figure 10.4). Test the links and any other essential components, fix them, and then publish.

TIPS FROM A PRO: A second way to preview a Web presentation before you actually publish it on the Web is to open it directly from the browser. Open the browser and click the **File** menu to find the item that will open a Web page. (The actual name will vary among browsers, but it will be something like Open or Open Page.) A dialog box opens, directing you to search for the saved file. When you select and open the file, it opens in the browser window. Now you can inspect the page to see whether any changes are required before you go to the trouble of uploading it to the Web.

TASK 4 — *Send a Presentation via Email*

CORE OBJECTIVE: Send a presentation via email

What: There's no need to save your work on a disk, package it up, and risk sending it through the mail when you want to collaborate with someone. Thanks to the Internet and PowerPoint, you can forward a presentation as email without leaving your desk or exiting the program.

Why: In addition to the obvious benefit—time saved—this is also a low-cost way to share information (and, no licking stamps or waiting in line to mail off your disk). In no time at all, your colleague can have the presentation, make changes, and send it back, whether your collaborator is in Australia, Montana, or just across the hall.

SEND A COPY OF A SINGLE SLIDE

How: When you want to forward a single slide, follow these steps:

1. Select the slide, and then choose either of these methods to open the email header shown in Figure 10.10.
   - Click the **E-Mail button**.
   - Choose **File|Send To|Mail Recipient**.
2. Complete the **To:** and **Cc:** boxes, like the example in Figure 10.10. When you are sending to multiple recipients, separate their names with semicolons. If you have addresses saved in a list, you can opt to click **To:** or **Cc:** and select the desired names. By default, the slide name is used in the Subject line, but you can click in the box and type to add something different.
3. When you're ready to send the slide, click **Send This Slide**.

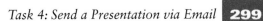

Figure 10.10
Sending a single slide as email

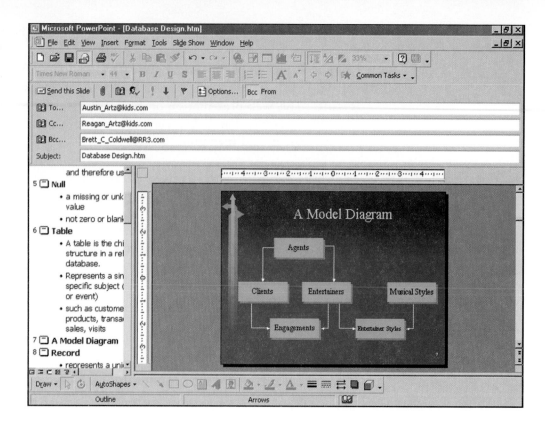

Result: The slide is immediately sent to the recipient, the email header closes, and you are returned to the regular PowerPoint window.

 TIPS FROM A PRO: Depending on your email configuration, a dialog box *may* appear when you click the **E-Mail** button with the following two check box options:

* Send the entire presentation as an attachment.
* Send the current slide as the message body.

If message doesn't appear, and you want to send an attachment in addition to this slide, click the **Insert File** button.

SEND A PRESENTATION AS AN ATTACHMENT

How: When you want to send an entire presentation using email, it's more efficient to attach the presentation to an email message and send it on its way. You can send a presentation as an *attachment* by opening your default email program, or you can send it without exiting PowerPoint, as follows:

1. Open the presentation that you want to send and choose **File|Send To|Mail Recipient (as Attachment)**. An email window like or similar to the one shown in Figure 10.11 appears (depending on the email program that you are using).
2. Complete the **To:**, **Cc:**, and **Subject** lines as necessary. You can also add an email message if you want to.

 3. Additional attachments can be added as well when you choose **Insert|File Attachment** or click the **Insert File** button or use the relevant button in your program.
4. When you are ready to transmit the email and attachments, click **Send**.

Figure 10.11
Sending a
presentation as an
email attachment

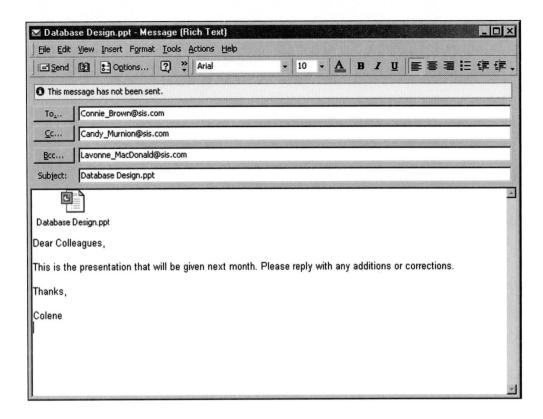

Result: As soon as you click the button, your email and its attachments zip away in the blink of an eye, leaving you staring at the PowerPoint window and your active presentation.

TIPS FROM A PRO: It goes without saying that you must have a network or modem connection to the Internet to take advantage of this feature. Before you can send email from within PowerPoint, however, you must have some additional software. First, you must be using PowerPoint 2000 and one of the following:

- A 32-bit email program compatible with the *Messaging Application Programming Interface* (MAPI). In addition, the Mapi32.dll driver must be included in the Windows system folder.
- An email program compatible with *Vendor Independent Messaging* (VIM). In this case, Mapivi32.dll, Mapivitk.dll, and Mvthksvr.exe must be in the Windows system folder for this feature to work properly.

Use Windows Explorer to see whether you have these components.

Use PinPoint

After gaining the skills in this chapter, you can set up and save a regular PowerPoint presentation as a Web page, publish the presentation, and send a presentation or slide using email. Now it's time to see what you can do with the PinPoint software. Remember, anytime you are unsure of what to do next, reread the relevant portion of the chapter, or you can click Show Me for a live demonstration. Try these skills in PinPoint:

- Web formatting
- Save as HTML
- View a Web presentation
- Publish to the Web

Key Terms

Attachments
File Transfer Protocol (FTP)
HyperText Markup Language (HTML)
Uniform Resource Locator (URL)
Upload
Web browser

Review Questions

You can use the following review questions and exercises to test your knowledge and skills. Answers are given in Appendix D, "Answers to Review Questions."

True/False

Indicate whether each statement is true (T) or false (F).

___ 1. HyperText Markup Language is the language of the WWW.

___ 2. After you have created a regular slide show, it is very difficult to convert it to a Web page.

___ 3. Saving a file as a Web page means converting it to HyperText Markup Language.

___ 4. FedEx presents that fastest way to get your presentation file to Singapore by tomorrow morning.

___ 5. The PowerPoint feature that enables you to send a single slide to a friend is called the intranet.

___ 6. Some special effects do not work in Web browsers.

___ 7. Adding navigational controls to your Web presentation enables you to publish it quickly.

___ 8. To broadcast your visual aids to the world, use PowerPoint and a local television station.

___ 9. Before you can publish a presentation on the Web, you must attach it to an email message.

___ 10. Checking hyperlinks, special effects, and the like by previewing your Web page before you publish it is a good idea.

Multiple Choice

Select the letter that best completes the statement.

___ 1. To publish a slide show on the Web, you must first:
    a. Designate it as a Web page the first time that you save.
    b. Save it as a Web page.
    c. Download special software so that you can save it correctly.
    d. Only a and c.
    e. a, b, and c.

___ 2. Navigational controls refer to features that:
    a. Enable Web presentation viewers to easily move from slide to slide.
    b. Help you save your presentation as a Web page.
    c. Enable a PowerPoint file to be converted to a Web page.
    d. Attach it to an email message.
    e. Only a and b.

___ 3. The quickest way to send a PowerPoint presentation to a colleague in London is to:
    a. Catch the next flight out of your local airport, disk in hand.
    b. Copy it to a disk, package it, and send it via an express mailing service.
    c. Make a hard copy (printed copy) and send it.
    d. Attach it to an email message.
    e. Only a and b.

___ 4. To format a presentation for the Web, choose:
    a. Format|Web Page.
    b. Tools|Options and click Web Options.
    c. File|Save As.
    d. Format|Web Options.
    e. Only a and b.

___ 5. When you send a presentation as an email attachment:
    a. You can only send one slide at a time.
    b. You can send the entire presentation file.
    c. You can't send a presentation using this method.
    d. Choose File|Send To|Recipient (as an attachment)
    e. Both b and d.

___ 6. When you want the outline and notes pane to have a different background color than the slide pane:
    a. You must add navigational controls in the Web Options dialog box.
    b. Choose Format|Background and change them.
    c. Choose Edit|Web page and change the colors.
    d. Open the page in a browser and change the pane colors.
    e. Both b and c.

___ 7. To convert a regular PowerPoint file to HTML:
    a. Choose File|Save As and choose Web Page as the Save As file type.
    b. Choose File|Save as Web Page.
    c. Choose File|Save As and rename the file Web Page.
    d. Both a and b.
    e. All of the above.

___ 8. When you publish a Web page:
  a. You send it to a location Web server.
  b. You upload it to a Web server.
  c. You store it on a Web server.
  d. You place it on a Web server and potentially anyone with Internet access can view it.
  e. All of the above.

___ 9. When you designate to have a supporting folder created when you save as a Web page:
  a. All the graphic files that you used on your page are placed in the folder.
  b. A copy of your presentation is created in case you misplace the original.
  c. Your Web page includes hyperlinks to each graphical object that you used.
  d. All of these.
  e. Both a and c.

___ 10. The Web Options dialog box enables you to:
  a. Publish your presentation.
  b. Save your presentation as a Web page.
  c. Open a browser to preview your Web presentation.
  d. Designate to have animated objects shown in the Web presentation.
  e. Both a and b.

Screen Review

Match the letters in Figure 10.12 with the correct items in the list.

Figure 10.12

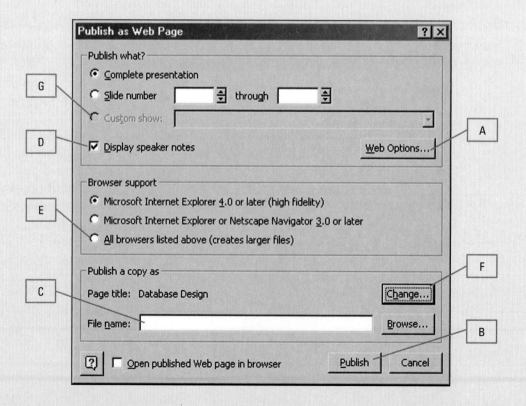

____ 1. Click to open the Publish As dialog box.

____ 2. Click here to view the presentation with any popular browser.

____ 3. Click to access another dialog box and add navigational controls.

____ 4. Click to show the speaker notes that you have typed.

____ 5. Click here to type in the URL of the Web server where you want to store place your presentation.

____ 6. Publish a custom show only.

____ 7. Change the title of the Web page.

Exercise and Project

Follow these step-by-step instructions to practice the skills that are included in this chapter. If you are working in a computer lab, you may have to ask your instructor where to save or print your work.

Exercise

1. Start PowerPoint and open **PPT10** from the Student\Chapter 10 folder of the PinPoint CD-ROM that came with this book.

2. Click the **E-Mail** button or choose **File|Send to**. Address the appropriate fields to send Slide 1 to a friend.

3. Save the file as **Exercise 10A**. Press **Print Screen**, open a blank PowerPoint presentation, and press **Paste**. Drag the image and the title placeholder to move and resize them until you can add your name into the placeholder. Save the file as **Exercise 10B**.

4. Access the Web Options dialog box. Add navigational controls to the slide show. Choose the option that shows text in the outline pane in white text on a black background. Clear the appropriate checkbox so that animated objects will not show while the presentation is being browsed.

5. Save the file as a Web page in your PowerPoint 2000 folder with a file name of **Home**.

6. Choose **File|Save as Web Page**. Find the folder and file location of Web page and its supporting folder. Press **Print Screen**, add a second slide to Exercise 10B and then press **Paste** to add the printed screen onto the new slide.

7. Open your Web presentation in a browser. Press **Print Screen**, and then return to the file that you saved as Exercise 10B. Add a third slide to the presentation and again press **Paste** to add the screen that you just copied.

8. Save the file, print the three slides, and Exit PowerPoint.

Project

You have just received the latest profit figures for your division, along with a call from the corporate office. The bottom line: You must lay off 20 percent of your staff within the next 30 days. To accomplish the staff reduction, you have been authorized to offer a severance package with the hope that a sufficient number of workers will leave. You are going to have a meeting in two days to present the financial situation and the severance offer to your entire staff. Create a presentation for the meeting to convey the following:

- The company's financial situation that has led to the layoff
- How this will affect this office in the short term (layoff and so on)
- The severance package
- What will happen if an insufficient number of people opt for the package

Save the file as **Project 10,** add your name to the title page, and print in the format of your choice.

Chapter 11

Use Advanced Features

In this book, you have seen many of the features available to PowerPoint users. You know how to create and give an effective professional-looking presentation in person or on the Internet. Before you slip on your PowerPoint crown, however, you should learn a few final features to help simplify your work in the program.

At the end of this chapter, you will be able to:

- [ ] ☑ Save a slide as a graphical image
- [ ] ☑ Customize the toolbar
- [ ] ☑ Create a new toolbar

EXPERT OBJECTIVE: Save a slide as a graphic

What: You can save a PowerPoint slide as a graphical image and then insert it as a picture onto another slide, or into another program.

Why: Sometimes you want to add a diagram, such as a flowchart or an org chart, to another file even if was created in a program that doesn't enable these types of figures. With this PowerPoint feature, you can save the slide that contains the diagram as a graphic and then insert it into your document or Web page just as you would any other picture. Not only does this save you from having to re-create your work, but it also enables you to include special diagrams where it would otherwise be impossible.

How: You can create graphical images from one slide or from every slide in a presentation as follows:

1. Open the PowerPoint file and select the slide (If you want to make pictures out of all of the slides, there is no need to select any of the slides).
2. Choose **File|Save As.**
3. When the Save As dialog box appears, as shown in Figure 11.1, choose the **Save in** location, enter a filename, and click the **Save as type** drop-down arrow.
4. Browse to find the graphics file type that you want, click to select it, and then click **Save.**
5. When prompted, indicate whether you want to save only the selected slide or all slides in the presentation.

Figure 11.1
Saving a slide as a picture

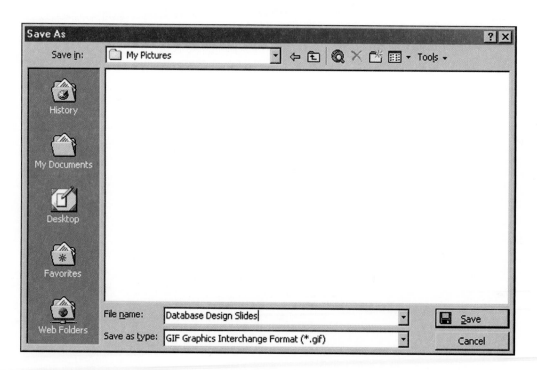

TIPS FROM A PRO: You should consider several factors before you choose a graphics file type. If you are going to insert your graphic onto a Web page, or if size is an issue, choose JPG, PNG, or GIF. On the other hand, if you aren't worried about file size and you are going to be embedding your picture in another Office document, save the graphic as a TIF, BMP, or WMF. Remember, if you think that you will want to modify the picture later on, save it as a WMF file. That way you can double-click the inserted graphic and change it using the methods that you learned in Chapter 6, "Elements of Sight and Sounds."

Result: Each slide that you selected has been saved as a graphical image. If you saved the entire presentation, PowerPoint has created a new folder for you with the filename that you choose in Step 4. In this case, each slide represents a separate graphics file within the folder (Figure 11.2). Now you can insert the images into a presentation or into a file created in another program, and size them as you would any other picture.

Figure 11.2
Inserting a slide saved as a picture

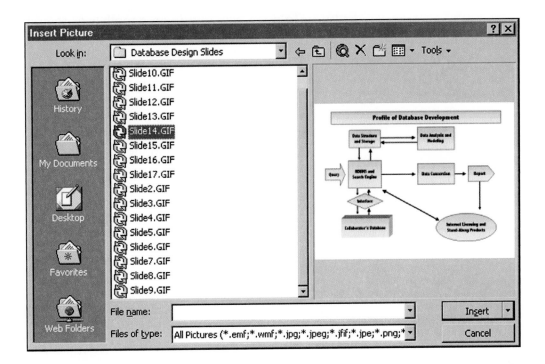

TASK **2**   *Customize the Toolbars*

EXPERT OBJECTIVE: Customize toolbars

What: In Chapter 1, "Get Started with PowerPoint," you learned how to make the Standard and Formatting toolbars share one row. You also know how to turn on toolbars and then shut them off. Still, you can customize the existing toolbars in many other ways, such as adding buttons to or deleting commands, or you can create your own unique toolbar. (You learn how to do this in Task 3.)

Toolbars can be positioned two ways on the PowerPoint window; they can be fixed, or **docked** within one of the edges of the PowerPoint window, or they can be floating, or free to move over the text.

Why: You can tailor the toolbars so that they are the most convenient for your work style. Although it would be impossible to fit all the available button commands or menus onto a toolbar (and still see any portion of the program window), you can add those that you use frequently, or remove those that you use infrequently. In addition, the flexibility to move toolbars around the window to the location handiest for you can save time and keep you from tiring and repetitive motions.

ADD A BUTTON OR BUILT-IN MENU TO A TOOLBAR

How: To put a new button on a toolbar or to add one of the built-in menus, first access the dialog box in one of the following ways:

○ Choose **View|Toolbars|Customize**.
○ Choose **Tool|Customize**.
○ Place the mouse pointer in a blank area between the toolbars (or the menu bar) at the top of the PowerPoint window and right-click.
  1. When the Customize dialog box appears, click the **Commands** tab to see the options in Figure 11.3. The left side of the dialog box displays command categories. Click an item to see which commands are associated with that topic. To see a description of a particular button command, click the command, and then click **Description**.
  2. When you have located a button icon or built-in menu that you want to add to a toolbar, click to select it.

Figure 11.3
Toolbar commands

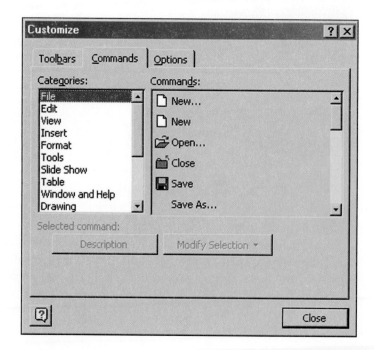

3. Press and hold the left mouse button and drag the button or menu towards the desired location. As soon as you begin to drag, the mouse pointer changes to include a small 3-D rectangle and a plus sign (Figure 11.4). When the pointer reaches one of the toolbars, a bold I-beam also appears to help direct the exact placement of the item. Release the mouse button to add it to the toolbar.

4. Repeat this process to add more items or click **Close** to close the dialog box.

Figure 11.4
Adding buttons or menus to a toolbar

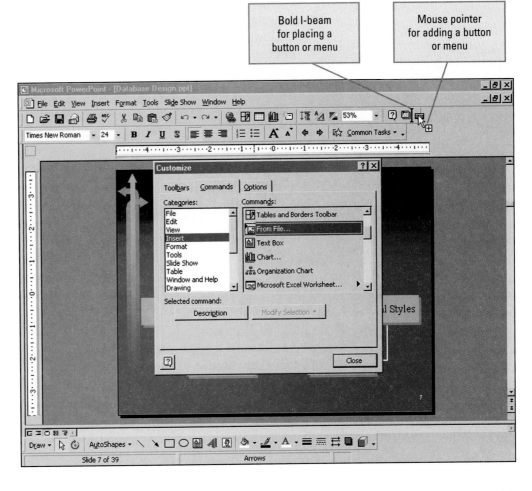

Result: The item that you added is positioned on the toolbar (Figure 11.5). If it is not where you would like it to be or you would like to change it in some other way, refer to the next sections in this task.

Figure 11.5
Standard toolbar with new button and menu

ADD A NEW MENU

How: When you don't want to use one of the built-in menus, use the following steps to create your own distinct version:

1. Access the **Customize** dialog box, and then click the **Commands** tab.
2. Scroll through the Categories to locate and then select **New Menu.**
3. On the right side of the dialog box, under Commands, click to select **New Menu.**
4. Drag it to the desired location on one of the toolbars.

Result: You have added a new menu to one of the toolbars. You can continue building the menu using the skills described in the remainder of this task.

MOVE OR DELETE A BUTTON OR MENU

How: To reposition or remove an item from one of the toolbars, follow these steps:

1. Access the Customize dialog box in one of the ways described previously in this task.
2. Click on the toolbar to select the item that you want to move or remove. You know when a button or menu has been selected because a bold black border surrounds it (refer back to Figure 11.5).
   - To delete the button or menu, right-click the item and choose **Delete** from the shortcut menu or drag the item downward onto the viewing window.
   - To reposition the button or menu, hold down the right mouse button and drag the selected item to the desired new location.

Result: The button icon or menu that you selected has been moved or deleted from the toolbar.

MODIFY A BUTTON ICON OR MENU ITEM

How: You can alter the toolbars in other ways too, like changing a button's icon image, starting a command group by adding a *separator line* (the lines that separate groups of icons or menu items) to a bar, or by adding text to a button area.

1. Access the Customize dialog box, and then click on the toolbar to select the button or menu item that you want to change.
2. Click the **Modify Selection** button to see the menu shown in Figure 11.6.
3. Select the menu item that you want to apply. (Not all options are available for each button.) Depending on the modification that you chose, you may see a second dialog box that requires additional inputs.

Result: You have changed the icon graphic for a command, reset a button to its original image, or changed the toolbar in some other way. Figure 11.7 shows few of the ways that you can change buttons and toolbars.

Figure 11.6
Modifying a button
or toolbar

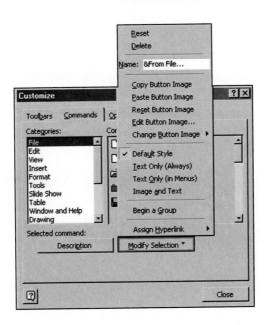

Figure 11.7
Modified toolbars

 TIPS FROM A PRO: In addition to the operations previously described, when you access the Modify Selection menus, you can reset buttons, delete buttons, and perform several other actions as well.

MOVE A TOOLBAR

How: Toolbars aren't static; you can relocate them. They can be docked, floating, or you can reposition them within the edges of the viewing window. To reposition a docked toolbar, follow these steps:

1. Move the mouse pointer over the *move handle* (the handle to move the toolbar) at the far left of the toolbar. The pointer turns into the familiar four-headed repositioning pointer.
2. Hold down the left mouse button and drag the toolbar to the desired new location (Figure 11.9). You can move right or left, or up and down but if you move the toolbar onto the viewing window, it changes to a floating toolbar.

 TIPS FROM A PRO: You don't have to use the move handles to relocate a docked toolbar. You can press and hold the mouse button, and then drag anywhere on the toolbar. However, this can be a bit tricky. The easiest place to grab is on one of the separator lines.

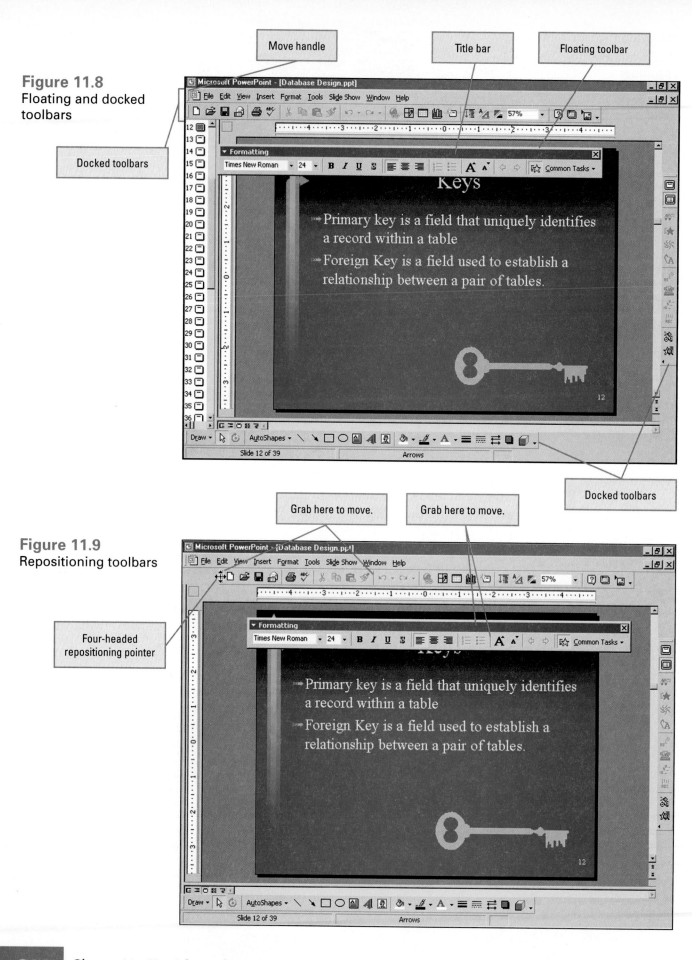

Figure 11.8
Floating and docked toolbars

Move handle

Title bar

Floating toolbar

Docked toolbars

Docked toolbars

Figure 11.9
Repositioning toolbars

Grab here to move.

Grab here to move.

Four-headed repositioning pointer

To reposition a floating toolbar, follow these steps:

1. Place the mouse pointer over the title bar (see Figure 11.8).
2. Press the left mouse button and drag the toolbar to its new home.

Result: The toolbar has been moved to a new location. If you want to return it to its original position, repeat the process. Figure 11.9 shows some toolbars that have been repositioned.

 TIPS FROM A PRO: Some toolbars can also be resized. (The leftmost docked toolbar on a horizontal row or the top toolbar on a vertical row are two exceptions.) That is, they can be made shorter or longer. However, this is only meaningful if the toolbar has buttons that are not visible (sharing a row), or is more than one row long.

- To resize a docked toolbar sharing a row with another toolbar, drag the move handle.
- To resize a floating toolbar, move the mouse pointer over any edge until it changes to a two-headed arrow, and then drag the edge of the toolbar. (If the pointer doesn't change, like with the Clipboard, the toolbar can't be resized.)
- To make the button icons larger, choose **View|Toolbars|Customize**. Check the **Large Icons** box.

RESET A TOOLBAR

How: If you find that you don't like the changes that you have made to a toolbar, you can easily reset it to its default status as follows:

1. Access the **Customize** dialog box and click the **Toolbar** tab.
2. Click to select the toolbar that you want to restore, and then click **Reset**.

Result: The selected toolbar has been restored to its original default position.

TASK **3**   *Create a New Toolbar*

 CORE OBJECTIVE: **Create a new toolbar**

What: Yes, you can move, add, and delete buttons or menus to customize the existing toolbars; sometimes you may want to create a new toolbar rather than redesign one of the existing models.

Why: Maybe you are working on a special project that requires constant repetition of the same operations. Or perhaps, you see a configuration that would be more logical for you. If the buttons that you want to group together are now placed helter-skelter, in various locations or not on a regular toolbar at all, you can save time by creating a new toolbar. Later if it is in your way, just close or delete it.

ADD A TOOLBAR

How: To add a new toolbar to the existing selection, follow these steps:

1. Access the Customize dialog box using one of the methods provided in Task 2.
2. Click the **Toolbars** tab, and then click **New**. The New Toolbars dialog box appears (Figure 11.10).
3. Click in the **Toolbars name** box to name your toolbar. Click **OK** to close the dialog box and add the toolbar to the existing set.

Result: Your new toolbar appears in the PowerPoint window as a floating object (Figure 11.11). When you access the Toolbars tab in the Customize dialog box, you will find the new toolbar has been added to the bottom of the list. Now you can reposition your creation or continue building it as described in the remainder of this task.

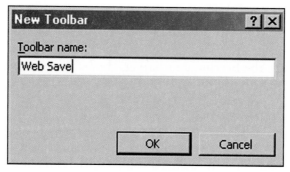

Figure 11.10 Adding a toolbar

Figure 11.11
New toolbar

ADD BUTTONS OR MENUS TO THE TOOLBAR

How: After you create the toolbar, you will want to add buttons or menus to it. Refer to earlier sections in this task and to Task 2 to carry out any of the following operations to complete the toolbar:

- ○ Add buttons.
- ○ Delete buttons.
- ○ Reposition or dock.
- ○ Add and build a new menu.
- ○ Add built-in menus (such as File or Edit).

Result: What your new toolbar looks like or where it is positioned depends on the choices that you have made. Figure 11.12 displays one example of a custom toolbar that can be created to shorten the process of saving and publishing a Web presentation.

Figure 11.12 Custom toolbar

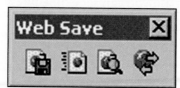

Use PinPoint

After gaining the skills in this chapter, you can save a slide as a picture and fully customize the toolbars. Now it is time to see what you can do with the PinPoint software. Remember, anytime you are unsure of what to do next, reread the relevant portion of the chapter, or you can click Show Me for a live demonstration. Try these skills in PinPoint:

- Save a slide as a graphic
- Create a new toolbar
- Customize the toolbar

Key Terms

You can find definitions for these words in this chapter:

Docked
Floating
Move handle
Separator line

Review Questions

You can use the following review questions and exercises to test your knowledge and skills. Answers are given in Appendix D, "Answers to Review Questions."

True/False

Indicate whether each statement is true (T) or false (F).

____ 1. After you have customized a toolbar, it can never be returned to its default position.

____ 2. Adding a new toolbar enables you to quickly access frequently used commands.

____ 3. A docked toolbar is one that is not visible on the screen.

____ 4. If you save a slide as a Windows Metafile, you can modify some of its characteristics by ungrouping the image.

____ 5. A move handle helps you reposition a slide.

____ 6. When a toolbar is floating, it can be placed over the text on the viewing window.

____ 7. The Customize dialog box enables you to change existing toolbars or add new ones.

____ 8. When you elect to save an entire slide show as a graphics file, PowerPoint creates one big picture for you.

____ 9. The folder created when you save slides as pictures helps keep your files organized.

____ 10. The quickest way to close a floating toolbar is to click the Close button.

Multiple Choice

Select the letter that best completes the statement.

___ 1. To access the toolbar Customize dialog box:
   a. Choose Tools|Options.
   b Right-click on the taskbar and choose Customize.
   c. Choose View|Toolbars|Customize.
   d. Both and b.
   e. All of the above.

___ 2. You can create a new toolbar:
   a. In the Customize dialog box.
   b. In the Options dialog box.
   c. In the Toolbars dialog box.
   d. You can't create new tool-bars!
   e. Both a and b.

___ 3. To save a PowerPoint slide as a picture:
   a. Click the Save button on the Standard toolbar.
   b. Choose File|Save As, and then select Design Template as the Save As type.
   c. Choose File|Save As a Web Page.
   d. Choose File|Save As, and then select a graphics Save As file type.
   e. Both a and b.

___ 4. If you right-click in the blank edge area at the top of the screen, you can:
   a. Turn on or off toolbars.
   b. Access the Customize dia-log box.
   c. Save a slide as a graphical image.
   d. Move the toolbars.
   e. Both a and b.

___ 5. A move handle:
   a. Enables you to reposition a docked toolbar.
   b. Enables you to reposition a floating toolbar.
   c. Enables you to move a graphical image.
   d. Helps you use the Cut, Copy, and Paste functions.
   e. Both a and b.

___ 6. A toolbar button that has been selected:
   a. Appears all black.
   b. Appears all white.
   c. Appears with a dark black border.
   d. Is clear.
   e. Both a and b.

___ 7. To move or delete a button on a toolbar, you must first:
   a. Select it and drag down-ward, off of the toolbar.
   b. Select it and press the Cut button on the formatting toolbar.
   c. Select it and press Delete.
   d. Access the Customize dia-log box.
   e. Right-click the button and press Delete.

___ 8. To reposition a floating tool-bar:
   a. Position the mouse pointer over one of the buttons and drag.
   b. Position the mouse pointer over the title bar and drag.
   c. Choose Tools|Customize|Reposition.
   d. Choose Tools|Customize, and then click the Characteristics tab.
   e. Both c and d.

___ 9. To turn off a floating toolbar:
  a. Choose View|Toolbars, click Toobars tab and clear the appropriate check box.
  b. Click the Close button on the toolbar.
  c. Right-click the toolbar and click the toolbar description.
  d. Right-click on the title bar and clear the applicable check mark.
  e. All of the above.

___ 10. To delete a custom toolbar, access the Toolbar tab in the Customize dialog box, and then:
  a. Select the toolbar and click Reset.
  b. Select the toolbar and click Delete.
  c. Select the toolbar and clear the check box.
  d. Any of these methods will work.
  e. Both a and b.

Screen Review

Match the letters in Figure 11.13 with the correct items in the list.

Figure 11.13

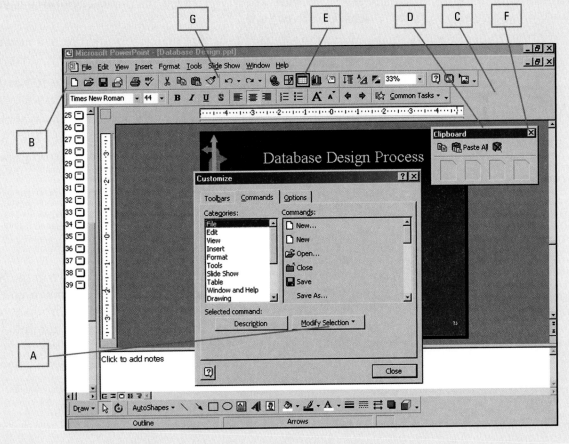

___ 1. Click here to turn on a toolbar.

___ 2. Drag here to undock the Standard toolbar.

___ 3. Click here to turn off the floating toolbar.

___ 4. Drag here to reposition the Formatting toolbar.

___ 5. A button icon that has been selected.

___ 6. Drag here to move a floating toolbar.

___ 7. Click here to modify the button icon.

Exercise and Project

Follow these step-by-step instructions to practice the skills that are included in this chapter. If you are working in a computer lab, you may have to ask your instructor where to save or print your work.

Exercise

1. Start PowerPoint and open **PPT11** from the Student\Chapter 11 folder of the PinPoint CD-ROM that came with this book.
2. Choose **File|Save As** and save the slide as a Windows Metafile.
3. Add a new slide at the end of the presentation.
4. Access the Open File dialog box and insert one of the slide pictures onto the slide. Add your name and the date in the title placeholder.
5. Save your file in the PowerPoint 2000 as **Exercise 11A** in your PowerPoint 2000 folder.
6. Select the slide where you added the picture, choose **File|Print,** and click to check **Current Slide.**
7. Access the toolbar Customize dialog box and create a new toolbar.
8. Rename the toolbar **Quick Edits.**
9. Add the Repeat, Duplicate, and Delete Side buttons to the toolbar. Close the dialog box.
10. Access the Customize dialog box and turn on all the available toolbars.
11. Press **Print Screen,** add another slide to the end of the presentation, and paste the screen print onto the slide. Add your name and other pertinent information to the title placeholder.
12. Save the presentation as **Exercise 11B** and print this slide only.
13. Turn off all the extra toolbars and exit PowerPoint.

Project

As a successful entrepreneur, you are somewhat of a hero in the small town where you grew up. Now you have been asked to give the commencement address at the high school that you attended. Remembering all those dry speeches that you have sat through, you would like to say something meaningful. Develop a short PowerPoint presentation for the occasion. Create a toolbar to simplify the process and save the slides as graphic images. Make sure that your name is on the title slide. Save the file as **Project 11.**

MOUS Skill Guides for Core and Expert Objectives

Each MOUS exam involves a list of required tasks you may be asked to perform. This list of possible tasks is categorized by skill area. The following tables list the skill areas and where their required tasks can be found in this book. Table A contains the Core-level tasks. Table B contains the Expert-level tasks. While most expert-level objectives are covered in this guide, there is currently not an expert-level PowerPoint 2000 MOUS exam. Expert objectives are included in this book to help you become an advanced user.

C Table A — MOUS Core Skill Guide

Skill Set	Required MOUS Activity	Chapter	Task	Page #
CREATING A PRESENTATION				
	Delete slides	3	6	102
	Create a specified type of slide	2	5	78
	Create a presentation from a template and/or a Wizard	1 / 5	2 / 1	44 / 138
	Navigate among different views (slide, outline, sorter, tri-pane)	1	5	52
	Create a new presentation from existing slides	1	7	57
	Copy a slide from one presentation into another	3	5	100
	Insert headers and footers	5	4	154
	Create a blank presentation	2	1	69
	Create a presentation using the AutoContent Wizard	1	2	44
	Send a presentation via e-mail	10	4	299
MODIFYING A PRESENTATION				
	Change the order of slides using Slide Sorter view	3	7	104
	Find and replace text	3	8	107
	Change the layout for one or more slides	2	5	78
	Change slide layout (Modify the Slide Master)	5	5	156
	Modify slide sequence in the outline pane	3	7	104
	Apply a design template	5	1	138
WORKING WITH TEXT				
	Check spelling	2	6	79
	Change and replace text fonts (individual slide and entire presentation)	4	2, 3, 4	118, 123, 124

Skill Set	Required MOUS Activity	Chapter	Task	Page #
	Enter text in tri-pane view	2	2	71
	Import text from Word	9	8	279
	Change the text alignment	4	1	116
	Create a text box for entering text	2	8	83
	Use the Wrap text in TextBox feature	2	8	83
	Use the Office Clipboard	3	3	97
	Use the Format Painter	4	5	125
	Promote and Demote text in slide and outline panes	2	2	71
WORKING WITH VISUAL ELEMENTS				
	Add a picture from the ClipArt Gallery	6	1	166
	Add and group shapes using WordArt or the Drawing Toolbar	6	3, 4, 6	176, 178 187
	Apply formatting	6	4	178
	Place text inside a shape using a text box	2	8	83
	Place text inside a shape using a text box	6	5	186
	Scale and size an object including ClipArt	6	2, 4	171, 178
	Create tables within PowerPoint	9	2	261
	Rotate and fill an object	6	4	178
CUSTOMIZING A PRESENTATION				
	Add AutoNumber bullets	4	6	125
	Add speaker notes	2	2, 3	71, 75
	Add graphical bullets	4, 6	6, 6	125
	Add slide transitions	6	10	197
	Animate text and objects	6	11	199
CREATING OUTPUT				
	Preview presentation in black and white	8	3	237
	Print Slides in a variety of formats	8	1	234
	Print audience handouts	8	4	239
	Print speaker notes in a specified format	8	6	241

C Table A   MOUS Core Skill Guide
(continued)

Skill Set	Required MOUS Activity	Chapter	Task	Page #
DELIVERING A PRESENTATION				
	Start a slide show on any slide	8	7	242
	Use on screen navigation tools	8	8	244
	Print a slide as an overhead transparency	8	2	235
	Use the pen during a presentation	8	8	244
MANAGING FILES				
	Save changes to a presentation	1	6	55
	Save as a new presentation	1	7	57
	Publish a presentation to the Web	10	2	294
	Use Office Assistant	1	9	60
	Insert hyperlink	7	1	209

E Table B   MOUS Expert Skill Guide

Skill Set	Required MOUS Activity	Chapter	Task	Page #
CREATING A PRESENTATION				
	Automatically create a summary slide	7	4	218
	Automatically create an Agenda Slide	7	5	219
	Design a template	5	6	157
	Format presentations for the Web	10	1	290
MODIFYING PRESENTATION				
	Change tab formatting	4	7	129
	Use the Wrap text in AutoShape feature	2	8	83
	Apply a template from another presentation	5	1	138
	Customize a color scheme	5	2	142
	Apply animation effects	6	11	199
	Create a custom background	5	3	145
	Add animated GIFs	6	1	166
	Add links to slides within the presentation	7	1	209
	Customize clip art and other objects (resize, scale, etc.)	6	2, 4	171, 178

Table B   MOUS Expert Skill Guide
(continued)

Skill Set	Required MOUS Activity	Chapter	Task	Page #
	Add a presentation within a presentation	7	3	216
	Add an action button	7	2	213
	Hide Slides	7	7	223
	Set automatic slide timings	7	6	221
WORKING WITH VISUAL ELEMENTS				
	Add textured backgrounds	5	3	145
	Apply diagonal borders to a table	9	4	268
USING DATA FROM OTHER SOURCES				
	Export an outline to Word	9	8	279
	Add a table (from Word)	9	2	261
	Insert an Excel Chart	9	8	279
	Add sound	6	8	190
	Add video	6	9	195
CREATING OUTPUT				
	Save slide as a graphic	11	1	308
	Generate meeting notes	8	9	251
	Change output format (Page setup)	8	2	235
DELIVERING A PRESENTATION				
	Save presentation for use on another computer (Pack 'N Go)	7	9	226
	Electronically incorporate meeting feedback	8	8	244
	View a Presentation on the Web	10	3	298
MANAGING FILES				
	Save embedded fonts in presentation	7	8	225
	Save HTML to a specific target browser	10	2	294
WORKING WITH POWERPOINT				
	Customize the toolbar	11	2	309
	Create a toolbar	11	3	315

E Table B MOUS Expert Skill Guide
(continued)

Skill Set	Required MOUS Activity	Chapter	Task	Page #
WORKING WITH CHARTS AND TABLES (OBJECTIVES MOVED FROM PROFICIENT LEVEL)				
	Build a chart or graph	9	5	271
	Modify charts or graphs	9	7	277
	Build an organization chart	9	1	257
	Modify an organization chart	9	1	257
	Modify PowerPoint tables	9	3	265

Use MOUS PinPoint 2000 Software

PinPoint 2000 is a software product that provides interactive training and testing in Microsoft Office 2000 programs. It is designed to supplement the projects in this book and will aid you in preparing for the MOUS certification exams. PinPoint 2000 is included on the CD-ROM in the back of this text. PinPoint 2000 Trainers and Evaluations currently run under Windows 95, Windows 98, and Windows NT 4.

The MOUS PinPoint software consists of Trainers and Evaluations. Trainers are used to hone your Office user skills. Evaluations are used to evaluate your performance of those skills.

PinPoint 2000 requires a full custom installation of Office 2000 to your computer. A full custom installation is an option you select at the time you install Microsoft Office 2000, and means that all components of the software are installed.

In this Appendix, you'll learn to:

- Install and start the PinPoint Launcher
- Start and run PinPoint Trainers and Evaluations
- View Trainer and Evaluation results
- Recover from a crash
- Remove PinPoint from your computer

Introduction to PinPoint 2000

The PinPoint 2000 Launcher

Your PinPoint 2000 CD contains a selection of PinPoint 2000 Trainers and Evaluations that cover many of the skills that you may need for using Word 2000, Excel 2000, PowerPoint 2000, and Access 2000.

Concurrency

PinPoint 2000 Trainers and Evaluations are considered "concurrent." This means that a Trainer (or Evaluation) is run simultaneously with the Office 2000 application you are learning or being tested in. For example, when you run a Pinpoint PowerPoint 2000 Trainer, the Microsoft PowerPoint 2000 application is automatically started and runs at the same time. By working directly in the Office 2000 application, you master the real application, rather than just practice on a simulation of the application.

Today's more advanced applications (like those in Office 2000) often allow more than one way to perform a given task. Concurrency with the real application gives you the freedom to choose the method that you like or that you already know. This gives you the optimal training and testing environment.

Trainer/Evaluation Pairs

Trainers and Evaluations come in pairs. For example, there is a Trainer/Evaluation pair for Word 2000 called "Expert Creating a Newsletter." This means that there is both a Trainer and an Evaluation for "Expert Creating a Newsletter."

Pinpoint Word 2000, Excel 2000, PowerPoint 2000, and Access 2000 all have such sets of Trainers and Evaluations.

Tasks

Each Trainer/Evaluation pair, or *module*, is a set of tasks grouped according to level (Core or Expert) and skill set.

Trainers

If you need help to complete the task, you can click the Show Me button and activate the Show Me feature. The Show Me will run a demonstration of how to perform a similar task.

After you attempt the task, the program checks your work and tells you if you performed the task correctly or incorrectly. In either case you have three choices:

- Retry the task.
- Have the Trainer demonstrate with the task's Show Me an efficient method of completing the task.
- Move on to the next task.

After you have completed all of the tasks in the module, you can study your performance by looking at the report that appears when you click the Report tab on the Launcher.

You may take a Trainer as many times as you like. As you do so, the Launcher keeps track of how you perform, even over different days, so that when you run a Trainer another time, the Trainer is set up to run only those tasks that were performed incorrectly on all of your previous run(s).

Evaluations

Since an Evaluation is really a test, it does not give you immediate feedback. You also cannot go back to a previous task or watch a demonstration of how to do the current task. You simply move from task to task until you have attempted all of the tasks in the Evaluation.

When you have finished, you can look at the report in the Reports section to see how you performed.

You can take an Evaluation as many times as you like. While you do so, the Launcher program keeps a record of how you have performed. As a result, if you take a Trainer after the corresponding Evaluation has been taken, the Trainer will set up to run only those tasks that were performed incorrectly on the Evaluation.

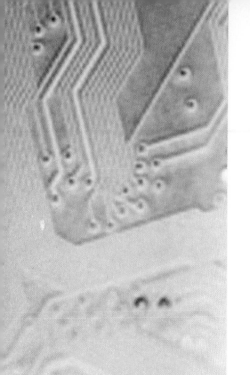

System Requirements

Table B.1 shows the system requirements to run PinPoint 2000 software on your computer.

Table B.1 PinPoint 2000 System Requirements

Component	Requirement
CPU	Minimum: Pentium Recommended: 166 MHz Pentium or better
Operating System	Windows 95, Windows 98, or Windows NT 4.0 sp5
Installed Applications	Full Custom Installation of Office 2000* Printer
RAM	Minimum: 16 MB Recommended: 32 MB or higher
Hard Drive Space	Minimum: Installing PinPoint 2000 software requires about 4 MB of hard drive space. Recommended: For efficient operation, however, you should make sure you have at least 100 MB of unused drive space after installing PinPoint 2000.
CD-ROM Drive	4X speed or faster
Video	Minimum: Color VGA video display running at 640x480 resolution with 16 colors. Recommended: Color VGA video display running at 800x600 (or higher) resolution with 16 colors. Note for Gateway computer users: If running a P5 90 (or less) Gateway computer, obtain the latest ATI "Mach 64" video driver from Gateway. This can be downloaded from Gateway's Web site.

*Office 2000 must be installed before installing PinPoint 2000. If a Full Custom Installation of Office 2000 has not been performed, some tasks will not be available because the components required for those tasks will not have been installed. The tasks will not be counted as right or wrong but recorded as N/A.

Run PinPoint 2000

Now that you know what PinPoint 2000 is and what is required to use it, you now see how to install and use the Launcher, and start and run Trainers and Evaluations. You also see how to view Trainer and Evaluation reports. Lastly, you find out how to recover from a crash of PinPoint 2000, if one occurs.

INSTALL THE LAUNCHER ON YOUR COMPUTER

To run the PinPoint 2000 Trainers or Evaluations, you must first install the Launcher program.

1. Start Windows on your computer.
2. Be sure that Office 2000 has already been installed to your computer with a Full Custom Install. If this is not the case, perform this installation before you continue with step 3.
3. Insert the PinPoint 2000 CD into your CD-ROM drive.
4. From the Start menu, select Run.
5. In the Run dialog box, enter the path to the SETUP.EXE file found in the root directory of the CD. For example, if your CD-ROM drive has been assigned the letter E, you would enter E:\setup.exe as shown in Figure B.1.

Note: If your CD-ROM drive has been assigned a letter different from E, use that letter to begin the path in this dialog box. For example, if your CD-ROM drive has been assigned the drive letter D, enter D:\setup.exe in this dialog box.

Figure B.1

6. Click OK.
7. When the Setup Type screen appears, select Normal Single-User Installation.
8. Click Next to continue.

You are given a choice concerning the location of the PinPoint 2000 folder.

The recommended location of the PinPoint 2000 folder is shown as the default. (*Note:* Two files that initially take up only 109 KB will be placed in this folder.)

If you prefer to use a different path or name for the PinPoint 2000 folder, click the Browse button and navigate to the location you prefer, or rename the folder.

9. Click Next to continue.

After the installation is complete, the PinPoint 2000 program group window appears.

10. Close the PinPoint 2000 program group window.

If the installation has occurred correctly, the following changes have been made to your computer:

- ○ A PinPoint 2000 shortcut icon has been installed that will enable you to run the Launcher program via the Start menu.
- ○ A new folder called PinPoint 2000 has been created on the hard drive of your computer (see Figure B.2).

Figure B.2

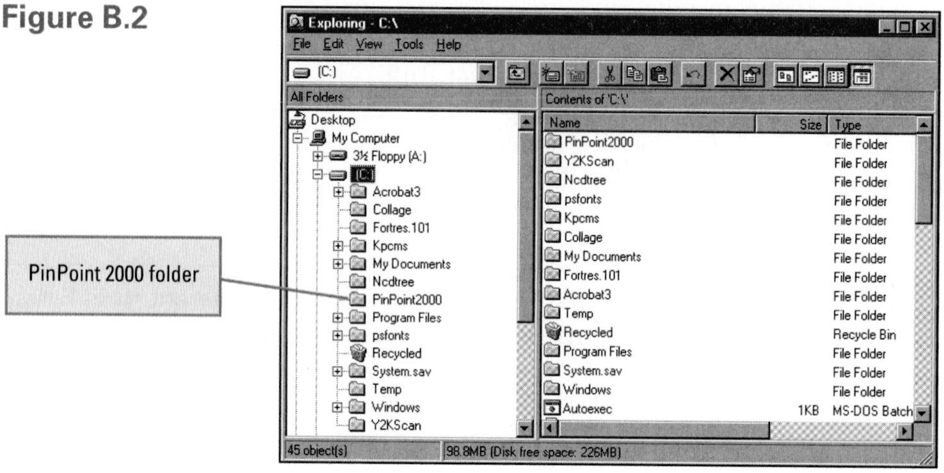

PinPoint 2000 folder

The PinPoint2000 folder contains:

- ○ An empty database file, CC_Admin.mdb. As you run Trainers and Evaluations, this file records your performance.
- ○ A small file, Uninst.isu, that is used for removing PinPoint 2000 from your computer.

Note: If your computer is configured so that file extensions are turned off, the CC_Admin.mdb file will appear without the .mdb extension.

Some files necessary for database access have been added to the Windows\System folder.

PREPARE TO RUN THE PINPOINT 2000 LAUNCHER

Before running the PinPoint 2000 Launcher, it is necessary to initialize each of the Microsoft applications (Word 2000, Excel 2000, PowerPoint 2000, and Access 2000) at least one time. If you have already used each of these applications, you can ignore this section.

Initializing these applications enables PinPoint training and testing to run in a more stable environment. You will need to provide user information in the first application that you run.

1. Start Microsoft Word 2000.
2. When the User Name dialog box appears type your Name and Initials.
3. Click OK to confirm.
4. When the Word window is completely set up and ready for use, you can close the application.
5. Start Microsoft Excel 2000.
6. When the Excel window is completely set up and ready for use, you can close the application.
7. Start Microsoft PowerPoint 2000.
8. When the PowerPoint window is completely set up and ready for use, you may close the application.
9. Start Microsoft Access 2000.
10. When the Access window is completely set up and ready for use, you can close the application.

You are ready to run the Launcher program and begin Trainers and Evaluations.

START THE PINPOINT 2000 LAUNCHER

The Launcher program enables you to run Trainers and Evaluations. It also gives you a performance report after you have taken a Trainer or Evaluation.

1. Select Start, Programs, PinPoint 2000, PinPoint 2000 (see Figure B.3).

Figure B.3

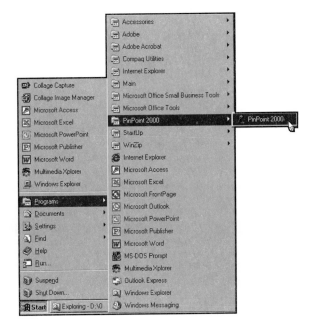

2. Enter a user name and password (see Figure B.4).

Figure B.4

The user name and password can consist of any characters, as long as neither of them exceeds 50 characters. They are NOT case sensitive: It doesn't matter if you use upper- or lowercase letters.

If more than one person will be running PinPoint 2000 from your computer, each person must enter a different user name. However, passwords can be the same.

3. Click OK in the Logon dialog box.

If you are logging on for the first time, you need to enter some information in the User Information dialog box.

4. Enter the requested information and click OK.

The PinPoint 2000 Launcher screen appears (see Figure B.5). Please note that this screen will only show the application for the text you are using.

Figure B.5

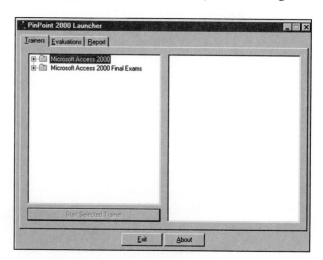

You are now ready to run PinPoint Trainers and Evaluations.

START PINPOINT 2000 TRAINERS AND EVALUATIONS

1. From the PinPoint Launcher, click the Trainers tab if you want to start a Trainer, or the Evaluations tab if you want to start an Evaluation (see Figure B.6).

Figure B.6

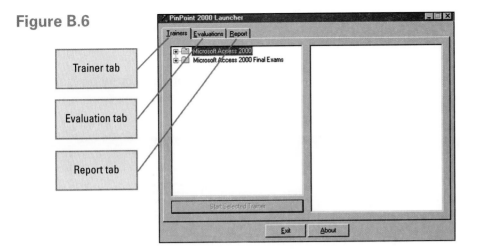

Trainer tab

Evaluation tab

Report tab

Note: Before you run a Trainer or Evaluation for the first time you must initialize each of the applications (Word 2000, Excel 2000, PowerPoint 2000, and Access 2000) at least one time.

---

2. Click the plus sign (+) to open an application's modules and exams. The plus sign becomes a minus sign (-), as shown in Figure B.7.

Figure B.7

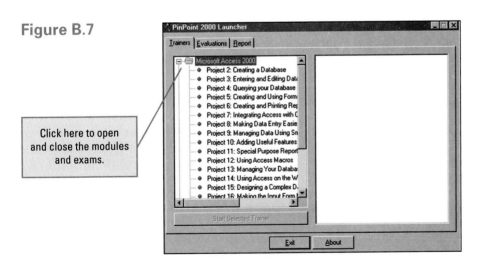

Click here to open and close the modules and exams.

3. Select the module or exam that you want to run.

The individual tasks that are part of the Trainer or Evaluation appear in the pane on the right.

4. If you are running a Trainer without an Evaluation, you can select or deselect individual training tasks by clicking on the box beside the task name (see Figure B.8).

The tasks that are deselected will not run during the Trainer. This enables you to adjust your training to include only those tasks that you do not already know how to do.

When running an Evaluation, however, you cannot deselect individual tasks. All tasks will run.

Figure B.8

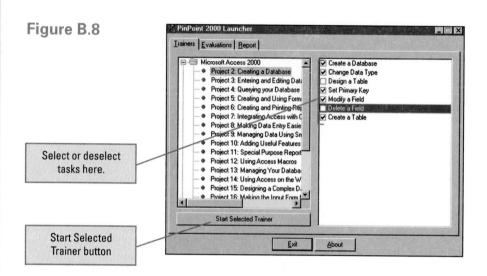

Select or deselect tasks here.

Start Selected Trainer button

5. Click the Start Selected Trainer button if you are starting a Trainer. Click the Start Selected Evaluation button if you are starting an Evaluation.

6. When you start the Trainer, you might encounter a warning message instructing you to change your computer's Taskbar settings (see Figure B.9).

If this message appears, follow its instructions before proceeding. Changing your taskbar settings in this way is necessary for proper functioning of a PinPoint Trainer. You can carry out the instructions given without canceling the box.

Figure B.9

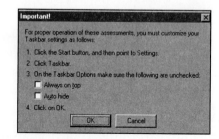

The PinPoint 2000 Launcher dialog box with your name and module selection appears (see Figure B.10).

Figure B.10

      7. Click Yes to continue.

The Trainer or Evaluation starts.

Proceed to the next two sections to see how to run Trainers and Evaluations.

RUN A TRAINER

This lesson shows you how to run a Trainer. It also details how to handle some of the situations you might encounter during a Trainer.

      1. Once your name and the selected module are displayed, click OK to begin the trainer.

The PinPoint 2000 launcher dialog box appears before a Trainer runs (see Figure B.11).

Figure B.11

      2. Click Yes to continue.

The first thing you see is an introduction to how all PinPoint 2000 Trainers work. If you want to see the demonstration of how a PinPoint Trainer works and how to use the PinPoint 2000 controls, press any key or click the mouse to continue.

      3. Press Esc to skip the introduction for now and go directly to a task.

 TIPS FROM A PRO: You can exit the introduction at any time by pressing **Esc** and moving straight to the training.

After initializing, the Trainer opens the first selected task.

The task instructions are displayed in a moveable instruction box that hovers over the application (see Figure B.12).

Figure B.12

The instruction box can be moved to different parts of the screen.

TIPS FROM A PRO: If the instruction box is blocking your view of something, you can drag it to another part of the screen. To instantly move the box to the other side of the screen, right-click the instruction box.

Notice the PinPoint control buttons that appear on the perimeter of the instruction box. Use these buttons to interact with the Trainer according to your needs (see Figure B.13).

Figure B.13

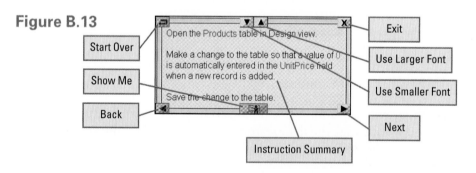

The features of the instruction box in Figure B.13 and their descriptions are listed here:

- The Instruction Summary displays the task to be completed. Instructions remain visible during the task.
- The Start Over button starts the current task again.
- The Back button returns you to the previous task.
- The Show Me button gives you a step-by-step demonstration using a similar example.

- The Use Larger Font and Use Smaller Font buttons enlarge or reduce the size of the box and text.
- The Quit button ends the current training session and returns you to the Launcher.
- The Next button checks a finished task for correct performance and moves you to the next task.

   4. Try to do the task exactly as instructed in the PinPoint instruction box.
   5. Click the Next button (refer to Figure B.13).

PinPoint 2000 gives you feedback in the Results dialog box.

Whether you performed the task correctly or not, you now have three choices:

- Click the Show Me button to display a step-by-step demonstration using a similar example.
- Click the Try Task Again button to set up the task so you can attempt it again.
- Click the Next Task button to move on and attempt the next task.

If you click the Show Me button, a demonstration of how to perform a similar task is given. This demonstration, called a Show Me, begins with a summary of the steps required to perform the task.

   6. Press any key or click the mouse to advance the next Show Me box.

Usually the key concept behind the particular skill is explained during the Show Me.

After the instruction summary (and possibly a key concept), each of the instructions in the summary is explained and demonstrated in detail.

 TIPS FROM A PRO: If you want to exit from the Show Me demonstration at any point, press **Esc** to return to the PinPoint task.

During the Show Me demonstration, the mouse pointer moves and text is entered automatically when appropriate to the demonstration, but whenever the description or action is completed the demonstration halts until the user prompts it to continue with either a mouse click or a key stroke.

After the demonstration is complete, you can perform the task yourself.

   7. Continue through the PinPoint Trainer at your own pace, attempting each task and watching Show Me demonstrations when you need help.

When you have finished with the training session, the Trainers screen of the Launcher is visible again. You can see a report of your performance by clicking the Report tab in the Launcher.

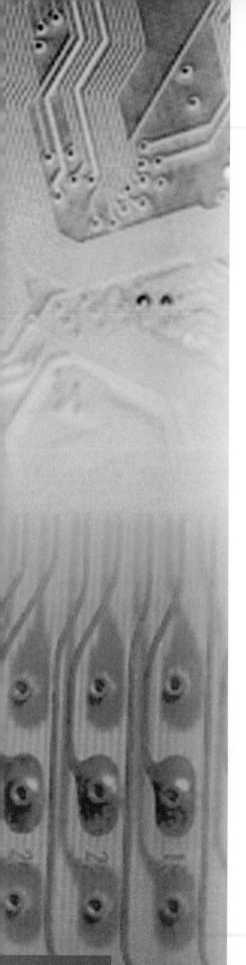

 TIPS FROM A PRO: You are free to exit from the training at any time by clicking the Exit button (refer to Figure B.13). When you attempt to exit a Trainer before it is finished, you are asked to confirm this decision (see Figure B.14).

Figure B.14

If you want to exit from the trainer at this point, click Yes.

RUN AN EVALUATION

This lesson shows you how to run an Evaluation. It also details how to handle some of the situations you might encounter during an Evaluation.

1. When you start the Evaluation, you might encounter a warning message instructing you to change your computer's Taskbar settings (refer to Figure B.9).

If this message appears, follow its instructions before proceeding. Changing your taskbar settings in this way is necessary for proper functioning of a PinPoint Trainer. You can carry out the instructions given without canceling the box.

2. After you have carried out the steps listed, click OK to continue.

The Pinpoint 2000 Launcher dialog box appears before an Evaluation runs (refer to Figure B.11).

3. Click Yes to continue.

The first thing you see is an introduction to how all PinPoint 2000 Evaluations work. If you want to see the demonstration of how an Evaluation works and how to use the PinPoint 2000 controls, press any key or click the mouse to continue past each screen. If you do not need to see the demonstration, press **Esc** to go straight to the testing.

Like a Trainer, an Evaluation presents you with a task to perform. In an Evaluation, however, the Start Over, Back, and Show Me buttons are all disabled. Therefore, you cannot restart a task, return to a previous task, or run a Show Me demonstration of how to perform the task.

4. After attempting a task, click the Next button to continue to the next task.

Normally, you would attempt all of the tasks in the Evaluation. But if you need to finish early and click the Exit button before you have attempted all of the tasks, the message box in Figure B.14 will display. Click the Yes button if you want to exit the Evaluation and go back to the Launcher program.

5. You can view a report of your performance by clicking the Report tab in the Launcher.

See the next section for details about viewing reports.

 TIPS FROM A PRO: Keep the following in mind for PinPoint 2000 Trainers and Evaluations to run properly:

- Only perform actions that the PinPoint task instructions ask you to perform.
- Do not exit from the Microsoft Office 2000 application in which you are training or testing unless you are told to do so.
- Do not close the example document (the document that PinPoint opens for you when you begin a task) unless you are told to do so.
- Do not run other programs (such as email, Internet browsers, virus shields, system monitors, and so on) at the same time as running PinPoint, unless you are asked to do so.
- Do not change views in one of the Office 2000 applications unless you are asked to do so.
- Do not change the way your Windows operating system or Office 2000 applications are configured by default.
- Do not turn off your computer in the middle of a PinPoint Trainer or Evaluation. Instead, first exit from the Trainer or Evaluation, and then turn off your computer.

VIEW REPORTS IN THE LAUNCHER

After you have taken at least one PinPoint 2000 Trainer or Evaluation, you can view detailed reports at any time concerning your performance on any of the modules that you have taken.

1. If the Launcher is not running, click Start, Programs, PinPoint 2000, PinPoint 2000 to run it. Then log on.
2. Click the Report tab.

The Report screen appears (see Figure B.15).

Figure B.15

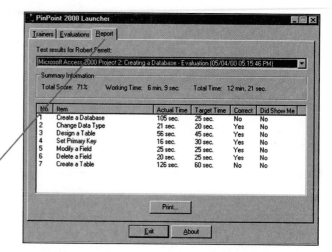

Click the Report tab to view a detailed report of your performance.

The very last Trainer or Evaluation that you ran is displayed on screen. The information displayed in the Report screen is as follows:

- *Total Score*—The percentage of the correctly performed tasks out of the total number of tasks set to run.
- *Working Time*—The total time you actually spent working on all of the tasks in the Trainer or Evaluation.
- *Total Time*—The total time you spent running the entire Trainer or Evaluation.
- *Item*—The name of the task.
- *Actual Time*—The time you took to perform the task.
- *Target Time*—A reasonable amount of time required to perform the task by an efficient method.
- *Correct*—Displays Yes if you performed the task correctly; No if you did not.
- *Did Show-Me*—Displays Yes if you ran a Show Me demonstration for that task; No if you did not.

Note: A blank or dotted line running through the task line, or N/A, indicates that the task was not taken.

---

3. If you want to print a report, click the Print button.
4. If you want to see a report for a Trainer or Evaluation that you took previously, select it from the Test results for *<your name>* drop-down list.

The reports are listed in the order in which they were taken.

Note: You will see only your own reports on the Reports screen and not the reports for anyone else using PinPoint on your computer.

Note: An important feature of the PinPoint 2000 Launcher is its capability to keep track of your history of running Trainers and Evaluations. The Launcher uses your history to reconfigure a Trainer each successive time you run it. To "reconfigure" means to change the tasks that will run.

The Launcher does not reconfigure an Evaluation the same way it does a Trainer. No matter which tasks you have performed correctly in the past (on either a Trainer or Evaluation), all tasks are automatically selected to be run when you attempt to take an Evaluation.

RECOVER FROM A CRASH DURING A TRAINER OR EVALUATION

If your computer crashes while you are running a Trainer or Evaluation, all the work you have already done is not wasted. You do not need to start the Trainer or Evaluation over again from the beginning. To recover from a crash during a Trainer or Evaluation, follow these simple instructions.

1. Reboot your computer.
2. Start the Launcher again and log on as usual.
3. When a message like the one in Figure B.16 appears, close the Office application you were working on (if it's still running in the background) by clicking the Close button in the top right corner of the application window.

Figure B.16

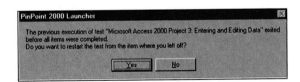

4. Click Yes to close the message box and return to the test.

The Trainer or Evaluation with which you were working will resume at the point where your computer crashed. Continue working on the Trainer or Evaluation as before.

Remove PinPoint 2000

When you have finished training and testing with PinPoint 2000, you may want to remove the Launcher program from your computer. PinPoint 2000 can be removed using the procedure for removing most other applications from your computer.

1. From the Start menu, select Settings, Control Panel.
2. Double-click the Add/Remove Programs icon.

The Add/Remove Programs Properties dialog box is displayed.

3. Select PinPoint 2000.

4. Click the Add/Remove button.
5. Confirm the removal of PinPoint 2000 by clicking Yes in the dialog box.
6. If the Remove Shared File? dialog box appears, click the Yes To All button (see Figure 17).

Figure B.17

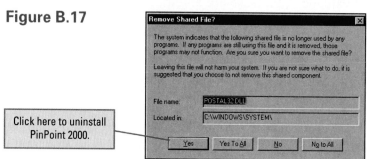

Click here to uninstall PinPoint 2000.

7. When the Remove Programs From Your Computer dialog box reports that the uninstall was successfully completed, click OK.
8. Click OK in the Add/Remove Programs Properties dialog box.
9. Close the Control Panel window.

PinPoint 2000 has now been completely removed from your computer.

Summary

PinPoint 2000 is a very valuable tool for preparing yourself for a MOUS Exam. You've learned how to install and start the PinPoint Launcher. You can now run Trainers and Evaluations, and view a report of their results. You also know what to avoid while running Trainers and Evaluations. You've seen how to recover if PinPoint crashes. And finally, you've learned how to uninstall PinPoint when you no longer need it. You are now equipped to take full advantage of the PinPoint 2000 training and testing software.

Prepare for MOUS Certification

This appendix gives you information that you need regarding the certification exams—how to register, what is covered in the tests, how the tests are administered, and so on. Because this information may change, be sure to visit www.mous.net for the latest updates.

How to Prepare for the Exams

This text is certified for both levels of certification:

- **Core**—You are able to manage a wide range of real world tasks efficiently.
- **Expert**—In addition to the everyday tasks at the Core level, you are able to handle complex assignments and have a thorough understanding of a program's advanced features.

In addition to the Core and Expert levels, Microsoft now offers a Master certification, which indicates that you have a comprehensive understanding of Microsoft Office 2000 and many of its advanced features. A Master certification requires students to successfully pass all five of the required exams: Word, Excel, PowerPoint, Access, and Outlook.

Each exam includes a list of tasks you may be asked to perform. The lessons in this book identify these required tasks with an icon in the margin. You can also review the MOUS Skill Guide in the front of this book to become familiar with these required tasks.

In addition to these icons, this book contains various study aids that not only help you pass the test, but also teach you how the software functions. You can use this book in a classroom or lab setting, or you can work through each chapter on your own using the PinPoint CD-ROM.

The PinPoint CD-ROM includes Chapter Review Tests for each MOUS Exam skill set. The coverage has two parts: a Task and a Show Me. The Task requires you to do something, (for example, format a document) and the Show Me demonstrates how to perform that task. In addition, each PinPoint has a practice test that mirrors the actual MOUS exams.

Use the PinPoint software as an evaluation of your comprehension. If you get stuck, be sure to use the Show Me demonstration.

Registering for and Taking the Exam

All MOUS exams are administered by a MOUS Authorized Testing Center (ATC). Most MOUS ATCs require pre-registration. To pre-register contact a local ATC directly. You can find a center near you by visiting the MOUS Web site at *www.mous.net*. Some ATCs accept walk-in examination candidates, allowing on-the-spot registration and examination. Be sure to check with a specific ATC to make certain of their registration policy.

The exam is not written and there are no multiple choice or true-false questions. You perform the required tasks on a computer running the live Microsoft application. A typical exam takes 45 to 60 minutes to complete. You must work through each task in the exam as quickly as you can.

All examination data is encrypted, and the examination process is closely monitored so your test scores are completely confidential. Examination results are provided only to the candidate and to Microsoft.

The Day of the Exam

Bring the following items with you to the testing center on exam day:

- **Picture ID**—driver's license or passport
- **Your MOUS identification number** (if you have take a previous MOUS certification exam)
- **ATC Student ID**, if applicable

At the exam center, you can expect to first complete the candidate information section, which provides the information necessary to complete your MOUS certificate.

After confirming your ID, the administrator will seat you at the test computer, log you onto the test system, and open your test module. You are now ready to begin.

To start the test, click the "Start Test" button and you're ready to begin your certification exam.

The Exam Itself

Instructions are displayed in a separate window on the screen. You can close the instruction window by clicking on it. You can restore it by clicking "Instructions" on the test information bar at the bottom of the screen. Read the test instructions carefully. Once you have started, a box in the bottom right corner of the screen indicates the question on which you are currently working. (For example, "question 3 of 50.")

If anything abnormal happens during the exam, or if the application "crashes," stop immediately and contact the administrator. The administrator will restart the test from where you left off. You will not be penalized any time for this.

When you have completed your exam, the computer will calculate your score. The scoring process takes a short time, and you will be notified onscreen whether you passed or failed. You may then ask the administrator to give you a printed report.

If you complete the exam successfully, your MOUS certificate will be delivered within 2-3 weeks.

General Tips

Unlike earlier MOUS exams, the results of the Office 2000 MOUS exams are expressed as a value on a 1000-point scale, rather than a percentage.

Each activity or question on the Office 2000 MOUS exams is comprised of several individually scored subtasks. A candidate's score is derived from the number of subtasks successfully completed and the "weight" or difficulty assigned to each.

Pay close attention to how each question is worded. Answers must be precise, resolving the question exactly as asked.

You can use any combination of menus, toolbars, and shortcut keys to complete each assigned task. Answers are scored based on the result, not the method you use or the time taken to complete each required task. Extra keystrokes or mouse clicks will not count against your score as long as you achieve the correct result within the time limit given.

Remember that the overall test is timed. While spending a lot of time on an individual answer will not adversely affect the scoring of that particular question, taking too long may not leave you with enough time to complete the entire test.

Answers are either right or wrong. You do not get credit for partial answers.

Important! Check to make sure you have entirely completed each question before clicking the NEXT TASK button. Once you press the NEXT TASK button, you will not be able to return to that question. A question will be scored as wrong if it is not completed properly before moving to the next question.

Save your Results Page that prints at the end of the exam. It is your confirmation that you passed the exam.

 TIPS FROM A PRO: Take note of these cautions:

- DON'T leave dialog boxes, Help menus, toolbars, or menus open.
- DON'T leave tables, boxes, cells "active or highlighted" unless instructed to do so.
- DON'T click the NEXT TASK button until you have "completely" answered the current question.

Lastly, be sure to visit the *mous.net* Web site for specific information on the Office 2000 exams, more testing tips, and to download a free demo of the exams.

Appendix D

Answers to Review Questions

Start with Windows

True/False		Multiple Choice		Screen Review	
1.	F	1.	B	1.	D
2.	T	2.	A	2.	H
3.	T	3.	D	3.	C
4.	F	4.	B	4.	A
5.	F	5.	A	5.	G
6.	F	6.	A	6.	F
7.	T	7.	E	7.	E
8.	T	8.	E	8.	B
9.	T	9.	A		
10.	F	10.	A		

Chapter 1

True/False		Multiple Choice		Screen Review	
1.	F	1.	D	1.	C
2.	T	2.	C	2.	B
3.	F	3.	A	3.	D
4.	F	4.	E	4.	A
5.	F	5.	C	5.	G
6.	F	6.	D	6.	E
7.	T	7.	E	7.	F
8.	F	8.	B		
9.	F	9.	C		
10.	T	10.	B		

Chapter 2

True/False		Multiple Choice		Screen Review	
1.	T	1.	B	1.	A
2.	T	2.	B	2.	B
3.	F	3.	B	3.	D
4.	T	4.	B	4.	G
5.	T	5.	B	5.	H
6.	T	6.	E	6.	F
7	F	7.	C	7.	C
8.	T	8.	D		
9.	F	9.	E		
10.	F	10.	D		

Chapter 3

True/False
1. T
2. F
3. F
4. T
5. T
6. F
7. T
8. T
9. T
10. F

Multiple Choice
1. E
2. A
3. B
4. A
5. E
6. B
7. E
8. E
9. D
10. A

Screen Review
1. D
2. A
3. E
4. F
5. G
6. B
7. C

Chapter 4

True/False
1. F
2. F
3. T
4. T
5. F
6. F
7. T
8. T
9. T
10. F

Multiple Choice
1. E
2. D
3. E
4. C
5. E
6. E
7. C
8. D
9. E
10. D

Screen Review
1. B
2. F
3. E
4. D
5. G
6. C
7. L
8. K
9. A

Chapter 5

True/False
1. F
2. T
3. F
4. T
5. F
6. F
7. T
8. T
9. T
10. F

Multiple Choice
1. E
2. C
3. B
4. D
5. B
6. A
7. E
8. C
9. E
10. E

Screen Review
1. A
2. F
3. H
4. D
5. C
6. E
7. G

Chapter 6

True/False

1. T
2. F
3. T
4. F
5. F
6. T
7. F
8. T
9. T
10. F

Multiple Choice

1. E
2. C
3. C
4. A
5. D
6. E
7. B
8. E
9. A
10. E

Screen Review

1. H
2. I
3. B
4. G
5. F
6. E
7. J
8. C
9. D
10. A

Chapter 7

True/False

1. F
2. T
3. T
4. F
5. T
6. T
7. F
8. T
9. T
10. F

Multiple Choice

1. D
2. E
3. C
4. E
5. B
6. E
7. C
8. A
9. E
10. D

Screen Review

1. B
2. A
3. A
4. D
5. E
6. C

Chapter 8

True/False

1. F
2. T
3. F
4. T
5. F
6. T
7. T
8. F
9. T
10. F

Multiple Choice

1. B
2. E
3. B
4. E
5. C
6. B
7. E
8. A
9. B
10. C

Screen Review

1. G
2. E
3. D
4. C
5. A
6. A
7. F

Chapter 9

True/False

1. T
2. F
3. F
4. T
5. T
6. T
7. F
8. T
9. F
10. T

Multiple Choice

1. D
2. B
3. A
4. D
5. A
6. A
7. B
8. A
9. D
10. B

Screen Review

1. C
2. B
3. E
4. F
5. D
6. A

Chapter 10

True/False

1. T
2. F
3. T
4. F
5. F
6. T
7. F
8. F
9. F
10. T

Multiple Choice

1. B
2. A
3. D
4. B
5. E
6. A
7. D
8. E
9. E
10. D

Screen Review

1. B
2. E
3. A
4. D
5. C
6. F
7. G

Chapter 11

True/False

1. F
2. T
3. F
4. T
5. F
6. T
7. T
8. F
9. T
10. T

Multiple Choice

1. C
2. A
3. D
4. E
5. A
6. C
7. D
8. B
9. E
10. B

Screen Review

1. C
2. G
3. F
4. B
5. E
6. D
7. A

Index

SINGLE PC LICENSE AGREEMENT AND LIMITED WARRANTY

READ THIS LICENSE CAREFULLY BEFORE USING THIS PACKAGE. BY USING THIS PACKAGE, YOU ARE AGREEING TO THE TERMS AND CONDITIONS OF THIS LICENSE. IF YOU DO NOT AGREE, DO NOT USE THE PACKAGE. PROMPTLY RETURN THE UNUSED PACKAGE AND ALL ACCOMPANYING ITEMS TO THE PLACE YOU OBTAINED. *THESE TERMS APPLY TO ALL LICENSED SOFTWARE ON THE DISK EXCEPT THAT THE TERMS FOR USE OF ANY SHAREWARE OR FREEWARE ON THE DISKETTES ARE AS SET FORTH IN THE ELECTRONIC LICENSE LOCATED ON THE DISK:*

1. GRANT OF LICENSE and OWNERSHIP: The enclosed computer programs and data ("Software") are licensed, not sold, to you by Prentice-Hall, Inc. ("We" or the "Company") and in consideration of your purchase or adoption of the accompanying Company textbooks and/or other materials, and your agreement to these terms. We reserve any rights not granted to you. You own only the disk(s) but we and/or our licensors own the Software itself. This license allows you to use and display your copy of the Software on a single computer (i.e., with a single CPU) at a single location for <u>academic</u> use only, so long as you comply with the terms of this Agreement. You may make one copy for back up, or transfer your copy to another CPU, provided that the Software is usable on only one computer.

2. RESTRICTIONS: You may <u>not</u> transfer or distribute the Software or documentation to anyone else. Except for backup, you may <u>not</u> copy the documentation or the Software. You may <u>not</u> network the Software or otherwise use it on more than one computer or computer terminal at the same time. You may <u>not</u> reverse engineer, disassemble, decompile, modify, adapt, translate, or create derivative works based on the Software or the Documentation. You may be held legally responsible for any copying or copyright infringement which is caused by your failure to abide by the terms of these restrictions.

3. TERMINATION: This license is effective until terminated. This license will terminate automatically without notice from the Company if you fail to comply with any provisions or limitations of this license. Upon termination, you shall destroy the Documentation and all copies of the Software. All provisions of this Agreement as to limitation and disclaimer of warranties, limitation of liability, remedies or damages, and our ownership rights shall survive termination.

4. LIMITED WARRANTY AND DISCLAIMER OF WARRANTY: Company warrants that for a period of 60 days from the date you purchase this SOFTWARE (or purchase or adopt the accompanying textbook), the Software, when properly installed and used in accordance with the Documentation, will operate in substantial conformity with the description of the Software set forth in the Documentation, and that for a period of 30 days the disk(s) on which the Software is delivered shall be free from defects in materials and workmanship under normal use. The Company does <u>not</u> warrant that the Software will meet your requirements or that the operation of the Software will be uninterrupted or error-free. Your only remedy and the Company's only obligation under these limited warranties is, at the Company's option, return of the disk for a refund of any amounts paid for it by you or replacement of the disk. THIS LIMITED WARRANTY IS THE ONLY WARRANTY PROVIDED BY THE COMPANY AND ITS LICENSORS, AND THE COMPANY AND ITS LICENSORS DISCLAIM ALL OTHER WARRANTIES, EXPRESS OR IMPLIED, INCLUDING WITHOUT LIMITATION, THE IMPLIED WARRANTIES OF MERCHANTABILITY AND FITNESS FOR A PARTICULAR PURPOSE. THE COMPANY DOES NOT WARRANT, GUARANTEE OR MAKE ANY REPRESENTATION REGARDING THE ACCURACY, RELIABILITY, CURRENTNESS, USE, OR RESULTS OF USE, OF THE SOFTWARE.

5. LIMITATION OF REMEDIES AND DAMAGES: IN NO EVENT, SHALL THE COMPANY OR ITS EMPLOYEES, AGENTS, LICENSORS, OR CONTRACTORS BE LIABLE FOR ANY INCIDENTAL, INDIRECT, SPECIAL, OR CONSEQUENTIAL DAMAGES ARISING OUT OF OR IN CONNECTION WITH THIS LICENSE OR THE SOFTWARE, INCLUDING FOR LOSS OF USE, LOSS OF DATA, LOSS OF INCOME OR PROFIT, OR OTHER LOSSES, SUSTAINED AS A RESULT OF INJURY TO ANY PERSON, OR LOSS OF OR DAMAGE TO PROPERTY, OR CLAIMS OF THIRD PARTIES, EVEN IF THE COMPANY OR AN AUTHORIZED REPRESENTATIVE OF THE COMPANY HAS BEEN ADVISED OF THE POSSIBILITY OF SUCH DAMAGES. IN NO EVENT SHALL THE LIABILITY OF THE COMPANY FOR DAMAGES WITH RESPECT TO THE SOFTWARE EXCEED THE AMOUNTS ACTUALLY PAID BY YOU, IF ANY, FOR THE SOFTWARE OR THE ACCOMPANYING TEXTBOOK. BECAUSE SOME JURISDICTIONS DO NOT ALLOW THE LIMITATION OF LIABILITY IN CERTAIN CIRCUMSTANCES, THE ABOVE LIMITATIONS MAY NOT ALWAYS APPLY TO YOU.

6. GENERAL: THIS AGREEMENT SHALL BE CONSTRUED IN ACCORDANCE WITH THE LAWS OF THE UNITED STATES OF AMERICA AND THE STATE OF NEW YORK, APPLICABLE TO CONTRACTS MADE IN NEW YORK, AND SHALL BENEFIT THE COMPANY, ITS AFFILIATES AND ASSIGNEES. HIS AGREEMENT IS THE COMPLETE AND EXCLUSIVE STATEMENT OF THE AGREEMENT BETWEEN YOU AND THE COMPANY AND SUPERSEDES ALL PROPOSALS OR PRIOR AGREEMENTS, ORAL, OR WRITTEN, AND ANY OTHER COMMUNICATIONS BETWEEN YOU AND THE COMPANY OR ANY REPRESENTATIVE OF THE COMPANY RELATING TO THE SUBJECT MATTER OF THIS AGREEMENT. If you are a U.S. Government user, this Software is licensed with "restricted rights" as set forth in subparagraphs (a)-(d) of the Commercial Computer-Restricted Rights clause at FAR 52.227-19 or in subparagraphs (c)(1)(ii) of the Rights in Technical Data and Computer Software clause at DFARS 252.227-7013, and similar clauses, as applicable. Should you have any questions concerning this agreement or if you wish to contact the Company for any reason, please contact in writing:

Director, New Media

Prentice Hall

1 Lake Street

Upper Saddle River, New Jersey 07458